Sharon L. McMillan, S.N.D. de N.

EPISCOPAL ORDINATION AND ECCLESIAL CONSENSUS

A PUEBLO BOOK

Liturgical Press   Collegeville, Minnesota
www.litpress.org

A Pueblo Book published by the Liturgical Press.

Cover design by David Manahan, O.S.B. Photo courtesy of Joyce McKenzie Photography and the Diocese of Fairbanks, Alaska.

The Scripture texts contained herein are from the New Revised Standard Version Bible, Catholic Anglicized edition, © 1999, 1995, 1989, Division of Christian Education of the National Council of the Churches of Christ in the United States of America, and are used by permission. All rights reserved.

| 1 | 2 | 3 | 4 | 5 | 6 | 7 | 8 |

Library of Congress Cataloging-in-Publication Data

McMillan, Sharon L., 1948–
    Episcopal ordination and ecclesial consensus / Sharon L. McMillan.
        p. cm.
    "A Pueblo book."
    Summary: "This study provides the historical and liturgical foundations for the election of bishops"—Provided by publisher.
    Includes bibliographical references and index.
    ISBN-10: 0-8146-6195-5 (pbk. : alk. paper)
    ISBN-13: 978-0-8146-6195-6 (pbk. : alk. paper)
        1. Ordination—Catholic Church—History.   2. Catholic Church—Bishops—History.   I. Title.

BX2240.M26 2005
264'.02084—dc22

2005002926

To the members

of the

St. Patrick's Seminary Community

Menlo Park, California

1994–2004

Contents

CHAPTER 6

**The Presentation of the Bishop-Elect in the
Rite of Episcopal Ordination according to the
Reform of the Second Vatican Council**   240

Conclusion   277

Acknowledgments

Remembering the humble beginnings of this work around a seminar table in Decio Hall on the University of Notre Dame campus in November 1989, and conscious of all who nurtured the project directly or who in the blessings of their friendship and kindness nurtured the author, I offer loving gratitude to:

Dr. Paul Bradshaw for the initial inspiration about the authentic nature of the sacrament of orders and for his consistent encouragement;

Abbot Marcel Rooney, O.S.B., who suggested narrowing the focus of this work to episcopal ordination and who was confident my notes from Notre Dame would have merit;

Fr. Anscar Chupungco, O.S.B., who corrected the course and affirmed the insights;

Fr. Ephrem Carr, O.S.B., who saved the day and brought the first project to a joyous conclusion;

Dr. Glenn C. J. Byer, S.L.D., who was a source of unfailing advice, good humor, and daring as we both "stood upon the heights" of those years at Sant'Anselmo;

Fr. Cassian Folsom, O.S.B., and Fr. Keith Pecklers, S.J., for the blessings of their work on my behalf and for their numerous points of improvement for the text;

Mr. Robert L. Volz, Custodian of the Chapin Library of Rare Books, Williams College, Williamstown, Massachusetts, who, "against [his] better judgement," copied for me the whole of 33v-57r of the Roman Pontifical of 1485;

Anne E. Grycz for life-giving friendship and for finding a way to get an early copy of the 2003 ICEL translation of the 1990 revision of the rite;

wise and patient friends who assisted with the translation:
>the late Fr. Frank Norris, s.s., Archbishop John R. Quinn,
>Dr. Martin Connell, Bishop Raymond Lahey, Fr. Bruce Harbert,
>Fr. Don Sharp, s.j., Mr. Peter Finn, and especially Fr. Dennis
>Smolarski, s.j.;

Mr. Peter Dwyer for coming to the lecture at the Institute for Ecumenical
>and Cultural Research at Saint John's University, Collegeville,
>and for his generous interest and support;

the Sisters of Notre Dame de Namur of the Generalate Community in
>Rome: via Monte Altissimo (1990–1994) and via Raffaello Sardiello
>(summer 1998 and January 1999) for the precious gift of their
>accompaniment in the common life;

Sisters of Notre Dame de Namur of the Waverley Street Community in
>Palo Alto, California (1994–2004), for their faithful witness to the
>goodness of God;

Fr. John Talesfore, s.l.l., Sr. Joyce Ann Zimmerman, c.p.p.s., and
>Ms. Bernadette Gasslein who shared a commitment to the subject,
>read manuscripts for other projects, and even printed them;

and in a most special way, the members of the St. Patrick's Seminary
>Community, 1994–2004: faculty, staff, Oblate Sisters, and students
>for the rich liturgical life that made sense of everything, for great
>hearts and great voices, for being living icons of servant leader-
>ship.

Ah! qu'il est bon le bon Dieu!
August 5, 2004
Dedication of the Basilica of Santa Maria Maggiore

Abbreviations

AAS	*Acta Apostolica Sedis*
BLE	*Bulletin de Littérature Ecclésiastique*
CCL	Corpus Christianorum (Series Latina)
DOL	*Documents on the Liturgy: 1963–1979. Conciliar, Papal, and Curial Documents.* International Commission on English in the Liturgy. Collegeville: Liturgical Press, 1982.
EL	*Ephemerides Liturgicae*
GeV	Gelasianum Vetus, *Liber sacramentorum romanae aeclesiae ordinis anni circuli (Cod. Vat. Reg. lat. 316/Paris, Bibl.Nat. 7193, 41/56) (Sacramentarium Gelasianum)*, L. C. Mohlberg, L. Eizenhöfer, and P. Siffrin, eds.
Greg	The Gregorian Sacramentary, *Le Sacramentaire Grégorien: Ses principales formes d'après des plus anciens manuscrits*, 3 vols. J. Deshusses, ed.
ITQ	*Irish Theological Quarterly*
J	*The Jurist*
JEH	*Journal of Ecclesiastical History*
JTS	*Journal of Theological Studies*
LG	*Lumen Gentium*
LJ	*Liturgisches Jahrbuch*
LMD	*La Maison-Dieu*
LQF	*Liturgiewissenschaftliche Quellen und Forschungen*
N	*Notitiae*
NRT	*Nouvelle Revue Théologique*
OR	*Les Ordines romani du haut moyen âge,* 5 vols. M. Andrieu, ed.
PGD	The Pontifical of Guillaume Durand, *Le Pontifical de Guillaume Durand.* Vol. III of *Le Pontifical romain au moyen âge.* M. Andrieu, ed.
PRC	The Pontifical of the Roman Curia, *Le Pontifical romain de*

la Curie romaine au XIIIe siècle. Vol. II of *Le Pontifical romain au moyen âge*. M. Andrieu, ed.

PRG   The Romano-Germanic Pontifical, *Le Pontifical Romano-Germanique du dixième siècle*, 3 vols. C. Vogel and R. Elze, eds.

PRXII   The Roman Pontifical of the Twelfth Century, *Le Pontifical romain du XIIe siècle*. Vol. I of *Le Pontifical romain au moyen âge*. M. Andrieu, ed.

PR1485   The Pontifical of 1485, *Pontificalis ordinis liber incipit in quo ea tantum ordinata sunt que ad officium pontificis pertinent* . . . , 3 vols. Romae, apud Steph. Planck, 1485.

PR1595   The Pontifical of 1595, *Pontificale romanum Clementis VIII P.M. iussu restitum atque editum*, 3 vols.

QL   *Les Questions Liturgiques et Paroissiales*

RED   Rerum Ecclesiasticarum Documenta

RHE   *Revue d'Histoire Ecclésiastique*

RL   *Rivista Liturgica*

RSPT   *Revue des Sciences Philosophiques et Théologiques*

RSR   *Revue des Sciences Religieuses*

SC   *Sacrosanctum Concilium*

SEA   *Statuta Ecclesiae Antiqua*. C. Munier, ed. CCL 148. Pp. 162–188. Turnhout: Brepols, 1963.

SJT   *Scottish Journal of Theology*

SL   *Studia Liturgica*

SSL   Spicilegium sacrum lovaniense

ST   Studi e testi

ST   *Summa Theologica*

SVe   *Sacramentarium Veronense (Cod. Bibl. Capit. Veron. LXXXV[80])*, L. C. Mohlberg, ed.

TS   *Theological Studies*

W   *Worship*

ZKT   *Zeitschrift für katholische Theologie*

Note to the Reader

I have kept the translation of the Latin texts as literal as possible so that the reader might encounter the texts without (too many) additional layers of interpretation from the author. But to this end, I have also maintained many Latin words and phrases both for their precision and their conciseness, and because the same words appear in subsequent texts throughout the development of the rite. For example, it is helpful to identify the collect following the litany as *Propitiare* and the initial words of the address as *Episcopum oportet* for the consistent use of these ritual elements through the centuries. I have also retained numerous Latin words (*apostolicus* and *consecrandus/consecratus,* for example) to highlight the underlying ecclesial and theological realities as well as to be accurate. When the texts use specific liturgical terms (*Kyrie eleison, Gloria, Alleluia),* those are retained as well.

As much as possible the translations include the original punctuation. For example, the critical edition of the letter of Archbishop Hincmar uses << >> to denote quotations, the *Lanalet Pontifical* characteristically inserts periods every few words, and the *Roman Pontifical of 1485* uses colons instead of commas. Very rarely, I will add a punctuation mark in brackets to make the meaning clearer.

I have also reproduced the capitalization as closely as possible, not using "Lord" when the text has "domine," for example, and retaining "Church" (the building) as the *Roman Pontifical of 1595* uses throughout. The one exception is to render "God" as capitalized though often the texts do not do so.

In order to make the lengthy sections of liturgical texts easier to read in both the Latin and the English, I have frequently added spaces between various sections which the original texts (even the critical editions) do not do. The copist of the *Roman Pontifical of 1485,* for example, deliberately saved space by cramming as many letters as possible on each page, and used abbreviations to do it. I have added new configurations of space as aids to the reader.

The inconsistencies of Latin spelling are generally transcribed as they are in the texts. The reader will note that the episcopal ceremonial shoes called *campagos* are also identified by a wide variety of spellings and that the *Benedictional of Robert* consistently adds additional marks to several vowels (e.g., ę). When describing the proclamation known as *Seruanda est* from the *Missale Francorum*, I maintain that spelling, but when it continues into the pontifical tradition, it becomes *Servanda est*. However, although the *Roman Pontifical of 1485* frequently employs abbreviated forms of words, these are not continued in the transcription but the words are reproduced in full.

Copies of the original Latin texts are appended to each individual section for the benefit of those readers who find them helpful. The ordination rite from the *Roman Pontifical of 1485* is not easily accessible, though the others are. Overall, whatever might assist the reader in discerning the evolving structure of episcopal ordination is what guided the presentation of these texts.

Introduction

In his fascinating and provocative memoirs, *Le mouvement liturgique: Témoignage et souvenirs*,[1] Bernard Botte allows his readers a rare glimpse into the insights and conflicts, the triumphs and aggravations behind the reform of the ordination rites during the years following the Second Vatican Council, 1965–72. He describes the extent of the project as he understood it:[2]

> The reform of these rites posed some ticklish problems. The Pontifical took shape progressively, from the fifth to the end of the thirteenth centuries, to a great extent outside Rome. It contained elements of very different origin and value. . . . Furthermore, certain formulas were inspired by medieval theology and needed correction. . . . The instructions given by the [Second Vatican] Council prescribed restoring simplicity and genuineness to the rites, so that the rites and prayers might catechize the people on holy orders. For this reason we had set aside the radical solution of restoring the ordinations to the fifth century state by suppressing the secondary rites added on through the ages. When judiciously chosen, these rites could be an element of catechesis. So we took the Roman Pontifical as it stood for our point of departure, and critiqued it to determine what could be retained of the Roman tradition.

Several decades after the initial reform of 1968 and many years since a further revision in 1990, it may be instructive to reconsider the consequences of using what Botte disclosed as the "point of departure" for the reform and its method.

A. THE PRESENTATION OF THE BISHOP-ELECT

The research for this work initially concentrated on a goal of presenting an extensive study of the sources for each element of the revised rite for the ordination of a bishop, *De Ordinatione Episcopi* (1968).[3] Following

Botte's illuminating comments, I began with a comparison of the 1968 rite with the texts from *Regarding the consecration of the elect as bishop [De Consecratione electi in episcopvm]* from the Roman Pontifical of 1595,[4] the "point of departure" for Botte and members of Study group 20 who were charged with the reform. The first ritual element of the 1595 Pontifical is the presentation of the bishop-elect; the research never went beyond it!

Study of the 1595 texts of *De Consecratione electi in episcopvm* brought to light not just one but two presentations of the bishop-elect, an unexpected discovery and the beginning of this present work. Why would a candidate for episcopal ordination be presented twice in one liturgy to the same ordaining bishop?

Further investigation into the relevant texts revealed his first presentation to the bishop to be related to the concluding elements of the selection of the bishop-elect. Use of the word "Selection" throughout this study is deliberate and meant to indicate a broad range of possible procedures by which the new bishop might be chosen. Selection does not denote democratic "election" nor any modern day political processes, but refers to choice of the elect by whatever means.

The 1595 texts indicated that the second presentation of the bishop-elect to the ordaining bishop introduced all the ritual elements of his consecration. Use of the word "Consecration" here is also deliberate and employed to identify the second stage of ordination (the laying on of hands and prayer) no matter what the title of the rite may be in any of the various liturgical books we will examine.

The significant distinction is this: the liturgical act of episcopal ordination possesses an essential structure consisting of two stages: Selection and Consecration. The two-stage structure of episcopal ordination is made known through the two-part structure of the presentation of the bishop-elect.

B. THE STRUCTURAL ANALYSIS OF
LITURGICAL UNITS

The fact of two presentations of the bishop-elect in the Pontifical of 1595 suggested that the most fruitful method of study would be structural analysis: to trace the presentation unit, which bridges Selection and Consecration, back to its sources by comparing the evolution of the presentation of the bishop-elect as a coherent ritual structure in itself. The methodology guiding this study owes a great deal to the method proposed by Robert Taft as "the structural analysis of liturgical texts."[5] I intend to follow Taft in his method and his motivation as he expresses it:

"I am seeking primarily the structure itself. For in the history of liturgical *development,* structure outlives meaning."[6]

Taft continues to explain the method:[7]

> . . . I have found the structural analysis of liturgical units to be the most useful first step after the gathering of initial data. That is, I have found it preferable to identify, isolate, and hypothetically reconstruct individual liturgical structures, then trace their history as such, rather than attempt to study complete rites as a unity in each historical period. For it has been my constant observation that liturgies do not grow evenly, like living organisms. Rather, their individual elements possess a life of their own.

The method then is one of structural analysis. To be more precise, it is the study of the evolution of one key ritual structure within the rite of episcopal ordination: the presentation of the bishop-elect. Study of this structure will rely upon the comparison of forms of the structure as it develops (often well after it has outlived its original meaning) in the major liturgical texts in the West from the fifth century to the present.

The task of tracing the evolution of liturgical texts confronts the reader with a double dynamic. On the one hand, liturgical texts are "living literature,"[8] constantly rewritten to express the developing self-awareness of different ecclesial communions through successive generations, adapted and revised to include felicitous elements borrowed from sister communions.

On the other hand, these "living" liturgical texts are uniquely conservative. "By the very process of their production,"[9] they copy, retain, and hand on ritual patterns and structures from age to age, long after their meaning is forgotten and long after the rituals themselves have ceased to be used.[10] And those transmitted structures themselves, as we will see, bear meaning, bear theological significance, and in particular, bear ecclesiological significance. As Aidan Kavanagh insightfully comments:[11]

> Another thing I have learned is that our Catholic tradition of worship is carried far more in the *structures* we observe in our worship than in the words, phrases, and verbal images with which we clothe those structures. Words, phrases, and verbal images, important as they are, are more malleable than structures. Words come and go from era to era. But structures, which also have a certain life of their own, tend to abide, and their influence on us is therefore more continuous, pervasive, subtle, and tough than we usually realize.

C. THE STRUCTURE OF EPISCOPAL ORDINATION

In this study of episcopal ordination rites, the structure is a deceptively simple one. Throughout the approximately 1500 years represented by the texts to be investigated below, even if all that remains are the "vestigial traces"[12] of the consensual selection process, the structure of episcopal ordination is revealed as twofold: Selection and Consecration.

Awareness of the two-stage nature of ordination is not new. Liturgical historians and theologians have recognized the traditional, multistage nature of the sacrament of ordination and have published their findings. Some of the most convincing statements over the last century include the following:

1907: a section of a lengthy article on episcopal consecration entitled "The influence of episcopal election on the rites of the consecration";[13]

1923: "Two actions belong to the ordination. . . . The first action is a choice for the commission (*electio*), the second is the commission itself (*ordinatio* in the strict sense). The two actions cannot be separated from each other";[14]

1937: "Episcopal ordination in the ancient Roman rite was marked by a great simplicity. . . . election, litany, imposition of hands, consecration prayer and kiss of peace";[15]

1953: "Ordination of bishops comprises two distinct times: a) the election; b) the consecration";[16]

1962: "What 'made' a man a bishop was due election and consecration in combination";[17]

1967: "[T]he admission of men to the ordained ministry involved in ancient times three main elements. First, a candidate was elected by the local Church. Secondly, there was the ordination itself. . . . Thirdly, the Eucharistic liturgy was celebrated";[18]

1972: "I use the term 'election–ordination' to describe the way a bishop was created in the early Church";[19]

1973: "[A] bishop is made so by his election and consecration, and as such he succeeds the apostles";[20]

1980: "Within the Spirit-filled Church authorization for a leadership function takes place through a spiritual event which includes election, ordination and reception of the newly ordained";[21]

4

1982: "From the councils of the fourth century on, the church held that election and consecration were the two principal acts in the making of a bishop";[22]

1986: "[O]rdination involves two distinct but related procedures: choice and election by the people, and a liturgical rite whose principal elements are the laying on of hands and prayer";[23]

1990: "[T]he older practice . . . saw ordination as a twofold process—the election as the means by which the candidate was actually appointed to the office, with the prayers then being made for his successful fulfillment of that into which he had already entered";[24]

1996: "[A]ll the elements of the process of admission to ordained ministry (electio-ordinatio-jurisdictio) form an indissoluble unity, particularly apparent in the case of the episcopacy."[25]

Key texts on which these scholars based their analyses of ancient church practice include the ordination rites described in (among others[26]) the *Apostolic Tradition*[27] and the *Canons of Hippolytus*.[28] These early texts provide excellent evidence of ordination as a two-stage process in one liturgical act that consists of communal choice and communal prayer at its core:

Apostolic Tradition 2. Concerning Bishops
Let him be ordained bishop who has been chosen by all the people, and when he has been named and accepted by all, let him assemble the people together with the presbytery and those bishops who are present, on the Lord's day. When all give consent, let them lay hands on him, and let the presbytery stand by, being still. And let all keep silence, praying in the heart for the descent of the Spirit; from whom let one of the bishops present, being asked by all, laying [his] hand on him who is being ordained bishop, pray, . . .[29]

Canons of Hippolytus 2. Of Bishops
Let the bishop be chosen by all the people, and let him be without reproach, as it is written concerning him in the Apostle. The week when he is ordained, all the clergy and the people say, 'We choose him.' There shall be silence in all the flock after the approbation, and they are all to pray for him and say, 'O God, behold him whom you have prepared for us.' They are to choose one of bishops and presbyters; he lays his hand on the head and prays. . . .[30]

The ancient two-stage structure may be traced back even further than the texts noted above. New Testament texts reveal the same original structure. The context in which the earliest structure takes shape is well described by Raymond Brown:[31]

> The only thing of which we can be reasonably sure is that someone must have presided at the eucharistic meals and that those who participated acknowledged his right to preside. How one got the right to preside and whether it endured beyond a single instance we do not know; but a more plausible substitute for the chain theory is the thesis that sacramental "powers" were part of the mission of the Church and that there were diverse ways in which the Church (or the communities) designated individuals to exercise those powers—the essential element always being church or community consent (which was tantamount to ordination, whether or not that consent was signified by a special ceremony such as the laying on of hands).

Patrick McGoldrick further identifies the converging elements in the New Testament which will become "Selection" and "Consecration": participation of the entire community, diversity of ministries, prayer, fasting, laying on of hands in a liturgical setting.[32] H. Boone Porter concurs: "The principal elements in this procedure begin to appear in the New Testament (Acts 1.21-6; 6.2-6; 1 Tim. 3.1-13; 4.14; 2 Tim. 1.6,7). These Biblical passages . . . have had such a great influence on later practice that apart from them the developed rites of later times cannot be fully understood."[33]

The ordination prayer for bishop from the *Apostolic Tradition* alludes to a very clear New Testament example of the two-stage structure of what will become the communal act of ordination in Acts 1:23-26:[34]

> So they proposed two, Joseph called Barsabbas, who was also known as Justus, and Matthias. Then they prayed and said, "Lord, you know everyone's heart. Show us which one of these two you have chosen to take the place in this ministry and apostleship from which Judas turned aside to go to his own place." And they cast lots for them, and the lot fell on Matthias; and he was added to the eleven apostles.

This primitive Selection stage consists of: the necessity of replacing a specific community leader; consensual choice of candidates; communal prayers recognizing God's choice; and a method of selection. What will become the Consecration stage is here described as a communal act of incorporation into leadership. This seminal two-stage structure, set by the author of Acts in the very earliest days of the Christian community, even before Pentecost itself, comes to mature expression in the patristic texts and is preserved in the liturgical books centuries beyond its actual use.

What does this current study hope to contribute if the New Testament and patristic two-stage structure of ordination is so well recognized? The initial work of this study, aiming at an understanding of *De Ordinatione Episcopi* (1968) as a reform of the base text of the rite in the 1595 Pontifical, discovered in the two presentations of the bishop-elect the bridge element between Selection and Consecration, i.e., the ritual element which made evident the two-stages of episcopal ordination even (surprisingly) in the Tridentine text. The research into the sources of this liturgical unit proceeded in reverse chronological order, marked by wonder at its complexity and tenacity. The investigation came to an end in the texts of *Ordo Romanus* XXXIV[35] and the *Missale Francorum*,[36] texts which stand as the earliest Western witnesses to the same two-stage structure handed on by the patristic tradition, the structure manifest by the presentation of the bishop-elect.

No longer would the New Testament and patristic pattern of episcopal ordination necessarily be considered a structure doomed to oblivion by the fifth century in the West. Careful attention to the development of this one structure of the presentation of the bishop-elect (once the reader knew what to look for) will reveal the remnants of its primitive form in all the major liturgical texts in the West through *De Ordinatione Episcopi* (1990).[37] This fact holds great promise for the recovery of this ancient structure and its full meaning for the life of the contemporary church. As David Power writes: "[I]t is worth noting how elements of an earlier polity remained on in the practice and celebration of ordination, thus becoming an available tradition allowing for retrieval."[38]

D. ECCLESIOLOGICAL IMPLICATIONS

Although the six chapters of this work are taken up in the comparative analysis of this one liturgical structure, it is ultimately the ecclesiology expressed by the changing forms of this structure which are of abiding interest, as well as the perspective this study provides within which to offer recommendations for further reform. To return to Fr. Taft, he explains that not only is structural analysis a valuable tool for historical understanding, but it has broader implications as well: "Not only can it provide paradigms for the reading of obscure texts and the reconstitution of debased remnants into their original shape; it can also help one identify an organic rhythm and theology of community prayer, ministerial roles, and so on, underlying the ancient structures. . . ."[39] The structure of the presentation of the bishop-elect reveals just such a theology, even when comparative analysis uncovers "regressive evolution"[40] of the rite and discloses how primitive elements were submerged and suppressed throughout the medieval period in particular.

While the focus of this study is primarily a structural analysis of the development of the presentation of the bishop-elect, ecclesiological implications of the various shifts within this liturgical unit will be indicated throughout the chapters. Descriptions of the development of additional elements of the rite are also included for the sake of completeness, because of the fascinating nature of this history, and because of the impact of the development of each ritual element upon the reform following the Second Vatican Council.

E. GOAL OF THIS STUDY

The chapters that follow take as a starting point the quotation of Bernard Botte that opened this Introduction and his comment about "the radical solution of restoring the ordinations to the fifth century state." The goal is to analyze the structure of the early texts of episcopal ordination (*Sacramentarium Veronense*,[41] the Gregorian Sacramentary,[42] *Ordo Romanus XXXIV, Ordo Romanus XXXV,* and *Ordo Romanus XXXVI,*[43] the *Missale Francorum,* the Old Gelasian Sacramentary (Gelasianum Vetus),[44] the *Gellone* Sacramentary[45] and the *Angoulème,*[46] and the letter of Hincmar of Rheims describing his ordination[47]); to study how the structure of the presentation of the bishop-elect becomes embedded in the tenth-century Romano-Germanic Pontifical,[48] in related *ordines romani* (*Ordo Romanus XXXV A* and *Ordo Romanus XXXV B,*[49]), and in selected English liturgical books (*The Leofric Missal*[50] *The Egbert Pontifical,*[51] the *Pontificale Lanaletense*[52] and *The Benedictional of Archbishop Robert*[53]); to see how the structure continues to change through the pontificals of the Middle Ages (the Pontifical of the Twelfth Century,[54] the Pontifical of the Roman Curia,[55] the Pontifical of Guillaume Durand de Mende,[56] the Pontifical of 1485,[57] and the Pontifical of 1595); and finally, to learn how the structure of the presentation of the bishop-elect is configured within the rites following the reform of the Second Vatican Council (*De Ordinatione Episcopi* [1968 and 1990]). The Conclusion will highlight selected historical and ecclesiological underpinnings and offer commentary regarding further reform of the rite of episcopal ordination.

These words of Michel Andrieu offer a helpful perspective as the structural analysis of the liturgical unit of the presentation of the bishop-elect begins. He suggests that in the course of studying each liturgical rite in turn, if the reader is sensitive to the diverse accents of the texts, one can catch the distinct voices of all the successive Christian ages:

> A sentence, a phrase, a single word can evoke distant resonances and carry our imagination back to that precise moment of the past when that word first resounded. Listening to the bishop repeat the sacred formularies, we forget the times in which we live and rejoin, across the centuries, the community of faithful who heard the bishop pray in that way for the first time. The rubrics themselves contain an evocative power. They describe rites whose original meaning is not always apparent: if we want to discover it and not be satisfied by a facile symbolism, it is necessary to restore the circumstances in which they were created, to revive the thoughts and purposes they inspired. The objects used by the celebrant and his ministers, the sacred vessels, the liturgical vestments: all of them have a history as well. Some apparently insignificant details can be remnants filled with history.[58]

Such a detail is the presentation of the bishop-elect.

NOTES

[1] Published by Desclée et Cie (Paris) in 1973; trans. J. Sullivan, *From Silence to Participation* (Washington, D.C.: Pastoral Press, 1988).

[2] Ibid., 134.

[3] From *De Ordinatione Diaconi, Presbyteri et Episcopi in Pontificale Romanum, ex decreto Sacrosancti Oecumenici Concilii Vaticanii II instauratum, auctoritate Pauli PP. VI promulgatum, editio typica* (Urbs Vaticana: Typis Polyglottis Vaticanis, 1968).

[4] *Pontificale romanum Clementis VIII P.M. iussu restitutum atque editum* (Romae: Iacobum Lunam, impensis Leonardi Parasoli et Sociorum, 1596); Paris, Bibl. Fac. O. P. Rés XVI A.-2° Centre international de publications oecuméniques des liturgies. The choice of 1595 as the date for this pontifical follows that given on the title page and several references to 1595 within the body of the text. 1595 is also the date the text was published.

[5] "The Structural Analysis of Liturgical Units: An Essay in Methodology" in his *Beyond East and West: Problems in Liturgical Understanding* (Washington, D.C.: Pastoral Press, 1984) 151–164.

[6] Ibid., 152 (emphasis in the original).

[7] Ibid., 154.

[8] Paul Bradshaw, "Shifting Scholarly Perspectives," in his *The Search for the Origins of Christian Worship*, second edition (New York: Oxford University Press, 2002) 5.

[9] Thomas Talley, *The Origins of the Liturgical Year* (New York: Pueblo, 1986) 189.

[10] Bradshaw, "Shifting Scholarly Perspectives," 5.

[11] "Reflections on Confirmation," *Professional Approaches in Christian Education* 17 (February 1986) 16 (emphasis in the original).

[12] Paul Bradshaw, *Ordination Rites of the Ancient Churches of East and West* (New York: Pueblo, 1990) 23.

[13] "Influence de l'élection épiscopale sur les rites de la consécration." Pierre de Puniet, "Consécration épiscopale," *Dictionnaire d'Archéologie Chrétienne et de Liturgie* III/2, 2582. Gen. eds. F. Cabrol and H. Leclercq (Paris: 1914).

[14] A quote by Rudolf Sohm, *Kirchenrecht*, vol. 2 (München-Leipzig: n.p.: 1923), 263, cited by Pierre-Marie Gy in his "Ancient Ordination Prayers," in *Ordination Rites*, eds. W. Vos and G. Wainwright (Rotterdam: The Liturgical Ecumenical Center Trust, 1980) 78.

[15] "La consécration épiscopale dans l'ancien rite romain était empreinte d'une grande simplicité. . . .: élection, litanies, imposition des mains, prière de consécration et baiser de paix." Vincent Leroquais, *Les Pontificaux manuscrits des bibliothèques publiques de France*, t. I (Paris: n.p., 1937) LXXXV.

[16] "L'Ordinazione dei vescovi comprende due tempi distinti: a) La elezione; b) La consacrazione." Mario Righetti, *I Sacramenti–I Sacramentali*, v. IV of *Manuale di Storia Liturgia* (Milano: Àncora, 1953) 426.

[17] Gregory Dix, "The Ministry in the Early Church," in *The Apostolic Ministry: Essays on the History and the Doctrine of Episcopacy*, ed. K. Kirk, second edition (London: Hodder and Stoughton, 1962) 212.

[18] H. Boone Porter, *The Ordination Prayers of the Ancient Western Churches* (London: SPCK, 1967) 78.

[19] Hervé-Marie Legrand, "Theology and the Election of Bishops in the Early Church," *Concilium* 7/8 (1972) 35.

[20] George Tavard, "Episcopacy and Apostolic Succession according to Hincmar of Rheims," *TS* 34 (1973) 615.

[21] Edward Kilmartin, "Episcopal Election: The Right of the Laity," in *Electing Our Own Bishops*, eds. P. Huizing and K. Walf (New York: Seabury, 1980) 41.

[22] Vivian Green, "Elections, church" in *The Dictionary of the Middle Ages*, volume 4, gen. ed. Joseph Strayer (New York: Charles Scribner and Sons, 1982) 421.

[23] Nathan Mitchell, *Mission and Ministry* (Wilmington, Delaware: Michael Glazier, 1986) 224.

[24] Paul Bradshaw, *Ordination Rites*, 57.

[25] James Puglisi, *The Process of Admission to Ordained Ministry: A Comparative Study*, volume I: *Epistemological Principles and Roman Catholic Rites*, trans. M. Driscoll and M. Misrahi (Collegeville: Liturgical Press, 1996) 200.

[26] For additional patristic texts, see Bradshaw, *Ordination Rites*.

[27] Bernard Botte, ed. *La Tradition apostolique de Saint Hippolyte: essai de reconstitution*, 5. Auflage, eds. A. Gerhards and S. Felbecker, *LQF* 39 (Münster: Aschendorff, 1989) and Paul Bradshaw, Maxwell Johnson, and L. Edward Phillips, *The Apostolic Tradition: A Commentary* (Minneapolis: Augsburg Fortress, 2003).

[28] *The Canons of Hippolytus*, ed. P. Bradshaw, trans. C. Bebawi, Alcuin/GROW Liturgical Study 2 (Bramcote, Nottingham: Grove Brooks Limited, 1987) 11–12. Critical edition is by René-Georges Coquin, *Les Canons D'Hippolyte, Patrologia Orientalis* tome XXXI.–Fascicule 2 (Paris: Firmin-Didot et Cie, 1966) 348–351 (Arabic and French).

[29] Bradshaw and others, *The Apostolic Tradition*, 24.

[30] The *Canons of Hippolytus*, ed. Bradshaw, 11–12.

[31] *Priest and Bishop: Biblical Reflections* (Paramus, New Jersey: Paulist Press, 1970) 41–42.

[32] "Orders, Sacrament of," in *The New Dictionary of Sacramental Worship*, ed. P. Fink (Collegeville: Liturgical Press, 1990) 898.

[33] *The Ordination Prayers of the Ancient Western Churches*, xi. Willy Rordorf adds Acts 20:28, a passage testifying that the Holy Spirit is the one instituting bishops in their ministry. Cf. "L'Ordination de l'évêque selon la Tradition apostolique d'Hippolyte de Rome," *QL* 55 (1974) 139 n. 7. The Chanoines Reguliers de Mondaye also suggest Hebrews 5:1, 4, which describe the high priest as called by God and chosen from among the people. See "L'Evêque d'après des prières d'ordination," in *L'Episcopat et L'Eglise universelle*, eds. Y. Congar and B.-D. Dupuy, Unam Sanctam 39 (Paris: Cerf, 1962) 752.

[34] *The New Oxford Annotated Bible*, New Revised Standard Version (New York: Oxford University Press, 1991).

[35] From *Les Ordines romani du haut moyen âge, III. Les Textes (Suite) (Ordines XIV–XXXIV)*, ed. Michel Andrieu, SSL Etudes et Documents 24 (Louvain: Spicilegium Sacrum Lovaniense, 1951; reprinted, 1961).

[36] *(Cod. Vat. Reg. lat. 257)*, eds. Leo Cunibert Mohlberg, Leo Eizenhöfer, and Petrus Siffrin, RED, series maior, fontes II (Roma: Herder, 1957).

[37] From *De Ordinatione Episcopi, Presbyterorum et Diaconorum, editio typica altera* (Città del Vaticano: Libreria Editrice Vaticana, 1990).

[38] "Power and Authority in Early Christian Centuries," in *That They May Live: Power, Empowerment and Leadership in the Church*, ed. M. Downey (New York: Crossroad, 1991) 32.

[39] Taft, "The Structural Analysis of Liturgical Units," 156.

[40] Robert Taft, "How Liturgies Grow: The Evolution of the Byzantine Divine Liturgy" in his *Beyond East and West*, 177.

[41] *(Cod. Bibl. Capit. Veron. LXXXV [80])*, eds. Leo Cunibert Mohlberg, Leo Eizenhöfer, Petrus Siffrin, third edition, RED, series maior 1 (Roma: Herder, 1978).

[42] Specifically, the *Hadrianum ex authentico in Le Sacramentaire Grégorien, Ses principales formes d'après les plus anciens manuscrits, I*, ed. Jean Deshusses, deuxième édition, Spicilegium Friburgense 16 (Fribourg: Editions universitaires, 1979).

[43] These latter two *ordines* are found in *Les Ordines romani du haut moyen âge, IV. Les Textes (Suite) (Ordines XXXV–XLIX)*, ed. Michel Andrieu, SSL Etudes et Documents 28 (Louvain: Spicilegium Sacrum Lovaniense, 1956).

[44] *Liber sacramentorum romanae aeclesiae ordinis anni circuli (Cod. Vat. Reg. lat. 316/Paris bibl. Nat. 7193, 41/56) (Sacramentarium Gelasianum)*, eds. Leo Cunibert Mohlberg, Leo Eizenhöfer, Petrus Siffrin, third edition, RED, series maior 4 (Roma: Herder, 1981).

[45] *Liber Sacramentorum Gellonensis*, eds. A. Dumas and J. Deshusses, CCL 159–159A Turnhout: Brepols, 1981).

[46] *Liber Sacramentorum Engolismensis: Le Sacramentaire gélasien d'Angoulême*, ed. Patrick Saint-Roch, CCL 159C (Turnhout: Brepols, 1987).

[47] The text and commentary by Michel Andrieu, "Le sacre épiscopal d'après Hincmar de Reims" *RHE* 48 (1953) 22–73, is considered the critical edition.

[48] *Le Pontifical romano-germanique du dixième siècle, I. Le Texte (I–XCVIII)*, eds. Cyrille Vogel and Reinhard Elze, ST 226 (Città del Vaticano: Biblioteca Apostolica Vaticana, 1963).

[49] These *ordines* are also found in volume IV cited in n. 38.

[50] *The Leofric Missal as used in the Cathedral of Exeter during the Episcopate of its first bishop A.D. 1050–1072*, ed. F. E. Warren (Oxford: Clarendon Press, 1883).

[51] *Two Anglo-Saxon Pontificals (The Egbert and Sidney Sussex Pontificals)*, ed. H.M.J. Banting, Henry Bradshaw Society, v. 104 (London: Henry Bradshaw Society, 1989).

[52] (*Bibliothèque de la ville de Rouen a. 27. Cat. 368*), ed. Gilbert Doble, Henry Bradshaw Society, v. 74 (London: Henry Bradshaw Society, 1937).

[53] Ed. H. A. Wilson, Henry Bradshaw Society, v. 24 (London: Henry Bradshaw Society, 1903).

[54] *Le Pontifical romain au moyen-âge, I. Le Pontifical romain du XIIe siècle*, ed. Michel Andrieu, ST 86 (Città del Vaticano: Biblioteca Apostolica Vaticana, 1938; reprinted, 1983).

[55] *Le Pontifical romain au moyen-âge, II. Le Pontifical de la Curie romaine au XIIIe siècle*, ed. Michel Andrieu, ST 87 (Città del Vaticano: Biblioteca Apostolica Vaticana, 1940; reprinted, 1984).

[56] *Le Pontifical romain du moyen-âge, III. Le Pontifical de Guillaume Durand*, ed. Michel Andrieu, ST 88 (Città del Vaticano: Biblioteca Apostolica Vaticana, 1940; reprinted, 1984).

[57] *Pontificalis ordinis liber incipit in quo ea tantum ordinata sunt que ad officium pontificis pertinent. . . .* (Romae: apud Steph. Planck, 1485).

[58] "Une phrase, une expression, un simple mot peut éveiller de lointaines résonances et transporter notre imagination vers le moment précis du passé où cette parole a d'abord retenti. En écoutant l'évêque qui redit les formules sacrées, nous oublions le temps où nous sommes et nous rejoignons, à travers les siècles, la communauté de fidèles qui, la première fois, entendit le pontife prier ainsi. Les rubriques elles-mêmes gardent une puissance évocatrice. Elles décrivent des rites dont la signification primitive n'est pas toujours apparente: si on veut la

découvrir et ne pas se contenter d'un symbolisme complaisant, il faut ressusciter les circonstances dans lesquelles ils furent créés, faire revivre les pensées et les intentions qui les inspirèrent. Les objets employés par le célébrant et ses ministres, les vases sacrés, les vêtements liturgiques, tout cela aussi a une histoire. Des détails en apparence insignifiants peuvent être des vestiges chargés de souvenirs." *Le Pontifical romain au moyen-âge, IV. Tables Alphabétiques*, ST 99 (Città del Vaticano: Biblioteca Apostolica Vaticana, 1941; reprinted, 1985) ix.

Chapter 1

The clergy and the people of the city consenting,
with their neighboring sees:

The Roman Model of Episcopal Ordination

I. The *Sacramentarium Veronense*[1]

A. THE *SVE* AND THE RITUAL CONTEXT OF EPISCOPAL ORDINATION

By the rite's "fifth century state," Dom Bernard Botte meant the ordination of bishops found in the collection known to him by the name "Leonine Sacramentary."[2] The source of those prayer texts is now identified as the *Sacramentarium Veronense,* most of whose original *libelli* date from the fifth and sixth centuries.[3]

The ordination texts occur in a descending order that is somewhat unusual: bishops, deacons, and presbyters—an order "reflecting the prestige of the diaconate at Rome."[4] There are no texts for the ordination of subdeacons nor any other orders.

The *SVe* follows the calendar of the civil year for the arrangement of its prayer texts. The ordination prayers are placed at the beginning of the month of September, one of four traditional times for diaconal and presbyteral ordinations in Rome.[5]

B. ANALYSIS OF THE LITURGICAL UNITS

Chapter XXVIII. *Consecratio Episcoporum* provides only a series of six prayer texts without titles and without rubrics:

no. 942 an oration: *Exaudi*

no. 943 an oration: the *secreta* of the Mass

no. 944 the *Hanc igitur* (of the Roman Canon)

no. 945 an oration: *Adesto*

no. 946 an oration: *Propitiare*

no. 947 the consecration prayer: *Deus honorum omnium*

The structure evident in the *SVe* is minimal. The following analysis will highlight a few points of interest regarding these texts, particularly those which continue in use in the pontifical tradition.

1. no. 942 an oration: *Exaudi*

Hear, Lord, the prayers of your humble people, that what is to be carried out by our ministry, may be established further by your power; through. . . .[6]

H. Boone Porter comments aptly on the identity of *Exaudi*:

"[D]ue to the rather haphazard arrangement of the *[SVe]*, it is not clear whether this prayer is there intended to be the first ordination collect, or the opening collect of the Mass."[7] In the Old Gelasian Sacramentary, the *Missale Francorum*, and the Sacramentary of *Angoulême*, *Exaudi* is the first ordination oration after the bidding, a fact suggesting that it may well have had the same purpose in *SVe* but was simply misplaced because of the "haphazard arrangement." The *Exaudi* will not continue in use in the pontifical tradition.

2. no. 943 (probably) the *secreta* of the ordination Mass

3. no. 944 the *Hanc igitur* (of the Roman Canon)

4. no. 945 another oration: *Adesto*

Assist [us], merciful God, so that what is done by our obedient office may be established by your blessing; through. . . .

In the *SVe, Adesto* is the first of two orations which characteristically occur before the consecration prayer in Roman episcopal ordination rites. In the *Missale Francorum*, however, it will be given the place of the post-communion prayer (even though it begs God's blessing for what is still to be done).

5. no. 946 another oration: *Propitiare*[8]

Graciously hear our petitions, O Lord, and pour out upon these, your servants, the power of your blessing, flowing from the horn of priestly grace; through. . . .

Propitiare is always the second of the two orations found before the consecration prayer in the Roman ordination rites. It will become the oration at the end of the litany of the saints in the later pontifical rites and remains in use in this same position in the current rite (1990).

6. no. 947 the consecration prayer: *Deus honorum omnium*

God of all honors, God of all the worthy ranks, which serve to your glory in hallowed orders; God who in private familiar converse with Moses your servant also made a decree, among the other patterns of heavenly worship, concerning the disposition of priestly vesture; and commanded that Aaron your chosen one should wear a mystical robe during the sacred rites, so that the posterity to come might have an understanding of the meaning of the patterns of the former things, lest the knowledge of your teaching be lost in any age; and as among the ancients the very outward sign of these symbols obtained reverence, also among us there might be a knowledge of them more certain than types and shadows. For the adornment of our mind is as the vesture of that earlier priesthood; and the dignity of robes no longer commends to us the pontifical glory, but the splendor of spirits, since even those very things, which then pleased fleshly vision, depended rather on these truths which in them were to be understood.

And, therefore, to these your servants, whom you have chosen for the ministry of the high-priesthood, we beseech you, O Lord, that you would bestow this grace; that whatsoever it was that those veils signified in radiance of gold, in sparkling of jewels, in variety of diverse workmanship, this may show forth in the conduct and deeds of these men. Complete the fullness of your mystery in your priests, and equipped with all the adornments of glory, hallow them with the [flow] of heavenly unction. May it flow down, O Lord, richly upon their head; may it run down below the mouth; may it go down to the uttermost parts of the whole body, so that the power of your Spirit may both fill them within and surround them without. May there abound in them constancy of faith, purity of love, sincerity of peace. Grant to them an episcopal throne to rule your Church and entire people. Be their strength, be their might; be their stay. Multiply upon them your blessing and grace, so that fitted by your aid always to obtain your mercy, they may by your grace be devoted to you; through. . . .

Until the conciliar reform of 1968, this venerable Roman text (with its later Gallican addition) served as the consecration prayer for well over a millennium of episcopal ordinations in the West.[9]

C. CONCLUSION

Botte concludes from this simple list of prayer texts that the structure of episcopal ordination at this early stage consisted of the imposition of hands joined to a prayer of consecration.[10] To make this assertion, however, Botte appears to be conflating the rubrics from chapters 2. (imposition of hands by the bishops present) and 3. (prayer of consecration) of the *Apostolic Tradition*[11] with the prayers of the "Leonine Sacramentary."

Such a conflation comes as no surprise since it is Botte whom we credit for the Latin reconstruction of the *Apostolic Tradition* and for the inspiration to substitute the consecration prayer from *The Apostolic Tradition* for that in the 1595 Pontifical. But Botte's outline of the structure of "the fifth century state" of the rite is somewhat less than accurate. For more precise textual evidence of the structure and rubrics for the Roman model of the ordination of bishops, we need to turn to *Ordo Romanus XXXIV*. But first let us examine the other Roman source for liturgical texts for episcopal ordination: the Gregorian sacramentary known as the *Hadrianum*.

Texts of the *Sacramentarium Veronense:*

SVe 942 an oration: *Exaudi*

Exaudi, domine, supplicum praeces, ut quod nostro gerendum est ministerio, tua potius uirtute peragatur: per.

SVe 945 another oration: *Adesto*

Adesto, misericors deus, ut quod actum est nostrae seruitutis officio, tua benedictione firmetur: per.

SVe 946 another oration: *Propitiare*

Propitiare, domine, supplicationibus nostris, et inclinato super hos famulos tuos cornu[m] gratiae sacerdotalis benedictionis tuae in eos effunde uirtutem: per.

SVe 947 the consecration prayer: *Deus honorum omnium*

Deus honorum omnium, deus omnium dignitatum quae gloriae tuae sacratis famulantur ordinibus, deus qui Mosen famulum tuum, secreti familiaris adfatu, inter cetera caelestis documenta culturae de [h]abitu quoque indumenti sacerdotalis instituens, electum Aharon mystico amictu uestiri inter sacra iussisti, ut intellegentiae sensum de exemplis priorum caperet secutura posteritas, ne eruditio doctrinae tuae ulli deesset aetati; cum et aput ueteres reuerentiam ipsa significationum species optineret, et aput nos certiora essent experimenta rerum quam enigmata figurarum. Illius namque sacerdotii anterioris habitus nostrae mentis ornatus est, et pontificalem gloriam non iam nobis honor commendat uestium, sed splendor animorum: quia et illa, quae tunc carnalibus blandiebantur obtutibus, ea potius quae in ipsis erant intellegenda poscebant.

Et idcirco his famulis tuis, quos ad summi sacerdotii ministerium deligisti, hanc, quaesumus, domine, gratiam largiaris, ut quidquid illa uelamina in fulgore auri, in nitore gemmarum, in multimodi operis uarietate signabant, hoc in horum moribus actibusque clariscat. Conple in sacerdotibus tuis mysterii tui summam, et ornamentis totius glorificationis instructos caelestis unguenti fluore sanctifica. Hoc, domine, copiosae in eorum caput influat, hoc in oris subiecta decurrat, hoc in totius corporis extrema descendat, ut tui spiritus uirtus et interiora horum repleat et exteriora circumtegat. Abundet in his constantia fidei, puritas dilectionis, sinceritas pacis. Tribuas eis cathedram episcopalem ad regendam aeclesiam tuam et plebem uniuersam. Sis eis auctoritas, sis eis potestas, sis eis firmitas. Multiplices super eos benedictionem et gratiam tuam, ut ad exorandam semper misericordiam tuam tuo munere idonei, tua gratia possint esse deuoti:

II. The Gregorian Sacramentary: *Hadrianum ex authentico*[12]

A. *GREGH* AND THE RITUAL CONTEXT OF EPISCOPAL ORDINATION

Michel Andrieu explains in his masterful commentaries on the *ordines romani* that the sacramentary which was employed concurrently with the *ordines* of the Roman "Collection A" was the Gregorian Sacramentary.[13] More precisely, it was the eighth-century *Hadrianum ex authentico*: "a Mass book compiled for the exclusive use of the *domnus apostolicus* ["the apostolic lord," the pope] when he celebrated *de iure* at the Lateran and in the stational churches of the City."[14]

The ordination rites for bishops, presbyters, and deacons occur in descending order at the beginning of Part I, immediately after the order of Mass. There are no ordination rites for any other ministry in this earliest form of the Gregorian except for the ordination of a pope (Part III, no. 226).

B. ANALYSIS OF THE LITURGICAL UNITS

The ordination texts from chapter 2, *Benedictio Episcoporum*, are these:

no. 21 an oration: *Adesto*

no. 22 an oration: *Propitiare*

nos. 23a and 23b the consecration prayer: *Deus honorum omnium*

no. 24 the *super oblata*

no. 25 the *Hanc igitur*

no. 26 the *ad completa* (postcommunion prayer)

1. no. 21 an oration: *Adesto*

Attend to our supplications, Almighty God, and may what is to be carried out by our humble ministry be fulfilled by the work of your power. Through. . . .

The *Hadrianum ex authentico* evinces the characteristic Gregorian pattern of three prayers for each Mass: in this case, *Adesto* (the collect), *super oblata*, and *ad completa*. It is this *Adesto* prayer from the *GregH*, with its echoes of the *SVe Exaudi*, which will be taken up into all the major pontificals as the collect of the ordination Mass until the 1968 reform.

2. no. 22 an oration: *Propitiare*

Except for a change in the number of bishops-elect from plural to singular, this is the text of the *SVe* 946 that will be consistently listed as the second oration before the consecration prayer in future episcopal ordination rites, becoming the litany oration.

3. nos. 23a and 23b the consecration prayer: *Deus honorum omnium*

The text of the Roman consecration prayer in the *GregH* is that of *SVe* 947 but with the addition of three crosses to indicate the appropriate times for the anointing of the head of the elect during the mention of spiritual anointing in the prayer:

. . . Complete the fullness of your mystery in your priest, and equipped with all the adornments of glory, hallow him with the [flow] of heavenly unction. + May it flow down, O Lord, richly upon his head; + may it run down below the mouth; + may it go down to the uttermost parts of the whole body, so that the power of your Spirit may both fill him within and surround him without. . . .[15]

4. no. 24 the *Super oblata*

This text is not derived from the *SVe*. It is taken up into the Romano-Germanic Pontifical as an alternative *secreta*, but then falls into disuse.

5. no. 25 the *Hanc igitur*

An expansion of the *SVe* text, this prayer will be accepted into the *Missale Francorum* and from there it will be copied into the major pontificals.

6. no. 26 the *Ad completa*

The *GregH* has composed a new prayer for the postcommunion; no other sacramentaries will include it in episcopal ordination rites.

C. CONCLUSION

Analysis of the prayer texts of the Roman sacramentaries, the *SVe* and the *GregH*, does not yield the structure that Botte recognizes. For a more complete description of the Roman model of the entire rite, we turn to an analysis of selected *ordines romani*.

Texts of the Gregorian Sacramentary:

GregH 21 an oration: *Adesto*

Adesto supplicationibus nostris omnipotens deus, et quod humilitatis nostrae gerendum est ministerio tuae uirtutis impleatur effectu. Per dominum.

GregH 23b the consecration prayer: *Deus honorum omnium*

. . . Comple in sacerdote tuo mysterii tui summam et ornamentis totius glorificationis instructum, caelestis unguenti flore sanctifica. + Hoc domine copiose in eius caput influat, + hoc in oris subiecta decurrat, + hoc in totius corporis extrema descendat, ut tui spiritus uirtus et interiora eius repleat, et exteriora circumtegat. . . .

III. *Ordo Romanus XXXIV*[16]

A. *OR34* AND THE RITUAL CONTEXT OF EPISCOPAL ORDINATION

OR34 ("In the name of the Lord the ordo by which an acolyte is ordained in the holy roman church") presents the rites for the ordination of acolyte, subdeacon, deacon, presbyter, and bishop in ascending order and in summary fashion. Nos. 1–13 include only two brief prayer texts; they concern themselves chiefly with the rubrics for the first four ordination rites. Nos. 14–45 describe the ordination of a bishop.

Andrieu consigned the manuscripts of *OR34* to his "Collection A" of *ordines* that are Roman in origin,[17] a provenance that is especially obvious in the rite of episcopal ordination: the ordaining bishop is the pope, the "apostolic lord" *(domnus apostolicus)*, and the elect swears an oath before the tomb of Saint Peter.

From the time period reflected by the practices recorded in *OR34*, Andrieu proposed that the *ordo* is the work of a Lateran cleric summarizing the ordination rituals of his day—the year 750 at the latest.[18] More significant, however, is Andrieu's further comment that, regarding the preliminary acts of the ordination on Saturday and preceding days, the redactor is handing on a practice established at least from the sixth century enduring well into the eighth.[19] Vogel concurs, stating that although

OR34 does not record original Roman practices before the sixth century, it "contains the Roman rites of ordination as they were performed in the early Middle Ages."[20] Thus *OR34* preserves the earliest unquestionably Roman *ordo* for the ordination of a bishop.[21]

B. ANALYSIS OF THE LITURGICAL UNITS

The rite for ordaining a bishop in *OR34* is remarkably comprehensive. Of the thirty-two elements of nos. 14–45 ("Again how a bishop is ordained"), more than half (17) occur before the Sunday consecration liturgy. Do these preliminary elements indicate merely imprecision in the title of the rite, or do they point to a significant fact about the underlying structure of the rite? What are the elements of ordination outlined in this section of the texts?

In *OR34*, the bishop-elect is presented twice to the ordaining bishop (in this case, the metropolitan, the Bishop of Rome). The first presentation completes and confirms his selection by the several sees involved; the second presentation introduces his consecration. The terms "Selection Presentation" and "Consecration Presentation" will be used to identify these two fundamental liturgical elements which characterize the Roman model of episcopal ordination.

1. *Selection Presentation*

a. SELECTION PRESENTATION: TEXT
OR34.14. Again how a bishop is ordained. When the bishop of a city or place has died, another is chosen by the people of the city and a decree [of election] is made by the priests, clergy and people.

15. And they come to the apostolic lord, bringing also with them the *suggestio*, this is the petitionary letters, that he may consecrate as bishop for them [the elect] whom they have brought with them.

16. Then the apostolic lord commands the *sacellarius*[22] or the *nomenculator* that he direct [the elect] to the archdeacon and he examines him regarding the four capital [sins] according to the canons, . . .

17. And, after the [book of the] gospels has been brought into their midst, the elect himself takes an oath before the archdeacon, provided that he has been aware of none of these things in himself.

18. And after this, having handed [the book] over to the subdeacon, he proceeds with the above-mentioned elect to the hall of the blessed apostle Peter, and there facing his most holy body he confirms that he is not acquainted with the above-named capital [sins].

19. On another day however, it is announced by the archdeacon that it has been done.

20. Then the apostolic lord vests himself with the pallium and sits in the chair and, after the bishops and presbyters have been called, he asks them to be seated with him, while all the clergy stand.

21. He commands his *sacellarius* that the people of the city should come in. While he proceeds leading them in, the apostolic lord chooses from them, that is, from the priests, the person who renders the account when he is being questioned.

22. And, when they have been brought in, they are questioned by the apostolic lord in this way:
What is it, brothers, that concerns you? They respond: That you, lord, would grant us a patron.

The apostolic lord responds: Do you have yours. They answer: We have. Which rank has he exercised? They respond: Deacon, presbyter or whatever it was.

They are asked: How many years has he in the diaconate or presbyterate? They respond how many and how well.
The apostolic lord says: Is he from the church itself or from another? They respond: From [the church] itself.
And, if he says: From another, the apostolic lord says: Does he have the dimissorial [letter] from his bishop? They respond: He has. And thereupon they present it.
The apostolic lord says: Did he have a spouse? Has he taken care of his household? They answer: He has taken care of it.
The apostolic lord says: What about him has pleased you? They respond: Chastity, hospitality, goodness and all good things that are pleasing to God.
The apostolic lord says: Consider, brothers, that he must not have made any promise to you. You know that simony is against the canons. They respond: Far be it from us. The apostolic lord says: You yourselves will see [to it].
And again he says: Do you have the decree [of election]? They respond: We do.

23. And, when they present it, he commands the *sacellarius* that it be read again.

24. And when it has been read again, the apostolic lord orders that the elect be led in.

25. When the elect has been led in by the subdeacon, he prostrates himself three times on the ground at a distance.

26. Then the apostolic lord says the prayer in this way: May the lord protect us. All respond: Amen.

27. The apostolic lord questions him: What concerns you, brother? He responds: To what I am not worthy, these fellow servants of mine have brought me.
He says: What rank have you exercised? He responds: Deacon or presbyter or whatever it is.

And he questions him: How many years do you have in the diaconate or in the presbyterate? He responds with how many. Again the apostolic lord questions him: Did you have a spouse and have you taken care of your household? He answers if he had, or not, and if he has taken care of his household.

And again he is questioned by the apostolic lord if he has made any gift or promise [in return for being selected]. He answers: Far be it [from me]. Again the apostolic lord asks him: Which codices [of scripture] are read in your church? He responds: The octateuch,[23] kings, prophets, acts of the apostles, the gospel and the apostle.

28. The apostolic lord asks: Do you know the canons? He responds: Teach us, lord. The apostolic lord says: If you hold an ordination, do it at the appropriate times, that is, at the first, fourth, seventh and tenth months. Do not promote bigamists or curiales[24] to sacred orders. Nevertheless the edict from the archives will be given to you regarding how you ought to live.[25]

29. Then the apostolic lord commands the archdeacon and he rereads the petition, which the elect himself presented to the apostolic lord from the people.

30. And when it has been read again, the apostolic lord says: Because the desires of all have agreed upon you, today you will abstain and tomorrow, if it is pleasing to God, you will be consecrated. The archdeacon answers: As you have commanded, lord.

31. The apostolic lord gives the kiss [of peace] to the elect and goes out.

b. SELECTION PRESENTATION: THE JOURNEY TO ROME

The first stage in the ordination of a bishop begins with the death of his predecessor and the selection of the new bishop by the community of the "widowed" church: its presbyters, clergy, and people. Representatives of the vacant see then accompany the bishop-elect on the journey to Rome for subsequent components of the ordination: they present their decree (verifying the legitimacy of the selection), the *suggestio* or petitionary letters (requesting the consecration of the elect), and they present the elect himself to the local metropolitan (the apostolic lord, the pope).

After the archdeacon has testified to the elect's innocence of the four capital sins which would prevent his ordination, the pope calls into assembly other bishops and presbyters with all the clergy. The people of the vacant see also gather that they may testify to the choice and so that the elect they have chosen may be questioned before them.[26] The apostolic lord first interrogates those who accompanied the elect, using the words of a ritual dialogue regarding his worthiness: is the elect worthy canonically, spiritually, personally? Was the election free? In the dialogue, members of the widowed church make their postulation: "That you, Lord, would grant us a patron."

Finding their testimony to be trustworthy, the pope then calls for the presentation of the elect himself. A subdeacon leads him before the pope, and the elect responds humbly to the questions of his worthiness:

OR34.27. . . . To what I am not worthy, these fellow servants of mine have brought me.

c. SELECTION PRESENTATION:
   PROCLAMATION OF CONSENSUS AND CONSECRATION

In addition to the identical questions previously asked of those accompanying the elect, further questions are put to the elect regarding the scriptural texts proclaimed in his church and his knowledge of ecclesiastical canons. The decree verifying the selection is then read in his hearing.

The questions, the documents and reports, and the interrogations confirm the consensus reached by the sees involved in the ordination: the presbyters, clergy, and people of the vacant see and the metropolitan see (which in this case is also the apostolic see). The presence of other bishops is noted for the Selection Presentation; they are also present for the consecration. James Puglisi offers this concise summary of the significance of the bishops' participation during the selection as well as the consecration:

> [T]heir involvement means several things: they bear witness for the whole Church, and stand guarantors of the faith of the ordinand; they are ministers of the gift of the Holy Spirit within the epiclesis of the assembly; and by their action they transmit the apostolic ministry to the elect by receiving him as the representative of his Church among the other apostolic Churches. . . .[27]

Once the consensus of all is clear, the pope announces it and thereby introduces the second stage of the ordination which follows the completed consensual process. The pope declares:

OR34.30. . . . Because the desires of all have agreed upon you, today you will abstain and tomorrow, if it is pleasing to God, you will be consecrated.

It is important to note the basis for the pope's assent. The worthiness of the elect for consecration is ratified by his previous selection by members of the vacant see and by the consent of the sees represented by the neighboring bishops. Thus it is by reason of the completed consensual process of selection (which the pope acknowledges and confirms) that the consecration of the bishop-elect may proceed. The first stage of ordination is consensual selection; only when consensus is established does the pope allow the second stage, the consecration, to begin.

The overriding concern of the ancient church, Santantoni explains, is clearly evident in the wording of the pope's proclamation of consensus:

> [O]ne cannot and must not impose on a Church a bishop who is not wanted; it is necessary that the faithful be in agreement with the choice. Only in these circumstances will the *Apostolic Lord* give his consent: *Because the desires of all have agreed upon you, you will be consecrated.* It is the principle of Pope Celestine I: *no bishop may be imposed on the unwilling; the consensus and desire of the clergy[,] people, and [civil] authority is required.*[28]

Completing and then proclaiming the consensus, the pope allows the consecration to take place the following day.

d. SELECTION PRESENTATION: STRUCTURE

The structure of the first stage of episcopal ordination in *OR34* follows this outline:

OR34

1st Stage

Selection Presentation

	Saturday[29]
presentation:	members of the vacant See
postulation:	grant us a patron
	decree
	examination

proclamation of consensus and consecration:

	the desires of all/
	you will be consecrated

This initial presentation of the elect by members of his local church acts as part of the ritual bridge between the selection and the consecration; it is the first formal act that links selection with the liturgy of consecration. The Selection Presentation also witnesses to the authenticity of the postulation, i.e., those who choose and present the elect are those who have found him worthy; their presentation confirms their postulation.

2. *Consecration Presentation*

a. CONSECRATION PRESENTATION: TEXT

OR34.32. On the next day, which is Sunday, the apostolic lord goes forth into the church, and there the bishops and presbyters and the other orders of clerics assemble with him.

33. And the apostolic lord enters the vesting room and orders the schola to sing.

34. And he processes with all decorum from the vesting room into the church itself, as is the custom.

35. When the introit is completed, they do not then sing *Kyrieleison*, but directly the apostolic lord says the prayer.

36. Then the apostle to Timothy is read: Dearly beloved, the saying is true: if anyone desires the episcopate, he desires a good work, and so on.

37. And while the gradual is sung, the archdeacon goes out with acolytes and subdeacons and vests him in the dalmatic, chasuble and campobos[30] and leads him in.

38. And when he has been led in, the apostolic lord addresses him thus: The clergy and people of the city of N. consenting, with their neighboring sees, have chosen for themselves N., the deacon, or presbyter, to be consecrated bishop. Therefore let us pray for this man, that our God and lord Jesus Christ may grant to him the episcopal chair for ruling over his church and all the people.

39. Then the schola begins *Kyrieleison*, with the litany, while the apostolic lord prostrates with the priests and the elect himself on the ground before the altar.

40. When the litany is completed, they rise and then he blesses him.

41. When the blessing is finished, he gives him the kiss and the archdeacon holding him brings him and thus he gives the kiss to the bishops, [and] presbyters.

42. And then the apostolic lord bids him to sit above all the bishops.

43. And when he is seated, the *Alleluia* is sung, then the gospel, and the mass is completed.

44. When he comes to communicate, the apostolic lord presents to him the *formata*[31] as well as a consecrated host and, receiving it, the bishop himself communicates from it at the altar and the rest he preserves to communicate himself from it for forty days.[32]

45. And afterward by the command of the apostolic lord he communicates all the people.

b. CONSECRATION PRESENTATION: SILENT ACCOMPANIMENT

While the first presentation was for reasons of verifying and completing the consensus as to the elect's worthiness and selection, the second presentation introduces the consecration (in *OR34*.41 called the blessing *[benedictio]*).[33] On Sunday, the pope enters the church in the company of bishops, presbyters, and the other clerical orders. Although *OR34* is silent on the subject, it is likely that members of the vacant see are also present, as the rubrics indicated their presence the evening before. Following the introit, the apostolic lord offers the collect, (probably) *Adesto* (= *GregH* 2.21).[34]

c. CONSECRATION PRESENTATION:
EPISCOPAL VESTMENTS

The Consecration Presentation of the elect occurs after the gradual: wearing episcopal vestments, the elect is led forward by the archdeacon with acolytes and subdeacons. The change in vesture at this point is not insignificant. Preceding any consecratory prayer, preceding any ritual gesture, the elect enters the church for consecration already vested as a bishop. The validity of this vesting lies in the significance of the Selection Presentation that occurred the previous day. Because of the consensus which elected this man and further confirmed his selection, a substantial part of his ordination has already occurred. He has been constituted bishop-elect by the desires of all; what remains to be accomplished is "the second half of the ordination process, the service of prayer for the ordinand."[35] For this stage of the process, he vests according to the order he already possesses in a real sense: the elect is presented vested as a bishop.

d. CONSECRATION PRESENTATION:
PROCLAMATION OF CONSENSUS AND PROCLAMATION

After the silent accompaniment, there occurs a proclamation of consensus and consecration by the pope:[36]

OR34.38. The clergy and people of the city of N. consenting, with their neighboring sees, have chosen for themselves N., the deacon or presbyter, to be consecrated bishop. *Therefore* let us pray for this man, that our God and lord Jesus Christ may grant to him the episcopal chair for ruling over his church and all the people.

The first half of this text is a statement of the consensus of the clergy and people of the vacant see as well as that of the adjacent sees in choosing this man for episcopal ministry. The pope acknowledges that the first constitutive element of the ordination has occurred: the consensus of the ecclesial communions involved in the choice of bishop—the vacant see, adjacent sees, and metropolitan (apostolic) see.

The second half of the text is actually a bidding, inviting the assembly to pray for the elect. Once the consensus of the sees involved is completed and acclaimed, only then does the assembly gather to pray for the elect.[37] As the pope and presbyters prostrate in prayer with the elect, the schola begins the *Kyrieleison* and the entire community enters into the prayer of the litany of saints as the consecration continues.

OR34 summarizes the remaining elements of the ordination quite succinctly: "then he blesses him" (no. 40). The consecration concludes with the kiss of peace and seating the new bishop in a special place above the other bishops present.

e. CONSECRATION PRESENTATION: STRUCTURE

We find the structure of the Consecration Presentation in this early Roman document to be as follows:

OR34

2nd Stage

Consecration Presentation:

	introt to gradual
	episcopal vestments
presentation:	archdeacon
proclamation of consensus and consecration:	
	clergy + people + bishops consent/
	bidding *OR34*
consecration:	litany
	blessing
	consecration continues

C. CONCLUSION

The earliest Roman tradition of episcopal ordination as preserved in *OR34* is characterized by an integrated process from the death of the previous bishop to the selection, presentation, and consecration of the next. Episcopal ordination is described as a two-stage ecclesial act extending over a period of time, involving consensus of the vacant see, adjacent sees, and the metropolitan see. Confirmation of the consensus then introduces the second stage: the consecration.

The liturgical units consist of, first, a Selection Presentation composed of a presentation of the elect to the ordaining bishop as the concluding stage of selection: i.e., an examination of his worthiness culminating in the proclamation of consensus and consecration. The second unit is the Consecration Presentation: a presentation of the elect for consecration beginning with the ordaining bishop's second proclamation of consensus and consecration (statement and bidding) which introduces the elements of consecration proper (litany, consecration prayer, etc.).

The consensus statements of the ordaining bishop highlight the function of the two presentations as the ritual bridge between the two stages of ordination. This bridge component is then visually represented by the vesting of the elect in episcopal garb before his consecration. It is the communion of consensus attested by all the participants in the ordination which is the catalyst for the consecration to begin. The pope confirms the consensus in his statement addressed to the entire assembly, and calls for the prayers of all to begin the second stage of the ordination, the consecration.

The following outline of the structure of the Roman model of episcopal ordination is offered as an alternative to what Botte considered "the fifth century state":

OR34

1st Stage

Selection Presentation
	Saturday
presentation:	members of the vacant See
postulation:	grant us a patron
	decree
	examination
proclamation of consensus and consecration:	
	the desires of all /
	you will be consecrated

2nd Stage

Consecration Presentation
	Sunday
	introit to gradual
	episcopal vesture
presentation:	archdeacon
proclamation of consensus and consecration:	
	clergy + people + bishops consent /
	bidding *OR34*
consecration:	blessing
	consecration continues

Texts of *Ordo Romanus 34:*

Selection Presentation:

14. Iterum quomodo episcopus ordinatur. Dum a civitate et loco episcopus fuerit defunctus, a populo civitatis elegitur alius et fiet a sacerdotibus, clero et populo decretus.

15. Et veniunt ad domnum apostolicum, adducentes secum et suggestionem, hoc est rogatorias litteras, ut eis episcopum consecret, quam secum deportati sunt.

16. Tunc domnus apostolicus praecipit sacellario vel nomenculatori, ut eum ad archidiaconum dirigat et eum inquirat de quattuor capitulis secundum canones, . . .

17. Et, dum se nulli horum ipse vir conscius fuerit, evangeliis ad medium deductis, iurat ipse electus archidiacono.

18. Et post haec, tradito subdiacono, pergit cum praefato electo apud aulam beati Petri apostoli, ibique in eius sacratissimum corpus confirmat quod non cognovisset superius nominata capitula.

19. Alio vero die, nuntiatur ab archidiacono sicut actum est.

20. Tunc domnus apostolicus induit se palleo et sedet in sede et, vocatis ad se episcopos vel presbiteros, iubet eos sibi consedere, stante autem universo clero.

21. Praecipit vero sacellario suo, ut plebs civitatis ingrediatur. Ille dum perrexerit eos introducendum, elegit ex illis, id est ex sacerdotibus, personam qui rationem reddat, dum fuerit interrogatus.

22. Et, dum fuerint introducti, interrogantur a domno apostolico sic: Quid est, fratres, quod vos fatigastis? Illi respondent: Ut nobis, domine, concedas patronem. Respondit domnus apostolicus: Habetis vestrum; Respondent Habemus.
Quo honore fungitur? Resp: Diaconus, presbiter, aut quod fuerit.
Interrogantur: Quantos annos habet in diaconato aut presbiterato? Resp. quantos et quomodo.
Domnus apostolicus dicit: De ipsa ecclesia est, an de alia? Resp. De ipsa. Et, si dixerit: De alia, dicit domnus apostolicus: Dimissoriam habet ab episcopo suo? Resp.: Habet. Et mox offerunt eam.
Domnus apostolicus dicit: Coniugem habuit? Disposuit de domo sua? Resp. Disposuit.
Domnus apostolicus dicit: Quid vobis complacuit de eo? Resp.: Et castitas, hospitalitas, benignitas et omnia bona quae Deo sunt placita.
Domnus apostolicus dicit: Videte, fratres, ne aliquam promissionem fecisset vobis. Scitis quod simoniacum est et contra canones. Resp.: Absit a nos. Domnus apostolicus dicit: Vos videritis.
Et iterum dicit: Habetis decretum? Resp.: Habemus.

23. Et, dum eum offerunt, iubet sacellario ut relegatur.

24. Et, dum relectus fuerit, iubet domnus apostolicus introducere electum.

25. Dum vero introductus fuerit electus a subdiacono a longe tertia vice se in terra prosternet.

26. Tunc domnus apostolicus orationem dicit sic: Protegat nos dominus. Respondent omnes: Amen.

27. Domnus apostolicus interrogat eum: Quid te fatigasti, frater? Resp.: Ad quod non sum dignus isti confamuli mei me adduxerunt.
Et dicit: Quod honore fungeris? Respondet: Diaconus, aut presbiter, vel quod est. Et interrogat eum domnus apostolicus: Quantos annos habes in diaconatu aut in presbiteratu. Resp. quantos.
Iterum interrogat eum domnus apostolicus: Habuisti coniugium et de domo tua disposuisti? Ille resp. si habuit, aut non, et si de domo sua disposuit. Et iterum interrogatur a domno apostolico si aliquam dationem aut promissionem fecisset. Resp.: Absit. Iterum domnus apostolicus interrogat eum: Quales codices in ecclesia tua leguntur? Resp.: Octatheucum, regnorum, prophetarum, actuum apostolorum, evangelium et apostolum.

28. Domnus apostolicus interrogat: Nosti kanones? Resp.: Doce nos, domine. Dicit domnus apostolicus: Ordinationem si feceris, aptis temporibus fac, id est primi, quarti, septimi et decimi mensis. Bigamos aut curiales ad sacros ordines ne promoveas. Attamen dabitur tibi edictum de scrinio quomodo debeas conversari.

29. Tunc praecipit archidiacono domnus apostolicus et relegit petitionem, quam ipse electus a populo domno apostolico offerreret.

30. Et dum relecta fuerit, dicit domnus apostolicus: Quoniam vota omnium in te conveniunt, hodie te abstinueris et crastino, si placuerit Deo, consecrandus eris. Resp. archidiaconus: Iussisti, domne.

31. Et dat domnus apostolicus ipso electo osculum et egredietur foras.

Consecration Presentation:

32. Alia vero die, quod est dominica, procedit domnus apostolicus in ecclesia, ibique episcopi et presbiteri cum eo vel ceteri ordines clericorum consistunt.

33. Et ingreditur domnus apostolicus secretario et iubet scolam psallere.

34. Et procedit de secretario cum omni decore in ecclesia ipsa, sicut mos est.

35. Completo vero introitu, non dicunt tunc Kyrieleison, sed mox domnus apostolicus dat orationem.

36. Deinde legitur apostolum ad Timotheum: Karissime, fidelis sermo: si quis episcopatum desiderat, bonum opus desiderat, et cetera.

37. Et dum psallitur gradale, egreditur archidiaconus cum acolitis et subdiaconis et induit eum dalmatica, planeta et campobos et introducit eum.

38. Dumque introductus fuerit, vocat eum domnus apostolicus sic:
Clerus et plebs consentiens civitatis talis, cum adiacentibus parrochiis suis, elegerunt sibi Illum talem, diaconum, vel presbiterum, episcopum consecrari. Oremus itaque pro eodem viro, ut Deus et dominus noster Iesus Christus tribuat ei cathedram episcopalem ad regendam ecclesiam suam et plebem universam.

39. Deinde scola incipit Kyrieleison, cum laetania, prostrato domno apostolico cum sacerdotibus et ipso electo in terra ante altare.

40. Completa vero laetania, surgent et tunc benedicet eum.

41. Benedictione expleta, dat osculum domnus apostolicus et tenens eum archidiaconus deportat eum et sic dat osculum episcopis, presbiteris.

42. Et tunc iubet eum domnus apostolicus super omnes episcopos sedere.

43. Et dum sederit, dicitur Alleluia, deinde evangelium, et expletur missa.

44. Dum vero venerit ad communicandum, domnus apostolicus porrigit ei formatam atque sacratam oblationem et, eam suscipiens, ipse episcopus ex ea communicat super altare et caeterum ex ea sibi reservat ad communicandum usque ad dies quadraginta.

45. Et postmodum ex praecepto domni apostolici communicat omnem populum.

IV. *Ordo Romanus XXXV*[38]

A. *OR35* AND THE RITUAL CONTEXT OF EPISCOPAL ORDINATION

Bernard Botte concisely evaluates the transition from *OR34* to *OR35*. He explains that, while OR34 remained faithful to the structural simplicity of episcopal ordination evident in the *Apostolic Tradition*, "the Roman liturgy was not confined to Rome. It spread out into Italy, into Gaul, into Germany. But what it gained by expansion, it risked losing in purity. It became loaded down with foreign elements."[39]

By the first quarter of the tenth century, *OR34* had been recast as *OR35*, a document "already contaminated at Rome itself, under the influence which the ultramontane liturgy had begun to exercise."[40] *OR35* still maintained the essence of the ancient Roman tradition but also represented liturgical practice of a period of transition not lasting beyond the mid-tenth century.[41] While the compiler of *OR35* had *OR34* "under his eyes," so the compiler of the Romano-Germanic Pontifical (as we will see) worked with a copy of *OR35*.[42]

Although "In the name of the most high God, the ordo by which a lector is ordained in the holy roman church" is the title of *OR35*, it contains detailed rubrical directives and prayer texts for the ordination of lector, acolyte and subdeacon, and the rites for use during the four Ember seasons of the year for the ordination of deacons and of presbyters. Nos. 38–74 ("How a bishop is ordained") concludes this sequence of ascending order. The slightly larger print that Andrieu uses to distinguish the additions of *OR35* from the text of *OR34* reveals that the later rites are meant for use outside the city of Rome.[43] Here the predominant reference is not to the apostolic lord but to the lord pontiff (*domnus pontifex*).

B. ANALYSIS OF THE LITURGICAL UNITS

1. *Selection Presentation*

a. SELECTION PRESENTATION: TEXT[44]

OR35.38. How a bishop is ordained. When the bishop of a city or place has died, another is chosen by the people of the city and a decree [of election] is made by the priests, clergy and people.

39. And they come to the lord pontiff, bringing with them the *suggestio,* that is, the petitionary letters, that he may consecrate [the elect] as bishop for them, that is that one they have brought with them.

[40.–42. The interrogation regarding the four capital sins; the elect swears on the gospel book; the elect swears again before the body of Saint Peter.]

43. On another day, which is Saturday, it is announced by the archdeacon that it has been done.

[44.–50. The pontiff calls in the other bishops and presbyters and all the clergy; the people are led in with one priest chosen to speak for them; the people of the local church are interrogated by the pontiff; the decree of election is read again; the elect enters and greets the pontiff humbly.]

51. The lord pontiff asks him: What concerns you, brother? He responds: To what I am not worthy, these fellow servants of mine have chosen me. [The interrogation continues.]

52. [The pontiff asks about the canons, and discusses the time for ordinations, who may be advanced (to higher rank) and the edict from the pontiff's archives which the elect will be given to advise him in his new ministry.]

53. [The petition is read again]

54. And when it has been read again, the lord pontiff says: Because the desires of all have agreed upon you, today you will abstain and tomorrow, if it is pleasing to God, you will be consecrated. He responds: As you have commanded, lord.

55. And then the lord pontiff gives the kiss to the elect and, having given the command, goes out.

b. SELECTION PRESENTATION:
   THE ROMAN MODEL OUTSIDE ROME

The structure as well as the wording of OR35 are almost identical to that of OR34. The process of ordination begins with the selection of another bishop after the death of the previous one and the creation of a decree of election by the presbyters, clergy, and people. Their written postulation is presented to the lord pontiff along with the elect himself. The investigation of the elect's moral standing by the archdeacon is described as it is in OR34, although OR35 explicitly mentions that it is on Saturday that the findings are reported.

The ordaining bishop then begins his own examination of the worthiness of the elect during the Saturday synaxis at which other suffragan bishops, presbyters, all the clergy and the people from the widowed church are gathered. One of their number (a presbyter) is chosen to answer the bishop's questions regarding the elect. This spokesman is the one who voices their request: That you, Lord, grant us a patron.

A subdeacon presents the elect for the final stage of the selection process. With the elect's words (To what I am not unworthy, these fellow servants of mine have chosen me), the bishop's examination begins. The questions for the interrogation are those of OR34 with provision still made that the elect might be a deacon or a presbyter. Only a few minor alterations[45] distinguish the examination of OR35 from its predecessor.

Satisfied that the selection of this man is valid and appropriate, the bishop makes his proclamation that consensus exists and therefore the consecration may proceed:

OR35.54. Because the desires of all have agreed upon you, today you will abstain, and tomorrow, if it is pleasing to God, you will be consecrated.

Thus the liturgical unit of the Selection Presentation evident in OR34 remains intact in OR35: presentation, interrogation, proclamation of consensus and consecration. The first stage of ordination involves a presentation of the elect for a final examination, the successful outcome of which is followed by a proclamation that consensus is now complete. The communion of consensus permits the second stage, the consecration, to commence.

2. *Consecration Presentation*

OR35.[56.–60. The next day, Sunday, the pontiff comes to the church and vests; the introit is sung but the *Kyrie* is omitted; the *Gloria* and collect take place. The epistle is from 1 Timothy 3:1ff.]

61. After this, the gradual is sung. Then the archdeacon goes out with acolytes or subdeacons, and vests the elect in dalmatic, chasuble and *campagos* and brings him in further, next to the entrance to the *presbyterium.*

62. Then finally the pontiff comes down from the chair and gives his hand to the deacon, and coming before the altar turns to the people and says:

The clergy and people of the city of N. consenting, with their neighboring sees, have chosen N., the deacon or presbyter, to be consecrated bishop. Therefore let us pray for this man, that our God and lord Jesus Christ may grant to him the episcopal chair for ruling over his church and all the people.

63. Then the schola begins: the *Kyrie eleyson,* with the litany. Then the pontiff bows before the altar with the elect and the deacons, until the *Agnus Dei* [section of the litany] is said.

64. At the conclusion of the litany, with the elect bowing before the pontiff, the archdeacon places the closed [book of the] four gospels upon his neck and between his shoulders. When a pope is consecrated, however, the open [book of the] gospels is placed upon him.

65. And apostolic lord alone blesses him himself, imposing the hand upon his head.

66. A bishop cannot be blessed by less than three other bishops, one who gives the blessing and the other two who impose the hand on the head of him who is blessed.

67. The bishop should be blessed in this way:
The Lord be with you. They respond: And with your spirit.
Prayer. *Propitiare. . . .*

68. The consecration. *Deus honorum omnium. . . .*

69. When this is completed, he consecrates his hands if they have not already been consecrated, according to the rite we have determined above [in the consecration of presbyter *OR35.*31].

70. Then [the newly ordained bishop] gives the kiss to the pontiff and deacons and taking hold of him, the archdeacon brings him into the *presbyterium* and he gives the kiss to the bishops and the presbyters.

71. And then the lord pontiff bids him to be seated at the head of the chairs of the bishops.

72. The lord pontiff returns to the chair. When he is seated, the *Alleluia* is sung, or the tract, then the gospel, and the Mass is completed according to its rite.

73. When [the new bishop] has come to communicate, the lord pontiff presents to him the *formata* as well as an entire consecrated host, and the bishop himself receiving it, communicates from it at the altar. When he is seated again, he preserves it and also [communicates] from it continually until forty days are over.

74. And afterward, at the command from the lord pontiff, he communicates the people with the other bishops.

b. CONSECRATION PRESENTATION:
   GALLICAN ADDITIONS IMPOSED ON THE ROMAN MODEL

Although greatly expanded with rubrics from the *ordo* of the solemn papal Mass and with prayer texts from *GregH*, the elements of the Consecration Presentation (occurring after the gradual of Sunday's liturgy) also follow the same structure as in *OR34*. The rubrics add that the proclamation of consensus and consecration is said to the people; the wording of the proclamation itself is that of *OR34*:

OR35.62. . . . The clergy and people of the city of N. consenting, with their neighboring sees, have chosen N., the deacon or presbyter, to be consecrated bishop. Therefore let us pray for this man, that our God and lord Jesus Christ may grant to him the episcopal chair for ruling over his church and all the people.

Following the proclamation, the litany begins and the consecration continues.

With only the briefest phrase, *OR34* depicted the consecration of the bishop-elect: "And then he blesses him." *OR35* extends this description to include significant Gallican additions: the imposition of the gospel book by the archdeacon on the neck and between the shoulders of the elect,[46] the rubric for imposition of hands by other bishops present while one of them offers the blessing, and the anointing of hands if that has not already been done (i.e., at the presbyteral ordination).[47] The elements of the consecration previously seen in *OR34* (the kiss of peace, the seating of the new bishop above the other bishops, and insertion of two prayer texts from *SVe* [*Propitiare* and the consecration prayer, *Deus honorum omnium*[48]]) complete the rite.

C. CONCLUSION

The structure of *OR35* then is the same as that outlined for *OR34*:

OR35

1st Stage

Selection Presentation

	Saturday
presentation:	members of the vacant see
postulation:	grant us a patron
	decree
	examination

proclamation of consensus and consecration:

	the desires of all /
	you will be consecrated

2nd Stage

Consecration Presentation

	Sunday
	introit to gradual
	episcopal vestments
presentation:	archdeacon and others

proclamation of consensus and consecration:

	clergy + people + bishops consent /
	bidding *OR34*
consecration:	litany
	Propitiare
	consecration prayer
	consecration continues

The significance of *OR35* does not lie in recording any changes in the structure of the two presentations of the bishop-elect, but in being the transition document between *OR34* and the eventual Germanic transformation of the ordination rite which further chapters will explore. As Andrieu explains what is to come:

> The preliminaries of episcopal ordination, with the double interrogation on Saturday, do not offer any notable modification compared with *OR34*. In the description of the first part of the Mass, up to the ordination, here and there a few minor details are recorded which do not relate to the original model, but which change nothing of the arrangement of the ceremony. It is after the litany that the innovations appear.[49]

The hybrid nature of the Romano-Gallican *OR35* thus helps us trace the evolution of the Roman liturgy of episcopal ordination as it gradually accumulates the "foreign elements" that Botte criticized. In his own examination of episcopal ordination in *OR34*, *OR36*, and *OR35*, Santantoni agrees with Botte and Andrieu when he writes that these three *ordines* "present a substantial affinity. In fact, only the last demonstrates the first symptoms of an evolution that is already under way and is by now unstoppable."[50]

Texts of *Ordo Romanus 35*:

Selection Presentation:

38. Quomodo episcopus ordinatur. Dum a civitate vel loco episcopus fuerit defunctus, a populo civitatis eligitur alter et fiet a sacerdotibus, clero et populo decretum.

39. Et veniunt ad domnum pontificem adducentes secum et suggestionem, id est rogatorias litteras, ut eis episcopum consecret, id est illum quem secum deportati fuerint.

[40.–42.]

43. Alia vero die, quod est sabbatum, nuntiatur ab archidiacono sicut actum est.

[44.–50.]

51. Domnus pontifex interrogat eum: Quid te fatigasti, frater? Resp.: Ad quod non sum dignus, isti confamuli mei me elegerunt. . . .

[52.–53.]

54. Et dum relecta fuerit, dicit domnus pontifex: Quoniam omnium vota in te conveniunt, hodie te abstinebis et crastina die, si Deo placuerit, consecrandus eris. Res.: Iussisti, domne.

55. Et tunc dat domnus pontifex ipso electo osculum et iussus egreditur foras.

Consecration Presentation:

OR35.[56.–60.]

61. Post haec, psallitur gradale. Tunc egreditur archidiaconus cum acolytis vel subdiaconibus, induet ipsum electum dalmatica, planeta et campagos et deportat superius, iuxta rugas altaris.

62. Tunc demum descendit pontifex de sede et dat manum diacono, veniensque ante altare vertit se ad populum et dicit:
Clerus et plebs consentiens civitatis Illius, cum adiacentibus parrochiis suis, elegerunt sibi Illum talem, diacconum vel presbiterum, episcopum consecrari. Oremus itaque pro eodem viro, ut Deus et dominus noster Iesus Christus tribuat ei cathedram episcopalem ad regendam ecclesiam suam et plebem universam.

63. Deinde scola incipit: Kyrie eleyson, cum letania. Tunc pontifex inclinat se ante altare cum ipso electo et diaconibus, usquedum dicatur Agnus Dei.

64. Finita vero laetania, inclinatus ipse electus ante pontificem, ponit archidiaconus quattuor evangelia super cervicem eius et inter scapulas clausa. Nam quamdo apostolicus consecratur, aperta ponuntur evangelia super eum.

65. Et benedicet eum domnus apostolicus solus per semetipsum, inposita manu super caput eius.

66. Nam a ceteris episcopis episcopus benedici non potest minus quam a tribus, unus qui dat benedictionem et alii duo qui inponunt manum super caput ipsius qui benedicitur.

67. Ita debet benedici episcopus: Dominus vobiscum. Resp.: Et cum spiritu tuo. Or[atio]. Propitiare. . . .

68. Consecratio. Deus honorum omnium. . . .

69. Hac expleta, consecrat ei manus si nondum habuit consecratas, ordine quo supra prefiximus.

70. Tunc dat osculum pontifici et diaconibus et tenens eum archidiaconus deportat in presbiterium et dat osculum episcopis et presbiteris.

71. Et tunc iubet eum dominus pontifex in capite sedium episcoporum sedere.

72. Domnus vero pontifex redit ad sedem. Dum enim sederit, dicitur Alleluia, aut tractus, deinde evangelium, et expletur missa ordine suo.

73. Cum autem venerit ad communicandum, domnus pontifex porrigit ei formatam atque sacratam oblationem integram, suscipiensque eam episcopus ipse ex ea communicat super altare. Quod vero residuum fuerit, sibi reservat de eo quoque die usque quadraginta dies expletos.

74. Et postmodum, iussus a domno pontifice, communicat populum cum ceteris episcopis.

V. *Ordo Romanus XXXVI* [51]

Do the liturgical units of other *ordines romani* that describe episcopal ordination confirm the two-part structure of ordination evident in *OR34* and *OR35?* The other relevant *ordines* are *Ordo Romanus XXXV A, Ordo Romanus XXXV B,* and *Ordo Romanus XXXVI.* Since both *Ordo Romanus XXXV A* and *Ordo Romanus XXXV B* are dependent upon the Romano-Germanic Pontifical,[52] the commentary on their structure will be included at the end of chapter 2 which is an analysis of that pontifical.

A. *OR36* AND THE RITUAL CONTEXT OF EPISCOPAL ORDINATION

Although from its title, "Concerning the ranks of the roman church," *OR36* appears to be a Roman document, "it is actually a Romano-Frankish rite of ordination making a bit more explicit the prescriptions of the *Statuta Ecclesiae Antiqua* which, since the late VI century, had been normative for the Frankish church."[53] Beginning with a brief mention of minor orders, *OR36* then presents the ordination rites for deacons, presbyters, and bishop in ascending order, and concludes with the rite for the ordination of a pope.

Vogel proposes the year 897 for the compilation of *OR36* and suggests that the compiler is a Frankish liturgist writing from firsthand experience of papal ceremonies.[54] The result is a mixed description of genuinely Roman elements (e.g., the description of the procession of the papal entourage from the basilica of Saint Peter up to the monastery of Saint Martin for the ordination) with non-Roman ones (e.g., Frankish vestment names and use of the title "pontiff" for the ordaining bishop rather than "apostolic lord" of *OR34*).

B. ANALYSIS OF THE LITURGICAL UNITS

1. *Consecration Presentation*

a. CONSECRATION PRESENTATION: TEXT
OR36 Concerning the ranks of the roman church.

29. Bishops however are blessed at every [liturgical] season. But now the practice is that they would be blessed during the night.

30. For at the second section [of the night office], that is at the sixth reading, the pontiff departs from the church of saint Peter and goes up to the monastery of saint Martin which is situated near the [outside of the] apse[55] of that church, and the elect who is to be blessed follows, entering in simplicity with the rest of the clergy, and stands outside the door of the oratory.

31. The schola of singers begins the introit. Afterward the pontiff intones: *Gloria in excelsis Deo.* The oration follows.

32. And leaving the altar, one presbyter and another deacon vest [the elect] in pontifical vestments, first in linen [alb] and cincture, then the large amice; then the smaller dalmatic and cincture, the maniple and short stole; then the greater dalmatic, with the clergy meanwhile singing the response Render to God. The tract is Those who sew.

33. The gospel: He sent them on ahead of him, two by two.

34. And then [the elect] is called into the basilica, a presbyter on his right and a deacon on his left. He bows his head in their midst and approaches and comes as far as the altar.

35. Then taking off the cope the pontiff vests him in chasuble[56] and reads a brief statement in this uninterrupted way: He says, our citizens have chosen this pastor for themselves. Therefore let us pray for this man that almighty God may pour into him the grace of his spirit and he may be considered worthy to rule the chair of the episcopacy.

36. And the schola responds: Christ, hear us. And they sing the litany.

37. And then [the elect] comes closer to the altar, with head bowed. The pontiff imposes a hand on his head and says an oration in the manner of a collect, and another [prayer] for him chanted with the modulations customary for a preface.

38. And the pontiff sits in his chair. The elect kisses his foot and receives the [kiss of] peace and his consecration is completed.

39. And that day wherever the pope celebrates Mass, [the new bishop] is to receive communion from his hand.

b. consecration presentation:
introductory rites

There is no description of a Selection Presentation of the bishop-elect in *OR36*. The initial prescriptions include the admonition that bishops may be ordained any time during the church year, i.e., in contrast to the four Ember Saturdays specified for presbyters and deacons. But the customary time for episcopal ordination according to *OR36* is the end of Saturday night vigils, with a variant of the text identifying the same Ember Saturdays when the episcopal ordination is held at the basilica of Saint Peter.[57]

The rite itself begins with the introit as the elect with the rest of the clergy stands at the threshold of the oratory. Following the *Gloria* and opening collect, the elect is vested as a bishop; the compiler of *OR36* meticulously notes each item of vesture in proper sequence.

Regarding the order of the ritual elements, however, the compiler seems less meticulous. He lists the gradual, and then the tract and gospel as occurring while the elect is being vested outside the basilica proper. Is the elect meant to be absent for the proclamations of Scripture?

Placement of the Consecration Presentation of the bishop-elect after the gospel in *OR36* is unique. None of the other Roman *ordines* nor the Romano-Germanic Pontifical vary from the pattern of the Consecration Presentation following the gradual, a pattern that will take firm hold in the pontifical tradition. Only the reform of the ordination rites in 1968 will break this venerable practice and place the rite after the gospel. Perhaps placement of the presentation at the conclusion of the gospel proclamation in *OR36* is a copyist's error (or perhaps faulty memory on the part of the Frankish eyewitness). It may also be a unique form that quickly fell into disuse.

c. CONSECRATION PRESENTATION: SILENT ACCOMPANIMENT

After donning episcopal vestments, the elect is called back into the basilica, accompanied by a presbyter on his right and a deacon on his left, and comes before the pontiff (not the pope). No relationships between the celebrants of the liturgy are important enough to specify in these rubrics. "Our citizens" have chosen the elect, but are these present? Are the presbyter, deacon, and clergy mentioned in the text members of any see involved in the selection? *OR36* gives no indication of such.

d. CONSECRATION PRESENTATION: PROCLAMATION OF CONSENSUS AND CONSECRATION

Immediately after the presentation, the elect receives the chasuble from the ordaining bishop who then makes a proclamation of consensus and consecration that leads into the bidding (neither of which have identical textual parallels in any other known document):

OR36.35. He says, our citizens have chosen this pastor for themselves. Therefore let us pray for this man that almighty God may pour into him the grace of his spirit and he may be considered worthy of the ruling chair of the episcopacy.

The introductory words of this proclamation ("Our citizens") indicate that this rite occurs in the cathedral city of the vacant see itself and not in Rome. Some type of previous selection process involving the faithful has occurred, but it is not described in *OR36*. The two-part dynamic of episcopal ordination, however, is evident: it is because "this man" has been chosen that the consecration may now begin, i.e., the litany, the imposition of hands with an oration (probably *Propitiare* = *SVe* 946) and the consecration prayer (probably the Roman formula *SVe* 947 with the Gallican interpolation) which is to be sung with modulations like the eucharistic preface (called the *contestata*.)[58]

e. CONSECRATION PRESENTATION: STRUCTURE

The structure of the presentation described in *OR36* is as follows, confirming the same two-part structure of ordination as that witnessed by *OR34* and *OR35:*

OR36

1st stage

2nd stage
Consecration Presentation:

	Sunday (Saturday evening)
	introit to collect
	episcopal vestments
	gradual to gospel
presentation:	presbyter and deacon
	additional vestments

proclamation of consensus and consecration:

	our citizens have chosen/
	bidding
consecration:	litany
	laying on of hands
	oration *(Propitiare?)*
	consecration prayer
	consecration continues

C. CONCLUSION

The pattern of episcopal ordination in the Roman tradition, drawn from *OR34, OR35,* and *OR36,* reveals two stages: the first characterized by a presentation of the bishop-elect for purposes of selection, the second characterized by a presentation for consecration. Both stages are described in *OR34* and *OR35,* while in *OR36* only the Consecration Presentation is included. However, a prior stage of ordination (the selection) is referred to in the words of the proclamation of consensus and consecration of *OR36.*

In each of the three Roman *ordines* discussed in this chapter, the ordaining bishop at the time of the Consecration Presentation announces the consensus achieved by the previous selection process and then, with the words of the bidding, introduces the consecration stage of the ordination. The Roman tradition of episcopal ordination consists of a two-stage process, selection and consecration; the bridge between them is the presentation of the bishop-elect, in particular the bishop's proclamation of consensus and consecration, the change to episcopal vestments, and the bishop's second proclamation.

The similarity in the structure of the liturgical units is clear in this outline:

OR34	OR35	OR36
1st stage	*1st stage*	*1st stage*
Selection Presentation	**Selection Presentation**	
Saturday	Saturday	
presentation:	**presentation:**	
Church of the elect	Church of the elect	
postulation:	postulation:	
grant us a patron	grant us a patron	
decree	decree	
examination	examination	
proclamation of consensus and consecration	**proclamation of consensus and consecration**	
desires of all/	desires of all/	
you will be	you will be	
consecrated	consecrated	
2nd stage	*2nd stage*	*2nd stage*
Consecration Presentation	**Consecration Presentation**	**Consecration Presentation**
Sunday	Sunday	Sunday
		(Saturday evening)
introit to gradual	introit to gradual	introit to gradual
episcopal vestments	episcopal vestments	episcopal vestments
presentation:	**presentation:**	**presentation:**
archdeacon	archdeacon and others	presbyter and deacon
proclamation of consensus and consecration	**proclamation of consensus and consecration**	**proclamation of consensus and consecration**
clergy + people	clergy + people	our citizens
+ bishops consent/	+ bishops consent/	have chosen/
bidding OR34	bidding OR34	bidding
consecration:	**consecration:**	**consecration:**
litany	litany	litany
	Propitiare	*(Propitiare?)*
blessing	consecration prayer	consecration prayer
consecration continues	consecration continues	consecration continues

Chapter 2 explores the texts that offer evidence of a Gallican model of episcopal ordination: the *Missale Francorum* and the Old Gelasian Sacramentary, and the letter of Hincmar of Rheims describing his own episcopal ordination. How do the Gallican churches adapt the structure (and texts) of the Roman model? Is the two-stage process of episcopal ordination evident in these texts as well?

Texts of *Ordo Romanus XXXVI:*

Consecration Presentation:

OR36 De gradibus romanae ecclesiae.

29. Episcopi autem omni tempore benedicuntur. Nunc vero mos est ut nocturno tempore benedicentur.

30. Secunda namque incisione, id est lectione sexta, egreditur pontifex de ecclesia sancti Petri et ascendit monasterium sancti Martini, quod sub tegna ipsius ecclesiae situm est, et subsequitur ipse electus qui benedicendus est, simpliciter cum reliquo clero incedens, et stat foris ostium oratorii.

31. Scola cantorum incipit introitum. Postea dicit pontifex: Gloria in excelsis Deo. Sequitur oratio.

32. Et exeuntes ab altare, unus presbiter et alter diaconus induunt eum vestimenta pontificalia, in primis linea et cingulo; deinde anagolagium grande; postea dalmatica minore et cingulo, brachiale et orarium brevem; deinde dalmatica maiore, clero interim canente responsorium Immola Deo. Tract. Qui seminant.

33. Evangelium: Misit illos binos ante faciem suam.

34. Et tunc advocatur in basilicam, presbiter a dextris eius et diaconus a sinistris. Ipse vero, inclinato capite in medio eorum, incedit usque dum veniat ante altare.

35. Tunc exuitur casula et induit eum pontifex planeta et legit brevem in hunc modum continentem:
Cives, inquit, nostri elegerunt sibi illum pastorem. Oremus itaque pro hoc viro, ut Deus omnipotens infundat in eo gratiam spiritus sui et dignus habeatur ad cathedram episcopatus regendam.

36. Et respondetur ab scola: Christe, audi nos. Et canunt laetaniam.

37. Et tunc accedit propius ad altare, subnixo capite. Pontifex vero ponet manum super caput eius et dicit unam orationem in modum collectae, alteram eo modulamine quo solet contestata cantari.

38. Et sedet pontifex in sella sua. Ipse vero osculatur pedem eius et suscipitur ad pacem et sic consummatur consecratio illius.

39. Et ipso die, ubicumque apostolicus missam celebrat, de manu eius communionem accipiat.

NOTES

[1] Hereafter *SVe*.

[2] "L'ordination de l'évêque," *LMD* 98 (1969) 113.

[3] Cyrille Vogel, *Medieval Liturgy: An Introduction to the Sources*, translated and revised by W. Storey and N. Rasmussen (Washington, D.C.: Pastoral Press, 1986) 43.

[4] Frank Hawkins, "The Early History of the Roman Rites of Ordination," in *The Study of Liturgy*, eds. C. Jones, G. Wainwright, E. Yarnold and P. Bradshaw, revised edition (New York: Oxford University Press, 1992) 362.

[5] "In the brief time which transpired from the death of Leo until the pontificate of Gelasius I (492–496), the ember days became certainly designated as the time for ordination to the priesthood and the diaconate." John Reiss, *The Time and Place of Sacred Ordination* (Washington, D.C.: The Catholic University of America Press, 1953) 8.

[6] Translation from Bradshaw, *Ordination Rites*, 215. The translations of *SVe* below are also from Bradshaw, 215–216, with the exception of *Propitiare* and of "fluore" (flow) in the consecration prayer. In the Gallican forms of the prayer, "fluore" will become "rore" (dew).

[7] H. Boone Porter, *The Ordination Prayers of the Ancient Western Churches*, 19.

[8] The translation is from *Ordination of a Bishop*, no. 43, in *Rites of Ordination of a Bishop, of Priests, and of Deacons*, second typical edition (Washington, D.C.: United States Conference of Catholic Bishops, 2003) adapted for the plural of the *SVe*. The *Propitiare* is the one oration in consistent use from the fifth or sixth century even to today.

[9] For excellent presentations of the theology of the composite prayer, see Antonio Santantoni, *L'Ordinazione episcopale*, Studia Anselmiana 69, Analecta Liturgica 2 (Roma: Editrice Anselmiana, 1976); Giuseppe Ferraro, *Le Preghiere di ordinazione al Diaconato, al Presbiterato, e all'episcopato* (Napoli: Edizioni Dehoniane, 1977); David Power, *Ministers of Christ and His Church* (London: Geoffrey Chapman, 1969); and Bradshaw, *Ordination Rites*.

[10] "Le Sacramentaire léonien ne nous en fait pas de description, mas les prières qu'il donne font supposer que c'était un rite très simple dont l'essentiel était l'imposition des mains par les évêques présents avec une prière de consécration." "L'ordination de l'évêque," 113.

[11] Botte, ed., *La Tradition apostolique de Saint Hippolyte*, 4–10.

[12] Hereafter *GregH*.

[13] Andrieu, *OR* III, 541.

[14] Vogel, *Medieval Liturgy*, 84.

[15] The first manuscript to introduce the crosses is Cambrai, bibl. mun., *codex* 164 (from 811–812): "the only surviving, complete, uncorrected copy of the *Hadrianum*." (See Vogel, *Medieval Liturgy*, 82; and A. Houssiau, "La formation de la liturgie romaine du sacre épiscopal," *Collectanea Mechliniensia* 33 [1948] 279–280, n. 7.) It is interesting to note that the Cambrai *codex* 164 was commissioned by the

same bishop (Hildoard) who probably commissioned the *Gellone* Sacramentary (790–800) (Vogel, ibid.) which is the oldest witness to the anointing of the head in episcopal ordination. The *Gellone* does not provide the obvious indication of three crosses within the text but merely an interruption in the middle of the prayer with the words Per [Christum Dominum nostrum]. The prayer then resumes with the section referring to spiritual anointing. (See Gerald Ellard, *Ordination Anointings in the Western Church before 1000 A.D.* [Cambridge: The Mediaeval Academy of America, 1933] 30–31.) Is it the connection of a Gallican bishop patron that explains why the crosses for anointing are in a manuscript of the Roman *Hadrianum* when the anointing of the head was unknown in the Roman episcopal ordination rite during the same time period [as we will see from *Ordo Romanus XXXIV*]? Translation of the text is adapted for the singular from Bradshaw, *Ordination Rites*, 216.

[16] Hereafter *OR34*.

[17] Andrieu, *OR* III, 535 and 541.

[18] Ibid., 595.

[19] Ibid. There is broad support for Andrieu's claim that *OR34* represents the authentic Roman ordination ritual. *OR* IV, viii. Pierre Salmon, for example, writes that the texts represent an epoch which must not be too distant from that of Gregory the Great. See "Le rite du sacre des évêques dans les pontificaux du moyen âge," in *Miscellanea Giulio Belvederi* (Città del Vaticano: Società "Amici delle Catacombe" presso Pontificio Istituto di Archeologia Cristiana, 1954–1955) 27. Bruno Kleinheyer agrees: "The *ordo* concerning Roman episcopal ordination for 'outside' candidates according to *OR34*.14-45 belongs to surely the oldest known elements of the ritual books." ("Das Verfahren bei der Bischofsweihe auswärtiger Kandidaten in Rom gemäß *OR34*, 14-45 gehört zu den ältesten sicher bezeugten Elementen des Rituals.") See "Ordinationen und Beauftragungen," in *Sakramentliche Feiern II*, B. Kleinheyer, B. Severus, and R. Kaczynski, Teil 8: *Gottesdienst der Kirche* (Regensburg: Pustet, 1984) 30.

[20] Vogel, *Medieval Liturgy*, 174.

[21] Liturgical scholars will cite the ordination of bishop in the *Apostolic Tradition* as the first complete ordination rite known to us. Its Roman provenance, however, has been questioned. See Marcel Metzger, "Nouvelles perspectives pour la prétendue Tradition apostolique," *EO* 5 (1988) 241–259, and Bradshaw and others, *The Apostolic Tradition*.

[22] As early as the end of the fourth century, specific offices within the papal households developed. The *sacellarius* had responsibilities for certain finances and the *nomenculator* oversaw the disposition of petitions addressed to the pope, for example, the petitionary letters for ordination. Johann Kirsch, "Palatini," volume XI, 417 of *The Catholic Encyclopedia*, eds. Charles Herbermann and others (New York: Robert Appleton Company, 1911). I am grateful to Fr. Dennis Smolarski, S.J., for this reference.

[23] The Octateuch is a collection of the first eight books of the Bible.

²⁴Curiales were powerful municipal appointees who were also clerics. Restriction against their ordination dates from the time of Constantine. See Andrieu, *OR* III, 577–579.

²⁵An example of this edict is included as an appendix to *Ordo Romanus XXXV*.

²⁶Note that this interrogation witnesses to a time when a deacon as well as a presbyter might be elected bishop. No. 27: He says: What rank have you exercised? He responds: Deacon or presbyter or whatever it is.

²⁷*Contemporary Rites and General Conclusions*, volume III of *The Process of Admission to Ordained Ministry* (Collegeville: Liturgical Press, 2001) 265.

²⁸"[N]on si può e non si deve imporre a una Chiesa un vescovo non desiderato e bisogna che gli animi siano concordi nella scelta. Solo allora, e proprio per questo, il *Domnus Apostolicus*, darà il suo consenso: *Quoniam vota omnium in te conveniunt consecrandus eris*. É'il principio di papa Celestino I: *nullus invitis detur episcopus: cleri plebis et ordinis consensus et desiderium requiratur*." Santantoni, *L'Ordinazione episcopale*, 129.

²⁹That the Selection Presentation occurs on a Saturday we know from the pope's proclamation of consensus and consecration. He charges the elect to fast today and then the following day he will be consecrated. No. 32 in the Consecration Presentation begins: On the next day, which is Sunday. . . .

³⁰*Campobos* (also spelled *campagos* or *cambagos* in subsequent texts) were a type of Roman footgear that was half-shoe, half-sandal. Made from a flat piece of leather, the *campobos* also covered only the toes and the heel, and were held in place by straps which crossed over the top of the feet. They eventually took on a strictly ceremonial use with elaborate ornamentation. See Eugène Roulin, *Vestments and Vesture: A Manual of Liturgical Art* (St. Louis: B. Herder Book Company, 1933) 190–193.

³¹Antonio Santantoni describes the *formata* as a type of directory to guide the newly ordained in episcopal ministry; originally it meant a certificate of ordination. See *L'Ordinazione episcopale*, 67.

³²Andrieu explains that the act of communicating from the host consecrated at this Mass recalls the intimate presence of the meals with the risen Christ with his disciples before his ascension. *OR* III, 589.

³³*OR34* is an excellent example of the lack of distinction between *benedictio*, *ordinatio*, and *consecratio* that characterizes the *ordines* and early sacramentaries. *OR34* gives the general title of "ordination" to the entire sequence of rites, while using the term "consecration" for the liturgy of Sunday, except for the consecration prayer itself which is called a blessing" *(benedictio)*. See Pierre Jounel, "Ordination," in *The Sacraments*, eds. R. Cabié and others, vol. III of *The Church at Prayer*, gen. ed. A.-G. Martimort (Collegeville: Liturgical Press, 1988) 173–174. See also Santantoni, *L'Ordinazione episcopale*, 51–52. Adolf Adam makes the point that the documents of Vatican II will also "use the Latin terms *ordinatio* and *consecratio* without distinction, as is already is clear in *S[acrosantcum] C[oncilium]* 76." See his *Foundations of Liturgy* (Collegeville: Liturgical Press, 1992) 211.

[34] As the apparatus notes, Deshusses recognizes the relation of this prayer to "*Le*" (i.e., the Leonine Sacramentary [= *SVe* 942]: *Exaudi*).

[35] Bradshaw, *Ordination Rites,* 34.

[36] Emphasis added.

[37] The wording of this bidding is adapted from the consecration prayer which was most probably used for the ordination: *GregH* 2.23a and 2.23b (= *SVe* 947) [before the Gallican addition]). Toward the end of the consecration prayer we find, "Grant to him an episcopal throne to rule your Church and entire people." We will hereafter refer to this invitation to prayer as bidding *OR34*.

[38] Hereafter *OR35*.

[39] ". . . la liturgie romaine ne s'est pas confinée à Rome. Elle a rayonné en Italie, en Gaule, en Germanie. Ce qu'elle gagne en étendue, elle risque de le perdre en pureté. Elle va se charger d'éléments étrangers." See "Le sacre épiscopal dans le rite romain," *QL* 25 (1940) 26.

[40] ". . . mais déjà contaminé à Rome même, sous l'influence que commençait à exercer la liturgie d'outremonts." Andrieu, *OR* IV, viii.

[41] Ibid., 27.

[42] Vogel, *Medieval Liturgy,* 176. See also Andrieu's comparative chart of *OR34*, *OR35* and the Romano-Germanic Pontifical on page 28 of *OR* IV which clearly indicates the dependence of the Romano-Germanic Pontifical on *OR35* (and *not* *OR34*).

[43] Even though the reference to the tomb of Saint Peter remains in the text.

[44] Since the text of *OR35* is so similar to *OR34*, only a few pertinent paragraphs will be repeated here.

[45] For example, in no. 51 the elect's formula of response to the interrogation calls for him to acknowledge his unworthiness of that to which he was *chosen* rather than of that to which he was *brought*, as in *OR34*.

[46] The imposition of the gospel book is from *Statuta Ecclesiae Antiqua* [hereafter *SEA*], ed. C. Munier, CCL 148 *Concilia Galliae A. 314-A. 506* (Turnhout: Brepols, 1963) 162–188. *SEA* "contains a collection of brief rubrical directions for the ordination of bishops, presbyters, and deacons, and also provides for the appointment of subdeacons, acolytes, exorcists, readers, doorkeepers, psalmists, and nuns." It may have been written by Gennadius of Marseilles ca. 490. See Bradshaw, *Ordination Rites,* 14–15.

[47] Anointing of the bishop's hands, included here to supply what was lacking when a deacon is ordained bishop, will continue into the medieval pontifical tradition as an essential additional ritual for every bishop until the rite of 1968. See Michel Andrieu, "L'onction des mains dans le sacre épiscopal," *RHE* 26 (1930) 346–347.

[48] This is the consecration prayer without the later Gallican addition *(Sint speciosi munere)* from the *Missale Francorum* 9.40 and the Old Gelasian Sacramentary 770.

[49] "Les préliminaires de l'ordination épiscopale, avec le double interrogatoire du samedi, n'offrent, par rapport à l'*Ordo XXXIV*, aucune modification notable.

Dans la description de la première partie de la messe, jusqu'à l'ordination, sont rapportés çà et là quelques menus détails, que ne signalait pas le modèle, mais qui ne changent rien à l'ordonnance de la cérémonie. Après le chant des litanies, les innovations apparaissent." Andrieu, *OR* IV, 18.

[50] ". . . presentano una sostanziale affinità. Soltanto l'ultimo, infatti, denuncia i primi sintomi di un'evoluzione già avviata e ormai inarrestabile." *L'Ordinazione episcopale*, 64.

[51] Hereafter, *OR36*.

[52] Vogel, *Medieval Liturgy*, 176 and Andrieu, *OR* IV, viii–ix.

[53] Vogel, *Medieval Liturgy*, 177.

[54] Ibid.

[55] See Andrieu, *OR* IV, 147: ". . . auprès du chevet de la basilique."

[56] Andrieu traces precise distinctions between the indigenous Gallican and Spanish *casula* (here understood as a type of cope) and the Roman *planeta*, the chasuble. Ibid., 149–153.

[57] Ibid., 147.

[58] Ibid., 154.

Chapter 2

*With the testimony of the presbyters and of all the clergy
and with the advice of the citizens and of those assembled:*

The Gallican Model of Episcopal Ordination

Excellent sources for understanding the Gallican model of episcopal ordination are the relevant texts in the early eighth-century *Missale Francorum*[1] (with parallel sections from the Old Gelasian Sacramentary[2]) and the letter of Archbishop Hincmar of Rheims to Bishop Adventius of Metz describing his episcopal ordination in 845. We will examine these texts for the structure they present and then compare that structure with the Roman model.

I. The *Missale Francorum*

A. THE *MF* AND THE RITUAL CONTEXT OF EPISCOPAL ORDINATION

The texts of "When a bishop is ordained" of the eighth-century *Missale Francorum* are a composite of Gallican and Roman elements; no purely Gallican rite exists. Antoine Chavasse's careful analysis of *Vaticanus Reginensis 316* (the Old Gelasian Sacramentary) confirms that the *MF* and the *GeV* are derived from a common Gallican source made up of both Roman and Gallican elements which dates from the end of the seventh century or the beginning of the eighth.[3] The Romano-Gallican episcopal ordination rite from this earlier source was added to the *GeV* when it was copied at Chelles.[4] The *MF* preserves even more of its contents.

The order in which the *MF* lists the ordination rites is worth noting. As we saw in the previous chapter, the earlier tradition is characterized by a descending order, evident from the *SVe*, *GregH*, and *SEA* (echoing the *Apostolic Tradition*?). Such a descending order suggests a theological basis for the arrangement: the ordination rite for bishop, source of all ministerial leadership, begins the list. Comparison of the ordination rites in the *GeV* and the *MF* highlights the shift in perspective that is to come.[5]

One indication of the close relationship between the *GeV* and the *MF* is the new *cursus* of ministries. "The ascending order (first the deacon, then the priest and last the bishop) appears in the *Missale Francorum* and becomes customary from the time of the Romano-Germanic Pontifical."[6] This reversal of the order signals a significant ecclesiological shift: ordination rites begin to be ranked on a continuum of advancement and promotion, each order a prerequisite for the next (as we will see prescribed by Hincmar). It is the ascending order which will prevail in the pontificals, even in the 1968 reform.

B. ANALYSIS OF THE LITURGICAL UNITS
Chapter 9 contains the following elements:

no. 35 an exhortation to the people

no. 36 the first bidding

no. 37 the first Roman oration: *Exaudi* = *SVe* 942

no. 38 the second Roman oration: *Propitiare* = *SVe* 946

no. 39 the extensive Gallican bidding

no. 40 the consecration prayer: *SVe* with Gallican interpolation

nos. 41–44 the orations for the Mass.

1. no. 35 an exhortation to the people: *Seruanda est*[7]
MF.9.35. Exhortation to the people when a bishop is ordained.

Dearly beloved brethren, at the death of priests the custom also of the ancient Church is to be kept, that when others have passed away, whoever are most worthy should be elected in their place, through whose teaching the Catholic faith and the Christian religion may stand fast, lest a violent robber break into the sheepfold of the Lord and, when the shepherd is absent, a thief in the night attack the scattered sheep. Since by the disposition of God your priest has thus been taken away, you must act carefully, in order that, into the place of the deceased, such a successor may be provided for the Church, that by his constant watchfulness and unceasing care, the order of the Church and the faith of the believers may, in the fear of God, grow stronger; a man who, as the Apostle teaches, may himself show in all his teaching the pattern of good works; whose character, speech, countenance, presence, teaching may be a source of strength; who as a good shepherd may instruct you in the faith, teach the example of patience, impart the doctrine of religion, and enforce the example of charity by means of every good work.

By the will of the Lord, therefore, in place of N., of pious memory, with the testimony of the presbyters and of the whole clergy and with the advice of the citizens and of those assembled, we believe that the reverend N. should be elected, a man honorable in his birth, as you know, exemplary in his demeanor, unblamable in religion, firm in faith, rich in mercy, humble, just, peaceful, patient, having charity, steadfast, abounding in all the good things together that are to be desired in priests. Therefore, dearly beloved brethren, acclaim this man, chosen by the testimony of good works, as most worthy of the priesthood, crying out your praises together, and say: He is worthy.

The text of the exhortation describes the first stage of the ordination of a bishop in terms strikingly similar to *OR34*. The exhortation offers evidence of a selection stage in the ordination process; selection progresses from the death of the previous bishop to the election of one who is "most worthy" by means of a consensual process involving the presbyters, entire clergy and people of the vacant see. Echoes of the Roman tradition are strong.

Missale Francorum provides no rubrics for the ritual setting of this exhortation to the people. It may occur immediately before the first bidding within the Sunday liturgy, but the exhortation may also be part of the selection process on a previous day. That would explain why several phrases within the text suggest that a significant part of the consensual process is still to come:

Since by the disposition of God your priest has been taken away, *you must act carefully,* in order that . . . such a successor *may be provided* for the Church. . . .
. . . we believe that the reverend N. *should be elected.* . . .
. . . *acclaim this man,* . . . crying out your praises together and *say: He is worthy.*

The elect has been nominated but full consensus is still to be achieved.

A separation in time between the elements of the rite may also be hinted at by the titles used in the *MF.* "Exhortation to the people when a bishop is ordained" is the first element; the texts that follow are listed and identified separately as "orations and prayers for bishops-elect." It is possible that the exhortation is to be used for the first stage of the ordination (the selection on a previous day?) and the orations and prayers are those needed for the second stage, the consecration: a two-part process.

2. no. 36 the first bidding

MF.9.36. Let us pray, our dearly beloved, that the goodness of almighty God may bestow the abundance of his grace upon these men appointed for the service of the church: through [our] lord.

This is not the bidding of *OR34* but a new composition also found in the *GeV* (= 766). Bradshaw comments that this bidding "was presumably composed in order to harmonize the Roman formularies for a bishop with those for presbyter and deacon, which included biddings"[8] (e.g., *SVe* 949 [deacon] and 952 [presbyter]).

It was in the bidding of the consecration stage that the Roman model combined the proclamation of consensus by the metropolitan (the pope) with the introduction of the prayer of the assembly (the litany). Does the Gallican pattern follow the Roman? The combined elements of a consensus statement with the beginning of the consecration are not as strong here as in the proclamation of consensus and consecration in the bidding from the *OR34*. Consensus is only indirectly implied ("these men appointed for the service of the church") as the consecration is introduced. An additional extended bidding (presented below) will better fulfill the double task of proclamation of consensus and consecration.

Whatever its origin and purpose, it is this first bidding which passes into use in the Romano-Germanic Pontifical and remains in use today in the reformed rites of 1968 and 1990. The more extensive Gallican bidding (no. 39 below) is only preserved here in the *MF*; it is not copied into the later eighth-century sacramentaries of *Gellone* and *Angoulême*.

3. no. 37 a Roman oration: *Exaudi* = *SVe* 942 = *GeV* 767

4. no. 38 a second Roman oration: *Propitiare* = *SVe* 946 = *GeV* 768

5. no. 39 the extended Gallican bidding[9]

MF.9.39. The collect follows.

Dearly beloved brethren, let us beseech God, conveyor of all holiness and piety, who has established his propitiation and sacrifices and rites, for this his servant whom he has willed to exalt in the Church and to place in the seat of the elders, by the harmonious decisions which he has inspired and by the loyal wishes spread forth among his people and by the testimony of their voices, setting him with the princes of his people; at their unanimous prayer may he now adorn this same man with the high priesthood, in the fullness of deserved honor, in the grace of spiritual gifts, in the abundance of sacred endowments, and especially in the virtue of humility; as a ruler may he not lift up himself too much, but humbling himself with regard to all, though he be greater, may he be among them as one of them, trembling at all the judgments of our Lord, not for himself alone but for the whole people entrusted to his care; may he be mindful of the souls that will be required of the hands of all who watch over them; may he keep watch for the safety of all, ever proving himself most zealous in his pastoral diligence on behalf of the sheep of the Lord entrusted to him.

That he who is to be raised up over the elect, chosen by all, may be made fit by each and every hallowed and hallowing rite, may we be aided by the most earnest and unanimous prayers of all in this rite of his consecration and of our supplication, which is a most complete and perfect blessing, the highest given to man through man. May the prayer of all rest on him, on whom is placed the burden of praying for all. May the yearning of the whole Church obtain for him virtue, piety, holiness, and the other sacred endowments of the high priesthood which are useful to the whole Church, of our Lord God, who is the flowing well-spring of holy gifts, who gives to all abundantly, bestowing most swiftly and most fully upon the priest what is asked with devout desire for the superabundant holiness of all his people; through our Lord himself.

The proclamation of consensus and consecration, only vaguely discernible in the first bidding, is recognizable here in full strength. The ordaining bishop announces that the consensual process has already occurred:

. . . by the harmonious decisions which he has inspired and by the loyal wishes spread forth among his people and by the testimony of their voices. . . .

Following the bishop's confirmation of the selection of the bishop-elect, the movement of the ritual is from consensus achieved to prayer invoked, from unanimous communal choice to unanimous communal prayer (as the bidding continues):

. . . at their unanimous prayer may he now adorn this same man with the high priesthood. . . .
That he who is to be raised up over the elect, chosen by all, may be made fit by each and every hallowed and hallowing rite, may we be aided by the most earnest and unanimous prayers of all in this rite of his consecration and of our supplication. . . .
May the yearning of the whole Church obtain for him virtue, piety, holiness, and the other sacred endowments of the high priesthood. . . .

In the second stage of ordination (the consecration), the Roman tradition of *OR34* combines a proclamation of consensus and consecration with a bidding before the assembly begins to pray the litany before the consecration prayer. The extended bidding of the *MF* repeats this Roman sequence of combining the proclamation of consensus and consecration with the first element of the consecration: the invitation to communal prayer in the bidding. The position of the Roman collects differs, however, between *OR34* and the *MF*:

Roman model [OR34 + SVe]	MF
	bidding *MF*
	Exaudi
	Propitiare
proclamation of consensus and consecration	**proclamation of consensus and consecration**
clergy + people + bishops consent/ bidding *OR34*	chosen by all/ extended bidding
Exaudi (= *SVe* 942)	
Propitiare (= *SVe* 946)	

Why are the two Roman orations placed before the bidding? We have already seen that the extended bidding in the *MF* was misidentified as a collect. Its length tended to enhance its importance, and thus it was inserted into the grouping of the other orations immediately before the similarly lengthy consecration prayer.

As Bradshaw has suggested, the brief "bidding *MF*" took its place as the first element of prayer in an attempt to systematize the components of the episcopal rite with the *SVe* presbyteral and diaconal rites whose consecration liturgies began with biddings. Episcopal ordination in the *MF* already included an extensive bidding (into which was woven the consecrator's announcement of consensus) but the compilers, unaware of its nature, added the new bidding also found in the *GeV*.

6. no. 40 the consecration prayer (the Roman formula *SVe* 947 with the Gallican interpolation also found in the *GeV* 770)[10]

MF.9.40. . . . May their feet, by your aid, be beautiful for bringing good tidings of peace, for bringing your good tidings of good. Give them, Lord, a ministry of reconciliation in word and in deeds and in power of signs and of wonders. May their speech and preaching be not with enticing words of human wisdom, but in demonstration of the Spirit and of power. Grant to them, O Lord, that they may use the keys of the kingdom of heaven for upbuilding, not for destruction, and may not glory in the power which you bestow. Whatsoever they bind on earth, may it be bound also in heaven, and whatsoever they loose on earth, may it be loosed also in heaven. Whose sins they retain, may they be retained; and whose sins they forgive, do you forgive. Whoever blesses them, may he be blessed; and whoever curses them, may he be filled with curses. May they be faithful and wise servants, whom you, Lord, set over your household that they may give them food in due season, in order that they may show forth an entire perfect man. May they be unwearied in watchfulness; may they be fervent in spirit. May they hate pride, love truth, and never be so overcome by faintness or fear as to abandon it. May they not put light for darkness nor darkness for light; may they not say evil is good nor good evil. May they be debtors to the wise and to the unwise, and may they have fruit of the benefit of all. . . .

This combined consecration text is taken up into the pontifical tradition from the tenth-century Romano-Germanic Pontifical until the revision mandated by the Second Vatican Council. The challenge of rewriting or replacing this venerable text as well as the accompanying prayer from the *SVe*, continually in use for a millennium, was one of the most significant and most daunting tasks of the reformers.

7. nos. 41–44 the orations for the Mass

The *Hanc igitur* and postcommunion prayer are from the *SVe* (944, 945); the *super oblata* is from the text common to the *GeV*.

C. CONCLUSION

The two lengthy exhortations are the key to an analysis of the liturgical structure of the *MF* episcopal ordination rite. The first *(Seruanda est)* introduces the final element of the selection stage (unanimous acclamation by the assembly); the second text (the extended Gallican bidding) confirms the consensual choice and then introduces the initial element of the consecration stage (unanimous prayer by the assembly). By means of even these few rubrics and texts, the two-stage process of the *Missale Francorum* is evident: a consensual selection followed by consecration. The elements may be outlined in this way:

Missale Francorum

1st stage

Selection
proclamation of consensus and consecration:
                    Seruanda est

2nd stage

Consecration

consecration: bidding *MF*
                                           Exaudi
                                           Propitiare

proclamation of consensus and consecration:
                                           extended Gallican bidding

consecration: consecration prayer (*SVe* + *MF/GeV*)
                                           consecration continues

Texts of the *Missale Francorum:*

no. 35 an exhortation to the people: *Seruanda est*

MF.9.35. Exortatio ad populum/cum episcopus ordinatur.

Seruanda est, dilectissimi fratres, in excessu sacerdotum et antiquae ecclesiae, ut decidentibus aliis quidem dignissime subrogentur, per quorum doctrina<m> fides catholica et religio christiana subsistat, ne ouile domini praedo uiolentus inrumpat, et dispersas absque pastore oues fur nocturnus inuadat. Receptu itaque dispensatione dei sacerdoti uestro, sollecite uobis agendum est, ut in locum defuncti talis successor praeparetur eclesiae, cuius peruigili cura et instanti sollicitudine ordo eclesiae et credentium fides in dei timore melius conualiscat. Qui praecipienti apostolo in omni doctrina formam boni operis ipse praebeat, cuique habitus, sermo, uultus, incessus, doctrina, uirtus sit; qui uos ut pastor bonus fide instruat, exemplum patientiae doceat, doctrinam religionis instituat, in omni opere bono confirmit caritatis exemplum. Secundum uoluntatem ergo domini in locum sanctae memoriae illi nomene uirum uenerabilem illum testimonio presbiterorum et totius cleri et consilio ciuium ac consistentium credimus eligendum, uerum (ut nostris) natalibus nobilem, moribus clarum, religione probum, fide[m] stabilem, misericordia habundantem, humilem, iustum, pacificum, pacientem, caritatem habentem, tenacem: cunctis que sacerdos elegenda sunt bonis omnibus exuberantem. Hunc ergo, dilectissimi fratres, testimonii boni operis electum, dignissimum sacerdotium consonantes laudibus clamate et dicite: Dignus est.

no. 36 the first bidding

MF.9.36. . . . Oremus, dilectissimi nobis, ut his uiris ad utilitatem eclesiae prouidendis benignitas omnipotentis dei gratiae suae tribuat largitatem: per dominum.

no. 39 the extended Gallican bidding

MF.9.39. Collectio sequitur.

Deum, totius sanctificationis actorem, qui plagationem suam et sacrificia et sacra constituit, fratres dilectissimi, depraecimur, uti hunc famulum suum, quem exaltare in eclesia et seniorum cathedra, concordibus sua inspiratione iudiciis et effusis super plebum suam uotis fidelibus ac uocum testimoniis, uoluit inponi, conlocans eum cum principibus populi sui, ad eorum nunc praecim uniuersam eundem summum sacerdotium, debita honoris plenetudine, carismatum gratia, sanctificationum ubertate hac praecipue humilitatis uirtute locupletit: ut rector putius non extollatur, sed in omnibus se quantum est maior humilians, sit in ipsis quasi unus ex illis: omnia iudicii domini nostri non pro se tantum, sed et pro omni populo qui sollicitutudini[s] suae creditur contremiscens: ut qui meminerit de speculatorum manibus omnium animas requirendas, pro omnium salute peruigilet, pastorali erga creditas sibi oues domini diligentiae eius semper se flagratissimum adprobans. Te delictorum adigitur praefuturus, ex omnbius elictus, ex omnibus uniuersis sacris sacrandisque idoneus fiat sub haec, que est homini per hominem postrima benedictio consummata atque perfecta suae consegrationis, nostrae subplecationis adtentissime, concordissimisque omnium praecibus adiouemur: omnium pro ipso oratio incumbat, cui exorandi pro omnibus pondus inponitur. Impetret ei affectus totius eclesiae uirtutem, pietate<m>, sanctificationem et ceteras summi sacerdotii sacras dotis uniuersae eclesiae profuturas domino deo nostro, qui sacrorum munerum profluus fons est, qui dat omnibus adfluenter, quod sacerdoti pio affectu poscitur, ad exundandam in omnibus sanctificationem suorum omnium prumtissime ac plenissime conferente[m]; per dominum nostrum sesum.

no. 40 the consecration prayer (the Roman formula *SVe* 947 with the Gallican interpolation also found in the *GeV* 770)

MF.9.40. . . . Sint speciosi muneri tuo pedes horum ad euangelizandum pacem, ad euangelezandum bona tua. Da eis, domine, ministerium reconciliationis in uerbo et in factis et in uirtutes et signorum et protigiorum. Sit sermo eorum et praedicatio non in persuasibilibus humanae sapientiae uerbis, sed in ostensione spiritus et uirtutis. Da eis, domine, claues regni caelorum; utantur nec glorientur potestate quam tribues in aedificationem, non in distructionem. Quodcumque legauerint super terram, sit legatum et in caelis; et quodcumque soluerint super terram, sit solutum et in caelis. Quorum detinuerint peccata, detenta sint; et quorum demiserint, tu demittas. Qui benedixerit eis, sit benedictus; et qui maledixerit eis maledictionibus repleatur. Sint serui fidelis et prudentes, quos constituas tu, domine, super familiam tuam, ut dent illis cibum in tempore necessario, ut exhibeant omnem hominem perfectum. Sint sollicitudine inpegri, sint spiritu feruentes. Oderint superbiam, diligant ueritatem, nec eam umquam deserant aut lasitudine aut timore superati. Non ponant lucem ad tenebras nec tenebris lucem, non dicant malum bonum nec bonum malum. Sint sapientibus et insipientibus debitores et fructum de profectu omnium consequantur.

D. EXCURSUS ON THE PATTERN OF THE
GELLONE AND THE *ANGOULÊME*

Two of the later "eighth-century Gelasian sacramentaries," the *Gellone* and the *Angoulême*, provide evidence for the next step in the evolution of the Gallican model of episcopal ordination found in the *MF*. Both follow this outline:

1st stage

Selection
proclamation of consensus and consecration:
                         Seruanda est

2nd stage

Consecration
proclamation of consensus and consecration:
                         [   ]
consecration: bidding *MF*
                                 Exaudi
                                 Propitiare
                                 consecration prayer
                                      (composite form *SVe* + *MF/GeV*)
                                 consecration continues

The proclamation of consensus marking the completion of the selection process remains in place, but the second proclamation (the extended bidding) has been omitted. Several forces are at work here. First, both stages of the ordination are eventually combined into one liturgy (a pattern found in the Romano-Germanic Pontifical, as we will see in chapter 3). Metropolitans will choose one lengthy address to the people for this single liturgy rather than two similar ones. And in the attempt to systematize the sequence and type of prayer texts in the consecration stage of all three ordination rites, the use of bidding *MF* prevails in its position before the two orations.

The loss of the extended Gallican bidding from the consecration stage is significant. Functioning ritually as a mirror text of the stirring exhortation to the people during the selection stage *(Seruanda est)*, it was a powerful witness of the two-stage process of ordination: an unambiguous testament to the vital participation of the vacant see in the prior selection process and in the unanimous communal prayer which is at the heart of the consecration.

But the *Gellone* and the *Angoulême* provide valuable testimony of another ordination component, a new element within the consecration stage: the anointing of the hands of the new bishop (in addition to the anointing he received at presbyteral ordination). The prayer text they preserve is found in the *MF* as a variant of the formulary for anointing in presbyteral ordination.

Kleinheyer explains that hand anointing was originally done as part of episcopal ordination only when the bishop-elect was a deacon (as we saw in *OR35*).[11] In order to distinguish between the two anointings in liturgical rites which retain both anointings, the presbyteral anointing will eventually be assigned the oil of catechumens, reserving chrism for the anointing of the hands in the episcopal rite.[12]

II. The Episcopal Ordination of Hincmar of Rheims

While *Missale Francorum* provides the necessary spoken texts for a bishop's ordination, the entire sequence of events and detailed rubrics are not included. For a clearer picture of those elements, we turn to an autobiographical account of episcopal ordination in the mid-ninth century. Michel Andrieu describes the letter of the archbishop of Rheims as a precise directory of the ceremony followed for the ordination of a metropolitan;[13] it is Hincmar's record of his own ordination on 3 May 845.

A. ANALYSIS OF THE LITURGICAL UNITS

1. *Selection Presentation*

a. SELECTION PRESENTATION: TEXT

Hincmar.3. On the Saturday preceding the Sunday, when the elect is to be ordained, the bishops of the neighboring Sees ought to assemble at the principal church of the metropolitan area and the decree [of election] should be read publicly before everyone and the bishops ought to inquire whether the desires of all, as contained there [in the decree] have come to agreement in this same elect.

And after their response, the bishops ought to ask if they believe or know these virtues, which are contained in the same [document], to be in this same elect.

And after the response is accepted, the bishops should inquire if there is anyone, who wishes to say anything against the same elect, or wishes to charge against him something contrary to episcopal ordination, that he may come forward and speak mindful of his communion. If anyone charges him with something, you have in the canons what is to be done from that moment.

4. But if however all are in agreement regarding his election, the praises of all are offered to God, and the same elect is to be examined by the bishops, according

to the chapter of the council of Carthage, by which is set forth the sort who should be ordained bishop, if he believes thus and professes the catholic faith in straightforward words, as is found written in that same [document]. And then the same elect is to be admonished, that that night, according to apostolic tradition, he will strive to commend himself to the Lord.

b. SELECTION PRESENTATION:
OBJECTIONS OF THE ASSEMBLY

The account begins with a Saturday assembly. In the cathedral of the metropolitan, the neighboring bishops gather, and in the presence of all, listen to the reading of the election decree, declare the consensus of their vote, and attend to any objections regarding the elect voiced by the assembly.

Archbishop Hincmar's description of the communal process for inquiring into possible charges against the bishop-elect bears a striking resemblance to a similar process in the Old Gelasianum Sacramentary (nos. 140–141)[14] in the ordination of presbyters, deacons, and subdeacons. The ordaining bishop addresses the assembly:

GeV.XX.141. With the help of the lord Jesus Christ, our God and savior, we choose for the order of deacon or presbyter N., subdeacon or deacon of the title N. If anyone has anything against these men, before God and for the sake of God let him come forward with confidence and speak. But truly let him be mindful of his communion.

Note the similar wording in Hincmar's description:

Hincmar.3. . . . the bishops must inquire whether anyone who is there wishes to say anything against the elect, or wishes to charge against him something contrary to episcopal ordination, that he may come forward and speak mindful of his communion.

Hincmar's letter is the only extant evidence for the use of this type of selection process ("election by the absence of objections") in episcopal ordination. It does not continue in use in the pontifical tradition for bishops, but prevails as the predominant initial element in presbyteral, diaconal, and subdiaconal ordination rites until 1968.

C. SELECTION PRESENTATION:
THE GALLICAN EXAMINATION

Following the wide variety of expressions of consensus, the bishops interrogate the elect himself.[15] Their formula is not of course the Roman examination from *OR34* but what the Romano-Germanic Pontifical will call "the examination for the ordination of bishop according to the Gauls" [examinatio in ordinatione episcopi secundum Gallos],[16] i.e., the Gallican examination according to the "chapter of the Council of Carthage."[17] This is the text that begins *Antiqua sanctorum patrum institutio docet et praecipit . . .* [The ancient instruction of the holy fathers teaches and prescribes . . .], copied in full in the Romano-Germanic Pontifical and retained in liturgical use up until 1968. Hincmar is the first evidence of its use.[18]

2. *Consecration Presentation*

a. CONSECRATION PRESENTATION: TEXT

*Hincmar.*5. Early Sunday the bishops of the [neighboring] dioceses and the clergy with the people must assemble at the place where the metropolitan bishop is usually ordained, according to custom. And when all has been prepared, and the bishops and ecclesiastical ministers are in the sacred vestments, and the bishops are standing beside the altar, the same elect, clothed in pontifical vestments, must be led in from the sacristy by the senior clerics of the metropolitan area and be stationed in the last place after the bishops.

6. This diocesan bishop, who is to pronounce the consecration over him, processes in for the Mass according to the practice when the introit is begun. When the introit is finished, <<*Kyrie eleison*>> is sung, the bishop then following with <<*Gloria in excelsis Deo*>>. And after <<*Gloria in excelsis Deo*>>, he says this oration which is the first in the scroll of the consecration. Immediately after this oration is completed however and before the Apostle is read, he admonishes the clergy and people, to pray for the elect to be ordained and for those ordaining him.

7. By his own hand, he takes the elect by his right hand and the litany is begun and both he and the elect with the other bishops who are present bow before the altar, until just after the end of the litany.

8. When the clergy begin to chant the <<*Agnus Dei*>> [section of the litany], the bishops straighten up and the one who pronounces the consecration [prayer] takes the [book of the] four gospels and opens it in the middle and with the elect bowed before the altar, places the gospels upon his shoulders and neck, and two bishops hold the gospels over him, one from one side, the other from the other side, and the consecrator as well as all the bishops hold their right hands over the head of the one to be ordained and the consecrator says: <<Let us pray. *Propitiare . . .*>>, and the rest.

9. With the prayer completed and all responding <<Amen>>, the consecrator intones: <<The Lord be with you. Lift up your hearts. Let us give thanks to the

lord our God>>. And the choir having responded to each one [of these acclamations], he begins the consecration [prayer] chanting: <<It is truly right and just>> up to <<eternal God>>, and then the consecration [prayer] follows, and the bishops at all times hold their right hands over the head of the one to be ordained.

Coming to the places [in the text] at which the crosses are marked, the consecrator takes the vessel of chrism in his left hand and with his right thumb, chanting what is found there, at each place he makes a cross with chrism on the crown of the head of the one to be consecrated.

And when the consecration [prayer] is completed and all have responded <<Amen>>, the [book of the] gospels is removed from his neck by the bishops.

b. CONSECRATION PRESENTATION:
   THE EXTENDED GALLICAN BIDDING

The second stage of the ordination occurs on Sunday, when in the presence of the bishops of the province, the clergy and people, the elect (vested as a bishop) is presented to the metropolitan once again. After the introit, *Kyrie, Gloria,* the collect is read from a *rotula consecrationis,* a scroll containing the particular prayers to be used for the consecration, chosen by Hincmar himself from all the texts available.[19]

Then the bidding occurs; here the metropolitan calls upon the clergy and people to pray for the elect and for those ordaining him. Is this the brief "bidding *MF*" ("Let us pray, our dearly beloved") or the extended Gallican bidding which only the *MF* preserved? The text of Hincmar (no. 6) notes that the metropolitan "admonishes the clergy and people, to pray for the elect to be ordained and for those ordaining him." Only the extended Gallican bidding from *MF* includes this double reference to the elect and to those ordaining him:

MF.9.39. . . . [T]hat he who is to be raised up over the elect, chosen by all, may be made fit by each and every hallowed and hallowing rite, may we be aided by the most earnest and unanimous prayers of all in this rite of his consecration and of our supplication, which is a most complete and perfect blessing. . . .

In compiling his *rotula consecrationis,* Hincmar seems to have substituted the extended Gallican bidding for the much briefer text of the bidding *MF.*

Following the litany and the litany oration *(Propitiare),* the consecrator chants the preface dialogue and then begins to sing the consecration prayer in the mode of a preface ("It is truly right and just . . ."). *Hincmar is the first witness to casting the consecration prayer in preface form,* complete with preface dialogue.[20] After the Romano-Germanic Pontifical brings the practice to Rome, it continues in the pontifical tradition until the reform of 1968.

c. CONSECRATION PRESENTATION:
 IMPOSITION OF THE GOSPEL BOOK

In chapter 1, we noted that *OR35* included the rubric originally from the fifth-century *Statuta Ecclesiae Antiqua:* the imposition of the gospel book over the neck of the elect before the consecration prayer. *Hincmar* is also a witness to this practice, although he assigns to the consecrator the duty of opening and placing the book on the neck of the elect:

*SEA.*90.(II)	*Hincmar.*8
When a bishop is ordained,	. . . the one who pronounces the
two bishops place and hold	consecration [prayer] takes the [book of the]
the book of the gospels	four gospels and opens it in the middle and
over his neck,	with the elect bowed before the altar, places
and one pours out	the gospels upon his shoulders and neck,
the blessing over him,	and two bishops hold the gospels over him,
all the rest of the bishops	one from one side, the other from the other
who are present	side, and the consecrator as well as all the
touch his head	bishops hold their right hands over the head
with their hands.	of the one to be ordained. . . .

This ritual gesture, taken up into the Romano-Germanic Pontifical from *OR35,* finds a permanent place in the episcopal ordination rite.[21] By following this rubric from *SEA, Hincmar* also witnesses to the simultaneous laying on of hands during the consecration prayer.

III. Conclusion

Even with the multiplication of ritual elements further on in Hincmar's letter (the anointing of the head in the middle of the consecration prayer [at those same points where the *GregH* has only a series of crosses], the giving of ring and crozier, the enthronement and first instruction to the local clergy[22]), it is possible to identify in this Gallican rite the same underlying structure evident in the earlier Roman rite: ordination as a two-stage process of consensual selection and consecration. Elements constituting the bridge between the two stages are the proclamation of consensus and consecration from the Selection Presentation, the vesting of the bishop in episcopal garb, the Consecration Presentation, and the bidding.

Comparison of the bridge section of the Roman and Gallican structures of episcopal ordination can be outlined in this way:

ROMAN	GALLICAN
1st stage	*1st stage*
Selection Presentation	**Selection Presentation**
Saturday	Saturday
presentation	**presentation**
postulation	
grant us a patron	
decree	decree
examination	examination
proclamation of consensus and consecration:	**proclamation of consensus and consecration:**
desires of all /	*Seruanda est*
you will be consecrated	
2nd stage	*2nd stage*
Consecration Presentation	**Consecration Presentation**
Sunday	Sunday
	presentation
	episcopal vestments
introit to gradual	introit to collect
episcopal vestments	
presentation	
proclamation of consensus and consecration:	**proclamation of consensus and consecration:**
clergy + people + bishops consent /	chosen by all /
bidding OR34	extended bidding
consecration	**consecration**
litany	litany
Propitiare	*Propitiare*
consecration prayer *(SVe)*	consecration prayer *(SVe + GeV/MF)*
consecration continues	consecration continues

As the Roman and Gallican two-stage structure of ordination is taken up into the pontificals from the twelfth to the fifteenth centuries (the Roman Pontifical of the Twelfth Century, the Pontifical of the Roman Curia, the Pontifical of Guillaume Durand, the Roman Pontifical of 1485), it is increasingly submerged by what Botte will call "a pile of secondary rites."[23] A document fundamental to the evolution of the two-stage structure is the Romano-Germanic Pontifical. Chapter III examines the expansion of the Roman/Gallican model in two recensions of the principal manuscripts of the Romano-Germanic Pontifical, and then considers the evidence provided by selected tenth-century English pontificals.

Texts of Archbishop Hincmar of Rheims:

Selection Presentation:

3. Sabbato autem praecedente dominicam, quando electus est ordinandus, convenire debent episcopi dioeceseos ad principalem ecclesiam metropolis et publice coram omnibus debet recitari decretum et interrogare debent episcopi si omnium vota, sicut ibi continetur in eundem electum concordent.

Et post responsionem illorum, debent interrogare episcopi si has virtutes, quae ibidem continentur, credunt vel sciunt esse in eodem electo.

Et accepta inde responsione, debent interrogare episcopi si aliquis ibi est, qui contra eundem electum aliquid dicere, vel ordinationi episcopali contrarium illi velit obiicere, ut exeat et dicat memor communionis suae. Quod si aliquis quiddam illi obiecerit, habetis in canonibus quid inde sit faciendum.

4. Sin autem omnes concordes fuerint in eius electione, referendae sunt ab omnibus Deo laudes, et examinandus est idem electus ab episcopis, secundum capitulum Carthaginensis concilii, quo manifestatur qualis debeat ordinari episcopus, si ita credat et simplicibus verbis catholicam fidem profiteatur, sicut ibidem scriptum habetur. Et tunc monendus est idem electus, ut ipsa nocte, secundum traditionem apostolicam, se studeat domino commendare.

Consecration Presentation:

5. Dominica autem die maturius episcopi dioeceseos et clerus ac plebs convenire debebunt ad locum, ubi secundum consuetudinem solet metropolitanus episcopus ordinari. Et praeparatis omnibus, et episcopis et ecclesiasticis ministris in vestibus sacris, et stantibus episcopis secus altare, idem electus indutus pontificalibus vestibus a primoribus clericis eiusdem metropolis de sacrario debet educi et in ultimo loco post episcopos collocari.

6. Is autem episcopus dioecesaneus, qui consecrationem fusurus est super eum, incepto introitu ad missam secundum morem procedat. Et finito introitu, dicatur <<Kyrie eleison>>, prosequente ab ipso episcopo <<Gloria in excelsis Deo>>. Et post <<Gloria in excelsis Deo>>, dicat hanc orationem quae prima est in rotula consecrationis. Statim autem post completam ipsam orationem, antequam legatur Apostolus, commoneat clerum et plebem, ut orent pro ordinando electo et pro ordinatoribus eius.

7. Et accipiat electum manu sua dextera per manum illius et incipiatur litania et tam ipse cum electo quam et ceteri qui adfuerint episcopi incurventur ante altare, usquedum breviter pro tempore finiatur litania.

8. Ut autem clerus inceperit dicere <<Agnus Dei>>, erigant se episcopi, et qui fundet consecrationem accipiat quatuor evangelia, et aperiat per medium, et

incurvato ipso electo ante altare, mittat ipse evangelia super collum et cervicem eius, et teneant ipsa evangelia super eum duo episcopi, unus ex una parte, alter ex altera, et tam consecrator quam omnes episcopi teneant manus dextras suas super caput ordinandi et dicat consecrator: <<Oremus. Propitiare, domine, supplicationibus nostris>>, et reliqua.

9. Et oratione completa et respondentibus omnibus <<Amen>>, dicat consecrator: <<Dominus vobiscum. Sursum corda. Gratias agamus domino Deo nostro>>. Et respondente choro ad singula, incipiat consecrationem cantando: <<Vere dignum et iustum est>>, usque ad <<aeterne Deus>>, et tunc sicut ipsa consecratio consequitur, et semper teneant manus dextras episcopi super caput ordinandi.

Ut autem ventum fuerit ad loca, in quibus sunt cruces signatae, accipiat consecrator vas chrismatis in sinistra manu et cum dextro pollice, cantans quae ibidem continentur, per singula loca faciat crucem de chrismate in verticem consecrandi.

Et perfecta consecratione et respondentibus omnibus <<Amen>>, tollantur ab episcopis evangelia de collo eius.

Text of the Old Gelasianum Sacramentary:

XX.141. Auxiliante domino deo et saluatore nostro Iesu Christo elegimus in ordine diaconi siue praesbyterii illum subdiaconum siue diaconum de titulum illum. Si quis autem habet aliquid contra hos uiros, pro deo et propter deum cum fiducia exeat et dicat. Uerumtamen memor sit communionis suae.

Text of *Statuta Ecclesiae Antiqua:*

90.(II)
Episcopus cum ordinatur, duo episcopi ponant et teneant euangeliorum codicem super ceruicem eius, et uno super eum fundente benedictionem, reliqui omnes episcopi, qui adsunt, manibus suis caput eius tangant.

NOTES

[1] Hereafter *MF.*

[2] Hereafter *GeV* (Gelasianum Vetus).

[3] Antoine Chavasse, *Le Sacramentaire Gélasien* (Tournai: Desclée, 1958) 6.

[4] Vogel, *Medieval Liturgy,* 175.

[5] How does one explain the ascending order of the *ordines romani?* These rites are for acolyte, subdeacon, deacon, presbyter, and bishop at a time when the orders were not prerequisites for each other. This arrangement may simply reflect ease of liturgical usage, i.e., placing the most frequently used rites first. But James Puglisi makes a strong case for another dynamic coming to the fore during this period. He writes that *OR34* "may indicate a change in the manner of under-

standing the different ministries in the church. We are in the presence of the birth of the hierarchy." *Epistemological Principles and Roman Catholic Rites*, 88.

[6] Pierre-Marie Gy, "Ancient Ordination Prayers," 76.

[7] Translations that follow are from Bradshaw, *Ordination Rites*, 228–230 (emphases added) and 242 (bidding, slightly adapted).

[8] Ibid., 283, n. 3.

[9] *MF* incorrectly titles the text a collect; "Gallican bidding" is the more accurate name given it by Bradshaw in "Medieval Ordinations," *The Study of Liturgy* (1992) 374. It is directed to dearly beloved brethren, despite its identifying rubric, "The collect follows."

[10] *MF* does not contain a purely Gallican consecration prayer but rather the Roman text with this Gallican insert. Bruno Kleinheyer makes an excellent case for a purely Gallican consecration prayer found in the *Leofric Missal*, a discussion of which begins on page 118.

[11] Bruno Kleinheyer, "La riforma degli ordini sacri," *RL* 56 (1969) 19.

[12] Bernard Botte, "Le nouveau rituel d'ordination," *QL* 49 (1968) 276.

[13] Andrieu, "Hincmar," 23.

[14] A variant of the text is found in *Ordo Romanus XXXVI.9*.

[15] In article 2 of his letter, Hincmar makes it clear that if a deacon should be elected, he must be ordained a presbyter before his episcopal consecration: Et si isdem electus in diaconii gradu adhuc est, canonico tempore debet presbyter ordinari. Hincmar is the first to attest to this requirement.

[16] *PRG.LXIII.(12)* and 12.

[17] The canons of "the fourth Council of Carthage" was the name erroneously given to the late fifth-century collection *Statuta Ecclesiae Antiqua* by the False Decretals. See Andrieu, "Hincmar," 32, n. 1.

[18] Andrieu, "Hincmar," 31.

[19] Ibid., 24.

[20] Ibid., 39–40.

[21] Studies of the history of this gesture are many and varied, as are the conclusions about the theological meaning of the act. Among others, see especially the summaries in Santantoni, *L'Ordinazione episcopale*, 138–147; and Bradshaw, *Ordination Rites*, 39–44, and his "Theology and Rite A.D. 200–400," in *The Study of Liturgy* (1992) 355–362. Also see the analyses of the Chanoines Réguliers de Mondaye (= the coming of the Spirit) in "L'évêque d'après les prières d'ordination," 739–780; Bernard Botte (= the equivalent of the imposition of hands) in "Le rituel d'ordination des *Statuta Ecclesiae Antiqua*," *Recherches de Théologie Ancienne et Médiévale* 11 (1939) 223–241 and "L'ordre d'après les prières d'ordination," *QL* 35 (1954) 166–179; Charles Munier, "Une forme abrégée du rituel des ordinations des *Statuta Ecclesiae Antiqua*," *RSR* 32 (1958) 79–84; and Joseph Lécuyer, "Note sur la liturgie du sacre des évêques," *EL* 66 (1952) 369–372. In a conversation on the subject ("Discussion" in *The Sacrament of Holy Orders* [Collegeville: Liturgical Press, 1962] 24–29), Pierre-Marie Gy recalls the medieval

symbolism of the gesture: the evangelical responsibility of preaching which was laid on the new bishop.

Bradshaw's commentary, however, in "Theology and Rite A.D. 200–400," 361, is worth remembering: "The diversity of all these interpretations gives the impression that they are attempts to find a meaning for an already ancient ceremony, the original sense of which has been forgotten. The practice was copied at Alexandria and at Rome, but in both places was restricted exclusively to the consecration of the patriarch. However, it also turns up in the Gallican *Statuta Ecclesiae Antiqua*, where it is directed to be used at all episcopal ordinations, and from here the custom eventually spread into all later Western rites for the episcopate, including that of Rome itself."

[22] Andrieu, "Hincmar," 63.

[23] Botte, *From Silence to Participation,* 134.

Chapter 3

With the consent of the clerics and laity and the
agreement of the bishops of the entire province:

The Evolution of the Roman and Gallican Models of Episcopal Ordination

I. The Presentation of the Bishop-Elect in the Romano-Germanic Pontifical of the Tenth Century[1]

A. THE *PRG* AND THE RITUAL CONTEXT OF EPISCOPAL ORDINATION

1. *The* PRG: *introduction*

The existence of the approximately fifty manuscripts of the *PRG* family[2] signaled an important stage in the evolution of liturgical books: this is the first "pontifical" in the modern sense. Up to this point, two distinctly different types of books were necessary to celebrate the Roman rite: the sacramentary and the *libelli* of the *ordines romani* (*OR34* and *OR35*, for example) which contained the rubrical descriptions of the rites.[3]

Cyrille Vogel and Reinhard Elze recount the process of the creation of the pontifical format in this way.[4] Collections of *ordines* (both Roman and Gallican) were eventually combined with theological and liturgical commentaries to create didactic works for the education of the clergy of the Middle Ages. The *ordines* were also joined to extracts of sacramentaries to create a second type of book for episcopal use, the pontifical, composed of ritual descriptions and prayer texts. Both types of documents, *ordines*-commentaries and *ordines*-sacramentaries, merged in the creation of the *PRG*.

A pontifical of over eight hundred pages of such material was compiled by the Benedictine monks of St. Alban's Abbey in Mainz in approximately the year 950.[5] In the general introduction to their critical edition of the *PRG* (which builds on the monumental work of Andrieu), Vogel and Elze summarize the extraordinary influence of this pontifical: "Thus the Romano-Germanic Pontifical of the tenth century occupies a hinge position of primordial importance in the development of Christian worship, at once a repository of cultic practices before its redaction or contemporary with it, and as the point of departure for further evolution."[6] The *PRG* will survive in many of the texts and structures of the medieval pontificals studied in this work, in the Roman Pontificals of 1485 and 1595, and in the Pontifical of the Vatican II reform.

2. The PRG: *two recensions*

Throughout chapter LXIII. [Ordination of a bishop] in their edition of the *PRG*, Vogel and Elze meticulously set before the reader two comparative columns of texts representing the different major recensions of the Pontifical identified by the initials [B G K L] and [A C D J T V]. For the analysis in this study, we will describe each of the two blocks separately and then compare their structures. An important first question concerns the relative age of the two sets of manuscripts.

Andrieu himself was convinced that manuscript C (Monte Cassino, Abbey Library, *codex* 451) and manuscript D (Rome, Biblio. Vallicelliana, *codex* D. 5) represent the two most faithful witnesses to the earliest arrangement of the *PRG*.[7] A different conclusion, however, is proposed by C. Erdmann and P. E. Schramm who agree with Vogel and Elze's analysis that the *PRG* provides numerous examples of divergent recensions of the same rite, singling out the ordination rituals, and in particular the ordination of bishop, as examples.[8]

Erdmann and Schramm then conclude, however, that for the texts of the blessing of a king and the ordination of a bishop another group of manuscripts (other than C and D) preserves the older recension.[9] These are the manuscripts identified as B (Bamberg, Oeffentl. Biblio., *codex lit.* 53), G (Eichstätt, Episcopal Archives, *Pontifical of Gondekar II*), L (Lucca, Biblio. capit., *codex* 607) and K (Pistoia, Biblio. capit., *codex* 141). Although C and D preserve the older forms of the *PRG* overall, B G L K represent the older recensions of the ordination of bishops. As Vogel explains, "[T]he recension of parts is quite different from the recension of the whole."[10]

A textual clue strengthening Erdmann and Schramm's hypothesis is a rubric found in *PRG* LXIII.20 and repeated in LXIII. 23. It describes the vesting of the elect as a bishop. This same ritual action occurs in the older texts of the *ordines romani* (*OR34* and *OR35*) immediately after the gradual and preceding the Consecration Presentation. Manuscripts B G K L maintain this Roman position, while manuscripts A C D J T V present a new pattern—vesting after the examination and consensus statement and before the epistle and gradual.

The unusual position of the ritual element of vesting reinforces Erdmann and Schramm's judgment that the block of manuscripts containing C and D represent the later recensions of the *PRG*. For the purposes of this study, we will conclude that the earlier rite of episcopal consecration in the *PRG* (from manuscripts B G K L) begins at no. a.(12), i.e., before the introductory rites of the Mass: "Beginning of the examination for ordination of a bishop according to the Gauls." This is the first set of texts we will examine.

3. *The* PRG: *ascending order*

The ascending arrangement of orders noted in *OR34* and *OR35* occurs in the *PRG,* but the *cursus* is far more extensive, with each stage a prerequisite for promotion to the next. The chapters begin with the rite of tonsure ("for the cutting of hair"), continue through "the ordo for how the sacred orders are made in the roman church" for psalmist, doorkeeper, lector, exorcist, and acolyte, and reach their apex with "the ordo for how presbyters, deacons and subdeacons are elected in the roman church," chapter XVI. These rites are then followed by over forty additional chapters unrelated to sacred orders: the rituals for the consecration of virgins, blessing of churches, dedication of baptisteries and cemeteries, among others.

Only much further on in chapter LVI does the first reference to bishop occur; the actual ordination rite of bishop is described even later on in chapter LXIII. Episcopal ordination is placed together with ceremonies for the blessings of king and emperor.[11] The *PRG* thereby introduces a strikingly new schema of sacred orders: subdeacon, deacon and presbyter have become the major orders; episcopacy is omitted.

4. *The* PRG: *introductory material for episcopal ordination*

The rite of episcopal ordination according to the *PRG* is preceded by a series of related juridical and canonical documents at the beginning of the relevant chapters. The first is the text of the decree of election which was presented to the metropolitan: LVI. "Decree which the clergy and people must sign regarding the bishop-elect." No. 4 of the decree begins with the phrase, "Whom we request be ordained pontiff for us as quickly as possible" ("Quem nobis quantotius petimus ordinari pontificem"), phrases which recall the *suggestio* or petitionary letters of *OR34.15*: "that he may consecrate as bishop for them [the elect]. . . ." However, no ritual formula for the postulation dialogue is recorded in the *PRG*[12] as it was in *OR34*.

The second text is the introductory formula for the electors' signatures on the decree: LVII. "Again the signature of the bishops for the election of a bishop." The formularies here indicate that the metropolitan archbishop signs first, then other bishops, demonstrating by their presence at the election their consensus regarding the one chosen.

Although chapter LVIII, the third text, is titled "From African council III. Chapter I," it is the prologue to the *Statuta Ecclesiae Antiqua* which provides in detail all questions necessary for the examination of the bishop-elect.[13] LVIII.2 is the source of a proclamation of consensus with elements similar to that from the second stage of ordination, the consecration liturgy, in *OR34.38*:

OR34.38	*PRG.LVIII.2*
	When he has been examined in all these [things], found fully prepared, then,
The clergy	with the consent of the clerics
and people of the city of N.,	and laity
with the consent of	and the agreement of
their neighboring sees,	the bishops of the entire province and especially of the metropolitan or by [his] authority or presence
have chosen N.,	
the deacon, or presbyter	
to be consecrated bishop.	he may be ordained. . . .

(We will find that a proclamation of consensus almost identical to LVIII.2 occurs within the liturgical texts in chapter LXIII [Ordination of a bishop].)

Chapter LIX, the fourth text in the series of juridical and canonical extracts that the *PRG* includes, is the metropolitan's invitation to the presbyters, deacons, honored clergy, nobility, and all the people of the vacant see to present their bishop-elect to him for ordination. The fifth text (LX) is taken from "chapter IIII" of the Council of Nicaea, often cited as the earliest canonical mandate for the presence of at least three bishops at the consecration of a bishop. The same text is also excellent evidence for the selection stage of ordination: the consensus of the neighboring bishops is required before the consecration may begin:

PRG.LX How a bishop is to be ordained. From the council of Nicaea, chapter IIII. It is especially suitable that a bishop be ordained by all the bishops who are in the province. If however this should be difficult, or because of present need, or because of lengthy travel, nevertheless when three of them have come together for this in any way and the absent also have decreed in like manner and consented in writing, then the ordination may be celebrated.

Paul Bradshaw summarizes this long tradition of the involvement of neighboring bishops in the ordination of a new bishop in their province:

> [F]rom at least the middle of the third century, if not earlier, a local church had to obtain from neighboring bishops their approval of the candidate proposed as their bishop, and this was usually signified by the presence of the bishops at the ordination itself. In the fourth century, the number of bishops requisite for a valid ordination was formalized. Canon 4 of the Council of Nicaea ruled that all the bishops of the province should be involved, but if that were not possible, then there should be a minimum of three, with the rest sending their approval in writing.[14]

Sunday is the day prescribed in the sixth text for the consecration of the elect; the feast day of an apostle is also appropriate. The seventh text (Chapter LXII. Ordination of a bishop) occurs only in the more recent recension (manuscripts C D J V); it is discussed together with those texts in section C below.

An overview of the interplay between the earlier and later recensions of the *PRG* may be helpful as the comparative analysis unfolds. Manuscripts B G K L are discussed in Section B immediately following, while manuscripts C and D are taken up in Section C. Here is a brief schema of the alignment of the texts:

C D

LXII. Ordination of a bishop.

1. First of all he is chosen.
2. "Collect."
3. Verses.
4. Afterwards he is seated on the cathedra.
5. Prayer.

B G K L

LXIII. [Ordination of a bishop.]   **LXIII. [Ordination of a bishop.]**

Gallican Examination.

a. (12) *Antiqua sanctorum patrum.* . . .

b. (13) Will you . . .?

c. (14) Do you believe . . .?

d. (15) May this faith be increased. . . .

e. (16) Another prayer.

f. (17) . . . the consent of the clerics and laity and the agreement of the bishops. . . .

B G K L and C D

How a bishop is ordained in the roman church.

1. Ministers and people gather.
2. Metropolitan vests.
3. Procession of ministers.
4. Procession of elect and others.
5. And after the scrutiny has been done. . . .
6. Entrance antiphon.
7. The *Gloria.*
8. *Adesto.*

B G K L   *C D*

9. Bishops gather.
10. Elect vested as a presbyter is presented.
11. . . . [T]he lord metropolitan says examining him thus:
12. Gallican Examination.
Antiqua sanctorum patrum. . . .
13. Will you . . .?
14. Do you believe . . .?
15. May this faith be increased. . . .
16. Another prayer.
17. . . . the consent of the clerics and laity and the agreement of the bishops. . . .
18. No bishop may be imposed. . . .
19. Elect is led into the sacristy.
20. Elect is vested as a bishop.

21. Epistle.
22. Gradual and tract.
23. Elect is vested as a bishop.

B G K L

C D

24. Prayer for vesting in sandals.
25. Prayer for vesting in gloves.
26. Prayer for vesting in dalmatic.

B G K L and C D

27. Presentation of the bishop-elect.

B. ANALYSIS OF THE LITURGICAL UNITS: THE EARLIER RECENSIONS B G K L

1. *Selection Presentation*

a. SELECTION PRESENTATION: TEXT

PRG.LXIII. [The ordination of a bishop].
Here begins the examination for the ordination of bishop according to the Gauls.

a. (12) *[Antiqua sanctorum patrum]* The ancient instruction of the holy fathers teaches and prescribes that he who is chosen for the order of the episcopacy, especially, as we read in the canon of Carthage, is to be most diligently examined beforehand with all charity regarding [his] faith in the holy trinity and questioned about [his] various motives and behaviors. . . .

b. (13) Interrogation. . . . Will you promise fidelity and submission to me and my successors of the holy church of Mainz?

c. (14) Interrogation. Do you believe in the holy trinity according to the understanding and capacity of your mind . . .?

f. (17) And thus examined and fully prepared with the consent of the clerics and laity and the agreement of the bishops of the entire province and especially of the metropolitan or by [his] authority or presence he may be ordained.

How a bishop is ordained in the roman church.

1. When a bishop is ordained, first the lord metropolitan makes his way with the elect and all the clergy and people to the church where he wants to hold that ordination.

5. And after the scrutiny has been done. . . .

b. SELECTION PRESENTATION:
  THE GALLICAN EXAMINATION

According to Vogel and Elze's alignment of manuscripts B G K L (the older recensions), episcopal ordination begins with an examination of the elect, the Gallican examination to be precise. Identified in this study by its opening words, *Antiqua sanctorum patrum,* the examination begins with an admonition that whoever is elected to the episcopacy must be most diligently examined in faith and morals. "The canon of the Council of Carthage" (actually *SEA*) is cited as precedent for this responsibility.

The examination includes a series of nine questions regarding the moral, canonical, and ecclesial worthiness of the elect *(Will you . . . ?)* and then a series of a further nine questions about the orthodoxy of his beliefs *(Do you believe . . . ?)*. The question regarding fidelity to the metropolitan and his successors uses the name of the holy church of Mainz *(sanctae Mogontiensi aecclesiae),* further underscoring the Germanic provenance of this rite.

There is no ritual context provided for the examination; it is simply inserted as nos. a.(12)–d.(15) before the consecration begins Sunday morning. Does the examination occur on a previous day, as in the Roman pattern, or earlier on the same day? Does it involve a prior interrogation of representatives of the electors? Do members of the vacant see participate? Do they present the elect?

Sparse information is provided thus far in the texts. At the end of the examination, we read:

PRG.LXIII.d. (15) And he says to him: Dearest brother in Christ, may this faith be increased within you by the lord for true and everlasting blessedness.
All respond: Amen.

We can state with certainty only that the elect has been chosen and that at some point he is presented to the metropolitan in a public liturgy for an examination. The dense descriptions of the Roman Selection Presentation in *OR34* and of Hincmar's letter regarding the Saturday before the consecration are absent here.

c. SELECTION PRESENTATION:
  PROCLAMATION OF CONSENSUS AND CONSECRATION

Following the examination is the consensus statement, taken originally from *Statuta Ecclesiae Antiqua:*

SEA (I) When he has been examined in all these things	PRG.LXIII.f. (17) And thus examined
and found fully prepared,	and fully prepared
then with the consent of the clerics and laity	with the consent of the clerics and laity
and the agreement of the bishops of the entire province	and the agreement of the bishops of the entire province
and especially of the metropolitan by authority or presence	and especially of the metropolitan by authority or present
the bishop may be ordained. . . .	he may be ordained.

This same canon was cited earlier in the *PRG* (chapter LVIII.2) where it was part of an extended quotation from *SEA*; it has now moved into the context of the ordination itself. This Gallican consensus statement within the selection process is quite distinct from the Roman:

OR34.30. . . . Because the desires of all have agreed upon you, today you will abstain and tomorrow, if it is pleasing to God, you will be consecrated.

The Gallican form specifies in even greater detail those involved in the consensual selection, yet it makes the same point: consecration follows immediately upon the final stage of selection, the consensus of all the sees involved.

For this proclamation of consensus, Vogel and Elze do not use italicized lettering which indicates a spoken text. However, the shift in the initial words of the statement (from *then,* with the consent) [in the canonical commentary of LVIII.2] to *and thus,* with the consent) [in the statement's reappearance in the liturgical description of LXIII.f.(17)] seems deliberate, and results in an appropriate introduction should the metropolitan read this text immediately after the examination, giving his own affirmation of the consensual selection and introducing the consecration. Perhaps spoken liturgical usage is the intent of such a subtle alternation in the text.

d. SELECTION PRESENTATION:
   INTRODUCTORY RITES

The title given to this section of Chapter LXIII of the *PRG* claims that what follows is the manner in which a bishop is ordained in the Roman Church. The site, however, is a church chosen by the archbishop of Mainz. The metropolitan, bishop-elect, all the clergy and people enter the church; the deacons and other ministers usually present at Sunday Eucharist are functioning as they ordinarily would.

e. SELECTION PRESENTATION:
   THE "SCRUTINY" AND ITS PLACEMENT

No. 5 presents an intriguing rubric which precedes the introit:

PRG.LXIII.5. And after the scrutiny has been done. . . .

What scrutiny? In the later manuscripts of the *PRG* (C D J T V), the word "scrutinizing" is found in no. 11 immediately before the Gallican examination. The Pontifical of the Roman Curia will use the expression "scrutiny" for the entire complex of elements in the Roman Selection Presentation from *OR34* which it reproduces. But the word scrutiny is not found in any other place in the *PRG* of these earlier recensions. To what ritual element does the word refer?

Pursuing the connection of "scrutiny" to the examination leads us to suggest that no. 5 of the earlier *PRG* recensions refers to the location of the "examination for the ordination of a bishop according to the Gauls" within the ordination ritual. The rubric "And after the scrunity has been done . . ." also provides us with evidence of the visible "seams" as elements of the Gallican ritual are woven into the older pattern of the *ordines romani*.

The earlier recensions of the *PRG* do not yet insert the text of the Gallican examination at the appropriate point within the consecration ritual from *OR35* that they copy. The complete examination formula is still placed separately and before the Roman texts describing the Sunday liturgy. But the newer rubric, "And after the scrutiny has been done" (written into the text of *OR35*), will make very clear to episcopal masters of ceremonies where the examination and consensus texts are to be inserted during the ordination liturgy.[15] Following this rubrical clue, we will place the Gallican examination in its liturgical context in the structure outlined below.

The juxtaposition of these diverse elements in the *PRG* reminds us of the hybrid nature of this Pontifical. Ritual compilers and copyists seem to be experimenting with the placement of the Gallican examination within the Romano-Germanic pattern of the ordination rite. The earlier pattern, as we have seen, is for an examination of the elect (as well as of members of the vacant see) taking place within a Selection Presentation structure on the Saturday before the consecration.

The later pattern, as we see it evolving here in the earlier manuscripts of the *PRG*, is transforming the previous tradition in light of its own needs. The Saturday synaxis is omitted, but the examination and proclamation of consensus and consecration are maintained are part of the selection process before the consecration liturgy. As Bruno Kleinheyer explains, ". . . in place of the evening examination, [the *PRG*] moves a long-winded inquiry which begins *Antiqua sanctorum patrum* directly to the beginning of the ordination liturgy."[16]

f. SELECTION PRESENTATION: STRUCTURE

For all the creativity of the Germanic genius, the earlier recensions of the *PRG* steadfastly maintain both the nature and the sequence of the structure of the Selection Presentation found in the earlier Roman and Gallican sources, i.e., an examination and proclamation of consensus and consecration *before* the introductory rites of the Mass begin.

PRG/B G K L

1st Stage

**Selection
(presentation)**
                                   examination
proclamation of consensus and consecration:
                                   with the agreement/
                                   he may be ordained

The elements of this section are somewhat meager: an examination followed by the (possible?) proclamation of consensus and consecration. There is no formal presentation nor ritual postulation in the rubrics though the reality of both is understood by the fact of the selection, the words of the postulating decree in Chapter LVI.4, and the examination. The proclamation of consensus and consecration may or may not be read aloud. Is it legitimate to identify the few texts above as a selection structure with a proclamation of consensus and consecration which parallels the Roman and early Gallican patterns?

The elements in *PRG*.LXII and LXIII are clearly the conclusion to a selection process for episcopal ordination. The nature of the examination is evident enough, and the proclamation which follows is a description of a consensual selection process, ending with the approval for the consecration. Immediately following the proclamation of consensus and consecration, the texts for the consecration stage begin. Although there is no textual dependency of any kind of the selection stage upon the Roman or earlier Gallican texts, the structural dependency is clear.

Thus the selection unit from the earlier recensions of the *PRG* parallels the type and the sequence of elements that exist in the Roman and earlier Gallican patterns:

OR34	Gallican	PRG/B G K L
1st stage	*1st stage*	*1st stage*
Selection Presentation	**Selection Presentation**	**Selection**
Saturday	Saturday	previous day?
presentation:	**(presentation)**	**(presentation)**
Church of the elect		
postulation:		
grant us a patron		
decree		
interrogation	examination	examination
proclamation of	**proclamation of**	**proclamation of**
consensus and	**consensus and**	**consensus and**
consecration:	**consecration:**	**consecration:**
desires of all/	*Seruanda est*	with the agreement/
you will be consecrated		he may be ordained

2. *Consecration Presentation*

a. CONSECRATION PRESENTATION: TEXT[17]

PRG.LXIII

5. And after the scrutiny has been done and with the bells of the church resounding, the lord metropolitan, as soon as he wishes, informs the cantor and thereupon he begins the antiphon for the introit.

7. And when they have finished the introit, they do not sing the *Kyrieleison* then but the lord metropolitan intones: *Gloria in excelsis Deo.*

8. That finished, he says: Peace be with you. R. And with your spirit. Then he offers the oration for the Mass: *Adesto.* . . .

[manuscripts B G K L skip from no. 8 to no. 21.]

21. Meanwhile the epistle is read.

22. After that the gradual is sung.

23. Then the archdeacon goes out with acolytes and subdeacons and vests the elect in sandals, dalmatic, chasuble and *cambagos*.[18]

27. The bishop-designate having then been solemnly prepared, two bishops wearing chasubles bring him back to a higher place, next to the altar.

28. And turning to the people the ordainer says: The exhortation to the people when the bishop is ordained. *Servanda est.* . . .

29. After these professions, he says this preface: *Oremus, dilectissimi nobis.* . . .

30. And immediately the clergy begin *Kyrieleison* with the litany. And the ordainer of the elect prostrates with the elect and the other bishops before the altar on the carpet until the schola sings *Agnus Dei*.

31. Then standing up, two bishops place and hold the closed book of the gospels over his neck and between his shoulders and one pouring out the blessing over him, all the rest of the bishops who are present touch their hands to his head and the ordainer says:

34. *Propitiare.* . . .

35. Then he says with a loud voice: Forever and ever. R. Amen. The Lord be with you. R. And with your spirit. Lift up your hearts. . . . Preface. It is truly right up to eternal God. Every honor. . . . Complete, lord, the fullness of your mystery in your priest, and equipped with all the adornments of glory, hallow him with the dew of heavenly unction.

Here he puts chrism on his head in the form of a cross and says: May your head be anointed and consecrated by the heavenly blessing in the pontifical order, in the name of the Father and of the Son and of the Holy Spirit. R. Amen. Peace be with you. R. And with your spirit. May it flow down, lord, richly upon his head. . . . [consecration prayer continues]

b. CONSECRATION PRESENTATION:
   INTRODUCTORY RITES

Following the "scrutiny" and the proclamation of consensus and con-secration, the introit of the Mass begins; the proclamation of consensus at the end of the selection stage introduces the consecration liturgy. The *Gloria* is sung, the greeting given, and the collect for the Mass (*Adesto* = *SVe* 942 = *GregH* 2.21) recited. The epistle, continuing the Roman pattern, is from 1 Timothy 3:1-8; the gradual follows.

c. CONSECRATION PRESENTATION:
   ARCHDEACON, ACOLYTES, AND SUBDEACONS,
   AND TWO BISHOPS

Nos. 23 and 27 provide a fascinating window on the process of Franco-Germanic adaptation of the earlier Roman rite. For the most part, no. 23 is a duplication of *OR*34.37 and *OR*35.61: a description of the vesting of the elect in episcopal garb by the archdeacon, acolytes and subdeacons before the Consecration Presentation:

OR35.61	OR34.37	PRG.LXIII.22, 23
After this, the gradual is sung. Then the archdeacon goes out with acolytes and subdeacons and vests the elect in dalmatic, chasuble and campagos and brings him in further, next to the entrance to the *presbyterium*.	And while the gradual is sung, the archdeacon goes out with acolytes and subdeacons and vests him in dalmatic, chasuble and campobos and leads him in.	After that the gradual is sung. Then the archdeacon goes out with acolytes and subdeacons and vests the elect in sandals, dalmatic, chasuble, and cambagos.

Manuscripts B G K L record this simple rubric at no. 23, and then proceed immediately to no. 27 in which the original set of ministers from the *ordines romani* (archdeacon, acolytes, subdeacons who vest and present the elect) have now been replaced for the presentation by the Germanic set of ministers: two bishops:

PRG.LXIII.27. The bishop-designate having then been solemnly prepared, two bishops wearing chasubles bring him back to a higher place, next to the altar.

These rubrics from the *PRG* have retained the archdeacon (probably from the vacant see) with acolytes and subdeacons for the task of vesting but have introduced two bishops for the actual presentation of the bishop-elect. In the Roman pattern as we have seen, only the pope's presence is necessary for consecration; other bishops are present in OR34 but they have no distinct liturgical role. As the expanded Romano-Germanic pontifical model evolves, it is evident that the suffragans are present and significant to the ritual action: two of them present the elect as an act of their consent to the selection.

d. CONSECRATION PRESENTATION:
   THE PROCLAMATION OF CONSENSUS AND CONSECRATION,
   SERVANDA EST

Following the presentation of the elect, the earlier recensions of the *PRG* include the metropolitan's extensive exhortation to the people, *Servanda est* (from the *Missale Francorum* 9.35). This eloquent address summarizes the selection process for a new bishop, stressing the vital importance of electing the one most worthy. The metropolitan confirms that the presbyters and entire clergy have participated in the choice as have the citizens and those assembled for the consecration. He states his own belief that "the reverend N. should be elected," and then calls upon the entire assembly to voice their consent by "crying out your praises together, and say: He is worthy."

What is somewhat curious in this choice of proclamation is the fact that it has been taken from the *selection* stage of the texts of the *MF*. The verbs within the exhortation refer to elements of the selection which are still to come. Yet ritually the next elements in sequence are the bidding, the litany and other texts for the consecration.

The compilers of the earlier recensions of the *PRG* recognize that a proclamation of consensus and consecration occurs traditionally at this point. They have already used the proclamation from *SEA* in the selection stage and either do not have access to the extended Gallican bidding from the *MF* or are dissuaded from using it by its inaccurate title. The stirring exhortation, *Servanda est,* is worth preserving. Since liturgical books often give evidence of retaining archaic liturgical forms long after those have fallen into disuse, it is not surprising to find this venerable text included. The exhortation, if actually used, would have provided the assembly the opportunity to confirm the selection once again as the consecration begins. In searching for a unit of proclamation of consensus and consecration/bidding, and intending to retain the older forms, the compilers choose the exhortation, *Servanda est,* and bidding *MF*.

e. CONSECRATION PRESENTATION:
    THE ROMANO-GERMANIC HYBRID RITE

This proclamation leads immediately to the bidding *MF,* here called a *praefatio.*[19] The litany follows. Roman elements of episcopal consecration elaborated by the Germanic genius begin their permanent hold on the tradition of the Roman Church: two bishops place and hold the gospel book over the neck and between the shoulders of the elect; the rest of the bishops impose hands while the metropolitan offers the Roman oration *Propitiare* (= *SVe* 946), begins the preface dialogue, and then the consecration prayer with the Gallican interpolation (= *SVe* + *GeV*/*MF*); he then anoints the head of the new bishop with chrism, recites the anointing formulary in the middle of the consecration prayer,[20] "confirms"[21] the thumb of him who only at this point is declared *consecratus* [consecrated], gives him the crozier, and imposes the ring.[22] The consecration rite concludes with the kiss of peace and the seating of the new bishop at the head of the other bishops.

The Mass resumes with the *Alleluia* and proclamation of the gospel. Following the prayer texts of the Mass, these older manuscripts provide a threefold blessing of the new bishop[23] and elements from Roman practice: giving the new bishop the *formata* (a guide to his episcopal ministry) and a consecrated host from which he will communicate for the next forty days.

f. CONSECRATION PRESENTATION: STRUCTURE

2nd Stage

Consecration Presentation

	introt to gradual
	episcopal vestments
presentation:	two bishops
proclamation of consensus and consecration:	
	Servanda est
	bidding *MF*
consecration:	litany
	gospel book
	laying on of hands
	Propitiare
	consecration prayer
	consecration continues

3. *Conclusion*

Analysis of the older recensions of the *PRG* reveals the gradual transformation of the earlier Roman and Gallican texts as these were successively copied to meet the needs of growing dioceses within the Romano-Germanic empire. The first compilers of the *PRG* seem intent on being faithful to the elements and to the sequence of the previous traditions while creating their own texts and revising others as needed.

Fidelity to the earlier Roman and Gallican structure of ordination by these *PRG* texts is witnessed by the titles given to sections of the ritual and placement of those titles in relation to the texts. Chapter LXIII, designated [Ordination of a bishop] in these older recensions, refers to the gathering of the metropolitan and suffragan bishops with all the clergy and people, an examination of the elect proper to the Gallican genius and needs of the times, and a proclamation of consensus regarding the choice of the elect by the vacant see, adjacent sees, and metropolitan see, which consensus then allows the consecration stage *(How a bishop is ordained in the roman church)* to begin.

Following the introductory rites of the consecration liturgy, the elect is vested as a bishop and is presented to the metropolitan by two bishops.

The metropolitan summarizes the entire selection process involved, restates the consensus of all the sees involved and invites the assembly to reaffirm its choice by acclaiming the worthiness of the elect. The bidding and litany follow, introducing the consecration. Thus episcopal ordination in the earlier recensions of the *PRG* includes both selection and consecration, a two-stage process.

Texts of the *PRG*:

Selection Presentation:

PRG.LX Qualiter episcopus debeat ordinari. Ex concilio Niceno, capitulo IIII. Episcopum convenit maxime quidem ab omnibus qui sunt in provincia episcopis ordinari. Si autem hoc difficile fuerit, aut propter instantem necessitatem, aut propter itineris longitudinem, tribus tamen omnimodis in idipsum convenientibus et absentibus quoque pari modo decernentibus et per scripta consentientibus, tunc ordinatio celebretur.

PRG.LXIII. [Ordinatio episcopi].

Incipit examinatio in ordinatione episcopi secundum Gallos.

a. (12) Antiqua sanctorum patrum institutio docet et praecipit ut is qui ad ordinem episcopatus eligitur, maxime, ut legimus in canone Cartaginensi, antea diligentissime examinetur cum omni caritate de fide sanctae trinitatis et interrogetur de diversis causis vel moribus. . . .

b. (13) Interrogatio. . . . Vis sanctae Mogontiensi aecclesiae, mihi et successoribus meis fidem et subiectionem exhibere?

c. (14) Interrogatio. Credis secundum intelligentiam et capacitatem sensus tui sanctam trinitatem . . .?

d. (15) Et dicatur ei: Haec tibi fides augeatur a domino ad veram et aeternam beatitudinem, dilectissime frater in Christo. Respondent omnes: Amen.

f. (17) Ita quoque examinatus et plene instructus cum consensu clericorum et laicorum ac conventu totius provinciae episcoporum maximeque metropolitani vel auctoritate aut praesentia ordinetur.

Qualiter episcopus in romana ecclesia ordinetur.

1. Episcopus cum ordinatur, primo progreditur domnus metropolitanus cum electo et cuncto clero et populo ad ecclesiam ubi ipsam fieri vult ordinationem.

5. Factoque ibi scrutinio . . .

Consecration Presentation:

5. Factoque ibi scrutinio et concrepantibus ecclesiae signis, domnus metropolitanus, mox ut vult indicet cantori et mox incipit antiphonam ad introitum.

7. Cumque introitum finierint, non dicitur tunc Kyrieleison sed dominus metropolitanus dicat: Gloria in excelsis Deo.

8. Quo finito dicit: Pax vobiscum. R. Et cum spiritu tuo. Deinde dat orationem ad missam: Adesto. . . .

21. Interim legatur apostolus.

22. Posthinc psallitur graduale.

23. Tunc egreditur arcidiaconus cum acolitis et subdiaconibus et induit ipsum electum sandalia, dalmaticam, planetam et cambagos.

27. Episcopo vero designato sollemniter praeparato duo episcopi casulis induti deportent eum superius, iuxta altare.

28. Et convertens se ad populum ordinator dicat: Exortatio ad populum cum episcopus ordinatur. Servanda est. . . .

29. His ita profitentibus dicat hanc praefationem: Oremus, dilectissimi nobis. . . .

30. Et statim incipit clerus Kyrieleison cum letania. Et prosternat se ordinator electi simul cum electo et ceteris episcopis ante altare super stramenta, usquedum dicat scola: Agnus Dei.

31. Ut autem surrexerint, duo episcopi ponunt et tenent evangeliorum codicem super cervicem eius et inter scapulas clausum et, uno super eum fundente benedictionem, reliqui omnes episcopi qui assunt manibus suis caput eius tangunt et dicit ordinator:

34. Propitiare. . . .

35. Tunc dicatur alta voce: Per omnia secula seculorum. R. Amen. Dominus vobiscum. R. Et cum spiritu. Sursum corda. . . .
Praephatio. Vere dignum usque aeterne Deus. Honor omnium. . . .
Comple, domine, in sacerdote tuo misterii tui summam et ornamentis totius glorificationis instructum caelestis unguenti rore sanctifica.

Hic mittat chrisma in caput eius in modum crucis et dicatur: Unguatur et consecretur caput tuum caelesti benedictione in ordine pontificali, in nomine patris et filii et spiritus sancti. R. Amen.
Pax tibi. R. Et cum spiritu tuo.

Hoc, domine, copiose in eius caput influat. . . .

Text of *Statuta Ecclesiae Antiqua:*
(I) Cum in his omnibus examinatus inuentus fuerit plene instructus, tunc consensu clericorum et laicorum et conuentu totius prouinciae episcoporum, maximeque metropolitani uel auctoritate uel praesentia ordinetur episcopus. . . .

C. ANALYSIS OF THE LITURGICAL UNITS: THE LATER RECENSIONS C D

1. *Selection Presentation*

a. SELECTION PRESENTATION: TEXT

PRG.LXII The ordination of a bishop.

1. First of all he is chosen. After the election this collect is recited by the archbishop:

2. Dearly beloved brothers, let us pray that our God and lord Jesus Christ may be pleased to enlighten us and our elect by the grace of the holy spirit. Through.

3. Then this verse is sung: Let them extoll him in the assembly of the people. R. And praise him in the seat of the elders.

4. Afterwards he is seated on the cathedra.

5. And he says this prayer: Almighty, holy father, eternal God, you have graciously ordained a man among the heavenly thrones. . . .

PRG.LXIII [The ordination of a bishop]
How a bishop is to be ordained in the roman church.

1. When a bishop is ordained, first the lord metropolitan makes his way with the elect and all the clergy and people to the church where he wants to hold that ordination.

5. And after the scrutiny has been done and with the bells of the church resounding, the lord metropolitan, as soon as he wishes, informs the cantor and thereupon he begins the antiphon for the introit.

10. Meanwhile the elect dressed in sacred vestments, comes out from the sacristy, two bishops leading him by the hand to before the altar.

11. . . . [T]he lord metropolitan says examining him thus:

12. Here begins the examination for the ordination of a bishop according to the Gauls. *Antiqua sanctorum patrum*. . . .

17. And thus examined and fully prepared with the consent of the clerics and laity and the agreement of the bishops of the entire province and especially of the metropolitan by [his] authority or presence he may be ordained.

18. No bishop may be imposed on the unwilling; the consent and desire of the clergy, people and [civil] authority is required.

19. With these things accomplished, two bishops coworkers in the sacred order lead the elect again in the sacristy.

b. SELECTION PRESENTATION:
   THE ELECTION AND ENTHRONEMENT

Manuscripts C and D of the *PRG* bring to light an entirely new chapter (LXII) for the ordination of a bishop absent from the earlier recensions. How well the title and first four words of this text summarize an essential dynamic in episcopal ordination: "The ordination of a bishop. First he is chosen": the first stage of ordination is selection. Chapter LXII underscores that fact by adding several ritual elements to the selection process: a bidding, chanting of verse 32 from Psalm 107, and a lengthy prayer recalling the divine vocation of the Old Testament priests, patriarchs, and prophets, and Christ's own choice of his apostles: Peter, first in the seat of honor, but also Matthias, who was counted in the company of apostles. Before the prayer, the bishop-elect is enthroned in the cathedra.

We have previously noted the importance of the elect vesting as a bishop before the consecration. In these later manuscripts of the *PRG*, he is also seated on the cathedra as part of the selection process, fulfilling the words of the psalm:

PRG.LXII.3. . . . Let them extoll him in the assembly of the people. And praise him in the seat of the elders.

It is the elect who enthroned as the archbishop prays that "our brother N." may be found worthy of the seat of honor through the same grace God bestowed on the holy apostles. By his selection, the elect is already constituted a bishop in significant ways; he has taken possession of the cathedra.

In their commentary on Chapter LXII in the apparatus, Vogel and Elze come to a conclusion about this initial section of the ordination rite that is worth noting. Although the title of Chapter LXII as given in the original text is "The ordination of a bishop," the editors dismiss this identification and direct the reader to regard these articles as having nothing to do with ordination but rather as referring only to the enthronement of the bishop after his election.[24] But this is precisely the point: selection of the elect and rituals confirming his choice have everything to do with ordination.

To strengthen their conclusion, Vogel and Elze decide to repeat the title but in brackets ["The ordination of a bishop"] and place that title at the head of the chapter that follows, a chapter which had no title in the original text. They thus indicate the judgment that the ordination of bishops does not begin at the point the texts indicate (with Chapter LXII:

his selection and seating in the cathedra) but only with the subsequent Chapter LXIII (the Gallican examination). An understanding of the two-stage structure of ordination would have allowed Vogel and Elze to recognize the *PRG*.LXII: "The ordination of a bishop" as accurate, as the beginning of the ordination rite.

This initial act of enthronement in the selection stage suggests that the election took place in the vacant see (site of the elect's cathedra); subsequent elements of the selection and consecration occur in the cathedral of the metropolitan (who does not relinquish his own cathedra to the newly ordained for the celebration of the Eucharist). The consecration stage of the ordination will conclude with the metropolitan seating the newly ordained at the head of all the other bishops gathered, but not in his own cathedra (LXIII.47). The original text of the *PRG* is correct as it stands: "The ordination of a bishop. First he is chosen."

Arthur Henderson offers a suggestion that is also helpful in identifying these initial texts. He writes that Chapter LXII is "a brief service presenting the bishop-elect" which includes what "may have been the closing prayer of a synod called to elect a new bishop."[25] These texts then (LXII: "The ordination of a bishop") are precisely that, the first elements in the ordination. In this instance, the original compiler (and not the later editors of the text) is correct.

Although the bidding from Chapter LXII also appears in *The Leofric Missal*, the archbishop's prayer after the enthronement is only found in these later recensions of the *PRG*; it does not appear to have been copied from any earlier work, and it does not reappear in any later pontificals.

c. SELECTION PRESENTATION:
    PLACEMENT OF THE ELEMENTS

The manuscripts of the *PRG* which Erdmann, Schramm, and Vogel conclude are the later recensions of the episcopal ordination rite (C and D) place the Gallican examination *(Antiqua sanctorum patrum)* and the proclamation of consensus and consecration (nos. 12–17) within the liturgical texts of the Sunday liturgy, i.e., after the collect. However, C and D insert these elements (with additional elaborate material now forming nos. 9–20) without removing the earlier rubric ("And after the scrutiny has been done . . .") which remains in its earlier place at no. 5. Only the redactor of manuscript T (Vienna, National-biblio., *codex lat.* 701) will notice this confusing and redundant rubric indicating in no. 5 an action that doesn't occur until no. 12. He omits it.

d. SELECTION PRESENTATION:
   TWO BISHOPS

The presentation of the bishop-elect in the selection stage is made explicit in these later manuscripts. After the introit of the Mass, *Gloria,* greeting, and collect, the elect is led by two bishops from the sacristy to the metropolitan for the Gallican examination. The bishops and their dioceses are not identified in the texts.

e. SELECTION PRESENTATION:
   THE GALLICAN EXAMINATION[26]

As indicated above, the examination in the later recensions has been moved from an initial position before any rubrics for the Sunday liturgy and newly inserted into the ritual texts after the opening prayer of the Mass:

PRG.LXIII.11. . . . [T]he lord metropolitan says examining him thus:

12. Here begins the examination for the ordination of a bishop according to the Gauls. *Antiqua sanctorum patrum.* . . .

The examination that follows is identical to that in B G K L except for very minor but interesting adaptations. C and D leave in the reference to "the holy Church of Mainz" in the promise of fidelity to the metropolitan; A (Rome, Biblio. Alessandr., *codex* 173) and V (Vendôme, Biblio. municip., *codex* 14) change the reference to Salzburg *[Iuvavensi]*; J (London, British Library, *codex addit.* 17004) has "the holy Church of N."; T (Vienna, Nationalbibl., *codex lat.,* 701) omits any reference at all to the local church and the present metropolitan and merely asks "Will you promise fidelity and submission to my successors?"

f. SELECTION PRESENTATION:
   PROCLAMATION OF CONSENSUS AND CONSECRATION

The examination is followed by the proclamation of consensus and consecration copied from *SEA* (as in B G K L) but with the addition of the forceful words of Pope Celestine I at no. 18:

PRG.LXIII.18. No bishop may be imposed on the unwilling; the consent and desire of the clergy [,] people and [civil] authorities is required.

Following the proclamation, the two assistant bishops lead the elect back into the sacristy.

g. SELECTION PRESENTATION: STRUCTURE

The later recensions of the *PRG* also follow the pattern of the earlier manuscripts: the same elements in the same sequence.

PRG/C D

1st stage

Selection Presentation

	Sunday
	introit to collect
presentation:	2 bishops
	examination

proclamation of consensus and consecration:

| | with the agreement/ |
| | he may be ordained |

The presentation of the bishop-elect for the concluding elements of his selection is more ritually defined in these texts: two bishops present him to the metropolitan for the examination. A clear statement of consensus and consecration (enhanced by the saying of Pope Celestine I) concludes the selection stage.

2. *Consecration Presentation*

a. CONSECRATION PRESENTATION: TEXT

PRG.LXIII.20. Then the archdeacon goes out with acolytes and subdeacons and vests the elect in *cambagos,* sandals, dalmatic, chasuble and gloves.

[21. Epistle: Timothy 3:1-8 and Titus 7, 10]

[22. Gradual and tract]

[23. The change to episcopal vestments]

24. This prayer is said when he is vested by the bishops in sandals: . . . .

25. Said when he is vested by the bishops with the gloves: . . . .

26. Said when he is vested by the bishops with the dalmatic: . . . .

27. The bishop-designate having been solemnly prepared two bishops wearing chasubles bring him back to a higher place, next to the altar.

28. And turning to the people the ordainer gives a sermon if he wishes.

29. After these professions with the consent of the clerics and laity and the agreement of the bishops of the entire province, and especially of the metropolitan or by [his] authority or presence he may be ordained.

[30. The litany begins; prostration of all bishops and the elect]

[31. Two bishops impose the gospel book on the neck of the elect; all other bishops present impose hands]

32. The prayer. *Adesto*. . . .

33. The preface follows. Let us pray, our dearly beloved, that the goodness of almighty God may bestow the abundance of his grace upon this man appointed for the service of the church. Through Christ our lord.

34. *Propitiare*. . . .

[35. The preface dialogue and consecration prayer]

b. CONSECRATION PRESENTATION:
   EPISCOPAL VESTMENTS

Following the Selection Presentation, the two bishops called coworkers lead the elect into the sacristy where he is vested as a bishop in *cambagos,* sandals, dalmatic, chasuble and pontifical gloves. This act of vesting marks the transition between the two stages of the ordination, as was true in the earlier models of ordination. The selection stage is concluded with the proclamation of consensus; the act of consecration begins with the elect vested as a bishop.

As noted above in connection with the earlier Roman and Gallican patterns, the vesting of the elect as a bishop at this point in the ordination is an act of critical significance. Unlike the ordination rites for psalmist ascending up through presbyter in the manuscripts of the *PRG*, the episcopal ordinand is clothed in the vestments of his new order *before* the consecration begins (i.e., not after the consecration prayer as an explanatory rite). His vesting follows the selection stage and the proclamation of consensus by the ordaining bishop: in some very real sense, the elect is already a bishop by virtue of the selection process. The placement of the act of vesting in episcopal garb *before* the consecration is consistent in every liturgical text studied in this work, up to and including the 1990 revision.

While the compilers of C and D clarify the roles of the assistant bishops as coworkers (who lead and present the elect) and the archdeacon, acolytes, and subdeacons (who vest the elect), they place the relevant rubrics in an awkward place: at no. 20 after the collect but before the epistle (a location only repeated in *OR35B*). The confusion is compounded when the reader discovers the identical rubrics for a duplicate vesting of the elect (but without gloves) occurring at no. 23 in all the manuscripts.

Manuscripts A C D J V aptly include prayers to accompany the vesting with sandals, gloves and dalmatic at what would be the more logical (and consistent) place, *after* no. 23 (the vesting) where it occurs in all the manuscripts. Taking the placement of the vesting prayers as evidence for the more probable location of the vesting itself, we will not include the first vesting rubric (before the epistle) in the outline of the structure that follows. The transformation of the earlier redactions of the *PRG* through these various recensions is an uneven one; copyists and compilers leave traces of their rearranging.

c. CONSECRATION PRESENTATION:
   PROCLAMATION OF CONSENSUS AND CONSECRATION
   AS AN OPTIONAL SERMON

After the elect is vested in episcopal garb, two bishops present him to the metropolitan. The earlier recensions (B G K L) as well as the later C D J and T cite the exhortation, *Servanda est* (from *MF* 9.35), as the proclamation of consensus and consecration. But A and V substitute this rubric:

PRG.LXIII.28. And turning to the people the ordainer gives a sermon if he wishes.

The compilers of A and V remove the exhortation, *Servanda est,* (because the selection process described no longer matched their reality?) and insert what appears to be an equivalent liturgical element: the sermon. And this they make optional! It is the texts of manuscripts A and V which the Roman Pontifical of the Twelfth Century will follow, signaling the end of the inclusion of *Servanda est* in any future pontifical text, signaling the permanent disappearance of an explicit proclamation of consensus and consecration within the Consecration Presentation stage of episcopal ordination. The conciliar reform of 1968 will not restore this constitutive structural element.

d. CONSECRATION PRESENTATION:
   A PATCHWORK OF ELEMENTS

In an odd arrangement, C D J include the proclamation of consensus and consecration from *SEA* again at this point (no. 29), rather than the bidding. The litany begins without any bidding; two bishops place and hold the gospel book over the neck and between the shoulders of the elect; the other bishops present lay on hands.

The copyists then add two elements in the wrong place: the ordaining bishop is to reread the collect of the Mass *(Adesto)* and follow this with the bidding *MF* which was to have introduced the previous litany. The copyists have also made the bidding into an oration by adding *Per Christum dominum nostrum* to its conclusion.

After this confusion, the elements of the consecration return to the earlier patterns described above: *Propitiare*, preface dialogue, consecration prayer (with the chrismal anointing accompanied by its own formulary inserted within the prayer). The later recensions of the *PRG* then add a prayer for the consecration of the hand[27] and a series of prayers for the blessing and giving of the ring and crozier.

All the manuscripts conclude the rite with a choice of two additional prayers for the giving of the ring, the kiss of peace, the seating of the new bishop at the head of the bishops present. The Mass then continues with the proclamation of the gospel.

e. CONSECRATION PRESENTATION: STRUCTURE

PRG/CD

2nd stage

Consecration Presentation

	episcopal vestments
	epistle to *Alleluia*
presentation:	two bishops
proclamation of consensus and consecration:	
	Servanda est
	[optional sermon AV] +
	with the agreement/
	he may be ordained

D. CONCLUSION

The hybrid nature of the *PRG* is even more evident in the two later manuscripts, C and D. We can observe the further steps in the evolution of the early Roman and Gallican models even to the extent of noticing the visible "seams" as the pastische of various elements takes uneven shape. Besides the increasing elaboration of prayers, formularies, and rubrics related to the consecration itself, several shifts in the presentations of the elect are worth emphasizing.

Of first concern is the presentation itself. Of the texts previously examined, the *ordines romani* (*OR34*, *OR35*, and *OR36*) highlight the presentation of the bishop-elect as an act by members of the vacant see after the consecrator has verified the worthiness of the elect in a dialogue with members of that see. The letter of Hincmar of Rheims, the *Missale Francorum,* and the Old Gelasian Sacramentary record ritual elements which imply at least a functional presentation during which the elect is examined and his worthiness proclaimed by the assembly. Manuscripts C and D of the *PRG* mark the canonization of the presentation of the bishop-elect by two bishops until the revision of 1968.

A second significant element is the shift in the nature of the proclamation of consensus and consecration which was such a dominant element in the early Roman and Gallican rites. Two recensions of the *PRG* (A and V) are witness to the loss of the proclamation in future pontifical texts, a loss that becomes permanent.

The earlier and later recensions of the *PRG* important for the study of episcopal ordination may be compared in this way:

PRG/B G K L	*PRG*/C D
1st stage	*1st stage*
Selection Presentation	**Selection Presentation**
Sunday	Sunday
(presentation)	**presentation:**
	two bishops
	introit to collect
examination	examination
proclamation of consensus and consecration:	**proclamation of consensus and consecration:**
with the agreement/	with the agreement/
he may be ordained	he may be ordained
2nd Stage	*2nd Stage*
Consecration Presentation	**Consecration Presentation**
introit to gradual	episcopal vestments
episcopal vestments	epistle to *Alleluia*
presentation:	**presentation:**
two bishops	two bishops
proclamation of consensus and consecration:	**proclamation of consensus and consecration:**
Servanda est	*Servanda est*
	[optional sermon AV] +
	with the agreement/
	he may be ordained
bidding *MF*	
consecration:	**consecration:**
litany	litany
gospel book	gospel book

PRG/B G K L	PRG/C D
laying on of hands	laying on of hands
	collect
	bidding *MF*
Propitiare	*Propitiare*
consecration prayer	consecration prayer
consecration continues	consecration continues

We study the further evolution of the presentation of the bishop-elect in Romano-Germanic hybrid rites in the *ordines romani, Ordo Romanus XXXV A* and *Ordo Romanus XXXV B.*

Texts of the *PRG,* manuscripts CD:

Selection Presentation:

*PRG.*LXII Ordinatio episcopi.

1. Primitus eligatur. Post electionem dicatur ab archiepiscopo haec collecta:

2. Oremus, dilectissimi fratres, ut Deus et dominus noster Iesus Christus nos et electum nostrum gratia sancti spiritus illustrare dignetur. Per.

3. Deinde dicatur iste versus: Exaltent eum in ecclesia plebis. R. Et in cathedra seniorum laudent eum.

4. Postea mittatur in cathedram.

5. Et dicat orationem: Omnipotens, pater sancte, Deus aeterne, tu hominem dignatus es in caelestibus sedibus ordinare. . . .

*PRG.*LXIII [Ordinatio episcopi]

Qualiter episcopus in romana ecclesia ordinetur.

1. Episcopus cum ordinatur, primo progreditur domnus metropolitanus cum electo et cuncto clero et populo ad ecclesiam ubi ipsam fieri vult ordinationem.

5. Factoque ibi scrutinio et concrepantibus ecclesiae signis, domnus metropolitanus, mox ut vult indicet cantori et mox incipit antiphonam ad introitum. . . .

10. Interim electus ille sacris vestibus indutus, procedit e sacrario, ducentibus eum per manus duobus episcopis ante altare.

11. . . . domnus metropolitanus ita eum scrutinando alloquitur:

12. Incipit examinatio in ordinatione episcopi secundum Gallos. Antiqua sanctorum patrum institutio docet. . . .

17. Ita quoque examinatus et plene instructus cum consensu clericorum et laicorum ac conventu totius provinciae episcoporum maximeque metropolitani auctoritate aut praesentia ordinetur.

18. Nullis invitis detur episcopus; cleri plebis et ordinis consensus et desiderium requiratur.

19. His ita peractis, duo episcopi cooperatores ordinis sacri reducant ipsum electum in sacrarium.

Consecration Presentation:

PRG.LXIII.20. Tunc egreditur archidiaconus cum acolitis et subdiaconibus et induit ipsum electum cambagos, sandalia, dalmaticam, planetam et manicas.

[21.–23.]

24. Quando induitur sandaliis dicatur ab episcopis haec oratio: . . . .

25. Quando induitur manicis dicatur ab episcopis: . . . .

26. Quando induitur dalmatica dicatur ab episcopis: . . . .

27. Episcopo vero designato sollemniter praeparato duo episcopi casulis induti deportent eum supeerius, iuxta altare.

28. Et convertens se ad populum ordinator faciat sermonem si velit.

29. His ita profitentibus cum consensu clericorum et laycorum et conventu totius provinciae episcoporum, maximeque metropolitani vel auctoriate vel praesentia ordinetur.

[30.–31.]

32. Oratio. Adesto. . . .

33. Sequitur praephatio. Oremus, dilectissimi nobis, ut huic viro utilitati ecclesiae providens benignitas omnipotentis Dei gratiae suae tribuat largitatem. Per Christum dominum nostrum.

34. Propitiare. . . .

II. The Presentation of the Bishop-Elect in *Ordo Romanus XXXV A* and in *Ordo Romanus XXXV B*

A. *ORDO ROMANUS XXXV A*[28]

1. OR35A *and the Ritual Context of Episcopal Ordination*

Both Andrieu and Vogel[29] concur that *OR35A* was drafted by a Roman master of ceremonies writing in approximately the year 970. He records the papal ceremonies he observes but with a copy of the *PRG* in hand which he does not follow faithfully. He removes some of the innovations from the *PRG* texts (the anointing of head, hands, and thumb, giving of ring and crozier) which had not yet gained acceptance in papal usage.[30]

Yet, while compiling the *ordo* for Roman usage, the redactor leaves in certain nonpapal elements. Andrieu calls the document a confused amalgam for its juxtaposed elements from *OR34*, from *OR35*, as well as from the *PRG*, and Vogel concludes, "*Ordo* XXXV A is a witness to the liturgical decadence that prevailed at Rome before all the sections of the RGP were imposed on the City."

2. *Analysis of the Liturgical Units: Consecration Presentation*

a. CONSECRATION PRESENTATION: TEXT

OR35A [The ordination of bishop]

1. The apostolic lord makes his way together with all the clergy to the stational church where he wants to hold that ordination. Proceeding to the altar, he signals first to the schola who presently begins the antiphon at the entrance . . . with the psalm . . . and the *Gloria*.

2. When the introit is finished, the *Kyrr[ie]* is not sung, but the *Gloria in excelsis Deo* is begun by the supreme pontiff.

3. When that is completed, Peace be with you is said and he goes into this prayer. The prayer of the Mass. *Adesto.* . . .

4. And then the reading of Paul the apostle is read. . . . Then the gradual is chanted. . . .

5. Meanwhile the apostolic lord signals to the archdeacon, who going down immediately walks outside of the choir, where the one to be ordained waits, and taking the vestments clothes him.

6. When the gradual is finished, with the elect having been presented [to him] and bowing, the apostolic lord goes up to the altar, saying to the assembly:

Preface of the bishop.
The clergy and people of city N., with their neighboring sees, request a bishop be consecrated for them. Now moreover in this work the elect is our venerable brother N.
Therefore let us pray for him that our God and lord Jesus Christ may bestow on him the episcopal chair for ruling his church and all the people.

7. Then the schola begins the litany and chants next to last: That you may be pleased to sanctify our brother N. chosen to be pontiff, we ask you, hear us.

8. With that finished, the apostolic lord raises the elect, imposing his head on the altar and two bishops holding onto the [book of the] gospels hold [it] over his head; with the rest of the bishops also holding their hands next to the hand of the supreme pontiff, this prayer is said slowly by the *apostolicus:*

9. His blessing. *[P]ropiciare.* . . .

10. With that completed, he intones in a loud voice: The consecration of the same one. *Deus honorum omnium, Deus omnium dignitatum.*

11. When this is finished, the archdeacon taking hold of him, raises him from the altar and, when the apostolic lord is seated, helps him down to his feet, and immediately raising [him], the blessing having been received, places him in the order of the bishops' choir.

[12. *Alleluia* or tract; gospel]

b. CONSECRATION PRESENTATION:
"THE SECOND HALF OF ORDINATION"

Michel Andrieu begins his description of *OR35A* by referring to the two stages of episcopal ordination. He explains that this *ordo* forms the second half of the ritual of episcopal ordination:[31] it describes only the consecration stage of ordination as celebrated by the pope.

c. CONSECRATION PRESENTATION:
INTRODUCTORY RITES

The title ("The ordination of a bishop") is given by Andrieu since the *ordo* begins without one. The pope with all the clergy enter the stational church of the pope's choice. The day of the week is not mentioned nor does the text indicate whether the clergy are from the vacant see. Following the introit, the *Gloria,* and greeting is the collect of the Mass, *Adesto* (= *SVe* 942 = *GregH* 2.21). The consecration occurs after the epistle (1 Tim 3:1-8) and the gradual.

d. CONSECRATION PRESENTATION:
THE PRESENTATION OF THE ELECT

Following the pattern set by *OR34,* the vesting of the elect occurs after the gradual; in this *ordo,* however, there is no mention of the names or types of vestments. Also according to the sequence of *OR34,* the archdeacon, after assisting the elect with his vestments, presents him to the pope for consecration.

e. CONSECRATION PRESENTATION:
PROCLAMATION OF CONSENSUS AND CONSECRATION

No. 6 calls the proclamation "the preface of the bishop," the introductory statement by the one ordaining. In it the pope, speaking to the assembly, uses a proclamation of consensus and consecration similar to that of *OR34* and *OR35* joined with the bidding:

OR35A.6. . . . The clergy and people of city N., with their neighboring sees, request a bishop be consecrated for them. Now moreover in this work the elect is our venerable brother N.
Therefore let us pray for him that our God and lord Jesus Christ may bestow on him the episcopal chair for ruling his church and all the people.

Although the text uses the verb "request" rather than "chosen" to be consecrated, the context of selection and consensus is clear. The clergy and people of the vacant see, together with the bishops of the adjacent dioceses, seek the consecration of this candidate. The pope announces the consensus and his own acceptance of this "venerable brother"; the consensus affirmed then introduces the consecration.

f. CONSECRATION PRESENTATION:
   BIDDING *SVE*
   With the consensus complete, the pope begins the consecration of the elect with the bidding whose text is from the consecration prayer in *SVe*. We have traced this Roman form of the proclamation of consensus/bidding from *OR34*, *OR35* and the Romano-Frankish *OR36* to its last inclusion here in *OR35A*. The Roman Pontifical of the Twelfth Century will not reproduce it. Recensions of the *PRG* will retain the Gallican unit of a proclamation of consensus and consecration followed by a bidding (*Servanda est* and bidding *MF* in recensions B G K L T), but the Roman form, the clearest example of these two elements joined together, goes out of existence with the adoption of the Roman Pontifical of the Twelfth Century.

g. CONSECRATION PRESENTATION:
   LITANY AND OTHER ELEMENTS
   The bidding introduces the litany which has added to it (for the first time in any of the liturgical texts studied here) an intercession for the elect:

OR35A.7. . . . That you may be pleased to sanctify our brother elect N. as pontiff, we ask you, hear us.

The rubrics in no. 8 reveal the nature of *OR35A* as, in Andrieu's words, a confused amalgam. Following the litany, the pope imposes hands on the elect, but then the source of the texts shifts to the *PRG*. According to the Gallican pattern, two bishops hold the gospel book over the neck of the elect, while the rest of the bishops join the pope in laying hands on his head. This multiplication of bishops and multiplication of hand-layings is not a Roman arrangement but is borrowed from the *PRG*.LXIII.31, following the rubrics of *SEA*:

SEA 90. (II)	*PRG.LXIII.*31	*OR*35A.8
When a bishop is ordained, two bishops place and hold the book of the gospels over his neck	. . . two bishops place and hold the closed book of the gospels over his neck and between his shoulders	. . . two bishops holding onto the [book of the] gospels hold [it] on his head;
and with one pouring out the blessing over him, all the rest of the bishops who are present, touch their hands to his head.	and with one pouring out the blessing over him, all the rest of the bishops who are present touch their hands to his head. . . .	with the rest of the bishops also holding their hands next to the hand of the supreme pontiff, this prayer is said slowly by the apostolicus:

The pope then offers the two orations from the Roman sequence: *Propiciare* (= *SVe* 946) followed by the consecration prayer, *Deus honorum omnium.* Even though the text indicates only the first words of the prayer, certainly the pope would have recited the long version of the prayer from the *PRG*, i.e., the Roman text (*SVe* 947) with the Gallican addition from *GeV/MF*.

The episcopal consecration concludes with an interesting new ritual element. In place of the kiss of peace offered to the newly ordained by the bishops and presbyters (the *PRG*.LXIII.46), the new bishop only kisses the feet of the pope. He is then seated among the other bishops but no longer given the first seat. The Mass resumes with the *Alleluia* and gospel.

A most curious rubric occurs at this point in the *ordo:*

*OR*35A.13. When that is finished, if the pope does not want to celebrate mass, when the archdeacon has proclaimed: Let us go, everyone leaves.

Andrieu remarks with surprise that this rubric does not even appear to shock the redactor who presents this as normal papal practice. How decadent indeed must the Roman liturgy of this era have become that the pope may or may not choose to consecrate a bishop within the context of the Eucharist.

h. CONSECRATION PRESENTATION: STRUCTURE

The confused amalgam of *OR35A* imposes Germanic elements from the *PRG* upon the older Roman outline. Within the second stage of episcopal ordination, the units of presentation and proclamation of consensus and consecration remain.

OR35A

2nd stage

Consecration Presentation

	[no day mentioned]
	introit to gradual
	[episcopal] vestments
presentation:	archdeacon
proclamation of consensus and consecration:	
	clergy + people + bishops ask
	bidding *OR34*
consecration:	litany
	laying on of hands
	gospel book
	Propiciare
	consecration prayer
	consecration continues

Texts of *OR35A:*

a. CONSECRATION PRESENTATION: TEXT

OR35A [Ordinatio episcopi]

1. Progreditur domnus apostolicus una cum cuncto clero ad stationis aecclesiam ubi ipsam vult fieri ordinationem. Procedens ante altare, innuit primo scolae, qui mox inchoat antiphonam ad introitum . . . cum psalmo . . . et Gloria.

2. Finito introitu, Kyrr[ie] non dicitur, sed a summo pontifice Gloria in excelsis Deo incipitur.

3. Qua expleta, Pax vobis dicitur et in hanc orationem intratur: Oratio ad missam. Adesto. . . .

4. Et deinde legitur lectio Pauli apostoli. . . . Inde cantatur gradale. . . .

5. Interim innuit domnus apostolicus archidiacono, qui mox descendens vadit extra chorum, ubi expectat qui ordinandus est, et accipiens vestimenta induit eum.

6. Finito gradale, domnus apostolicus ascendit ad altare, oblato sibi ab archidiacono electo atque curvato, dicens ad aecclesiam:

Prefatio episcopi. Clerus et plebs de civitate Illa, cum adiacentibus parochiis suis, rogant sibi episcopum consecrari. Nunc autem electus est venerabilis frater noster Ille in hoc opus. Oremus itaque pro eo, ut Deus et dominus noster Iesus Christus tribuat ei cathedram episcopalem ad regendam aecclesiam suam et plebem universam.

7. Tunc scola incipit laetaniam et in penultimo dicit: Ut fratrem nostrum Illum electum ad pontificem sanctificare digneris, te rogamus, audi nos.

8. Qua finita, domnus apostolicus elevat ipsum electum, imponens caput eius super altare et duo episcopi nitentes aevangelia tenent super verticem eius; reliquis etiam episcopis iuxta manum summi pontificis manus tenentibus, lenta voce ab apostolico haec oratio dicitur:

9. Benedictio eius. [P]ropiciare, domine, supplicationibus nostris.

10. Qua expleta, excelsa voce dicit:
Consecratio eiusdem. Deus honorum omnium, Deus omnium dignitatum.

11. Qua completa, adprehendens eum archidiaconus elevat de altari et, cum sederit domnus apostolicus, proicit eum ad pedes eius, moxque relevans, benedictione percepta, imponit eum in ordinem chori episcoporum.

13. Quo finito, si domnus apostolicus non vult missam celebrare, archidiacono exclamante: Procedamus, omnes discedunt.

B. *ORDO ROMANUS XXXV B*

1. OR35B *and the Ritual Context of Episcopal Ordination*

Analysis of the texts of *Ordo Romanus XXXV B* reveals it to be an extensive patchwork containing only the rituals for episcopal ordination. The compiler, writing in or near Rome during the last quarter of the tenth century,[32] had been charged with creating a rite of episcopal ordination for use in the suburbicarian dioceses. Ironically, he was to use the *PRG* to create this rite for Italian sees which had used *OR34* for centuries.

The first step was to recast for Roman usage the recension of the *PRG* that he did possess, a manuscript with characteristic variants from the Mainz archetype.[33] However, the result provided texts only for the second stage of the ordination structure—the Sunday liturgy of consecration. Further modifications were needed.

Aware that Roman tradition demanded a Saturday synaxis, the compiler of *OR35B* knit one together from major portions of the traditional Roman *OR34* along with elements of the Romano-Gallican *OR35* in order to provide texts for the Selection Presentation with an examination of the bishop-elect. Andrieu concludes that the tapestry of *OR35B* (with its Germanized Roman elements and Romanized Germanic sections) was precisely the vehicle whereby usage of the *PRG* becomes acceptable within the apostolic city itself.[34]

2. *Analysis of the Liturgical Units*

a. SELECTION PRESENTATION

i. Selection Presentation: text

OR35B In the name of Christ, here begins the order for calling and examining or consecrating the elect as a bishop.

1. On Saturday about vespers, when the apostolic lord is seated in the atrium next to the church, the archpresbyter comes vested in chasuble, with the clerics of that church whose elect is to be consecrated, and, genuflecting before the *apostolicus*, asks a blessing saying: Bid, lord to bless. The *apostolicus* responds: May the creator of the heavenly dwelling guide and save us. The archpresbyter then rising goes forth a little and, again asking a blessing, genuflects and says: Bid, lord. He responds: May the lord preserve, protect and govern us. He asks a blessing a third time in the same way, saying: Bid, lord. He responds: May their ruler give us the joys of the heavens.

2. When the blessing is finished, the apostolic lord questions them: What are all the things you are rightly concerned about, brothers? They respond: That our God and lord may grant us a pastor.
He asks: Do you have yours? They respond: We do.
He asks: Is he from the church itself or from another? They respond: From [the church] itself.
He asks: What rank has he exercised? They respond: The presbyterate.
He asks: How many years has he in the presbyterate? They respond: Ten.
He asks: Did he have a spouse? They respond: By no means.
He asks: Has he taken care of his household? They respond: He has taken care [of it].
He asks: What in him is pleasing to you? They respond: Sanctity, chastity, humility, goodness and all things that are pleasing.
He asks: Do you have the decree? They respond: We do.
And the *apostolicus* says: Let it be read.

3. Then the decree is brought out and read in this way: [text of the decree with accompanying signatures follows]

4. When this has been read, the *apostolicus* continues further: See to it that he has not made any promise to you. You know that simony is against the canons. They respond: Far be it [from us].

5. And he says: Let him be lead in. Then the elect comes, vested in chasuble, and three times asks a blessing as above.

6. When the blessing is completed, the *apostolicus* questions him: What are all the things you are rightly concerned about, brother? He responds: Although I was not worthy, these fellow brothers of mine have chosen me to preside over them as pastor.

[The *apostolicus* asks questions regarding the elect's church, rank and years in that rank, spouse and household.]

He asks: Which books are read in your church? He responds: *Eptaticus*,[35] prophets, gospel apocalypse, epistles of Paul, and the rest.

7. He asks: Do you know the canons? He responds: Teach us, lord. And the *apostolicus* says: See that if you hold ordinations, you hold them at certain times, that is, at the first, fourth, seventh and tenth months, do not promote Bigamists or curiales, or [those] from the condition of servitude to a sacred order. May you guard yourself totally from simoniacal heresy. Nevertheless the edict from our archives will be given to you [concerning] how you ought to live. See that you have not made any promise on behalf of this case, because simony is against the canons. He responds: Far be it [from me].

8. And the pope says: You will see [to it].

Therefore because the desires of all have agreed upon you, today you will abstain and tomorrow, God willing, you will be consecrated.

9. On Sunday the apostolic lord makes his way with the elect and clergy and all the people to the church. Then the cantors begin the introit. . . .

10. When the introit is finished, the *Kyrie* is not sung, but the *Gloria in excelsis.*

11. When that is finished, he says: Peace be with you. They respond: And with your spirit. Prayer. *Adesto.* . . .

12. When the prayer is finished, the lord pope sits in his chair; when silence has been achieved there, an examination such as this takes place: *Antiqua sanctorum patrum.* . . .

He asks: Will you promise fidelity and submission to me and to my successors of the holy church of Salzburg? He responds: I will.

[13.–14. The pope questions the elect in detail about specific doctrines of the faith; two prayers for an increase of faith conclude this section.]

15. And thus examined and fully prepared with the consent of the clerics and laity and the agreement of the bishops of the entire province, and especially of the metropolitan or by [his] authority or presence he may be ordained. No bishop may be imposed on the unwilling but the consensus and desire of the clergy, people, [civil] authority is required.

16. With these things accomplished, two bishops coworkers of the sacred order lead the elect again into the sacristy.

ii. Selection Presentation: the Roman model

Nos. 1–8 describe the Saturday synaxis in words borrowed from *OR34* and *OR35*. At the hour for Vespers, the pope (as local metropolitan) interrogates the clergy who have come from the vacant see as to the worthiness of the elect. No other bishops nor the laity seem to be present (as they were in *OR34* and *OR35*).

iii. Selection Presentation: the postulation

The assembled visiting clergy ask that God and the apostolic lord grant them a pastor. The only order from which the elect may come is the presbyterate (once again distinct from *OR34* and *OR35* which both also allow the diaconate) and he has not been married. While the older *ordines* recorded the pope's concern for the elect's chastity, hospitality, and good-ness, in *OR35B* the questions highlight sanctity and humility as well as chastity and goodness.

Assured that these qualities reside in the elect, the pope calls for the reading of the election decree, signed by those participating and attesting to the selection's validity. Satisfied that (in the words of the decree) the clergy and people of the widowed church unanimously have petitioned and requested the ordination of this man, the pope calls for the elect to be presented.

At the beginning of this second examination, the elect declares before the pope:

OR35B.6. . . . For what I was not worthy, these fellow brothers of mine have chosen me to preside over them as pastor.

Representatives of those who previously chose the elect also present him for consecration.

iv. Selection Presentation:
Proclamation of consensus and consecration

Concluding his interrogation and confirming the consensus of the valid choice and worthiness of the elect, the pope then makes his proclamation:

OR35B.8. . . . Therefore because the desires of all have agreed upon you, today you will abstain and tomorrow, God willing, you will be consecrated.

The apostolic lord's examination is the last element of the selection process; it is concluded with a consensus statement that introduces the consecration. With the consensus of the choice completed by the pope's affirmation, the consecration will follow; the examination/proclamation of consensus and consecration unit remains intact.

v. Selection Presentation:
  juxtaposition of the Germanic model
Sunday's liturgy is a recasting of appropriate elements from the *PRG* for Roman use which leaves evident the seams from the joining. For example, the apostolic lord with the elect, clergy and all the people proceed to "the church," not the Lateran cathedral nor the tomb of Saint Peter as one would expect in a genuinely Roman document.

The compiler of *OR35B* also leaves the traces from inserting elements of the Selection Presentation into the Mass (as the later recensions of the *PRG* do) by leaving duplicate elements in their original place. One element incorporated is the examination/proclamation of consensus and consecration unit from the first stage of selection. The compiler of *OR35B* places the introductory rites of the Mass before this unit (nos. 9–11), but then appears to forget this fact, and includes the very same collect once again at no. 25.

Following the introit, the *Gloria,* and collect (*Adesto* = *SVe* 942 = *GregH* 2.21), the apostolic lord (also called here the lord pope, *domnus papa*) begins the Gallican examination, *Antiqua sanctorum patrum,* taken directly from the *PRG*. Further betraying its Germanic origins, the text of the examination calls upon the elect to promise fidelity to the metropolitan of Salzburg and to his successors!

The patchwork character of *OR35B* is clearest at the beginning of the Sunday liturgy. The (Roman) examination/proclamation of consensus and consecration unit has concluded the Selection Presentation and immediately precedes the Sunday consecration liturgy of the second stage. *OR35B* now incorporates the (Gallican) examination/proclamation of the consensus and consecration unit after the introductory rites of the Mass. The Roman and Gallican models of the Selection Presentation are thus placed back to back. The second examination is from the *PRG*, followed by its proclamation of consensus from Chapter LXIII.(17) and 17:

OR35B.15. And thus examined and fully prepared with the consent of the clerics and laity and the agreement of the bishops of the entire province, and especially of the metropolitan or by [his] authority or presence he may be ordained.

with the addition of the saying of Pope Celestine I:

No bishop may be imposed on the unwilling but the consensus and desire of the clergy, people, [civil] authorities is required.

Nos. 12–16 then are the Gallican examination/proclamation of consensus and consecration unit (from the selection stage of the *PRG*) inserted in *OR35B* into the consecration stage before the presentation of the bishop-elect.

vi. Selection Presentation: structure

The Selection Presentation of *OR35B* retains the same structure as the earlier texts from which it was compiled: *OR34* and *OR35* followed immediately by duplicate elements of the *PRG/CD*:

OR35B

1st stage (Roman)

Selection Presentation

Saturday

presentation:

the vacant see

postulation:

grant us a pastor
decree
examination

proclamation of consensus and consecration:

desires of all/
you will be consecrated

1st stage (Gallican)

Selection Presentation

Sunday
introit to collect

(presentation)

examination

proclamation of consensus and consecration:

with the agreement/
he may be ordained

b. CONSECRATION PRESENTATION

i. Consecration Presentation: text

OR35B.17. Then the archdeacon goes out with acolytes, and subdeacons and vests the elect in cambagos, sandals, dalmatic, chasuble and gloves.

18. Meanwhile the apostle is read: Reading of the epistle of blessed apostle Paul to Timothy. . . . [text provided of epistle, gradual, *Alleluia* and verse]

[19.–21. prayers for vesting in sandals, gloves and dalmatic]

22. The bishop-designate having been solemnly prepared, two bishops wearing chasubles bring him back to a higher place next to the altar and turning to the people the ordainer gives a sermon, if he wishes.

23. Then the clergy introduce the litany and the ordainer of the elect together with the elect and the other bishops prostrate before the altar, on the carpet, until the schola sings: [the] *Agnus Dei* [section of the litany].

24. When they stand up, two bishops place and hold the closed book of the gospels over the top of [his] head and between [his] shoulders and, one pouring out the blessing over him, all the rest of the bishops who are present touch their hands to his head.

25. And the ordainer says: Prayer. *Adesto.* . . .

26. Let us pray, our dearly beloved, that the goodness of almighty God, may bestow the abundance of his grace upon this man, provided for the service of the church. Through him who.

27. Prayer. *Propitiare.* . . .

28. And then he begins in a loud voice: Forever and ever. Amen.
The Lord be with you. They respond: And with your spirit.
Lift up your hearts. They respond: We have [them to the Lord.]
Let us give thanks to the lord our God. They respond: It is right and just.

Truly right. Eternal God, honor of all worthy ranks. . . .
Complete the fullness of your mystery in your priest, and equipped with all the adornments of glory, hallow them with the flow of heavenly unction.

29. Here the chrism is put on his head in the form + and [the following] is said:
May your head be anointed and consecrated. . . . Peace be with you. They respond: And with your spirit.

30. May it flow down, lord, richly upon his head. . . .

ii. Consecration Presentation: two assistant bishops

The elect is led into the sacristy by two assistant bishops where the archdeacon, assisted by acolytes and subdeacons, vests the elect in his episcopal garb (nos. 16-17). The very fact of the presence of two (unidentified) bishops assisting at the consecration indicates the non-Roman provenance of this section of the ritual: the pope ordains alone[36] as was evident from *OR34*.

From no. 16 onward, with the first mention of the two assistant bishops, the term for the ordaining bishop also shifts from the papal titles (apostolic lord and lord pope [Roman elements earlier super-imposed on the Gallican *ordo*]) to the Romano-Germanic titles (ordainer and lord pontiff).

When the elect has been vested, the epistle (1 Timothy 3:1-7) is read, followed by the gradual and gospel acclamation. (The gospel itself [no. 41] is inexplicably separated from the *Alleluia* [no. 18]; it will be proclaimed at the conclusion of the ordination rite, after the new bishop has been seated among the other bishops.) Nos. 19–21 (specific formularies to accompany the vesting in episcopal sandals, gloves, and dalmatic) are also misplaced; the vesting occurred earlier at no. 17.

The two bishops then lead the elect back to the altar area; he is presented for consecration. Besides the presence of the two assistant bishops, OR35B notes the presence of the clergy and all the people in the church but does not identify them further. There is no evidence in the Consecration Presentation that members of the church of the elect are present at the (Romano-Germanic) consecration stage, although their presence was well established at the (Roman) selection stage.

iii. Consecration Presentation: a sermon

At this same point (immediately after the Consecration Presentation of the elect), the older recensions of the *PRG* as well as three of the more recent ones, cite the exhortation, *Servanda est*, from the *MF*. Two of the later *PRG* manuscripts simply state that the ordaining bishop delivers a sermon if he wishes.

OR35B follows this latter arrangement and omits the exhortation. Andrieu explains the probable reasoning: since this *ordo* is created for the papal city, members of the widowed church are not likely to be present in large numbers due to distance, and it is to them that the exhortation is addressed.[37] So the compiler of OR35B replaced the exhortation with what he considered an equivalent ritual element, the sermon. Thus the clear and extensive proclamation of consensus that the Gallican exhortation represents and that is such a strong parallel to the consensus process outlined in the earlier Roman *ordines* is absent from OR35B. The proclamation of consensus and consecration in the second stage (Consecration Presentation) has become an optional sermon.

iv. Consecration Presentation:
litany, bidding, other elements

Although the first element of the proclamation of consensus and consecration (the consensus statement) is missing, the second element is present, the bidding. The source of the bidding is the *MF*; it calls upon "our dearly beloved" to enter into prayer for the elect. But then appended to the bidding are the words "Through him who" as if the bidding were an oration, following the pattern of the later *PRG* manuscripts.

The bidding's placement too is further evidence of the erratic arrangement of this *ordo*. Following the optional sermon, *OR35* indicates that the litany occurs immediately (no. 23), even though the bidding to introduce the litany does not occur until no. 26. After the litany, two bishops place the gospel book upon the neck and between the shoulders of the elect, while one among them offers the consecration prayer and the rest of the bishops impose hands on his head.

Instead of presenting the consecration prayer at this point, *OR35B* provides the ordainer with the text of the collect of the Mass (*Adesto* = *SVe* 942 = *GregH* 2.21) for a second time and then gives the text of the bidding which it has turned into an oration. Following this series of confused elements, *OR35B* returns to the pattern of both *SVe* and *GeV/MF*: the oration *Propitiare* and the consecration prayer (slightly reworded), *Deus, honor omnium* (*SVe* + *GeV/MF*).

The consecration prayer begins with the Preface dialogue and includes rubrics for the anointing of the head of the elect with chrism together with the words for the accompanying formulary, all in the midst of the consecration prayer. Then, according to the pattern of the later recensions of the *PRG*, *OR35B* adds the consecration of the hand and "confirmation" of the thumb, blessing, giving and imposing of the ring, blessing, and giving of the crozier. The kiss of peace and seating of the new bishop among the other bishops concludes the consecration rite.

v. Consecration Presentation: structure

OR35B

2nd Stage

Consecration Presentation

	episcopal vestments
	epistle to alleluia
presentation:	two assistant bishops
proclamation of consensus and consecration:	
	optional sermon
consecration:	litany
	gospel book
	laying on of hands

collect
bidding *MF*
Propitiare
consecration prayer
consecration continues

3. *Conclusion*

The texts of *OR35B* juxtapose the Selection Presentation texts of the Roman model *(OR34/OR35)* and the later Romano-Germanic model (the *PRG/C D*); the rite now consists of two presentations, two examinations, two proclamations of consensus and consecration. The Roman texts will soon be consigned to the appendix of the Roman pontificals, while the hybrid pattern and texts from the *PRG* will take firm hold. The ritual elements of the two stages of ordination will be permanently joined within one liturgy.

In Vogel's analysis of *OR35B*, he provides a striking affirmation for the two-part structure of episcopal ordination when he characterizes the *ordo* as a "rite for episcopal consecration containing two distinct sections."[38] He cites the title of the rite itself as evidence for the characterization: "the *ordo* for calling and examining or consecrating the elect a bishop." The compiler of the *ordo* has summarized the episcopal ordination process: call, examination (completing and confirming the call), followed by consecration. Of all the documents included in this study, the title of *OR35B* is one of the clearest textual references that exist for the multi-stage process of episcopal ordination.

A comparative outline of the liturgical units we have been studying is helpful in tracing the tenth-century evolution of the rite of episcopal ordination. The earlier recensions of the *PRG* place the selection stage before the Mass of consecration begins; the later recensions move the entire Selection Presentation into the Mass itself (into the midst of the Scripture readings).

Two bishops now present the elect to the metropolitan at the end of the selection stage and again at the beginning of the consecration stage. The proclamation of consensus and consecration in the second stage has devolved into an optional sermon. *OR35A* and *OR35B* are a patchwork compilation of Roman, Gallican, and Germanic elements. It is the texts of *OR35B* (faithful to the later recensions of the *PRG*) which will be taken up into the Roman Pontifical of the Twelfth Century.

PRG/BGKL	PRG/CD	OR35A	OR35B	OR35B
1st stage	*1st stage*		*1st stage*	*1st stage*
Selection	**Selection**		**Selection**	**Selection**
Presentation	**Presentation**		**Presentation**	**Presentation**
Sunday	Sunday	[no day mentioned]	Saturday	Sunday introit to collect
presentation	**presentation** 2 bishops introit to collect		**presentation** vacant see **postulation** grant us a pastor decree	**presentation**
examination	examination		examination	examination
proclamation	**proclamation**		**proclamation**	**proclamation**
consensus/	**consensus/**		**consensus/**	**consensus/**
consecration	**consecration**		**consecration**	**consecration**
with the agreement/ he may be ordained	with the agreement/ he may be ordained		desires of all/ you will be consecrated	with the agreement/ he may be ordained
2nd stage	*2nd stage*	*2nd stage*		*2nd stage*
Consecration	**Consecration**	**Consecration**		**Consecration**
Presentation	**Presentation**	**Presentation**		**Presentation**
introit to gradual episcopal vestments	episcopal vestments epistle to *Alleluia*	[episcopal] vestments		episcopal vestments epistle to *Alleluia*
presentation	**presentation**	**presentation**		**presentation**
2 bishops	2 bishops	archdeacon		2 bishops
proclamation	**proclamation**	**proclamation**		**proclamation**
consensus/	**consensus/**	**consensus/**		**consensus/**
consecration	**consecration**	**consecration**		**consecration**
Servanda est	*Servanda est* [optional sermon AV] with the agreement/ he may be ordained	clergy + people + bishops ask		optional sermon
bidding *MF*		bidding *SVe*		
consecration	**consecration**	**consecration**		**consecration**
litany	litany	litany		litany
gospel book	gospel book	gospel book		gospel book
laying on of hands	laying on of hands collect	laying on of hands		laying on of hands

PRG/BGKL	PRG/CD	OR35A	OR35B	OR35B
	bidding *MF*			
Propitiare	*Propitiare*	*Propitiare*		*Propitiare*
consecration	consecration	consecration		consecration
prayer	prayer	prayer		prayer
consecration	consecration	consecration		consecration
continues	continues	continues		continues

Before turning our attention to the evolution of these texts within the pontifical tradition, we include for further examination the episcopal ordination rites in selected English pontificals. These liturgical books also draw on sources common to the *PRG* as did the *OR35A* and *OR35B*.

Texts of *OR35B*:

Selection Presentation:

OR35B In Christi nomine, incipit ordo ad vocandum et examinandum seu consecrandum electum episcopum.

1. Sabbati die circa vesperam, sedente domno apostolico in atrio iuxta ecclesiam, venit archipresbiter indutus casula, cum clericis illius ecclesię cui electus consecrandus est, et, flectens genua ante apostolicum, benedictionem petit dicendo: Iube, domne benedicere. Resp. apostolicus: Nos regat et salvet cęlestis conditor aulę.

Archipresbiter autem surgens procedit paululum et, iterum petens benedictionem, genua flectit et dicit: Iuve, domne. Resp.: Nos dominus servet, custodiat atque gubernet.

Tertia vero vice benedictionem simili modo petit, dicens: Iuve, domne. Resp.: Gaudia cęlorum det nobis rector eorum.

2. Benedictione completa, interrogat eos domnus apostolicus: Omnia recte, quod vos fatigastis, fratres? Resp.: Ut Deus et dominus noster concedat nobis pastorem. Interr.: Habetis vestrum? Resp.: Habemus.
Interr.: Est de ipsa ecclesia an de alia? Resp.: De ipsa.
Interr.: Quo honore fungitur? Resp.: Presbiteratus.
Interr.: Quot annos habet in presbiteratu? Resp.: Decem.
Interr.: Habuit coniugium? Resp.: Minime.
Interr.: Disposuit domui suae? Resp.: Disposuit.
Interr.: Quid vobis complacuit in ipso? Resp.: Sanctitas, castitas, humilitas, benignitas et omnia quę placabilia sunt.
Interr.: Habetis decretum? Resp.: Habemus.
Et dicit apostolicus: Legatur.

3. Tunc profertur decretum et legitur hoc modo: . . . .

4. Hoc lecto, prosequitur apostolicus: Videte ne aliquam vobis promissionem fecerit. Sciatis quia simoniacum est et contra canones. Resp.: Absit.

5. Et dicit: Ducatur.
Tunc venit ipse electus, planeta indutus, et ter benedictionem petit sicut superius.

6. Benedictione expleta, interrogat eum apostolicus: Omnia recte quod te fatigasti, frater? Resp.: Quod ego dignus non fui, isti confratres mei elegerunt me sibi preesse pastorem. . . .
Interr.: Qui libri leguntur in ecclesia tua? Resp.: Eptaticus, prophetarum, evangelium apochalipsis, epistole Pauli, et reliqui.

7. Interr.: Nosti canones. Resp.: Doce nos, domine. Et dicit apostolicus: Vide, ordinationes si feceris, ut certis temporibus facias, id est primi, quarti, septimi et decimi mensis, Bigamos aut curiales, aut de servili conditione ad sacrum ordinem non promoveas. A simoniaca vero heresi te omnino custodias. Tamen dabitur tibi edictum de scrinio nostro qualiter debeas conversari. Vide autem ne aliquam promissionem pro hac causa feceris, quia simoniacum est et contra canones. Resp.: Absit.

8. Et dicit papa: Tu videris. Quia ergo omnium in te vota conveniunt, hodie abstinebis et cras, Deo annuente, consecraberis.

9. Dom[inica] vero die progreditur domnus apostolicus cum electo et clero et cuncto populo ad ecclesiam. Tunc cantores incipiunt introitum: . . . .

10. Finito introitu, non dicatur Kyrie, sed Gloria in excelsis.

11. Quo finito, dicit: Pax vobis. Resp.: Et cum spiritu tuo. Oratio. Adesto. . . .

12. Finita oratione, sedeat domnus papa in sua sede; facto ibi silentio, fiat examinatio talis:
Antiqua sanctorum patrum. . . .
Interr.: Vis sancte Iuvavensi ecclesie et michi et successoribus meis fidem et subiectionem exhibere? Resp.: Volo.

15. Ita quoque examinatus et plene instructus cum consensu clericorum et laicorum ac conventu totius provincie episcoporum, maximeque metropolitani auctoritate aut presentia ordinetur. Nullis detur invitis episcopus, nisi cleri, plebis, ordinis consensus et desiderium requiratur.

Consecration Presentation:

OR35B.16. His ita peractis, duo episcopi cooperatores ordinis sacri reducant ipsum electum in sacrarium.

17. Tunc egreditur archidiaconus cum accolitis, et subdiaconibus et induit ipsum electum cambagos, sandalia, dalmaticam, planetam et manicas.

18. Interim legitur apostolus: Lectio epistole beati Pauli apostoli ad Timotheum. . . .

22. Episcopo vero designato sollemniter preparato, duo episcopi casulis induti deportent superius iuxta altare et convertens se ordinator ad populum faciat sermonem, si velit.

23. Deinde imponat clerus letaniam et prosternat se ordinator electi simul cum electo et cęteris episcopis ante altare, super stramenta, usquedum dicit scola: Agnus Dei.

24. Ut autem surrexerint, duo episcopi ponunt et tenent evangeliorum codicem super verticem et eius inter scapulas clausum et, uno fundente super eum benedictionem, reliqui omnes episcopi qui assunt manibus suis caput eius tangunt.

25. Et dicat ordinator:
Oratio. Adesto. . . .

26. Oremus, dilectissimi nobis, ut huic viro, utilitati ecclesię providens, benignitas omnipotentis Dei gratię suę tribuat largitatem. Per eum qui.

27. Oratio. Propitiare. . . .

28. Tunc incipit alta voce: Per omnia secula seculorum. Amen.
Dominus vobiscum. Resp.: Et cum spiritu tuo.
Sursum corda. Resp.: Habemus.
Gratias agamus domino Deo nostro. Resp.: Dignum et iustum est.
V[ere] D[ignum]. Ęterne Deus, honor omnium dignitatum, . . .
Comple in sacerdote tuo mysterii tui summam et ornamentis totius glorificationis instructum cęlestis unguenti flore sanctifica.

29. Hic mittatur chrisma in capite eius in modum + et dicatur:
Unguatur et consecretur caput tuum cęlesti benedictione in ordine pontificali, in nomine patris et filii et spiritus sancti.
Pax tibi. Resp.: Et cum spiritu tuo.

30. Hoc, domine, copiose in eius caput influat . . .

III. The Presentation of the Bishop-Elect in Selected English Pontificals

A. *THE LEOFRIC MISSAL*

1. The Leofric Missal *and the Ritual Context of Episcopal Ordination*
In 1042 when Leofric, first bishop of Exeter (1050–1072), accompanied the exiled Edward the Confessor home to England to assume the crown, Leofric brought with him a sacramentary of Gregorian origin. However, as it had been copied in the early tenth century in a monastic *scriptorium* in Lotharingia (the northern borderland between France and Germany),

the Franco-Germanic additions to the Gregorian book were much in evidence.[39] Thus the largest portion of the book (called *Leofric* A by editor F. E. Warren) "is not English in origin, only in use."[40] *Leofric* A is the source of the second section of the episcopal rite contained in the Missal: "Orations and prayers for the ordination of a bishop."

The entire first section of episcopal texts, "Oration for the election of a bishop," is identified by Warren as belonging to a separate collection, *Leofric* C, "a heterogeneous collection of Masses, manumissions, historical statements, etc., written in England partly in the tenth, partly in the eleventh century."[41] The majority of the texts of *Leofric* C (although set forth in a novel arrangement) have been copied from the *PRG*. Thus the section of *Leofric* titled "Oration for the election of a bishop" (Warren's *Leofric* C) has no English origin at all but is Franco-Germanic (with the sole exception of its Mass texts).

2. *Analysis of the Liturgical Units*

a. SELECTION STAGE

i. Selection: the text
Leofric C pp. 215–217 Oration for the election of a bishop

Let us pray, brothers, that God and our lord Jesus Christ may be pleased to enlighten us and our elect by the grace of the holy spirit. Who lives and reigns. Amen.
Bishop's admonition.
[Oration]
Oration after the profession.
[Text for the giving of the ring]
[Text for the giving of the crozier]
[Various antiphons for the Mass]
[Epistle]. . . .
[Gospel]. . . .

ii. Selection:
"Oration for the election of a bishop"
This initial section of *Leofric* (called *Leofric* C) gives ample evidence of its Franco-Germanic roots in the arrangement as well as in the source of the majority of its texts. This first section's title identifies the first stage of the ritual process: election. The second section (*Leofric* A) contains the rituals for the second stage: consecration. *The Leofric Missal* employs the same two-stage arrangement for its texts for episcopal ordination as noted previously in the Roman and Gallican traditions.

iii. Selection: the bidding

Of particular interest in *Leofric* C is the opening bidding, a direct borrowing from the *PRG* LXII.2:

Leofric C p. 215 Brothers, let us pray that God and our lord Jesus Christ may be pleased to enlighten us and our elect by the grace of the holy spirit. Who lives and reigns. Amen.

Not only is this immediate *PRG/Leofric* C relationship worthy of note but so is the specific source of the bidding. *Leofric* C draws its opening text not from the *PRG*.LXIII whose first element is "Here begins the examination for the ordination of bishop according to the Gauls," but from the *PRG*'s previous chapter, LXII (found in manuscripts C and D). Titled "The ordination of a bishop," *PRG*.LXII contains the ritual related to the new bishop's election, as its opening rubrics indicate:

PRG.LXII.1. First of all he is chosen. After the election this collect is recited by the archbishop:

"This 'collect'"[42] is the bidding. In both the *PRG* and in *Leofric*, this bidding stands as the very first liturgical text in the rite of episcopal ordination.

iv. Selection: ring and crozier

The elements themselves of which the selection stage in *Leofric* C consists (bidding, admonition, profession, collect, giving of ring and crozier) are not unusual; they are common to the majority of the liturgical books previously studied. What is entirely novel in *Leofric* C is their arrangement and the inclusion of some of them in the selection stage, not the consecration. Particularly striking here is the inclusion of the giving of the ring and the crozier within the selection stage.

The handing over of these two ritual elements occurs in every other liturgical text as explanatory rites, i.e., ritual elements which follow and further illuminate the meaning of the rite's core components, the laying on of hands and the consecration prayer. The placement of these two explanatory rites within the selection stage of *Leofric* C suggests the struggles of the investiture controversy.

Robert Benson's comprehensive study, *The Bishop-Elect: A Study in Medieval Ecclesiastical Office*,[43] relates historical and liturgical data about the investiture controversy relevant to the present study:

During the eleventh and early twelfth centuries, in the ceremonial act of investiture, the monarch granted to a new prelate the symbols of his office: the ring and the crosier. Investiture was the sign and symbol of the king's power over the episcopate and of his right to control episcopal appointments.[44]

Uta-Renate Blumenthal's work on the same subject situates the investiture controversy in Bishop Leofric's adopted homeland as well as in Germany:

Late ninth century sources for Western Francia mention that the king presented the successful candidate with his bishopric by handing the bishop-elect a symbolic staff, described by at least one source as a shepherd's crook. German kings, especially from the time of Otto I, strongly emphasized this ceremony, which later sources describe as investiture. . . . Under Henry III (1039–56) the episcopal ring was added to the crosier. . . . Episcopal consecration by the metropolitan bishop ordinarily followed investiture by the king. The formal aspects of initiation into ecclesiastical office had come to resemble closely the investiture of vassals with secular fiefs. . . . Investiture merely made evident that the bishop or abbot was under royal protection, and that he in turn had certain obligations toward the king.[45]

Incorporation of specific rubrics and formularies for the giving of the ring and crozier within episcopal ordination rites is consistent with the social and political dynamics of Bishop Leofric's time. In the *PRG*, however, the handing over of the symbols of episcopal authority belonged solely to the ordaining bishop, and as mentioned above, occurred as explanatory rites following the consecration. In the texts of *Leofric* C, the personal responsibility for the giving of ring and crozier is not identified. While the admonition belongs to the ordaining bishop, and while the formularies used in *Leofric* are the same as those spoken by the bishop in the *PRG*, it is possible that the giving of ring and crozier was the act of a secular ruler, hence their inclusion immediately after the election and before the rite of consecration, as Blumenthal suggests.[46]

b. CONSECRATION STAGE

i. Consecration: text

Leofric A pp. 217–218 Orations and prayers for the ordination of a bishop
Oremus, dilectissimi nobis. . . .
Another. *Adesto.* . . .
Another. *Propitiare.* . . .

The consecration.[47] Holy Father, almighty God, who through our Lord Jesus Christ have from the beginning formed all things and afterwards at the end of time, according to the promise which our patriarch Abraham had received, have also founded the Church with a congregation of holy people, having made decrees through which religion might be orderly ruled with laws given by you; grant that this your servant may be worthy in the services and all the functions faithfully performed, that he may be able to celebrate the mysteries of the sacraments instituted of old. By you may he be consecrated to the high priesthood to which he is elevated. May your blessing be upon him, though the hand be ours.

Command, Lord, this man to feed your sheep, and grant that as a diligent shepherd he may be watchful in the care of the flock entrusted to him. May your Holy Spirit be with this man as a bestower of heavenly gifts, so that, as that chosen teacher of the Gentiles taught, he may be in justice not wanting, in kindness strong, in hospitality rich; in exhortation may he give heed to readiness, in persecutions to faith, in love to patience, in truth to steadfastness; in heresies and all vices may he know hatred, in strifes may he know nothing; in judgments may he not show favor, and yet grant that he may be favorable.

Finally, may he learn from you in abundance all the things which he should teach your people to their health. May he reckon priesthood itself to be a task, not a privilege.[48] May increase of honor come to him, to the encouragement of his merits also, so that through these, just as with us now he is admitted to the priesthood, so with you hereafter he may be admitted to the kingdom; through. . . .

Again another consecration. *Deus honorum omnium.* . . .

ii. Consecration:
  "Orations and prayers for the ordination of a bishop"
  The bidding and the prayers contained in this second section are the texts for the consecration liturgy, and employ the same sequence of texts found in earlier sacramentaries. *Leofric* A (a century or more older than *Leofric* C) also gives evidence of another trait of early sacramentaries: the almost complete absence of rubrics.[49] The title itself most resembles that of the *Missale Francorum* which uses "Orations and Prayers for the Bishop-Elect." This is not an unusual similarity given their common Frankish roots.

iii. Consecration: bidding
  Oremus, dilectissimi nobis (which we have heretofore identified as bidding *MF*) introduces the litany before the consecration. The bidding, frequently misidentified in other liturgical books as a collect, also occurs

in this initial position in the *GeV* itself (766), in the *MF* (9.36), in the *Angoulême* (2103). In the *Gellone,* this same bidding (2546) immediately follows the exhortation, *Servanda est,* as it also does in the *PRG*.LXIII.29.

iv. Consecration: two orations

These are cited as if they were alternatives to the bidding "collect":

1. *Adesto* is the Gregorian version (*GregH* 2.21) of *SVe* 942 *(Exaudi)* which continues in use as the first (genuine) collect for the pontifical tradition begun by the manuscripts of the *PRG;* the sacramentary pattern (*GeV* 767, *MF* 9.37, *Gellone* 2547, *Angoulême* 2104) mirrors the Roman tradition of the *SVe* in citing *Exaudi* as the first oration.

2. *Propitiare* (*SVe* 946) is the prayer which the sacramentaries and pontificals uniformly cite as the second oration which follows the litany of the saints and occurs immediately before the consecration prayer itself.

v. Consecration: *Pater sancte*

With the first consecration prayer given in *Leofric* A (placed immediately before the hybrid text of *Deus honorum omnium* [*SVe* 947 with the Gallican interpolation]), *Leofric* A preserves a treasure: a unique consecration prayer first found in *Leofric* and then copied into later English liturgical books. It does not occur in any of the later liturgical books from the Continent, save the late tenth-century Sacramentary of Corbie.[50]

Despite Santantoni's careful comparison suggesting parallels with early Hispanic texts, both Bradshaw and Paul DeClerck find Kleinheyer's arguments more persuasive. They agree that *Pater sancte* appears to be of Gallican origin and perhaps may even be the "lost" Gallican consecration prayer for episcopal ordination, missing from the *Missale Francorum* and subsequent Gallican liturgical books.[51] Beyond creating euchological material merely for a Gallican interpolation within a predominantly Roman prayer, sixth-century Gallican Churches may have composed such a consecration prayer complete in itself: *Pater sancte.* In addition, Gy, Porter and Bradshaw go on to note characteristics of this prayer that seem similar to those in the *Apostolic Tradition.*[52]

vi. Consecration: "Again another consecration"

The second consecration prayer is the hybrid *Deus honorum omnium* (*SVe* 947 with Gallican interpolation). Warren notes that a more recent hand (in Leofric's time?) has added a rubric in the midst of the prayer indicating the anointing with oil.[53]

vii. Consecration: structure

For the consecration stage, *Leofric* A presents the simple skeletal outline of a sacramentary:

> bidding *GeV*
> *Adesto*
> *Propitiare*
> consecration prayer *Pater sancte*
> consecration prayer *Deus honorum omnium* + anointing
> Mass prayers

3. *Conclusion*

Although the *Leofric Missal* provides no texts which further the tradition of the presentation of the bishop-elect, it strengthens the pattern appearing here of the two-stage process of ordination: selection and consecration.

Texts of *The Leofric Missal*:

Selection Presentation:

Leofric C pp. 215–217 Oratio in electione episcopi
Oremus, fratres, ut deus et dominus noster ihesus christus nos et electum nostrum gratia spiritus sancti inlustrare dignetur. Qui uiuit et regnat. Amen.
Amonitio episcopi.
[Oration]
Oratio post profesionem.
[Oration]
Hic dandus est anulus.
Hic dandus est baculus.
Nunc inchoandum est introitum. . . .
[Epistola]. . . .
[Euangelium]. . . .

Consecration Presentation:

Leofric A pp. 217–218 Orationes et preces in ordinatione episcopi
Oremus, dilectissimi nobis. . . .
Alia. Adesto. . . .
Alia. Propitiare. . . .

Consecratio. Pater sancte, omnipotens deus, qui per dominum nostrum ihesum christum, ab initio cuncta formasti et postmodum in fine temporum, secundum pollicitationem quam abraham patriarcha noster acceperat, ecclesiam quoque sanctorum congregatione fundasti, ordinatis rebus per quas legibus a te datis discipline religio regeretur; presta, ut hic (hii) famulus(ti) tuus (tui) sit (sint) ministeriis cunctisque fideliter gestis officiis dignus(ni), ut antiquitus instituta possit(sint) sacramentorum mysteria celebrare. Per te in summum ad quod assumitur(muntur) sacerdotium consecre(cren)tur. Sit super eundem (eosdem) benedictio tua licet manus nostra sit. Precipe, domine, huic (his) pascere oues tuas, ac tribue ut commissi gregis custodia sollicitus(ti) pastor(es) inuigilet(lent). Spiritus huic (his) sanctus tuus caelestium carismatum diuisor adsistat, ut sicut ille electus gentium doctor instituit, sit (sint) iustitia non indigens(tes), benignitate pollens,(tes) hospitalitate diffusus(si), seruet(uent) in exortationibus alacritatem, in persecutionibus fidem, in caritate patientiam, in ueritate constantiam, in heresibus ac uiciis omnibus odium sciat(ant), in aemulationibus nesciat(ant), in iudiciis gratiosum(sos) esse non sinas, et tamen gratum(os) esse concedas. Postremo omnia a te largiter discat(cant) quae salubriter tuos doceat(ant). Sacerdotium ipsum opus esse existimet(ment) non dignitatem. Proficiant ei honoris augmenta, etiam ad incrementa meritorum, ut per haec sicut apud nos nunc adsciscitur(untur) in sacerdotium, ita apud te postea adsciscatur(antur) in regnum. Per.

Item alia consecratio. Deus honorum omnium. . . .

B. ADDITIONAL ENGLISH WITNESSES

Other early (i.e., tenth-century) English liturgical documents which contain the rite of episcopal ordination, *The Lanalet Pontifical*,[54] *The Benedictional of Archbishop Robert*,[55] *The Egbert Pontifical*,[56] and *The Dunstan and Brodie Pontificals*,[57] follow a pattern similar to sacramentaries and include few rubrics related to the presentation of the bishop-elect.

1. The Egbert Pontifical *and the* Pontificale Lanaletense

Egbert and *Lanalet*, the older documents,[58] begin the rite of episcopal ordination with a block of rubrics derived from the *Statuta Ecclesiae Antiqua*:

SEA.90. (II)	Egbert p. 8	Lanalet p. 57
When a bishop is ordained, two bishops place and hold the book of the gospels over his neck, and with one pouring out the blessing over him,	When a bishop is ordained, two bishops place and hold the book of the gospels over his neck and one pours out the blessing over him. and afterward	When a bishop is ordained, two bishops place the book of the gospels over his neck and one pours out the blessing over him
all the rest of the bishops, who are present,	all the bishops who are present must recite these three orations. The	all the rest of the bishops who are in place
touch his head with their hands.	rest hold their hands upon his head.	touch their hands over his head.

Robert, Dunstan, and *Brodie* follow the same pattern. Bradshaw explains the connection. "The relevant directions from the *Statuta Ecclesiae Antiqua* came to be placed at the head of the collection of formularies for each order in some sacramentaries, as a first step in the process of combining rubrics and texts, which would lead in time to the emergence of complete pontificals."[59] This particular directive from *SEA* will be copied into many later liturgical sources besides the English pontificals (*OR35* and the *PRG* as two key examples noted above), and will thus wield a powerful influence over the liturgical shape of medieval ordination rites.[60]

The familiar prayer texts of the consecration follow the opening rubrical block:

Egbert p. 8; Lanalet pp. 57–58

Oremus dilectissimi nobis. . . .
Adesto. . . .
Propitiare. . . .
[*Exaudi domine supplicum preces.* . . . *Egbert* only]
Deus honorum omnium. . . .

While neither of these pontificals adds to an understanding of the presentation of the bishop-elect, it is interesting to note that *Lanalet* begins the ordination rite for deacons and presbyters with a postulation dialogue copied from Manuscript A (Rome, Biblio. Alessandr., *codex* 173) of the *PRG,*[61] a document contemporary with *Lanalet*:

Lanalet p. 53

The Order for How Presbyters[,] Deacons are to be Ordained in the Roman Church. The Order for How to Ordain in Rome.

On saturdays. in the first. fourth. seventh. and tenth months. with twelve readings at Saint Peter's. [in the place] where masses are celebrated. After they sing the antiphon and the introit.

After the prayer provided the archdeacon says thus.

Holy mother catholic church asks that you ordain this subdeacon present to the responsibility of deacon or deacon to the responsibility of presbyter.

The bishop is to ask. Do you know him to be worthy?
The archdeacon is to respond.
As far as human frailty permits [one] to know. I know and testify he is worthy of the responsibility of this office.

2. The Benedictional of Archbishop Robert

a. THE POSTULATION DIALOGUE IN EPISCOPAL ORDINATION

Of even greater interest is the presence of this postulation dialogue within the episcopal ordination rite in the appendix of *The Benedictional of Archbishop Robert*. This is the text which will find its way into the episcopal ordination rite of the late thirteenth-century, *Pontifical de Guillaume Durand,* and from there into the current rite. H. A. Wilson, *Robert*'s editor, notes that the *Benedictional*'s appendix is an addition probably of the eleventh century.[62] The promise of obedience further on in the appendix identifies the text as an adaptation for the Diocese of Rouen,[63] clear evidence of the Norman usage of this liturgical book.

The introductory rubrics in the appendix prescribe the sequence and extremely elaborate style of the entrance procession of the metropolitan, other bishops, and accompanying ministers (two acolytes with thuribles, two subdeacons with crosses, seven acolytes with candelabra and candles, seven subdeacons with gospel books, seven deacons with holy relics, and twelve presbyters in chasubles). The bishop-elect is not yet to wear the episcopal sandals but is vested in alb, stole, and the *cappa,* a voluminous cape whose extensive train needed to be borne by one or more acolytes. The crozier and miter rest on the altar; as soon as the elect becomes *consecratus,* he will receive these from the archbishop. When all are properly seated, the Selection Presentation of the bishop-elect begins:

Robert p. 162

The fellow provincial bishops. offer the elect to the lord metropolitan with these words;
Reverend father. holy mother church. N. asks that you elevate this presbyter present to the responsibility of the episcopacy.
And the metropolitan should respond.
Do you know him to be worthy?
And the bishops [say].
As far as human frailty permits [one] to know. we know. and believe him to be worthy.
And all should respond.
Thanks be to God.

While similar postulation dialogues can be found in the texts for the ordination of presbyters and of deacons in the *PRG*, the Roman Pontifical of the Twelfth Century, the Pontifical of the Roman Curia, and the Pontifical of Guillaume Durand, only this latter pontifical will include this same dialogue for the presentation of the bishop-elect. The similarity of Durand's wording to the *Robert* text suggests that the archbishop of Mende, rather than merely rewriting the presbyteral/diaconal dialogue from the Pontifical of the Roman Curia to create a text appropriate for episcopal ordination, copied the text itself from older Gallican or English manuscripts not available (or of little interest) to the Roman compilers of the Roman Pontifical of the Twelfth Century or the Pontifical of the Roman Curia.

Robert p. 162	*PGD*.I.XIV.16
The fellow provincial bishops.	. . . two bishops . . .
offer the elect	offer him,
to the lord metropolitan	
with these words;	saying in a loud voice:
Reverend father.	Reverend father,
holy mother church. N. asks	holy mother catholic church asks
that you elevate	that you elevate
this presbyter present	this presbyter
to the responsibility	to the responsibility
of the episcopacy.	of the episcopacy.
And the metropolitan should respond.	And the consecrating [bishop] says:
Do you know him to be worthy?	Do you know him to be worthy?
And the bishops [say].	The bishops respond:
As far as human fraility permits [one]	As much as human fraility permits [one]
to know. we know. and believe him	to know, we know and believe him
to be worthy.	to be worthy.
And all should respond.	The consecrator and others respond:
Thanks be to God.	Thanks be to God.

b. POSTULATION DIALOGUE IN THE *PONTIFICAL OF BESANÇON*

One other source for the postulation dialogue in episcopal ordination, so rare before the Pontifical of Guillaume Durand, is an *ordo* later than *Robert* also with Norman roots. *Ordo* X in Martène's *De Antiquis Ecclesiae Ritibus*[64] (Lib.I, Cap.VIII, art. XI) contains the dialogue with the almost identical wording (*archiepiscopus* replaces *metropolitanus*). Santantoni identifies this rite as the *Pontificale di Besançon*;[65] Righetti and Kleinheyer date it as possibly twelfth century.[66] This is the only text of which this author is aware which combines both the Roman model for the Selection Presentation of the bishop-elect with the Gallican pattern of the selection examination.

Ordo X includes this text of the Selection Presentation, adapted for the Dioceses of Besançon and Tours from a recension of *OR34*:

Martène Lib. I. Cap. VIII. Art. XI. Ordo X.

. . . When the bishop has been buried, the elders of the church are to assemble together: clerics first, then acknowledged laity: and after the scrutiny has been done, the divine name invoked, favoritism of persons refused, with a common desire and equal consent, they are to choose whom they discover from their own congregation to be more holy and more beneficial, if it is possible to do so: . . . .

. . . [T]he lord is to command the archdeacon and the chancellor that they are to bring in the elect, and that he be led with great reverence before the lord. . . . For what have you come[,] brother? He responds: To what I am not worthy these brothers have summoned me. . . .

Then the lord [says] to the elect: Because, brother, the desires of all have agreed upon you, today you will fast, tomorrow you will abstain, on Sunday God granting at the third hour you will be consecrated.

Ordo X then combines the structure above with the Gallican pattern of the postulation dialogue from *Robert* at the beginning of the Sunday liturgy, to be immediately followed by the Gallican examination, *Antiqua sanctorum patrum:* a sequence we will not see again until the Pontifical of Guillaume Durand.

3. *Conclusion*

The tenth-century English pontificals make a fascinating study, given the unique prayers for episcopal ordination which they preserve and the variety of the arrangement of their prayer texts. M. Conn's edition and study of *The Dunstan and Brodie (Anderson) Pontificals,* for example, brings to light intriguing elements: a possible double anointing of the bishop-elect's head, a formula of unknown origin for giving the crozier, prayers for an archbishop who does not want to go to Rome for the pallium.[67] However, besides the definitive two-stage structure of *Leofric* and the early witness to the postulation dialogue in *Robert*'s appendix, the only elements of the presentation of the bishop-elect which they as a group confirm are the bringing forward of the elect by two bishops for the consecration presentation and the bidding which immediately follows.

Following this analysis of the tenth- and eleventh-century evolution of the Roman and Gallican models of the presentation of the bishop-elect in the later Franco-Germanic and English texts, we take up a study of episcopal ordination in the tradition of the pontificals.

Texts of the Lanalet Pontifical:

Ordo Qualiter in Romana Ęclesia Presbiteri Diaconi Ordinandi Sunt. Ordo Qualiter Ordinandum Romae.

Mensis primi. quarti. septimi. et decimi. sabbatorum die. in duodecim lectionibus ad sanctum petrum. ubi missę caelebrantur. Postquam antiphonam et introitum dixerint.

Data oratione dicat archidiaconus taliter.

Postulat sancta mater ecclesia catholica. ut hunc pręsentem subdiaconum ad onus diaconii uel diaconum ad onus presbiterii ordinetis.

Interroget episcopus.

Scis illum dignum esse?

Respondeat archidiaconus.

Quantum humana fragilitas nosse sinit. et scio et testificor ipsum dignum esse ad huius onus officii.

Texts of the Benedictional of Archbishop Robert:

Robert p. 162

[De Ordinatione Episcopi.]

In die ordinationis episcopi. . . .

Comprouinciales autem episcopi. offerant electum domno metropolitano his uerbis;

Reuerende pater. postulat sancta mater aecclesia. N. ut hunc presentem presbiterum ad onus episcopatus subleuetis.

Et respondeat metropolitanus.

Scitis illum dignum ess?

Et episcopi.

Scimus. et credimus illum esse dignum. quantum humana fragilitas sinit nosse.

Et respondeant omnes. Deo gratias.

p. 163 Vis sanctę rotomagensi aecclesię. michique et successoribus meis oboediens esse et subditus?

Texts from Martène:

Martène Lib. I. Cap. VIII. Art. XI. Ordo X.

. . . Sepulto episcopo, conveniant in unum majores ecclesiae: primum clerici, deinde probabiles laici: et facto scrutinio, invocato divino nomine, abjecta personarum acceptione, communi voto parique consensu, quem sanctiorem et utiliorem invenerint, eligant, si fieri potest, ex eadem congregatione: . . . .

. . . jubeat domnus archidiacono et cancellario ut introducant electum, et deducatur cum magna reverentia ante domnum. . . . Ad quid venisti frater? Respondet: Ad quod dignus non sum isti fratres me cogunt. . . .

Tunc domnus ad electum: Quia, frater, omnium vota in te conveniunt, hodie jejunabis, cras abstinebis, Dominica die Deo donante hora tertia consecraberis. . . .

NOTES

[1] Hereafter *PRG*.

[2] Vogel and Elze describe the *PRG* as a family of manuscripts consisting of recensions of an important liturgical collection of a hybrid nature ("une famille de manuscrits constituant les répliques d'une importante collection liturgique de nature hybride" *PRG* I, vii) to which Andrieu would give the hybrid name "Pontifical romano-germanique du Xe siècle." He explains the accuracy of his title: it purports to correspond to the state of things, or, in other words, that the model from which all our examples derive has been composed in Germanic regions in the tenth century using materials a large number of which are of Roman origin. ("Le titre proposé . . . répond à l'état des faits, ou, en d'autre termes, que le modèle dont dérivent tous nos exemplaires a été composé en pays germain, au Xe siècle, à l'aide de matériaux dont un grand nombre sont d'origine romaine.") *Les Ordines romani du haut moyen âge, I. Les Manuscrits,* SSL Etudes et Documents 11 (Louvain: Spicilegium sacrum Lovaniense, 1931; reprinted, 1957) 495.

[3] Bruno Kleinheyer, *Die Priesterweihe im römischen Ritus: eine liturgie-historische Studie* (Trier: Paulinus, 1962) 114.

[4] Vogel and Elze, *Le Pontifical romano-germanique du dixième siècle.* III, *Introduction générale et Tables,* ST 269 (Città del Vaticano: Biblioteca Apostolica Vaticana, 1972) 7.

[5] This was probably during the reign of the abbey's great friend and patron, archbishop and archchancellor of the empire, Wilhelm I (+968), son of Otto the Great. It is easy to imagine that prelates accompanying the emperor on his first trip to Rome (962–964) brought along copies of the *PRG*. See Niels Rasmussen, "Unité et diversité des Pontificaux latins au VIIIe, IXe et X siècles," in *Liturgie de l'Eglise particulière et liturgie de l'Eglise universelle,* Conférences Saint-Serge, Bibliotheca "Ephemerides Liturgicae" "Subsidia" 3 (Roma: Edizioni Liturgiche, 1976) 408; and Kleinheyer, *Die Priesterweihe,* 143 and 167.

[6] "Le Pontifical romano-germanique du Xe siècle occupe donc une place de charnière, d'importance primordiale, dans le développement du culte chrétien, à la fois comme collecteur d'usages cultuels antérieurs à sa rédaction ou contemporains de celle-ci, et comme point de départ de l'évolution ultérieure. . . . " Vogel and Elze, *PRG* III, 6.

[7] As reported by Vogel and Elze, *PRG* I, xiii.

[8] Ibid., xii.

⁹ Ibid., xiv.

¹⁰ Vogel, *Medieval Liturgy*, 236.

¹¹ As Pierre Jounel summarizes, "The successor of the apostles is thus turned into a feudal lord." See "Ordinations," 164.

¹² Only one of the fifty manuscripts of the *PRG* records the Roman scrutiny of *OR34*: Rome, Biblio. Alessandr., *codex* 173 ("copied in Italy, perhaps at Rome itself, from a Salzburg model; early XI century"). Vogel, *Medieval Liturgy*, 231. Vogel and Elze include the text of the Saturday synaxis in the Appendix to the *PRG.LXIII* in their edition, *PRG* I, 226–228.

¹³ Pierre de Puniet suggests that in creating the *examinatio* (*Antiqua sanctorum patrum*) the author did not make any great imaginative effort: he was content to copy the chapter from *SEA* which concerned the examination of the candidate for the episcopacy ("n'a pas fait grand effort d'imagination: il s'est contenté de copier le chapitre de ces *Statuta* où il est question de l'examen du candidat à l'épiscopat . . .)." "Consécration épiscopale," 2585.

¹⁴ Bradshaw, *Ordination Rites*, 39.

¹⁵ The compilers of the Roman Pontifical of the Twelfth Century and the Roman Pontifical of the Roman Curia must have seen this clear rubrical clue also, for the texts found in the *PRG.LXIII.a.*(12)-f.(17) are the texts placed immediately before the phrase *"And when the scrutiny has been done"* in each of these later pontificals. As Vogel explains, "The *scrutinium*, isolated at first, will be incorporated without alteration into the mass of consecration, after the collect." ("Le *scruinium*, d'abord isolé, sera incorporé sans retouches dans la messe de la consécration, après la collecte.") "Précisions sur la date et l'ordonnance primitive du Pontifical romano-germanique," *EL* 74 (1960) 161.

¹⁶ "An die Stelle des vorabendlichen Examens tritt unmittelbar zu Beginn der Ordinationsliturgie eine langatmige Befragung, die beginnt: *Antiqua sanctorum Patrum*. . . ." See "Ordinationen und Beauftragungen," 39.

¹⁷ Translation of the consecration prayer is from Bradshaw, *Ordination Rites*, 216 slightly adapted.

¹⁸ The addition of sandals as pontifical vesture is unusual at this point, particularly since the bishop-elect is also wearing *cambagos*. These hybrid texts of the tenth century bring together Roman and Germanic practices, here even including two types of footwear.

¹⁹ A curious title coming as it does after the lengthy introductory statement of *Servanda est*; the *PRG* also identifies the consecration prayer as a *praephatio*.

²⁰ Reference to the "flow of heavenly unction . . . richly upon his head" in the original prayer of the *SVe* inspires an actual anointing with chrism in the midst of the prayer, necessitating splitting the prayer into two separate elements to accommodate the new anointing rite which then generates its own formulary along with a sign of peace!

²¹ Further discussion of this curious element is found on page 197 n. 18 below in the context of similar texts in the Pontifical of the Twelfth Century.

[22] These older recensions of the *PRG* are the only texts which maintain this sequence of crozier/ring; *Hincmar* and the later *PRG* recensions present the order that will be followed in the Roman Pontificals: ring/crozier.

[23] This threefold, solemn blessing, together with an alternate form from the later recensions of the *PRG,* will fall into disuse until both texts are returned in the rite of 1968.

[24] LXII. "Il ne s'agit pas, dans ce tibre [sic], de l'ordination épiscopale proprement dite, mais de l'intronisation de l'évêque après son élection." Apparatus, *PRG* I, 199.

[25] See his doctoral dissertation, "Ordained Ministry in the American Lutheran and Roman Catholic Churches: A Study in Theological Method and a Proposal for Mutual Recognition" (Ann Arbor, Michigan: University Microfilms International, 1986) 117.

[26] Manuscript A (which Andrieu calls *Ordo Romanus XXXV B* [hereafter *OR35B*]) includes the texts for the Roman examination with its entire Saturday synaxis combined with the Gallican examination and the Sunday liturgy. Vogel and Elze place the Roman texts from this *ordo* in the appendix to chapter LXIII. A separate analysis of this *ordo* is included below on pages 105–114.

[27] A text originally from presbyteral ordination in the *MF* 8.34.

[28] Hereafter *OR35A.*

[29] The information for the paragraphs in this section is derived from Andrieu, *OR* IV, 61–69 and Vogel, *Medieval Liturgy,* 176.

[30] These ritual elements, transmitted through *OR35B* (as we will see below), will eventually take hold in the apostolic city through the use of the Roman Pontifical of the Twelfth Century.

[31] "*L'Ordo XXXV A* forme la seconde moitié du rituel de l'ordination épiscopale. . . ." Andrieu, *OR* IV, 61.

[32] Information for this and the following paragraph is taken from Vogel, *Medieval Liturgy,* 176–177 and Andrieu, *OR* IV, 79–93.

[33] Andrieu proposes that this recension is the manuscript Rome, Biblio. Alessandr., *codex* 173, copied from a model used at Salzburg. See Andrieu, *OR* I, *Les Manuscrits,* SSL Etudes et Documents 11 (Louvain: Spicilegium sacrum Lovaniense, 1931; reprinted, 1957) 282–287. Evidence of this provenance is found in *OR35B.*12, the elect's promise of fidelity to the metropolitan of Salzburg.

[34] Acceptance of the *PRG* for Roman papal ceremonies will be the stimulus for the eventual creation of the Roman Pontifical of the Twelfth Century. Thus the immediate source for the Selection Presentation of the elect in the Roman Pontifical of the Twelfth Century is *OR35B,* as we will see in chapter 4.

[35] The Heptateuch is a collection of the first seven books of the Bible.

[36] Santantoni, *L'Ordinazione episcopale,* 47; Salmon, "Le rite du sacre des évêques," 30, n. 5; D.L.B., "Constitution apostolique sur le rôle des évêques coconsécrateurs," *LMD* 5 (1946) 108.

[37] Andrieu, *OR* IV, viii.

[38] Vogel, *Medieval Liturgy,* 176.

[39] Warren, xx–xxvii, xl.

[40] Ibid., xxv.

[41] Ibid., xxvi.

[42] This original, incorrect designation has been copied from the *PRG*.

[43] Princeton: Princeton University Press, 1968.

[44] Ibid., 204.

[45] *The Investiture Controversy: Church and Monarchy from the Ninth to the Twelfth Century* (Philadelphia: University of Pennsylvania Press, 1988) 35–36.

[46] Vivian Green is even more specific when she writes, "In the eleventh and twelfth centuries an election sometimes preceded the investiture; sometimes an election followed the investiture, confirming the royal choice of a bishop; and occasionally the election was dispensed with altogether." "Elections, church," 422.

[47] Translation from Bradshaw, *Ordination Rites*, 236, adapted in part from H. Boone Porter, *The Ordination Prayers of the Ancient Western Churches*, 85–93.

[48] There is an echo of this phrase, May he reckon priesthood itself to be a task, not a privilege, in the homily from the 1968 rite: The title of bishop is one not of honor but of function. . . . Perhaps this was a suggestion from Bruno Kleinheyer who worked diligently over both texts.

[49] Warren, preface [n.p.].

[50] Bradshaw, *Ordination Rites*, 16. With the exception of *The Pontifical of Egbert*, the consecration prayer, *Pater sancte,* is found in the later English liturgical books: *The Pontifical of Magdalen College, The Benedictional of Archbishop Robert, The Pontifical of Winchester, The Pontifical of Lanalet,* and *The Pontifical of Sherborne or St. Dunstan.* See Santantoni, *L'Ordinazione episcopale*, 98–99.

[51] DeClerck's analysis is excellent. See "La prière gallicane 'Pater Sancte' de l'ordination épiscopale," in *Traditio et Progressio,* Studia Anselmiana 95, Analecta Liturgica 12 (Roma: Pontificio Ateneo S. Anselmo, 1988) 163–176. He presents a careful study of both Santantoni's and Kleinheyer's arguments, ultimately agreeing with Kleinheyer, as does Bradshaw, *Ordination Rites*, 15.

[52] Gy, "Ancient Ordination Prayers," 72; Bradshaw, *Ordination Rites,* 17; Porter, *The Ordination Prayers,* 73.

[53] *Leofric,* 218, n. 1. Warren notes that he found these words in the margin, by an editor's hand: Here the putting of oil over the head.

[54] Gilbert H. Doble, ed., *Pontificale Lanaletense* [hereafter *Lanalet*]: at use in Brittany, but from an English model of approximately 960.

[55] H. A. Wilson, ed., *The Benedictional of Archbishop Robert* [hereafter *Robert*]: a late tenth-century codex from Winchester that subsequently passed into use in Normandy.

[56] H.M.J. Banting, *Two Anglo-Saxon Pontificals*. Banting edited both *The Egbert Pontifical* [hereafter *Egbert*] and *The Sidney Sussex Pontifical* which includes no text for episcopal ordination. *Egbert* is of mid-tenth-century Anglo-Saxon origin.

[57] Marie Conn, "The Dunstan and Brodie (Anderson) Pontificals: An Edition and Study" (PH.D. diss., University of Notre Dame, 1993). *The Dunstan Pontifical,*

also called *The Sherborne Pontifical,* gives the usage of Canterbury from Dunstan's episcopacy there 960–988. *The Brodie Pontifical* is also from the end of the tenth century.

[58] *"Egbert* and *Lanalet* both retain what seems to have been the older order, which probably stood in the books from which they were copied. They seem, when regarded as representatives of those older books, to take their place within, and at the beginning of, the series of English Pontificals which illustrate the variations of usage, and the developments of this class of Service-books, not only in England, but also in the neighbouring parts of the Continent, in the period before the Norman Conquest" [1066]. H. A. Wilson, *Robert,* xviii.

[59] Bradshaw, "Medieval Ordinations," in *The Study of Liturgy,* 372.

[60] Ibid., 370.

[61] See the *PRG.*XVI.1. No manuscript of the *PRG,* however, includes this postulation dialogue in the ordination of a bishop.

[62] Wilson, *Robert,* 162, n. 1.

[63] "Will you be obedient and subject to me and my successors of the holy church of Rouen?" *Robert,* 163.

[64] Editio secunda (Antwerp: Bry, 1736; reprinted at Hildesheim: Georg Olms, 1967) 153–169. Page 153 has the postulation dialogue.

[65] Santantoni, *L'Ordinazione episcopale,* 16.

[66] Righetti, *I Sacramenti–I Sacramentali,* 324; Kleinheyer, *Die Priesterweihe im Römischen Ritus,* 254.

[67] Conn, *"The Dunstan and Brodie (Anderson) Pontificals,"* 448.

The Presentation of the Bishop-Elect in Selected Pontificals of the Middle Ages

I. The Presentation of the Bishop-Elect in the Roman Pontifical of the Twelfth Century[1]

A. THE *PRXII* AND THE RITUAL CONTEXT OF EPISCOPAL ORDINATION

With the liturgical reforms initiated by Gregory VII (+1085), Rome regained leadership in the area of worship which had been previously dominated by Carolingian reformers and Ottonian emperors.[2] Individual churches throughout the ancient *Italia suburbicaria* devised their own pontificals, using as "the common root of all the Roman episcopal books of the twelfth century"[3] the Romano-Germanic Pontifical of the Tenth Century. The separate pontificals compiled during the twelfth century were so distinctly different from each other, however, that no single compilation appeared as archetype. In fact, Andrieu collated nine of the surviving manuscripts for his critical edition of the *PRXII*, manuscripts he described as "the Roman family . . . a particular group, the members of which are easily recognizable."[4]

Of these nine manuscripts, four are particularly significant for the study of episcopal ordination. Manuscripts B (London, British Museum, *codex addit.* 17005), C (Rome, Biblio. Vat., *codex Barber.* 631), and O (Rome, Biblio. Vat., *codex Ottobon. lat.* 270 [the only one actually compiled at Rome]) arose from the beginning of the twelfth century and were probably created for the liturgical use of the pope himself.[5]

Manuscript L (Lyons, Biblio. municip., *codex* 570) seems to date from before the end of the twelfth century and had only limited influence. It is characterized by a marked attempt to reorder the rubrics, which "before that were organically built into the rite only in a minimal sense."[6] In the texts of the presentations of the bishop-elect, we find the manuscript block B C O frequently contrasted by Andrieu with the greatly expanded rubrics of manuscript L.

In its various recensions, the *PRXII* enjoyed a very broad distribution: from the *scriptoria* of the Lateran, throughout the pope's suffragan sees, ultimately into the entire Latin Church. Papal legates, for example, carried copies of the *PRXII* on their journeys north of the Alps to enforce the decrees of Lateran I (1123); the popes themselves brought copies on their journeys of political exile into the cities of northern Italy and southern France. The *PRXII* enjoyed certain but limited success, eventually giving way before the pontifical which was tied to the reforms of Innocent III: the Pontifical of the Roman Curia.

The first chapters of the *PRXII* are those of the *cursus honorum:* "In the name of the Lord, here begins the *ordo* of the seven ecclesiastical ranks." They are presented in the same ascending order as the *PRG.* The rites begin with "the making of a cleric," "the shaving of the beard," and the rite for being made a psalmist. The seven ecclesiastical ranks include doorkeeper, lector, exorcist, acolyte, subdeacon, and deacon; the apex of the grades is presbyter.

Although the liturgy for episcopal ordination follows immediately after that of presbyter (*PRXII.X.* "Here begins the ordo for the calling and examining or consecrating the elect a bishop according to the custom of the roman church"), this chapter remains outside the *cursus* of the seven ranks. It is followed by rites for the consecration of virgins and the blessing of abbots and abbesses.[7]

B. ANALYSIS OF THE LITURGICAL UNITS

1. Selection Presentation

a. SELECTION PRESENTATION: TEXT

PRXII.X. Here begins the order for the calling and examining or consecrating the elect a bishop according to the practice of the roman church.

1. On Saturday about vespers, when the apostolic lord is seated in the atrium next to the church, the archpresbyter comes vested in chasuble, with the clerics of that church whose elect is to be consecrated and, genuflecting before the *apostolicus,* asks a blessing saying thus:
[the formal, threefold blessing seen above in *OR35B*]

2. When the blessing is finished, the apostolic lord questions them: What are all the things you are rightly concerned about, brothers? They respond: That God and our lord may grant us a pastor.

[Questions identical to those in *OR35B* follow, regarding the elect's church, rank and years in it, spouse and household and pleasing qualities, with the reading of the decree, with the addition:]

If he would have more or less [than ten] years in the presbyterate, the exact time would be given.

3. Then the decree is brought out and read in this way:
[the text follows]

4. When this is read, the *apostolicus* continues further: Consider that he must not have made any promise to you: you know that simony is against the canons. They respond: Far be it [from us]. And the *apostolicus* says: Let him be led in.

5. Then the elect comes vested in chasuble, and three times asks a blessing as it is stated above.

6. Then the pontiff asks him: What are all the things you are rightly concerned about, brother? He responds: Although I will not be worthy, these fellow brothers of mine have chosen me to preside over them as pastor.

[Questions identical to those in *OR35B* follow, regarding the elect's church, rank and years in it, spouse and household, books read in his church and his knowledge of ecclesiastical canons.]

7. And the *apostolicus* says:
[The information identical to that given in *OR35B* regarding the times for ordination, those not to be promoted, the promise of giving the edict from the papal archives, and the warning about simony.]

Therefore because the desires of all have agreed upon you, today you will abstain and tomorrow God willing you will be consecrated.
He responds: As you have commanded. This done, they depart individually to their places.

b. SELECTION PRESENTATION:

In the critical apparatus referring to the beginning of this rite, Andrieu notes that nos. 1–7 are extracts from an ancient *ordo romanus* foreign to the genuine *PRG*. This ancient *ordo* is Manuscript A (Rome, Biblio. Alessandr., *codex* 173)[8] referred to above in the study of *OR35B* (page 133 n. 12). Andrieu and Kleinheyer suggest that the copyist of Manuscript A transcribed the work from a model of the *PRG* from Salzburg around the year 1000 in Rome itself, during which process the copyist added "an authentic Roman *ordo* describing the Saturday evening synaxis."[9] Subsequent copyists followed this example, particularly the four principal manuscripts from which Andrieu created his edition of the *PRXII* (B C O L). Thus it is that the *PRXII* presents preliminary rites of episcopal ordination that reflect *OR34* and not the *PRG*.

The entire Selection Presentation is almost identical to that of *OR35B*; there are a few very minor changes. An archpresbyter enters the atrium of the church where the apostolic lord is seated with the clergy from the church for whom the elect will be consecrated. The interrogation begins, and members of the vacant see request that God and the apostolic lord grant them a pastor. The representatives then offer testimony to the elect's worthiness. In this examination, the elect must have already achieved the orders of both deacon and presbyter.

The elect then enters alone.[10] The second interrogation begins with the elect's humble admission:

PRXII.X.6. Although I will not be worthy, these fellow brothers of mine have chosen me to preside over them as pastor.

Following the examination, the pope gives his proclamation of consensus and consecration:

PRXII.X.7. Therefore because the desires of all have agreed upon you, today you will abstain and tomorrow God willing you will be consecrated.

We see here the same structure for the Selection Presentation as was evident in *OR35B*:

PRXII

1st stage

Selection Presentation

Saturday

presentation: clergy of the vacant see

postulation: grant us a pastor

examination

proclamation of consensus and consecration:

the desires of all/

you will be consecrated

2. *A Second Selection Presentation*

a. SELECTION PRESENTATION: TEXT

PRXII.X.8. On Sunday, the apostolic lord makes his way with the elect and all the clergy and people to the church where he wants to hold that ordination. And going into the sacristy, he clothes himself in pontifical vestments.

9. After a little while, he goes forth from the sacristy with deacons and the rest of the ministers going forth as is the practice on Sundays. And the elect, clothed in sacred vestments, goes forth at the same time with him and the other bishops from the sacristy [to] before the altar. And once [all are] assembled, the examination is done:

10. *Antiqua sanctorum patrum.* . . .
He asks: Will you promise fidelity and submission in all things to blessed Peter, to whom the power to bind and to loose was given by God and to me his unworthy vicar and to my successors?

[11. Nine further questions concerning the details of the elect's doctrinal beliefs]

12. Therefore thus. examined and well prepared, with the consent of the clerics and laity and the agreement of the bishops of the entire province, in the name of the lord he may be ordained.

b. SELECTION PRESENTATION:
THE GERMANIC MODEL

The patchwork quality of *OR35B* that we previously observed is evident in the second set of texts from the *PRXII* as well. Having added the venerable Roman pattern of a Selection Presentation to the beginning of the ordination texts, the compiler now returns to copying the Germanic pattern of the Selection Presentation from the *PRG* but in a more rubrically precise manner than either *OR35B* or the *PRG*. The elements of the Selection Presentation (presentation/examination/proclamation of consensus and consecration) all occur immediately after the assembly gathers and before any other element of the Sunday consecration liturgy occurs.

c. SELECTION PRESENTATION: PAPAL USAGE

The elements of the Selection Presentation from the *PRG* are present here in the *PRXII*: the Gallican examination *(Antiqua sanctorum patrum)* with the same proclamation of consensus and consecration, but both adjusted for papal use. The redactor of the *PRXII* has added the reference that the pope himself interrogate the elect, and has removed the promise of fidelity that ordinarily follows at this point—a reference to the metropolitan see and the metropolitan (*PRG.LXIII.b.*[13], Mainz; *OR35B.12*, Salzburg). Separate mention of a metropolitan was then also excised from the proclamation of consensus and consecration originally from *SEA*, specifying the sees involved in the consensus. Such a recasting of the texts is understandable, since as Bishop of Rome and patriarch of the Latin Church, the pope acts as metropolitan in this ordination rite.

PRG.LXIII	PRXII.X
13. Will you promise fidelity and submission in all things to blessed Peter, to whom the power to bind and to loose was given by God, and to his vicar and his successors?	10. Will you promise fidelity and submission in all things to blessed Peter, to whom the power to bind and to loose was given by God, to me his unworthy vicar and to my successors?
Will you promise fidelity and submission to me and my successors of the holy church of Mainz?	
17. And thus examined and fully prepared with the consent of the clerics and laity and the agreement of the bishops of the entire province and especially of the metropolitan by authority or presence	12. Therefore thus. examined and well prepared, with the consent of the clerics and laity and the agreement of the bishops of the entire province,
	in the name of the lord
he may be ordained.	he may be ordained.

What was clearly titled "the examination according to the Gauls" (*Antiqua sanctorum patrum*) in the *PRG* is now included without that specific provenance identification; it has become "the examination." Through these texts of the *PRXII*, the Gallican examination will be permanently incorporated into papal liturgical practice. The copyist has adjusted these northern texts to reflect papal usage.

d. SELECTION PRESENTATION:
"AND ONCE [ALL ARE] ASSEMBLED, THE EXAMINATION IS DONE"
The *PRXII* has untangled the use of the curious rubric from the *PRG*.LXIII.5: "And after the scrutiny has been done. . . ." Following the earlier recensions of the *PRG*, the rubric was accurately placed—after the Gallican examination. But according to the later recensions, "And after the scrutiny has been done . . ." was set in place well before the examination, not after it. The compiler of the *PRXII* copied the rubric from both recensions but then wisely adjusted one of them.

"And after the scrutiny has been done . . ." remains well placed in the *PRXII* (no. 13) immediately after the Gallican examination and proclamation of consensus and consecration and before the entrance antiphon begins. Its confusing, previous position before *Antiqua sanctorum patrum* according to the later recensions has remained, but the text is fittingly reworded as "And once [all are] assembled, the examination is done," referring to the interrogation which is about to begin.

e. SELECTION PRESENTATION:
ROMAN AND LATER GERMANIC FORMS IN USE

The *PRXII* includes two separate Selection Presentations within its texts. Faithful to the textual tradition of *OR35B,* the pontifical presents the Roman Selection Presentation (with its liturgical units of presentation/examination/proclamation of consensus and consecration) but then immediately follows it with the Germanic block (presentation/examination/proclamation of consensus and consecration). So, as redundant as it may have been, certainly for part of its history, the complete rite of episcopal ordination contained within the *PRXII* appears to have been celebrated as it stands: with two Selection Presentations, two examinations (one Roman, one Germanic), and two proclamations of consensus by the pope.

The Germanic pattern would surely have been included as part of the overall acceptance of the *PRG* within Rome itself as the common source for a revitalized papal liturgy. The Roman pattern persisted at the beginning of the Germanic form as a way of retaining both authentic Roman liturgical tradition and papal authority in the choice of suffragan bishops. The conclusion of the selection process which takes place at the Saturday synaxis allowed the pope to assert control of the selection of all the bishops of central Italy as well as all the bishops of the other metropolitan dioceses within Italy, France, and Germany. This older, authentically Roman rite was too important politically to be allowed to lapse into disuse.[11] And as Santantoni explains, "Cases in which the same document would prescribe the two different types of examination are not rare,"[12] and lists the *PRXII,* the Pontifical of the Roman Curia, and the Pontifical of Guillaume Durand as examples.

f. GALLICAN SELECTION PRESENTATION:
EPISCOPUM OPORTET

In the apparatus, Andrieu notes that Manuscript O adds another sentence to the proclamation of consensus:

PRXII.X.12. Therefore thus. examined and well prepared, with the consent of the clerics and laity and the agreement of the bishops of the entire province, in the name of the lord he may be ordained.

[O] Regarding the office of bishop. A bishop is to *[Episcopum oportet]* judge, interpret, consecrate, consummate, ordain, offer and baptize.

In his extensive article entitled "The *De Officiis VII Graduum,*"[13] Roger Reynolds summarizes the conclusions of liturgical scholars about the tract of which *Episcopum oportet* is a part. It is not an authentic work of Isidore of Seville; it was written between the fifth and late-seventh centuries; the treatise is non-Roman (since it originally had no mention of the acolyte);[14] and it was written "in a region where Celtic and Gallican influences met and were mixed."[15] The addition of such florilegial and pedagogical tracts as the *De Officiis VII Graduum* to liturgical manuscripts was a significant factor in the creation of the *PRG* from the *ordines romani,* so it is not surprising to find the *Episcopum oportet* unit appearing at the end of the full tract in the *PRG.XIV.De officiis VII graduum Ysidori capitula.* After similar texts listing the duties of doorkeeper, lector, exorcist, subdeacon, deacon, and presbyter, there occurs this statement.

PRG.XIV.7. Concerning the bishop. A bishop is to judge, interpret, and consecrate, consummate, ordain, offer and baptize.

Reynolds explains that "originally the *De Officiis VII Graduum* was set *en bloc* before the ordination rites for the individual grades. . . ."[16] The later Roman pontificals inserted specific verses from the tract as "introductions to the ordinational rite for each grade" (as in the *PRXII*) "or as integral parts of the allocution directed by the bishop to the ordinand" (e.g., manuscript L of the *PRXII* and recension γ of the Pontifical of the Roman Curia). The later splitting up of the individual elements of the tract was possibly done "to adapt the tract to strictly liturgical use."

In the rite of episcopal ordination, the individual *Episcopum oportet* unit first appears in manuscripts O (Rome, Biblio. Vat., *Ottobon. lat.* 270) and B (London, British Museum, *codex addit.* 17005) of the *PRXII,* following the examination and proclamation of consensus and consecration of the Selection Presentation. Its suitability for a consecrator's optional sermon is eventually recognized, and the position of *Episcopum oportet* will shift (in a recension of the Pontifical of the Roman Curia) to the place of the proclamation in the Consecration Presentation. *Episcopum oportet* will remain as the only text for the proclamation (of consensus and consecration) through the Pontifical of Guillaume Durand, the Roman Pontifical of 1485, and the Roman Pontifical of 1595.

g. SELECTION PRESENTATION: STRUCTURE

PRXII.X.1-7 (Roman model)	PRXII.X.8-12 (Gallican model)
1st stage	*1st stage*
Selection Presentation Saturday **presentation:** clergy of the vacant see **postulation:** grant us a pastor decree examination **proclamation of consensus and 　consecration:** the desires of all/ you will be consecrated	**Selection Presentation** Sunday examination **proclamation of consensus and 　consecration:** with the agreement/ he may be ordained

3. *Consecration Presentation*

a. CONSECRATION PRESENTATION: TEXT

PRXII.X.13. And thus after the scrutiny has been done, the apostolic lord as soon as he wants informs the cantor. And immediately the entrance antiphon begins.

[14. The introit, the *Gloria*, and pontiff's greeting]

15. Prayer for the elect for the mass. *Adesto*. . . .

16. Reading of the epistle of blessed Paul the apostle to Timothy: . . . .

17. Afterward the gradual is sung. . . .

18. Then the archdeacon goes out with acolytes and subdeacons and vests the elect in dalmatic, chasuble and *cambagos,* and two bishops wearing chasubles bring him to a higher place next to the altar. And turning to those present the *apostolicus* says this exhortation:

19. *Oremus, dilectissimi nobis*. . . .

20. And immediately the *Kyrie eleison* begins with the litany and the ordainer of the elect together with the elect and other bishops prostrates before the altar on the carpet, up until the schola sings *Agnus Dei*.

21. Then standing up, two bishops place and hold the closed book of the gospels over his neck and between his shoulders and, one pouring out the blessing over him, all the rest of the bishops who are present touch their hands to his head and the ordainer says:

22. *Propitiare*. . . .

23. For ever and ever. Amen. Here he raises his voice in the manner of a preface. The Lord be with you . . . Truly right . . . Honor of every worthy rank. . . .

24. Here he puts chrism on his head in the form of a cross. May your head be anointed and consecrated. . . . Peace be with you. They respond: And with your spirit.

25. Similarly he says this in the manner of a preface: May it flow down, lord, richly upon his head . . . [consecration prayer continues].

b. CONSECRATION PRESENTATION: EPISCOPAL VESTMENTS

Only after the examination is concluded does the introit of the Sunday liturgy begin. The *Gloria* is sung, the greeting given, the collect (*Adesto* = *SVe* 942) offered. The epistle from 1 Timothy and the gradual follow.

The elect is then vested as a bishop in dalmatic, chasuble, and *campagos*. Two bishops accompany the elect to the pope. By this simple act, we see repeated a rubric originally from the Roman pattern: the addition of episcopal vestments as the ritual bridge between the Selection Presentation and the Consecration Presentation.

Selection Presentation:
presentation
examination
proclamation of consensus and consecration

episcopal vestments

Consecration Presentation:
presentation
proclamation of consensus and consecration
bidding
consecration: litany, etc.

c. CONSECRATION PRESENTATION: TWO BISHOPS

The Roman masters of ceremonies, while following the older Roman pattern of vesting which we trace from *OR34* and into the hybrid Germanic rites as well (the *PRG* [both sets of recensions] and *OR35B*), at this point chose to follow the Gallican custom of two bishops to present the elect for consecration. The Roman ritual texts of *OR34* mentioned the presence of bishops at both stages of the ordination but they had no separate liturgical role; the pope ordained alone.

The Germanic metropolitans, however, involved their suffragan bishops, supported by the canonical and liturgical texts from the Council of Nicaea and *SEA*. In accepting the rituals of the *PRG* for papal use, the

Roman liturgists adopt the Germanic rubrics regulating the presence and participation of Roman suffragans: they present the elect to the pope for consecration, and also (following Gallican custom) place and hold the gospel book over the neck and between the shoulders of the elect and lay hands on his head while the consecration prayer is offered. Thus we see the Germanic metropolitan practices imposed upon the older Roman pattern.

We also find increasing liturgical involvement of the two bishops in the ordination rites described in all the pontificals from the *PRXII* on. Paul Bradshaw describes at least part of the dynamic at work:

> One of the more obvious effects of the presence of several bishops at an episcopal ordination was that they were generally not content to remain merely as spectators, passively observing the proceedings, but took an increasingly active role. In some cases, they began to share in certain of the actions of the presiding bishop, especially the imposition of hands, and in other cases, they took over what were traditionally diaconal roles in the rite, especially the leading of the prayers of the people and the holding of the gospel book.[17]

d. CONSECRATION PRESENTATION:
   PROCLAMATION OF CONSENSUS AND CONSECRATION:
   "THE EXHORTATION"

After the elect is presented for consecration, the ritual indicates that the pope offers an exhortation. Surprisingly, the text included at this point is only the brief bidding *MF,* not the eloquent text of *Servanda est* which the *PRG* had titled an exhortation. In fact, however, there is no exhortation at all. A comparison with the *PRG* reveals that the genuine exhortation has simply been excised:

PRG.LXIII	*PRXII.X*
28. And turning toward the people the ordainer says: The exhortation to the people when a bishop is ordained.	18. Turning to those present the *apostolicus* says this exhortation:
Servanda est. . . .	
29. After these professions he says this preface:	
Oremus, dilectissimi nobis. . . .	*Oremus, dilectissimi nobis*. . . .

The exhortation, *Servanda est,* which described the Gallican selection process, had become useless for papal ceremonies, but no equivalent Roman proclamation of consensus and consecration (as we saw in the *ordines romani*) was created to replace it. So perhaps the copyist, told to remove the exhortation, did just that but left in the rubric that referred to it. Following the presentation and bidding, the litany begins. Thus in the *PRXII* the second stage of the ordination begins with no expression of the consensus achieved; only the second half of the proclamation structure remains, the bidding.

Perhaps the redactors of the *PRXII* found that having two proclamations of consensus and consecration in two selection presentations sufficed; a proclamation within the consecration presentation was not important. However, the absence of an acknowledgment of consensus and an expression of its necessary relation to the consecration is significant.

While it is unfortunate that the stirring Gallican exhortation, *Servanda est,* never finds a place in another pontifical text after the *PRG,* it is more than merely unfortunate that an entire structural element of the ordination process is omitted here. By naming the bidding that remains "the exhortation," the compilers of the *PRXII* betray the view that any exhortation will substitute for the one excised (just as *OR35B* supplied an optional sermon at this point). With the *PRXII,* the evolution of the ordination rite takes a substantial step away from the traditional necessity for an expression of consensus as a constitutive element in the second stage of episcopal ordination.

e. CONSECRATION PRESENTATION:
   GERMANIC ELEMENTS AND NEW ROMAN ELEMENTS
   OF THE CONSECRATION

As two bishops hold the gospel book over the elect and the rest of the bishops impose hands, the *ordinator* recites the Roman oration, *Propitiare,* and the consecration prayer *(SVe + GeV/MF)* in the middle of which there continues to be a separate formulary for the chrismal anointing of the head of the elect. The pope is directed to offer the consecration prayer with his voice raised "in the manner of a preface" *(in modum prefationis),* a rubric warranting the continued addition of the preface dialogue to the beginning of the consecration prayer (as noted first in Hincmar and then in the *PRG*).

The papal Pontifical at this point includes only some of the Germanic explanatory rites that came into the episcopal ordination liturgy by way of the *PRG:* anointing of the hand and thumb with accompanying prayer;[18] formula for the giving of the crozier; and formula for the imposition of the ring. But the creativity of the papal masters of ceremonies adds a new ritual at this point: the giving of the gospel book with accompanying formulary. It is an elegant and prayerful way to deal with the removal of the gospel book from the hands of the two assisting bishops while underscoring the preaching and teaching ministry of the bishop.

Manuscript L explains that the consecrator takes the gospel book from between the shoulders of the new bishop, gives him the closed book and says:

PRXII.X.29. . . . Receive the gospel book and go, preach to the people entrusted to you. God is powerful to increase grace within you. . . .

It is only at this point (after the hand anointing and giving of the crozier and ring) that the elect is identified as *consecratus* (while manuscripts B C O inexplicably continue to refer to him as still *electus*).

The consecration ends with a series of fascinating ritual elements. The kiss of peace is exchanged with the pope, all the deacons, bishops, and presbyters; manuscript L includes the pope's feet. After the *Alleluia,* gospel, and Creed, the *PRXII* makes the first mention of gifts from the new bishop to the consecrator: two loaves of bread and a flask of wine. Manuscripts B C O retain a custom first encountered in *OR35.73.* The new bishop receives Communion each day from the consecrated host given him by the pope, but the length of time for this practice has been extended from forty to fifty days. At the conclusion of the Mass, the new bishop offers reverence to the pope with the threefold acclamation: *multos annos.* The linen strips which bound the elect's head during the anointing are removed; the crown of his head is cleansed with bits of bread (which are then to be burnt, having absorbed the chrism), and the miter is imposed without formulary. The new bishop is then encouraged, if possible, to celebrate the Eucharist for the next forty days for the people entrusted to him.

f. CONSECRATION PRESENTATION: STRUCTURE

The absence of the proclamation of consensus and consecration is the only alteration in the structure of the Consecration Presentation from the *PRG* to the *PRXII.* The elements and sequence of the original Roman and early Gallican structures continue to be followed in this papal ritual as Germanic elaborations are adopted and rituals of papal reverence are added.

2nd stage

Consecration Presentation

　　　　　　　　　　　　　introit to gradual

　　　　　　　　　　　　　episcopal vestments
presentation:　　　　　　two bishops
proclamation of consensus and consecration:

　　　　　　　　　　　　　[　　　　　　　]

　　　　　　　　　　　　　bidding *MF*
consecration:　　　　　　litany

　　　　　　　　　　　　　gospel book

　　　　　　　　　　　　　laying on of hands

　　　　　　　　　　　　　Propitiare

　　　　　　　　　　　　　consecration prayer

　　　　　　　　　　　　　consecration continues

C. CONCLUSION

Before a comparison is made of the structures of the presentations of the bishop-elect in the texts studied thus far, it is necessary to discuss the existence of the two Selection Presentations in the *PRXII:* the Roman and the Gallican. Were there actually two separate scrutinies taking place within only a few hours of each other, both conducted by the pope? Did the elect appear two separate times in presbyteral vestments, even after the first proclamation of consensus and consecration ("you will be consecrated")? The texts of the *PRXII* contain no explicit qualifying commentary that suggest otherwise,[19] but the duplication of the presentations is worth exploring. Let us consider the textual evidence and the commentaries of liturgical scholars on the question.

1. *Two Selection Presentations: textual evidence*

Three sets of rubrical material seem to demonstrate that the Germanic Selection Presentation with its examination was a genuine element in the Sunday liturgy of episcopal consecration in the *PRXII.* The first set involves the rubrics "And once [all are] assembled, the examination is done" (no. 9) and "And after the scrutiny has been done" (no. 13). These occur just before and after the examination *(Antiqua sanctorum patrum),* suggesting that the Germanic form from the *PRG* has already been well integrated into the elements from the earlier Roman *ordo.*

The second rubrical clue is found in a comparison of the first set of nine questions in the examination of the *PRG* with the first set of eight questions in the *PRXII.* Which question was deleted? It is the fourth question from the *PRG* which asks for a promise of fidelity to the metropolitan of Mainz and his successors. The Lateran clerics took the trouble to omit this question altogether and altered the third question of the Gallican form to be used in Rome by the pope himself. So it seems likely that there was the Gallican examination before the introit of the Sunday consecration liturgy in Rome. With this very lengthy scrutiny, was there need for another the evening before, as the text indicates?

The third textual clue lies in the list of questions themselves which the Roman interrogation asks in the course of the previous evening. Would these still have been questions of concern in the twelfth century?

PRXII.X.6. . . . Did you have a spouse? . . . Have you taken care of your household?

PRXII.X.7. . . . Do not promote bigamists or curiales or [those] from a condition of servitude to a sacred order.[20]

Perhaps these very questions point *away* from any realistic use of the Roman Saturday scrutiny in the twelfth century, even in the apostolic city itself.

One significant contradictory element, however, is the evidence of the expanded rubrics in manuscript L from the end of the twelfth century. Not only does the meticulous rubricist carefully detail each aspect of the Germanic Selection Presentation for papal use, but thoroughly reworks the rubrics in the Roman texts for the Saturday scrutiny as well. The same hand seems to have adjusted the rubrics in both sets of texts. For example:

The Roman Selection Presentation:

PRXII.X.1. On Saturday about vespers, when the apostolic lord is seated in the atrium next to the church, the archpresbyter comes

B C O	L
vested in chasuble, with the clerics of that church whose elect is to be consecrated and,	of that church whose elect is to be consecrated, vested in alb and chasuble, since he ought to sing the mass, whom the younger cardinal deacon should lead and hold by the right hand and the subdeacon by the left hand. And others from the clerics of that same elect, with surplices or copes, follow the archpresbyter calmly and with decorum. Then the archpresbyter
genuflecting before the *apostolicus*, asks a blessing saying thus:	comes before the presence of the pontiff, genuflecting before the pontiff,

150

And the Germanic Selection Presentation:

B C O	L
PRXII.X.21. Then standing up, two bishops place and hold the closed book of the gospels over his neck and between his shoulders and, one pouring out the blessing over him, all the rest of the bishops who are present touch their hands to his head and the ordainer says:	*PRXII.X.21.* The bishops also rise and lifting up the elect lead him before the presence of the pontiff. And the pontiff receiving the text of the gospels places it open on the shoulders of the elect. And then he himself and all the bishops who are present touch the head of the elect himself and the pontiff in moderate voice says this prayer. The bishops also follow in this [prayer] and in the others with subdued voice until the end of the consecration.

Note that this inclusion of the Saturday scrutiny and its careful and deliberate rewriting in the *PRXII* occurred at a time when "the Roman liturgists aimed at eliminating a good deal of archaic and unnecessary material from the Mainz Pontifical: archaic *ordines* . . . which neither Rome nor its suffragans needed. . . ."[21] It would have been reasonable then for the copyist to have eliminated the entire Saturday synaxis. In fact he intentionally copies it back into the papal liturgy, presumably to use it.

Andrieu describes the situation as he understands it:

> One must conclude therefore that a liturgist working in Rome, having a pontifical of the form B C O to work from, decided to create a revised and expanded edition. He recast the rubrics and recorded a certain number of new details which he was aware of, having directly observed them himself at ceremonies performed in the apostolic city. Perhaps even, in certain cases, he did not limit himself to recounting verified practices and ventured some personal innovations which seemed to him desirable and justified. At a time when many ceremonial details (too summarily described in the present books) were still seeking their definitive form, such initiatives on the part of an authorized liturgist were nothing abnormal.[22]

The compiler of L rewrote the directives accompanying both the Roman and the Germanic Selection Presentations according to what he saw and perhaps also according to his imagination, but in neither case did he rewrite the spoken texts. His creative freedom was limited to rubrics.

Perhaps this was the case because the Roman and the Germanic presentations had come to have their own unassailable status: the Roman, essential for underscoring both the antiquity of its ritual tradition and the predominant power of the pope in the confirmation of the choice of a bishop, and the Germanic, the ritual tradition brought back to the apostolic see by the emperors and authorized under the title of "How a bishop is ordained *in the roman church*."[23]

One may conclude from these fragments of evidence that the two Selection Presentations which *PRXII* contains were both in use at least for some part of the Pontifical's brief history. Perhaps the best that can be said is that the *PRXII* is a document of transition, part of "the labor of adapting the *[PRG]* to the new Roman situation" of the twelfth century.[24] Liturgical scholars themselves seem convinced that the Roman scrutiny of Saturday eventually falls into disuse. Any lack of clarity concerns whether the cessation of the Saturday ritual occurred before or after the creation of the texts of the *PRXII*.

In assessing the use of duplicate presentations, Pierre Batiffol makes only a general comment: "This Gallican examination makes a useless repetition of the Roman evening scrutiny, and it is understood that, retained by the Roman liturgy, it pushed out the scrutiny."[25] Batiffol however does not specify when this happens. Andrieu too writes knowledgeably about the waning of the Roman practice but not about when it took place: "The ancient Roman ordination ritual fell into disuse and the learned clerics considered as the only norm that which the French or German books described and notably the Romano-Germanic Pontifical."[26]

Salmon is more precise. He assures the reader that, "The Pontifical of the Twelfth Century and that of the Curia of the Thirteenth Century always had the ceremony of Saturday evening; it took place principally in the atrium of the church."[27] But then in describing the interrogation, he goes on to clarify that, "whereas formerly it all took place the entire day before, in the pontificals of the twelfth and of the thirteenth centuries and in that of Guillaume Durand, it will be transferred in large part to the same day as the ordination."[28]

We conclude the commentaries with Kleinheyer's characterization of the Roman Saturday evening scrutiny (which continued to be found in the appendix of the Roman Pontifical up until the 1968 revision). He states that even in the *PRXII* the Saturday ritual "was already a relic; since with the *PRG* at the latest, in Rome as well one conformed to the other traditions."[29]

For purposes of comparing the structural units of the Selection Presentations in the *PRXII*, we will conclude that both Selection Presentations included in the text may have been part of the ritual actually celebrated, if only for a brief while. The examination of the bishop-elect copied from the *PRG* represented only the form any metropolitan would use; it was vital to the pope that the hundred bishops under special jurisdiction of the Roman See[30] have in their possession the ritual whose directives respected the authority of the pope. He himself would verify the validity of the selection process of the elect by interrogating the representatives who had been present and by accepting their decree, by examining the elect, and by affirming whether he was worthy of elevation to the episcopacy.[31]

But eventually, as Batiffol describes, the Gallican examination will "push out" the Roman evening scrutiny from papal practice. In the earlier period in which the manuscripts of the *PRXII* were being created, however, the gradual consolidation of papal authority relied on the texts for episcopal ordination to highlight the position of the pope as the last voice in the selection process of the bishop-elect.

The comparative outline that follows reflects the assumption that both Roman and Gallican Selection Presentations were included in papal practice. The development of the presentations of the bishop-elect in the liturgical documents examined thus far can be seen when their structures are juxtaposed:

OR34	*Gallican*	*PRG*	*PRXII*	*PRXII*
1st stage	*1st stage*	*1st stage*	*1st stage*	*1st stage*
Selection Presentation Saturday	**Selection Presentation** Saturday	**Selection Presentation** Sunday	**Selection Presentation** Saturday	**Selection Presentation** Sunday
presentation vacant see **postulation**	**presentation**	**presentation**	**presentation** vacant see **postulation**	**presentation**
examination	examination	examination	examination	examination
proclamation	**proclamation**	**proclamation**	**proclamation**	**proclamation**
consensus/ consecration	**consensus/ consecration**	**consensus/ consecration**	**consensus/ consecration**	**consensus/ consecration**
desires of all/	*Servanda est*	with the agreement/	desires of all/	with the agreement/
you will be consecrated		he may be ordained	you will be consecrated	he may be ordained

153

OR34	Gallican	PRG	PRXII	PRXII
2nd stage	*2nd stage*	*2nd stage*	*2nd stage*	
Consecration	**Consecration**	**Consecration**		**Consecration**
Presentation	**Presentation**	**Presentation**		**Presentation**
Sunday	Sunday	Sunday		Sunday
introit to	**presentation**	introit to		introit to
gradual	episcopal	gradual		gradual
episcopal	vestments	episcopal		episcopal
vestments	introit to	vestments		vestments
	collect			
presentation		**presentation**		**presentation**
archdeacon		2 bishops		2 bishops
proclamation	**proclamation**	**proclamation**		**proclamation**
consensus/	**consensus/**	**consensus/**		**consensus/**
consecration	**consecration**	**consecration**		**consecration**
clergy + people	extended	*Servanda est*		[ ]
+ bishops	bidding	[CD: with the		
with consent		agreement/		
		he may be		
		ordained]		
		[AV: optional		
		sermon]		
bidding *OR34*		bidding *MF*		bidding *MF*
consecration	**consecration**	**consecration**		**consecration**
litany	litany	litany		litany
		gospel book		gospel book
		laying on		laying on
		of hands		of hands
Propitiare	*Propitiare*	*Propitiare*		*Propitiare*
consecration	**consecration**	**consecration**		**consecration**
prayer	prayer	prayer		prayer
consecration	consecration	consecration		consecration
continues	continues	continues		continues

Important elements to note in the evolution of the Selection Presentation as recorded in the *PRXII* include:

- decline in the participation of the vacant see in the presentation and postulation of the elect whom they have assisted in choosing;

- predominance of the Gallican examination over the Roman examination of both electors and elect;

- omission of the mention of the metropolitan's consensus in the proclamation of consensus and consecration (thus facilitating papal usage);

- decline in the participation of the assembly in other elements of the selection process (through the loss of the Roman examination form and through the loss of the Gallican exhortation *Servanda est*);

- loss of a proclamation of consensus and consecration to be explicitly recited by the consecrator (as the strong Roman and Gallican proclamations are replaced by [recitation of?] the consensus statement from *SEA*);

- consistency in celebrating the selection stage before the introit of the consecration Mass;

- inclusion for the first time (in the *PRXII*, manuscript O) of the *Episcopum oportet* unit which will eventually move into the consecration stage, displace the optional sermon, and become the only "proclamation of consensus and consecration."

In the evolution of the Consecration Presentation as demonstrated by the *PRXII*, the following changes may be observed:

- juxtaposition of the selection and consecration liturgies on Sunday morning;

- consistency of the change to episcopal vestments functioning as the bridge between the two liturgies, the two stages;

- the beginning of the use of two bishops to present the elect;

- the substantive shift in the proclamation of consensus and consecration: from Roman and Gallican spoken proclamations joined to the bidding, to the substitution of *Servanda est* (from the selection stage) as the proclamation, to an optional sermon, to nothing in most manuscripts of the *PRXII*;

- the increasing multiplication and elaboration of secondary rites (especially within and after the consecration prayer);

- systematizing of the bidding to introduce the litany and *Propitiare* as the litany collect;

- correction of the chaotic and erroneous placement of several ritual elements.

We turn our attention from the *PRXII* to study the further evolution of the Selection Presentation and Consecration Presentation in the rite of episcopal ordination in the Pontifical of the Roman Curia.

Texts of the Pontifical of the Twelfth Century:

Selection Presentation:

PRXII.X. Incipit ordo ad vocandum et examinandum seu consecrandum electum in episcopum iuxta morem romanae ecclesiae.

1. Sabbati die circa vesperam, sedente domno apostolico in atrio iuxta ecclesiam, venit archipresbiter indutus casula cum clericis illius ecclesiae cui electus consecrandus est et, flectens genua ante apostolicum, benedictionem petit sic dicendo: . . .

2. Benedictione completa, interrogat eos domnus apostolicus: Omnia recte quod vos fatigastis, frates? Resp.: Ut Deus et dominus noster concedat nobis pastorem. Si plures vel pauciores in presbiteratu annos habeat, certum tempus respondebit.

3. Tunc profertur decretum et legitur hoc modo: . . .

4. Hoc lecto, prosequitur apostolicus: Videte ne aliquam vobis promissionem fecerit: sciatis quia symoniacum est et contra canones. Resp.: Absit. Et dicit apostolicus: Ducatur.

5. Tunc venit ipse electus planeta indutus, et ter benedictionem petit sicut superius dictum est.

6. Tunc interrogat eum pontifex: Omnia recte quod te fatigasti, frater? Resp.: Quod ego dignus non fui, isti confratres mei elegerunt me sibi preesse pastorem. . . .
. . . Habuisti coniugium? . . . Diposuisti domui tuae?

7. Et dicit apostolicus: . . . Bigamos aut curiales aut de servili conditione ad sacrum ordinem non promoveas. . . .
Quia ergo in te omnium vota conveniunt, hodie abstinebis et cras Deo annuente consecraberis.
Resp.: Praecepisti. Hoc facto, discedunt singuli in loca sua.

A Second Selection Presentation:

8. Dominica vero die, progreditur domnus apostolicus cum electo et cuncto clero et populo ad ecclesiam ubi ipsam fieri vult ordinationem. Et ingressus sacrarium, induit se vestimenta pontificalia.

9. Post pusillum, procedit a sacrario cum diaconibus et reliquis ministris sicut dominicis diebus mos est procedendi. Et electus, sacris vestibus indutus, procedit simul cum eo et ceteris episcopis e sacrario ante altare. Factoque conventu, fiat examinatio:

10. Antiqua sanctorum patrum. . . .

Interr.: Vis beato Petro, cui a Deo data est potestas ligandi atque solvendi, michique indigno eius vicario successoribusque meis fidem et subiectionem per omnia exhibere?

12. Ita igitur. examinatus et bene instructus, cum consensu clericorum et laicorum ac conventu totius provinciae episcoporum, in nomine domini ordinetur.

[O] De officio episcopi. Episcopum oportet iudicare, interpretari, consecrare, consumare, ordinare, offerre et baptizare.

Consecration Presentation:

PRXII.X.13. Facto itaque scrutinio, domnus apostolicus mox ut vult indicat cantori. Et mox incipit antiphona ad introitum.

15. Oratio pro electo ad missam. Adesto. . . .

16. Lectio epistolae beati Pauli apostoli ad Timotheum. . . .

17. Postea psallitur graduale. . . .

18. Tunc egrediatur archidiaconus cum acolitis et subdiaconibus et induat ipsum electum dalmaticam, planetam et cambagos, et duo episcopi casulis induti deportant eum superius iuxta altare. Et convertens se apostolicus ad circumstantes dicit hanc exhortationem:

19. Oremus, dilectissimi nobis. . . .

20. Et statim incipit Kyrie eleison cum letania et prosternit se ordinator electi simul cum electo et caeteris episcopis ante altare super stramenta, usquedum dicit scola Agnus Dei.

21. Ut autem surrexerint, duo episcopi ponunt et tenent evangeliorum codicem super cervicem eius et inter scapulas clausum et, uno super eum fundente benedictionem, reliqui omnes episcopi qui assunt manibus suis caput eius tangunt et dicit ordinator:

22. Propitiare. . . .

23. Per omnia secula seculorum. Amen. Hic elevat vocem suam in modum prefationis. Dominus vobiscum . . . Vere Dignum . . . Honor omnium dignitatum. . . .

24. Hic mittit chrisma in caput eius in modum crucis. Ungatur et consecretur caput tuum. . . . Pax tibi. Resp.: Et cum spiritu tuo.

25. Hic similiter dicit in modum prefationis: Hoc, domine, copiose in eius caput effluat. . . .

29. Accipe evangelium et vade, praedica populo tibi commisso. Potens est enim Deus augere tibi gratiam. . . .

The Roman Selection Presentation:

PRXII.X.1. Sabbati die circa vesperam, sedente domno apostolico in atrio iuxta ecclesiam, venit archipresbiter [L] illius ecclesiae, cuius electus consecrandus est, indutus alba et casula, sicut deberet missam cantare, quem iunior diaconus

157

cardinalis deducere debet et tenere per manum dextram et subdiaconus per manum sinistram. Et aliqui de clericis eiusdem electi, cum superpelliciis vel cappis, ipsum archipresbiterum modeste et decenter prosequantur. Ut autem venit ante conspectum pontificis, flectens genua ipse archipresbiter ante pontificem, benedictionem petit sic dicendo:

And the Germanic Selection Presentation:

PRXII.X.21. [L] Surgunt quoque episcopi et elevantes electum deducunt eum ante presentiam pontificis. Et pontifex accipiens textum evangeliorum ponit ipsum apertum super scapulas electi. Et tunc ipse et omnes episcopi qui adsunt tangunt caput ipsius electi et dicit pontifex media voce hanc orationem. Episcopi quoque in hac et in aliis ipsum prosequuntur voce suppressa usque in finem consecrationis.

II. The Presentation of the Bishop-Elect in the Pontifical of the Roman Curia of the Thirteenth Century[32]

A. THE *PRC* AND THE RITUAL CONTEXT OF EPISCOPAL ORDINATION

Michel Andrieu himself adopted the name *The Pontifical of the Roman Curia of the Thirteenth Century* for his edition of this work,[33] reflecting its origin in the "initiatives taken by the masters of ceremonies of the Lateran at the time of Innocent III"[34] (+1216). Although thirty-three manuscripts form the basis of Andrieu's edition, he describes them as forming "a coherent family" and "without any doubt, they are wholly dependent upon a common ancestor."[35] Three recensions exist: α from the pontificate of Innocent III; β which is impossible to date precisely;[36] and γ compiled probably in the middle of the thirteenth century, during the pontificate of Innocent IV (+1254).[37] This third and last recension then travels with the popes to Avignon (1305/1309) and eventually serves as a basis for the Pontifical of Guillaume Durand de Mende.[38] In fact, as Andrieu explains, Durand drew on many sources for his pontifical, "but the source on which he drew most of all was the Pontifical of the Curia."[39]

The initial chapter of the *PRC* is the "ordo of the seven ecclesiastical ranks"; its ascending arrangement begins with the preparatory rites for becoming a cleric, "cutting the beard," and being made a cantor or psalmist. The seven ranks themselves include doorkeeper, lector, exorcist, acolyte, subdeacon, deacon, and finally culminate in presbyter. The rite of episcopal ordination which follows is outside this *cursus;* it is placed together with the ordination of a pope, the blessing and coronation of an emperor, the blessing of abbots and abbesses. This is the same arrangement found in *PRXII*.

B. ANALYSIS OF THE LITURGICAL UNITS

1. *Selection Presentation*

a. SELECTION PRESENTATION: TEXT

PRC.XI. Here begins the *ordo* for the calling that is the examining or consecrating the elect as a bishop, but if he has been chosen by the roman church he will not be examined by reason of the prerogative of the roman church.

1. On Saturday about vespers, with the apostolic lord seated in the atrium next to the church, the archpresbyter comes vested in chasuble, with the clerics of that church whose elect is to be consecrated, and genuflecting before the *apostolicus* asks a blessing saying: . . .

[2.–3. The formal, threefold blessing seen above in *OR35B* and *PRXII*]

4. When the blessing is finished, the apostolic lord questions them: What are all the things you are rightly concerned about[,] brothers? They respond: That God and our lord may grant us a pastor.

[Questions identical to those in *OR35B* and *PRXII* follow, regarding the elect's church, rank and years in it, spouse and household and pleasing qualities, with the reading of the decree, with these additions]

And if he may have had more or less [than ten years in his rank], he may respond accordingly. And if he is not a presbyter, he is questioned and responds about the order which he has and how long he has been in that [order]. He asks: Did he have a spouse? He responds: By no means. Nevertheless if he had a spouse, let it be mentioned beforehand to the pontiff and let him respond: You know [of it], lord.

5. Then the decree is brought out and read in this way:
[a partial text follows]

6. When this is read, the *apostolicus* continues further and says: Consider that he must not have made any promise to you, because simony is against the canons. They respond: Far be it [from us]. And the *apostolicus* says: Let him be led in. Then the elect comes vested in chasuble and asks for a blessing saying: [the formal, threefold blessing as in *OR35B* above]

7. Then the *apostolicus* asks him: What are all the things you are rightly concerned about, brother? He responds: Although I was not worthy, these fellow brothers have chosen me to preside over them as pastor.

[Questions identical to those in *OR35B* and *PRXII* follow, regarding the elect's church, rank and years in it, spouse and household, books read in his church and knowledge of the canons, with the additions mentioned above regarding more or less years in the presbyterate and his spouse.]

8. [The pontiff gives the elect information identical to that given in *OR35B* and *PRXII* regarding the times for ordination, those not to be promoted, the promise to receive the edict, and the two warnings against simony.]

And the pope says: You will see [to it].
Therefore because the desires of all have agreed upon you, today you will abstain and tomorrow, God willing, you will be consecrated.
He responds: As you have commanded. Then they depart individually to their places.

b. SELECTION PRESENTATION: THE ROMAN PATTERN

Chapter XI of the *PRC* bears the same initial title as that of *OR35B* and the *PRXII*: "Here begins the *ordo* for the calling and examining or consecrating the elect a bishop" but with this significant addition: "but if he has been chosen by the roman church he will not be examined by reason of the prerogative of the roman church." Andrieu explains that at this point the preliminary synaxis of Saturday evening, the *serotinum scrutinium* (evening scrutiny), has fallen into disuse.[40]

Manuscripts of the block A P V Y Z, for example, insert these words before the title: "The following evening scrutiny is not held today in the roman church." Manuscripts B and H more precisely add that the entire Selection Presentation (nos. 1–8) consists of elements which "are not observed today." What could only be intimated regarding the future of the Saturday ritual in the *PRXII* here is explicitly stated in the *PRC*: the texts of the *serotinum scrutinium* are retained in the texts of the pontifical but are not retained in practice.[41] We will remark briefly on the contents of the Saturday *scrutinium* in the *PRC*, but its Selection Presentation will not be included in the overall structure.

Chapter XI includes nos. 1–41, of which nos. 1–8 describe the Saturday evening Selection Presentation of the bishop-elect. Alterations from the text of the *PRXII* are very few and minor. As Andrieu indicates in the apparatus, the *PRC*.XI.1-8 (the Saturday scrutiny) is drawn directly from the *PRXII*.X.1-7.[42]

Saturday evening at the hour of vespers an archpresbyter with the clergy from the church for whom the elect is to be consecrated enters the atrium of the church where the apostolic lord is seated. The presentation, postulation, and examination occur as recorded in the *PRXII*. The decree with the signatures of the electors is read; the elect enters alone and in presbyteral vestments. The interrogation of the elect concludes with the same proclamation:

PRC.XI.8. . . . Therefore because the desires of all have agreed upon you, today you will abstain and tomorrow, God willing, you will be consecrated.

c. SELECTION PRESENTATION: THE GERMANIC MODEL

PRC.XI.

9. Early on the following day the elect himself however should take care that with his own [things] there are also prepared at hand everything necessary for him in the consecration, namely the stockings, sandals, amice, alb, cincture, stole, maniple, tunic, dalmatic, chasuble and cope white in color, gloves, pontifical ring and another small ring, miter embroidered in gold, pastoral staff, two basins, cloths for wiping the hands, cloths for setting before the consecrator, cloths and comb for combing, morsels of bread for wiping the hands and head, two arm's lengths of cloth, two arm's lengths of curtain fabric for wrapping around the head for the anointing, two large loaves covered with two cloths, two large flasks full of wine and two large torches for offering, books of the mass and of the pontifical [rites], a low faldstool and carpet, a priest with surplice and cloths who is to assist the elect with the book and a palfrey [riding horse] covered in buckram.

10. On Sunday however and not on another feast day, the apostolic lord makes his way with the elect and all the clergy and people to the church where he wants to hold that ordination and going into the sacristy he clothes himself in pontifical vestments. After a little while he goes forth from the sacristy with deacons and the rest of the ministers processing as is the practice on sundays.

11. And the elect clothed in sacred vestments, namely amice, alb, maniple, stole and cincture and cope only processes together with him and the other bishops from the sacristy [to] before the altar, and having assembled, before the confession takes place, an examination such as this is done.

12. While that examination is read, however the consecrating bishops and pope ought to have miters on [their] heads, but not the one to be consecrated.

13. *Antiqua sanctorum patrum.* . . .
Will you promise fidelity and submission in all things to blessed Peter to whom the power to bind and to loose was given by God and to me his vicar and to my successors?
If another in place of the pope is to consecrate he says: Will you promise fidelity and submission in all things to blessed Peter to whom the power to bind and to loose was given by God and to his vicar the most holy father our lord N. supreme pontiff and to his successors?

14. Therefore thus examined and well prepared, with the consent of the clerics and laity and the agreement of the bishops of the entire province in the name of the lord he may be ordained.

15. Regarding the office of bishop. *[Episcopum oportet]* A bishop is to judge, interpret, consecrate, confirm, ordain, offer and baptize.

As with the Roman pattern of the Selection Presentation, the Germanic Selection Presentation also repeats the structure and wording of the *PRXII*. Sunday morning the pope, the elect, all the clergy and people, assemble in the church of the pope's choice. Deacons and other ministers are also present. In presbyteral vestments,[43] the elect proceeds to his place before the altar in the company of the other bishops present.

The Gallican examination *(Antiqua sanctorum patrum)* is read, and the elect responds to the exhaustive list of questions. The *PRC* records only one of the questions; it is that which calls for the promise of fidelity to the Roman Pontiff and his successors. The *PRC* provides two forms: one for use by the pope himself, and the second, for use in the churches subject to him.

No. 14 is the proclamation of consensus, exactly as preserved in the *PRXII*. Both the *PRC* and the *PRXII* removed the reference to the metropolitan which the *PRG* had preserved in its use of this canon from *SEA*. The removal of the reference to the metropolitan may indicate two distinct dynamics at work: the first is that the local metropolitan was already present in the person of the pope. Through his presidency over the examination (with its promise of fidelity), his consent was explicitly demonstrated. The second dynamic involved the increasing erosion of the ancient Roman and Gallican processes of episcopal election during this era. As Thomas O'Meara succinctly concludes, "The metropolitan and the bishops of the area lost in importance as pope and prince gained."[44]

There continue to be no rubrics provided for the proclamation of consensus and consecration. It appears to have been copied along with the Gallican examination to which it was appended by the *PRG*; it maintains its position there. Perhaps the existence of this isolated canonical element is what now draws the *Episcopum oportet* unit. We find it following the proclamation of consensus and consecration:

PRC.XI.14. Therefore thus examined and well prepared, with the consent of the clerics and laity and the agreement of the bishops of the entire province in the name of the lord he may be ordained.

15. Regarding the office of bishop. *[Episcopum oportet]* The bishop is to judge, interpret, consecrate, confirm, ordain, offer and baptize.

While only one manuscript of the *PRXII* had included *Episcopum oportet* at this point, fifteen manuscripts of the two earlier recensions of the *PRC* (α and β) place it here together with the proclamation of consensus. Batiffol takes it for granted that it was read to the assembly, but he judges it "a bizarre formula which is not a monition and which appears to be addressed to no one."[45]

d. SELECTION PRESENTATION: STRUCTURE

With the certain demise of the Roman Saturday evening scrutiny, the structure of the Selection Presentation of the *PRC* remains that of the Germanic model of the *PRG* (with the addition of the *Episcopum oportet* unit in two of the three recensions of the *PRC*):

PRC

1st stage

Selection Presentation

>Sunday
>examination

proclamation of consensus and consecration:

>with the agreement/
>he may be ordained
>[α β *Episcopum oportet*]

2. *Consecration Presentation*

a. CONSECRATION PRESENTATION: TEXT

PRC.XI.16. After the scrutiny has been done, the one to be consecrated is led to the pontiff, whose foot and face are kissed, if it is the pope; if it is another, hand and face. And then the apostolic lord with bishops and ministers of the altar and also the elect approaching the altar, makes the confession and as soon as [the pontiff] wishes he informs the cantor and he begins the antiphon for the entrance of that Sunday and the rest as usual and the elect returns to the place where he had been vested.

17. The prayer for the elect follows . . . Prayer. *Adesto.* . . .

18. . . . [T]he archdeacon with acolytes and subdeacon vests the elect in tunic, dalmatic, chasuble and *cambagos*. And two bishops wearing chasubles lead him to a higher place before the altar

before the *apostolicus*.

19. And sitting with miter he says:
[*Episcopum oportet*] A bishop is to judge,
interpret, consecrate, confirm, ordain,
offer and baptize.

20. Then rising and having taken off
the miter]

turning to those present, the *apostolicus* says this prayer: *Oremus, dilectissimi
nobis. . . . Per.*

21. And immediately the *Kyrie eleison* begins with the litany and the ordainer
prostrates as well as the elect reclining at his left and the other bishops and
ministers before the altar on the carpet, until the schola sings *Agnus Dei.*

b. CONSECRATION PRESENTATION:
   PROCLAMATION

"And after the scrutiny has been done" (the curious rubric from the
PRG) is here again correctly attached to the context of the examination as
it was in the *PRXII.* Following the Selection Presentation, the second
stage begins. The introit and usual introductory elements of the Mass
take place through the gradual.

The archdeacon with acolytes and a subdeacon assist the elect with
episcopal vestments; two bishops then accompany him for the presentation to the pope. At this point, the earlier recensions of the *PRC* duplicate
the rubrics of the *PRXII:*

PRXII.X.	PRC.XI.
18. . . . and two bishops wearing chasubles bring him to a higher place next to the altar. And turning to those present the *apostolicus* says	18. . . . And two bishops wearing chasubles lead him to a higher place before the altar turning to those present the *apostolicus* says

But the compiler of the *PRC*, realizing that what follows is *not* an exhortation, alters the *PRXII* text to read:

PRXII.X.	PRC.XI.
. . . the *apostolicus* says this exhortation:	. . . the *apostolicus* says this oration:

The "oration" is bidding *MF.* The *PRC* recensions α and β continue the
practice of the *PRXII* and omit any proclamation of consensus and

consecration before the bidding; they also omit the rubric which once referred to it.

The redactor of the later recension γ however makes an interesting substitution at no. 19. In the place once occupied by the exhortation, *Servanda est*, of the *MF* and the *PRG*, (the place left standing empty in the *PRXII* and the *PRC*), we find the brief canonical statement, *Episcopum oportet*, which has moved up from no. 15 in recensions α β. The *PRC* γ however presents it as an allocution:

PRC.XI.18 . . . And two bishops wearing chasubles lead him to a higher place before the altar

α β	γ
and	in the presence of the *apostolicus*.
	19. And sitting with miter he says: [*Episcopum oportet*] The bishop is to judge, interpret, consecrate, confirm, ordain, offer and baptize.
	20. Then rising and having taken off the miter

turning to those standing around the *apostolicus* says this oration.

It is this insertion of *Episcopum oportet* into recension γ which will later enter the Roman Pontificals of 1485 and of 1595 by way of the Pontifical of Guillaume Durand.

After the allocution, *Episcopum oportet*, all recensions merge for the following rubric and bidding:

PRC.XI.18. . . . turning to those present the *apostolicus* says this oration: Oremus, dilectissimi nobis. . . .

The *Kyrie* then begins the litany, and the consecration continues.

c. CONSECRATION PRESENTATION: STRUCTURE

The Consecration Presentation takes this form:

PRC

2nd stage

Consecration Presentation

Sunday
introit to gradual
episcopal vestments

presentation:	two bishops
proclamation of consensus and consecration:	
	[*Episcopum oportet* γ]
	bidding *MF*
consecration:	litany
	gospel book
	laying on of hands
	Propitiare
	consecration prayer
	consecration continues

C. CONCLUSION

The evolution of the presentation of the bishop-elect from the earlier Roman model through the three later pontificals can be demonstrated by the following outline:

PRG	*PRXII*	*PRC*
1st stage	*1st stage*	*1st stage*
Selection Presentation	**Selection Presentation**	**Selection Presentation**
Sunday	Sunday	Sunday
presentation	**presentation**	**presentation**
examination	examination	examination
proclamation of consensus and consecration	**proclamation of consensus and consecration**	**proclamation of consensus and consecration**
with the agreement/	with the agreement/	with the agreement/
he may be ordained	he may be ordained	he may be ordained
		[α β *Episcopum oportet*]
2nd stage	*2nd stage*	*2nd stage*
Consecration Presentation	**Consecration Presentation**	**Consecration Presentation**
Sunday	Sunday	Sunday
introit to gradual	introit to gradual	introit to gradual
episcopal vestments	episcopal vestments	episcopal vestments
presentation	**presentation**	**presentation**
two bishops	two bishops	two bishops
proclamation of consensus and consecration	**proclamation of consensus and consecration**	**proclamation of consensus and consecration**
Servanda est	[ ]	[γ *Episcopum oportet*]
[CD: with the agreement/ he may be ordained]		
[AV: optional sermon]		
bidding *MF*	bidding *MF*	bidding *MF*

PRG	PRXII	PRC
consecration	**consecration**	**consecration**
litany	litany	litany
gospel book	gospel book	gospel book
laying on of hands	laying on of hands	laying on of hands
Propitiare	*Propitiare*	*Propitiare*
consecration prayer	consecration prayer	consecration prayer
consecration continues	consecration continues	consecration continues

While the structural shifts between the *PRXII* and the *PRC* are slight,[46] there are evolutions in other patterns that are interesting to note at this point. The *PRC* marks the decisive end of the use of the Roman *scrutinium* and a change in the terms used to designate this episcopal rite.

We noted previously the lack of distinction in earlier liturgical texts between *ordinatio, consecratio,* and *benedictio*. The *PRC* prefers *consecratio* (following the pattern set by the title "the *ordo* for the . . . *consecrating the elect as a bishop*." The elect is called the *consecrandus* (no. 16) and the one who presides is *consecrator* (γ no. 25). Outside of the proclamation of consensus, the word *ordinare* appears only three times in the text: "to the church where he wants to hold that ordination" (no. 10) and "ordainer" (nos. 21 and 23). Santantoni explains that in fact from the thirteenth century on, the rite of episcopal ordination will only be called "consecration."[47] Thus with these three instances (and two later occasions where the Pontifical of Guillaume Durand borrows from the *PRC*), we are witnessing the last uses of *ordinare* in any such rite until *De Ordinatione Episcopi* of 1968.

In the texts of the *PRC*, the Roman Selection Presentation remains suppressed, and the Gallican examination continues to be the focus of the Selection Presentation in the *PRC*. However, the addition of the proclamation, *Episcopum oportet,* and two other rubrical shifts to the Consecration Presentation are noteworthy. Let us first consider two specific groups of alterations in the rubrics: one related to the reverence toward the consecrating bishop, the other to consecration of a number of bishops at one time. What were equivalent elements in the earlier *ordines romani* with which we might compare the later pontificals?

1. *Reverence to the Consecrator*
The marked simplicity of the Roman rite of *OR34* for example was not without signs of reverence toward the apostolic lord by the elect. His presentation at the Saturday evening scrutiny involved prostration three

times and a brief prayer with communal response. The chief concern, however, of the Selection Presentation was the integrity of the ecclesial process: had the widowed church chosen freely and had it chosen well?[48] The Saturday scrutiny and the Sunday consecration provided ritual expressions of the consent of the vacant see, neighboring sees, metropolitan (apostolic) see, and the elect himself. Then, as a new bishop, he was welcomed into his order by being given the first seat among the bishops present.

The shifts perceptible between the rubrics of *OR34* and the *PRC* are subtle but significant. Moving beyond general acts of reverence, the compilers of the *PRXII* and the *PRC* prescribe ritual elements which underscore the personal fidelity of the elect to the consecrating bishop. Several of these elements originate in the *PRG:* the promise of fidelity in the examination and the imposition of crozier and ring by the consecrator. The *PRXII* and the *PRC,* however, multiply this type of ritual by their innovation: presentation of the (increasingly elaborate) offertory gifts by the *consecratus* as a kind of personal gift for a personal favor, the threefold bow before the consecrator accompanied by the threefold *multos annos,* and the suppression of the seating of the new bishop at the head of the *ordo episcoporum.* Concern for multiple expressions of ecclesial consent seems to be rapidly giving way before ritual expressions of personal consent of the elect to the consecrator.

With the suppression of the Saturday evening scrutiny, the dialogic character of the Roman and early Gallican Selection Presentations is lost with the substitution of the almost monologic examination from the *PRG.* According to Santantoni, from this point on, the examination "will serve only to remind the one about to be consecrated at the threshold of his ordination what his new duties and his new responsibilities will be."[49] Although the examination takes place in a liturgical context, it suggests a narrowing of focus from the ecclesial to the individual, devoid as it is of elements more inclusive of the sees involved.

2. *Consent and Fealty*

Added to these admittedly minor rubrics is the occurrence of the phrase "and it is repeated as [often] as one pleases if there are more." This phrase is inserted four separate times during the explanatory rites after the prayer of consecration. When severed from selection and presentation by a vacant see, it seems that episcopal consecration can conveniently accommodate any number of elect. Thus, the simple phrase "if there are more" reveals the vastly different ecclesial contexts of the

earlier Roman and Gallican forms and the *PRC*. The first were characterized by a Selection Presentation of ecclesial consent, and the second by a
Selection Presentation structure of personal fealty (or fealties "if there
are more"!).

   The absence of any proclamation of consensus in the Consecration
Presentation in either the *PRXII* or the *PRC* highlights the shift that seems
to be occurring in these texts. The extensive dialogues of *OR34* and the
MF were accompanied by the presentation and reading of the decree
with the petitionary letters as well as by proclamations of consensus and
consecration by the ordaining bishop and proclamations by the assembly.
The *PRG*, though without a Saturday scrutiny, retained multiple written
documents testifying to a mutual consent evident in the selection of the
elect, and gave this consent vigorous expression in the metropolitan's
proclamation of consensus, *Servanda est,* which simultaneously called for
the assembly's acclamation: "He is worthy!" The *PRXII* and the *PRC*
(α and β) have no proclamation of consensus and consecration; the *PRC* γ
fills that void with the juridical unit, *Episcopum oportet.* The overall
Presentation structure has altered just enough between the Roman and
early Gallican models and the *PRC* to accommodate the shift that seems
to be occurring in the ecclesial understanding of the episcopacy.

   We next trace the evolution of the two presentations of the bishop-
elect through the texts of the Pontifical of Guillaume Durand de Mende.

Texts of the Pontifical of the Roman Curia:

Selection Presentation:

PRC.XI. Incipit ordo ad vocandum seu examinandum vel consecrandum electum
episcopum, quod si fuerit electus de ecclesia romana non examinabitur
prerogativa romane ecclesie.

1. Sabbati die circa vesperam, sedente dompno apostolico in atrio iuxta ecclesiam,
venit archipresbiter indutus casula, cum clericis illius ecclesie cui electus
consecrandus est, et flectens genua ante apostolicum benedictionem petit dicens:
. . .

4. Benedictione completa, interrogat eos dompnus apostolicus: Omnia recte quod
vos fatigatis fratres? Resp.: Ut Deus et dominus noster concedat nobis
pastorem. . . . Et si plures vel pauciores habeat, respondeat de illis. Et si non est
presbiter, interrogetur et respondeat de ordine quem habet et de tempore ipsius.
Interr.: Habuit coniugium? Resp.: Minime. Si tamen habuit, predicatur hoc
pontifici et respondeatur: Tu scis, domine.

5. Tunc profertur decretum et legitur hoc modo: . . . .

6. Hoc lecto, prosequitur apostolicus et dicit: Videte ne aliquam promissionem vobis fecerit, quia simoniacum est et contra canones. Resp.: Absit. Et dicit apostolicus: Ducatur. Tunc venit ipse electus planeta indutus et benedictionem petit dicens: . . . .

7. Tunc interrogat eum apostolicus: Omnia recte quod te fatigasti, frater? Resp.: Quod ego dignus non fui, isti confratres mei elegerunt me sibi preesse pastorem. . . . Et si plures vel pauciores habeat, respondeat de numero illorum. Interr.: Habuisti coniugium? Resp.: Minime. Si tamen habuerit, predicto hoc consecratori in examinatione vel alias respondeat:
Tu scis, domine.

8. . . . Et dicit papa: Tu videris.
Quia ergo omnium in te vota conveniunt, hodie abstinebis et cras, Deo annuente, consecraberis.
Resp.: Precepisti. Tunc descendunt singuli in loca sua.

Selection Presentation: the Germanic model
PRC.XI.
9. Provideat autem ipse electus cum suis quod mane diei sequentis parata sint et in promptu omnia sibi necessaria in consecratione, videlicet calige, sandalia, amictus, alba, cingulum, stola, manipulum, tunicella, dalmatica, planeta et pluviale albi coloris, cirothece, anulus pontificalis et alius anulus parvus, mitra aurifrixiata, baculus pastoralis, duo bacilia, tobalia pro manibus tergendis, tobalia ad ponendum coram consecratore, tobalia et pecten ad pectinandum, mica panis ad tergendum manus et caput, duo brachia tele de cortina ad circumligandum caput in unctione, duo magni panes involuti duabus tobaliis, due magne phyale plene vino et duo magna torticia ad offerendum, libri missalis et pontificalis, faldistorium bassum et tapetum, sacerdos cum superpellicio et tobalia qui serviat electo de libro et palafredus coopertus bocharamine.

10. Dominica vero die et non in alia festivitate, progreditur dompnus apostolicus cum electo et cuncto clero et populo ad ecclesiam ubi ipsam fieri vult ordina-tionem et ingressus sacrarium induit se vestimenta pontificalia. Post pusillum procedit e sacrario cum diaconibus et reliquis ministris sicut diebus dominicis mos est procedendi.

11. Et electus sacris vestibus indutus, scilicet amicto, alba, manipulo, stola et cinctorio et pluviali tantum procedit simul cum eo et ceteris episcopis e sacrario ante altare, factoque conventu, antequam fiat confessio, fiat examinatio talis.

12. Dum autem ista examinatio legitur, episcopi et papa consecrantes mitras debent habere in capite, sed consecrandi nequaquam.

13. Antiqua sanctorum patrum. . . .

. . . Vis beato Petro cui a Deo data est potestas ligandi atque solvendi michique eius vicario successoribusque meis fidem et subiectionem per omnia exhibere?

Si alius consecrat vice pape dicit: Vis beato Petro cui a Deo data est potestas ligandi atque solvendi et eius vicario sanctissimo patri nostro domino N. summo pontifici eiusque successoribus fidem et subiectionem per omnia exhibere.

14. Ita igitur examinatus et bene instructus, cum consensu clericorum et laicorum ac conventu totius provincie episcoporum in nomine domini ordinetur.

15. De officio episcopi. Episcopum oportet iudicare, interpretari, consecrare, confirmare, ordinare, offerre et baptizare.

Consecration Presentation:

PRC.XI.16. Facto itaque scrutinio, deducitur consecrandus ad pontificem, cuius, si sit papa, osculatur pedem et os; si vero alius, manum et os. Et deinde dompnus apostolicus cum episcopis et ministris altaris et ipso quoque electo accedens ad altare, facit confessionem et mox ut vult indicat cantori et ille incipit antiphonam eiusdem dominice ad introitum et cetera ex more et electus revertitur ad locum ubi fuerat indutus.

17. Sequitur oratio pro electo. . . . Oratio. *Adesto*. . . .

18. . . . archidiaconus cum acolitis et subdiacono et induat ipsum electum tunicam, dalmaticam, planetam et cambagos. Et duo episcopi casulis induti deducant eum superius ante altare et

[*PRC*γ coram apostolico. 19. Et ille sedendo cum mitra dicit: Episcopum oportet iudicare, interpretari, consecrare, confirmare, ordinare, offerre et baptizare.

20. Deinde surgens et deposita mitra]
convertens se apostolicus ad circumstantes, dicit hanc orationem:
Oremus, dilectissimi nobis, . . . Per.

21. Et statim incipit Kyrie eleison cum letania et prosternit se ordinator simul cum electo accumbente ad sinistram ipsius et ceteris episcopis ac ministris ante altare super stramenta, usquedum dicit scola: Agnus Dei.

III. The Presentation of the Bishop-Elect in the Pontifical of Guillaume Durand de Mende[50]

A. THE *PGD* AND THE RITUAL CONTEXT OF EPISCOPAL ORDINATION

"In the years 1292–1295 there arose in the small diocese of Mende in the south of France a pontifical which for the wider development of pontifical liturgy would become of as much decisive importance as the *PRG*, the *Pontificale Guilelmi Durandi* (the *PGD*)."[51] Its editor was the

Dominican canonist, Guillaume Durand, bishop of Mende in 1285, author of a famous compilation of criminal law (the *Speculum iudiciale*) and the *Rationale divinorum officiorum*.[52] He died in Rome in 1296 and was buried in the Dominican church, Santa Maria sopra Minerva.

His Pontifical was begun as early as 1292 and was published between 1293 and the autumn of 1295.[53] There is no title to the work other than "Here begins the book of pontifical *ordos*." Durand's genius showed itself in many aspects of the book, one of the most obvious being its division into three parts:

The first part concerns blessings of persons, ordinations and consecrations.

The second part concerns consecrations and blessings of other things both sacred and profane.[54]

The third part concerns those things related to ecclesiastical offices.[55]

Durand begins Book I with another innovation—moving the frequently celebrated rite of confirmation to the first place in the book. The rites for the seven ecclesiastical orders follow confirmation and the rites for psalmist and becoming a cleric. Before the chapters describing the ordination rites for the sacred orders, Chapter X articulates a few general canonical principles. Its first section, for example, states the theological understanding of the day regarding the sacramental status of the episcopacy:[56]

PGD.X.1. The sacred and major orders are subdiaconate, diaconate, and presbyterate. The episcopal order is not understood simply under the appellation of a sacred order, because it is called the summit, the culmination, the apex and the throne of the dignity of the priesthood.

Chapter XIV is "Concerning the examination, ordination and consecration of a bishop," comprising nos. 1–64. No. 65 is the promise of obedience by the new bishop to the metropolitan, and no. 66 is a brief rite for the imposition of the pallium. Rites for the ordination of the pope and for the various stages in monastic life fall after these.

Sources for the *PGD* certainly include the *PRXII* and the *PRG*,[57] but the *PRC* (particularly recension γ[58]) was an even more significant source. Throughout his work, Durand makes reference to "the roman *ordo*" and "use of the roman church" by which he means the *PRC*.[59]

Specifically regarding episcopal ordination, Luca Brandolini states that Guillaume Durand provided "the definitive touch to the already complex and confused rite [which was] then canonized by the Roman pontifical first published by Clement VIII,"[60] the Roman Pontifical of 1595. This is a reasonable conclusion, given that it is to Durand that we owe these additions to the rite of episcopal ordination: the consecrator's triple blessing in the midst of the litany, the imposition of hands before the consecration prayer with the words "Receive the holy spirit," the singing of the *Veni sancte spiritus* during the anointing of the head and "Behold how good" (Psalm 133) with its antiphon during the anointing of hands and thumb, the formulas for the blessing of the crozier and ring and for the blessing and imposition of miter and gloves, the return of the ritual for the enthronement of the new bishop, the singing of the *Te Deum* during the procession through the church, and the words of the pontifical solemn blessing *(Sit nomen domini benedictum.)*[61]

B. ANALYSIS OF THE LITURGICAL UNITS

1. *Roman Selection Presentation*

a. ROMAN SELECTION PRESENTATION: TEXT

PGD.I.XIV. Regarding the examination, ordination and consecration of a bishop.

1. . . . On Saturday before the Sunday set for him to be consecrated, at the hour for vespers, the metropolitan is to be in place on the faldstool in the atrium of the church. . . . And at least two suffragan bishops particularly called together for this are to be similarly in place on faldstools at his right and left.

2. Then the archpresbyter or archdeacon of the church for which he is the elect, . . . led by two canons of the same church one on each side they come before the metropolitan, . . .

[3.–4. The archpresbyter or archdeacon asks the threefold blessing of the metropolitan.]

5. And so when the blessing is finished, the metropolitan questions them. And the suffragans say the same silently: My son, what do you ask? The archdeacon responds: That God and our lord may grant us a pastor. Question: Do you have yours? He responds: We have. Question: Is he from the church itself or from another? He responds: From [the church] itself. Question: What in him pleases you? He responds: Sanctity, chastity, humility, goodness and all things that are pleasing to God. Question: Do you have the decree? He responds: We have. And the metropolitan says: Let it be read.

[6. The decree is read]

7. When the decree has indeed been read, the metropolitan continues and says: Consider that he must not have made any promise to you, because simony is also

against the canons. He responds: Far be it [from us]. And the metropolitan says: Let him be led in.

8. With lit candles, the elect still fasting, prepared in cope or chasuble if that is the practice, is led in procession before the metropolitan, with canons preceding him of the church for which he is the elect, the archdeacon and archpresbyter of the metropolitan church lead him one on each side. . . .

[9.–10. The elect asks a blessing with a threefold formula.]

11. Then the metropolitan questions him: My son, what do you ask? The elect responds: Most holy father, my fellow brothers have chosen me, although unworthy, to preside over them as pastor.
[The elect is questioned about his rank and years in that rank, spouse and household, the books read in his church, and knowledge of the canons.]

[12. The metropolitan advises the elect regarding times for ordinations and the danger of simony.]
He responds: Far be it [from me]. And the metropolitan says: You will see [to it]. Therefore because the desires of all have agreed upon you, today you will abstain and tomorrow, God willing, you will be consecrated.
He responds: You have commanded, lord. But, if it is desirable, he may dispense with that so that [the elect] may eat. Then he assigns to him a wise confessor from his church, to whom he may confess his sins.

[13. The *consecrandus* prostrates himself for the singing of a psalm and its antiphon and a concluding prayer]
Then, when he rises and is given the blessing May the name of the lord, and so on by the metropolitan, they depart individually to their homes. . . .

b. ROMAN SELECTION PRESENTATION:
   COPIED BUT NOT IN USE
   Guillaume Durand records the texts he had adapted for the Roman Selection Presentation as if they actually occur. Only after describing the entire scrutiny given above does he add:

PGD.I.XIV.13. . . . Certain churches do not hold the evening scrutiny above, but, on sunday morning, it occurs according to the following.

No. 18 is even more specific:
PGD.I.XIV.18. The roman church, which does not administer the evening scrutiny, begins the office of consecration here, before the confession occurs before mass.

Citing the example of the Roman Saturday scrutiny, Andrieu explains Durand's principle: "Often, after having described the Roman usage, he recounts the [usage] that is followed elsewhere. . . . Sometimes it is even the Roman usage which comes in second place, with the one presented earlier seeming to be considered the more usual."[62]

For the sake of completeness, a brief analysis of the *PGD* version of the Roman Selection Presentation follows below; however, it will not be included as part of the overall structure of the Selection Presentation.

C. ROMAN SELECTION PRESENTATION:
  SATURDAY SCRUTINY

Saturday evening at least two suffragan bishops, accompanied by the archpriest or archdeacon and two canons from the vacant see, present the elect to the metropolitan. After a series of detailed acts of reverence, the metropolitan begins the interrogation of the representatives from the widowed church but with the opening question (originally from *OR34*) rewritten by Durand:

PGD.I.XIV.5. . . . My son, what do you ask?[63]

Questions concerning the elect's years as presbyter, previous marital commitment and state of his domestic affairs have been omitted by Durand; this abbreviated inquiry has become even more formalistic. The archdeacon gives the prescribed answer about the elect's worthiness: he is known for his sanctity, chastity, humility, and kindness. Then the election decree is called for and read.

D. ROMAN SELECTION PRESENTION: THE DECREE

The canonist Durand has taken care to revise the wording of the decree that was preserved in the *PRC*. (Only the *PRXII* records the full text.)

PRC.XI.	*PGD*.I.XIV.
5. . . . The clergy and people of the church of N. in the servitude of complete alliegance to the most blessed pope N. of the apostolic see conspicuous in dignity.	6. . . . The chapter of the church of N. in the servitude of complete alliegance to the most reverend in Christ father lord N. of the metropolitan see conspicuous in dignity.

Durand's revision reflects the ecclesiastical polity of the time: electors are no longer the clergy and people of the vacant see, but the canons of the cathedral chapter.

The reading of the decree[64] (public verification of the legitimacy of the selection) prompts the metropolitan to call for the presentation of the elect. Now a small, candlelit procession forms: the two canons from the cathedral of the vacant see precede the metropolitan's own archdeacon or archpresbyter who accompanies the elect. He has been fasting and is vested as a presbyter. Together they approach the consecrator who initiates the interrogation of the elect. Except for Durand's initial rewriting, the text is that first seen in *OR35B*:

PGD.I.XIV.11. Then the metropolitan questions him: My son, what do you ask? The elect responds: Most holy father, my fellow brothers have chosen me, although unworthy, to preside over them as pastor.

After the same long series of questions, the consecrator concludes the Roman evening scrutiny with the proclamation of consensus and consecration from *OR35B*:

PGD.I.XIV.12. . . . Therefore because the desires of all have agreed upon you, today you will abstain and tomorrow, God willing, you will be consecrated.

Another series of versicles and responses ends with a blessing by the metropolitan and all depart. The *PGD* marks the last time the text of the Roman scrutiny will be included within the rite of episcopal ordination.[65]

2. *Gallican Selection Presentation*

a. GALLICAN SELECTION PRESENTATION: TEXT

PGD.I.XIV.14. And thus on Sunday the following day, around the middle of [the hour for] terce, the metropolitan going into the church, in which the elect should be consecrated, enters the vestibule or sacristy wearing pontifical apparel, just as [if he were] about to celebrate mass. Then he goes out from the sacristy with the bishops present wearing amices, albs or surplices, stoles and capes or copes, with miters and croziers and with deacons and subdeacons and the rest of the ministers, going forth solemnly according to the practice for mass on sundays.

15. And the elect, prepared in amice, alb or surplice, stole, cincture and cope only, is led by two bishops one on each side after them, and they process in this way as far as the altar. Then the consecrator is in place on the faldstool before the altar, [his] back turned to the altar. The other bishops also sit on their faldstools in rank order on each side at [his] right and at [his] left below in the choir of the church, as if making a choir, holding their pontifical books on their knees.

16. Then the two bishop escorts, standing in the lower part of the choir of the church behind the bishops, holding the elect in [their] midst before the face of the consecrator, they present him to him, saying in a loud voice:

Reverend father, holy mother catholic church asks that you elevate this presbyter to the responsibility of the episcopacy.

And the consecrating [bishop] says:
Do you know him to be worthy?
The bishops respond:
As far as human frailty permits [one] to know, we know and believe him to be
worthy.
The consecrator and all respond:
Thanks be to God.

17. . . . And the consecrator in a moderate voice, in the manner of a reading,
begins the following examination of the council of Carthage. The other bishops
however follow in subdued voice and say whatever the consecrator says. And all
ought then to hold [their] miters and to sit.

18. The roman church, which does not administer the evening scrutiny, begins
the office of consecration here, before the confession is done before mass. On the
preceding day, nevertheless the fast is imposed on the *consecrandus* and another
cardinal confessor is assigned to him.

19. The examination which is begun [is done] completely. *Antiqua sanctorum
patrum.* . . .

Will you promise fidelity, submission and obedience to blessed Peter the apostle
to whom the power to bind and to loose was given by God, to his vicars the
roman pontiffs and to me his minister of the holy church of Besançon and to my
successors according to canonical authority? . . .

20. And with the scrutiny thus finished, the above-mentioned two bishops, who
earlier led and presented the elect, bring him to the consecrator and his hand is
reverently kissed.

b. GALLICAN SELECTION PRESENTATION:
   THE POSTULATION DIALOGUE

Sunday morning (Durand specifies 9:00)[66] the metropolitan enters the
church; bishops (with their own copies of the rite in their laps), deacons,
subdeacons, and other ministers are present. The elect, vested as a
presbyter, is presented to the metropolitan by two bishops.

Here at the beginning of the Selection Presentation of the bishop-elect,
Durand introduces a liturgical unit completely new to the Roman
pontifical tradition of episcopal ordination we have been studying:
the postulation dialogue. The *PRG*, *PRXII*, and *PRC* all begin the Gallican
examination immediately, with no other preliminary element than a
silent accompaniment of the elect before the consecrator.

Durand, however, has at hand a source containing the dialogue
identical to that previously examined in chapter 3, the text found in the
appendix of *The Benedictional of Archbishop Robert*. His source is most

likely the twelfth-century Pontifical of Besançon. (The Diocese of Mende is in the Province of Besançon and the version of the Gallican examination which Durand uses includes the promise of obedience to the metropolitan of Besançon [Bituricense]).[67]

Robert	Pontifical of Besançon	PGD.I.XIV.16
The fellow provincial bishops. offer the elect to the lord metropolitan with these words;	The fellow provincial bishops offer the elect to the lord archbishop with these words:	. . . the two bishops leading him . . . before the face of the consecrator, present him to him . . .
Reverend father. holy mother church. N. asks that you elevate this presbyter present to the responsibility of the episcopacy.	Reverend Father, holy Mother church N. asks that you elevate this presbyter present to the responsibility of the episcopacy.	Reverend father, holy mother catholic church asks that you elevate this presbyter to the responsibility of the episcopacy.
And the metropolitan should respond.	And the archbishop should respond:	
Do you know him to be worthy?	Do you know him to be worthy?	Do you know him to be worthy?
And the bishops [say].	And the bishops should respond:	And the bishops should respond:
As far as human frailty permits [one] to know. we know. and we believe him to be worthy.	As far as human frailty permits [one] to know, we know and we believe him to be worthy.	As far as human frailty permits [one] to know we know and we believe him to be worthy.
And all should respond.	And all should respond.	The consecrator and others should respond.
Thanks be to God.	Thanks be to God.	Thanks be to God.

Employing the dialogue allows Durand to return to both the traditional concern for consensus among the sees involved and the importance of the worthiness of the elect. In his version, however, those who present the elect, make the postulation, and testify to the elect's worthiness are two bishops, but not the fellow provincial bishops (or suffragans) of the earlier texts. Neither is the vacant see named. The consecrator's voice (in the response of "Thanks be to God") has increased in importance over participation of the entire assembly (omnes). Durand has adjusted elements of the text to suit his purposes.

One of those purposes appears to be greater symmetry between the diaconal, presbyteral, and episcopal ordination rites. Rather than copying the postulation dialogue word for word from his older Gallican source, he aligns that model to the diaconal and presbyteral texts from the *PRC*. Those prior texts needed no mention of the name of the local church. The one who made the postulation was "holy mother catholic church"; there was no other See involved from which the local church needed to be distinguished. The response of the archdeacon regarding the candidates' worthiness began with the words "As far as human frailty permits [one] to know," so Durand adapted that arrangement for the two bishops in his own text.

When viewed side by side, the three postulation dialogues reveal the symmetry Durand achieved:

PGD.I.XII.4	*PGD*.I.XIII.3	*PGD*.I.XIV.16
Regarding the ordination of a deacon	**Regarding the ordination of a presbyter**	**Regarding the examination, ordination and consecration of a bishop**
. . . holy mother catholic church asks that you ordain these subdeacons present to the responsibility of deacon.	. . . holy mother catholic church asks that you ordain these deacons present to the responsibility of presbyter.	. . . holy mother catholic church asks that you elevate this presbyter to the responsibility of the episcopacy.
Do you know them to be worthy?	Do you know them to be worthy?	Do you know them to be worthy?
As far as human frailty permits [one] to know, I know and I affirm them to be worthy of the responsibility of this office.	As far as human frailty permits [one] to know, I know and I affirm them to be worthy of the responsibility of this office.	As far as human frailty permits [one] to know, we know and we believe him to be worthy.
5. . . . With the help of our lord God and savior Jesus Christ, we choose these subdeacons present for the order of deacon.	4. . . . Nor is it in vain that we recall the ordinance of the Fathers, that the people also should be consulted concerning the choice of those who are to be appointed to the regulation of the altar . . . . . . Therefore	Thanks be to God.
If anyone has anything against them. . . .	if anyone has anything against them. . . .	

Until the *PGD*, this form of the postulation dialogue did not exist in the Roman pontifical tradition of episcopal ordination. Following the texts created by the bishop of Mende, the Roman Pontificals of 1485 and 1595 will continue (but significantly alter) this postulation dialogue when used for the ordination of a bishop.

c. SELECTION PRESENTATION:
OTHER ELEMENTS

The Gallican examination *(Antiqua sanctorum patrum)* follows immediately and includes the promise of fidelity to the metropolitan of *Bituricense* (Besançon). Then for the first time through all the rites studied thus far, the proclamation of consensus is severed from the examination and omitted. The examination ends with no proclamation of any kind, not "with the consent of the clerics and laity . . ." from the *PRG* nor the *Episcopum oportet*. The examination concludes with the elect's act of reverence to the consecrator.

d. SELECTION PRESENTATION: STRUCTURE

In the pontifical of Guillaume Durand, the structure of the Selection Presentation evinces a truncated form:

PGD

1st stage

Selection Presentation

	Sunday
presentation:	2 bishops
postulation:	elevate this presbyter
	examination
proclamation of consensus and consecration:	
	[ ]

3. *Consecration Presentation*

a. CONSECRATION PRESENTATION: TEXT

PGD.I.XIV.21. Thus when the confession has been done, the metropolitan goes up to the altar, the cantor commencing the antiphon at the entrance. The bishop escorts however who were sent ahead lead [the elect] to behind the altar. After he has humbled himself there, they return to their chairs in the choir in the order of the bishops and the archdeacon and acolytes vest him in sandals, dalmatic, chasuble and all pontifical [apparel], except for the ring, miter, and gloves.

22. It is to be noted however that the roman church never changes the office of the day because of the ordination of bishops. One nevertheless says the collect *Adesto suplicationibus nostris,* and so on, for the office of consecration and the insert [for the eucharistic prayer] and the post communion [prayer] written below. Many other churches however say the mass of the holy spirit and others say the following mass. . . .

23. . . . Prayer. *Adesto.* . . .

24. The reading of the epistle of blessed Paul the apostle to Timothy. . . .

25. When the gradual is finished, the two bishops who were sent ahead, who led him earlier, vested in chasubles, lead him to the steps before the altar. Then the consecrator, sitting before the middle of the altar, says toward him: *[Episcopum oportet]* A bishop is to judge, interpret, consecrate, confirm ordain, offer and baptize.

26. Standing he then says to those present: Prayer. *Oremus, dilectissimi nobis.* . . . Through. They respond: Amen.

27. And immediately both the consecrator as well as the bishops and elect lie down upon the faldstools, before the altar so that the elect remains to the left of the consecrator. The ministers also and the others prostrate on the carpet and the cantor begins the litany saying: *Kyrie eleison,* and so on, going through the entire [litany] in sequence. Look above [for the text of the litany], under the ordination of subdeacon.

28. After however he has said, That the homage of our service, and so on, and the response has been made by the choir to him, then the consecrator rising from [this position of] lying down and turning to the *consecrandus,* holding the pastoral staff with the left [hand], says first:
That you may deign to ble + ss this elect present. We ask you, hear us.
He says second:
[That] you may deign to ble + ss and to sanc + tify.
He says third:
[That] you may deign to ble + ss and to sanc + tify and to consecrate + ,

continually making the sign of the cross over him, and the other bishops do and say the same, those prostrate still keeping [that position] however, the choir also continually responding to each [line of the litany] in the same way. Then [the consecrator] lies down again, with the cantor resuming the litany and saying: That you may deign to graciously hear us, and so on, going through the entire [litany] in sequence.

29. When it is finished, all rise and, with the consecrator standing before the altar, [his] face toward the choir and the elect kneeling before him, the consecrator opens the book of the gospels, placing it upon the head and shoulders of the *consecrandus,* and two bishops hold it in place, keeping the text facing downward.

30. Then the ordainer imposes both hands upon his head saying:
Accipe spiritum sanctum.
All the bishops do and say the same, with others as needed holding the book one after another.

31. When this is done, with [the *consecrandus*] kneeling, the ordainer says in moderate voice and the other bishops also, but in subdued voice, with him: Prayer. *Propitiare.* . . .

32. Then the consecrator says in moderate voice, hands joined before the chest, and the other bishops also, holding the books, say the same in subdued voice: Preface. For ever and ever, and so on. Truly right, and so on. Honor of all dignity . . . dew of heavenly unction.

33. Here the consecrator, kneeling, is to begin the sequence, *Veni sancte spiritus.* Then immediately standing, while it is sung, he puts chrism on [the elect's] head in the manner of a cross, having first bound a twisted linen cloth around the head . . . reading:
May your head be anointed and consecrated with the heavenly blessing in the pontifical order. In the name of the fa+ther and the son+ and the holy + spirit. Amen. Peace be with you. And with your spirit.
And if there are several who are consecrated, this is repeated individually with each person. But according to the practice of some churches, all the bishops who are present one after another anoint his head by their hands in the same way, each saying: May you be anointed and consecrated, and so on, as above. That is not suitable according to the law or the custom of the roman church.

34. When the anointing and the sequence are finished, the pontiff again resumes [the prayer] in the original tone and says: May it flow down, O Lord, richly upon his head. . . .

35. After this the consecrator begins, with the schola following, the antiphon: Anointing on the head. . . . Psalm Behold how good. . . .

36. After the antiphon has begun however, immediately he confirms and anoints both of [the elect's] hands and thumbs with chrism . . . just as in the anointing of priests' hands which is done with oil, as is stated above, in the Chapter regarding the ordination of a priest. And while anointing he says: Prayer. God and father of our lord Jesus Christ. . . .

37. In certain churches only the palm of the right hand is anointed with chrism and oil mixed together, first by the consecrator and after this by all the bishops one after another. And then only the thumb of the same hand is anointed with chrism by the consecrator alone. This nevertheless neither law nor the practice of the roman church recommends.

49. Then immediately the *consecratus* offers by institution of pope Melchiades and by practice two loaves [of bread], two pitchers full of wine and two lit candles and the other customary items.

b. CONSECRATION PRESENTATION: INTRODUCTORY RITES

Once again asserting his own rubrical sense, Durand moves the moment during the ritual when the elect is vested as a bishop. Up to this point, the majority of liturgical texts we have examined have consistently placed this act after the gradual. In the *PGD*, however, it is during the introit that the elect is vested in sandals, dalmatic, chasuble, and all pontifical vesture except for the ring, miter, and gloves. Perhaps it seems more reasonable to have the elect thus vested from the beginning of the Mass of consecration.

In the next section, Durand reminds the reader that the Roman Church does not alter the Mass texts of the day for an ordination, a prescription that will enter the Roman Pontifical of 1485. The collect for the consecration continues to be *Adesto* (= *SVe* 942); it will be added to the collect of the day. Epistle and gradual follow.

c. CONSECRATION PRESENTATION: PROCLAMATION OF CONSENSUS

After the gradual, the same two bishops present the elect to the metropolitan who turns and speaks (not to the people *[PRG]* nor to those present *[PRXII, PRC]*) but to the elect alone. And he reads (not the proclamation of consensus and consecration joined with a bidding *[OR34]* nor the stirring *Servanda est [PRG]*) but, once again using the *PRC* γ as a model, the *Episcopum oportet* unit. Thus Durand repeats the insertion of the allocution *Episcopum oportet* into the void left by the *PRXII* (which omitted the exhortation, *Servanda est*) and by *PRC* α and β.

PRG.LXIII.28	PRXII.X.18	PRC.XI.19 γ	PGD.I.XIV.25
And turning to the people the ordainer	And turning to those present the *apostolicus*	And sitting with miter	Then the consecrator, sitting before the middle of the altar, says
says:		he says:	toward him:
The exhortation to the people when the bishop is ordained. Servanda est . . .		*[Episcopum oportet]* A bishop is to judge, interpret, consecrate, confirm, ordain, offer and baptize.	*[Episcopum oportet]* A bishop is to judge, interpret, consecrate, confirm, ordain, offer and baptize.

PRG.LXIII.28	PRXII.X.18	PRC.XI.19 γ	PGD.I.XIV.25
29. After these professions,		20. . . . turning to those present the *apostolicus*	26. Standing he then says to those present:
he says this preface:	says this exhortation:	says this oration:	Oration.
Oremus, dilectissimi nobis. . . .	Oremus, dilectissimi nobis. . . .	Oremus, dilectissimi nobis. . . .	Oremus, dilectissimi nobis. . . .

The change to episcopal vestments, the act bridging the Selection and Consecration Presentations, has occurred. Durand's choice of *Episcopum oportet* to fill the position of the proclamation of consensus and consecration from the earlier Roman and Gallican traditions and to introduce the bidding proves decisive. *Episcopum oportet* remains in this position until the reform of 1968.

Durand's rewriting of the beginning of the Consecration Presentation is all the more unusual considering his changes to this same structure in the ordination rite for presbyters. This section of the *PRC* γ consists of the postulation dialogue, the *Sacerdotem oportet* unit, followed by a brief proclamation of consensus which asks the assembly for any objections to the candidates. The bidding and litany occur immediately afterward.

Durand has substantially rewritten the *PRC* pattern of these elements for presbyteral ordination. He begins with the same postulation dialogue but then brings in from the *PRG* an adaptation of the allocution to the people at the ordination of presbyters which emphasizes:

PRG.XVI.24. . . . the ordinance of the Fathers, that the people also be consulted concerning the choice of those who are to be appointed to the regulation of the altar.

This allocution includes the opportunity for the assembly to voice their objections. In addition Durand then writes his own admonition to the people on the ministry of the presbyterate, incorporating the *Sacerdotem oportet* unit. The bidding and litany follow.

To enrich the presbyteral ordination rite in his Pontifical, Durand has retrieved the allocution/proclamation of consensus from the *PRG* and has composed his own lengthy admonition to be the bridge into the consecration. Yet in the episcopal rite, Durand does neither of these things. He does not bring the proclamation of consensus and consecration *(Servanda est)* from the *PRG* nor does he write an admonition on episcopal ministry using the *Episcopum oportet* unit.

Instead he eliminates the proclamation of consensus and consecration from its traditional place in the Selection Presentation and maintains the absence of a proclamation of consensus from the Consecration Presentation (while creating one for presbyteral ordination). Thus it is with the *PGD* that we encounter an episcopal ordination rite with no proclamation of consensus and consecration in either the Selection Presentation nor the Consecration Presentation. All that remains of the original proclamation structure is the bidding *MF (Oremus, dilectissimi nobis)* which the consecrator addresses to those present.

d. CONSECRATION: NEW ELEMENTS IN THE *PGD*

It is ironic that Guillaume Durand eliminates primary elements from the presentations at the same time as he multiplies secondary elements during the consecration. All of his elaborations will find their way into the Roman Pontificals of 1485 and of 1595, and all of his deletions remain excluded.

i. litany blessing

An example of Durand's creative elaborations occurs after the phrase in the litany related to those who have died. The consecrator stands with crozier in hand and prays over the elect, making signs of the cross over him each time:

PGD.I.XIV.28. . . . That you may deign to ble + ss this elect present.
. . . [That] you may deign to ble + ss and to sanc + tify.
. . . [That] you may deign to ble + ss and to sanc + tify and to consecrate +

And all the bishops present stand and imitate this ritual action in the middle of the litany. An earlier form of this blessing within the litany can be found not in the *PRC*,[68] but in the *PRXII* (manuscript L). Here the subdeacon sings twice (as part of the litany):

PRXII.X.20. . . . That you deign to bless and to consecrate this elect. . . .

while all the bishops make the sign of the cross over him.[69] Durand has found an elaboration of words and gesture from an earlier text that seems to him appropriate to the solemnity, copies it, adapts it to general episcopal use, and then both clarifies and expands the rubrics.[70]

ii. *Accipe spiritum sanctum*

A second example of Durand's elaboration: with the conclusion of the litany, as we have seen in previous texts, the consecrator places the open gospel book upon the head and shoulders of the elect; the two assisting bishops hold it in place. At this point, Durand again employs his own genius.

After the litany and before *Propitiare* and the consecration prayer, the consecrator imposes one hand upon the head of the elect and prays (in the words of John 20:22) "Receive the holy spirit." The other bishops do and say the same.[71]

What might be the impetus (besides Scripture) for this unusual, unattached, and deprecative element addressed to the elect himself to be inserted between the litany of saints and its concluding oration? In attempting to answer that question, it is important to note that the bishop of Mende also created two similar statements for his rites of presbyteral and diaconal ordination:

PGD.I.XIII.25. . . . Receive the holy spirit,
whose sins you forgive they are forgiven them and whose you retain they are retained.

PGD.I.XII.10. . . . Receive the holy spirit
for power and for resisting the devil and his temptations.

Perhaps as with the postulation dialogue, Durand is seeking greater symmetry between these three ordination rites, and thus creates a similiar, shorter statement for episcopal ordination which has lacked any such element up to this point. Since theologians of the day considered that the two greatest sacramental powers had already been received through presbyteral ordination (*PGD.I.XIII.17.* "Receive power to offer sacrifice to God and to celebrate mass for the living and for the dead" and 25. "Receive the holy spirit, whose sins you forgive they are forgiven them and whose you retain they are retained"), there was little left for a consecrator to pray over the bishop-elect except simply: "Receive the holy spirit."[72]

The laying on of hands by all the bishops at this point seems to be the only imposition of hands in the rite. Durand specifies that for the offering of the consecration prayer the consecrator's hands are to be joined before his chest. In the *PRC*, the rubrics prescribed the laying on of (both) hands by the bishops immediately before *Propitiare*, but Durand has removed that rubric. The prayer *Propitiare* follows this new ritual action now severed from its role as the prayer concluding the litany. Then the consecration prayer which the bishops offer with the consecrator begins as usual with the preface dialogue.

iii. *Veni sancte spiritus*

A third example: at the usual point (the words "the dew of heavenly unction"), the anointing of the elect's head begins, but in the *PGD* this element now includes the consecrator's intoning the sequence, *Veni sancte spiritus*. Several manuscripts (M [= Metz, Biblio. munic., *codex* 47], V [= Rome, Biblio. Vat., *codex Regin.*, 1930] and E [= Aix-en-Provence, Biblio. Méjanes, *cod.* 13]) add the alternate hymn, *Veni creator spiritus*, which was the hymn used in the *PRC* presbyteral ordination rite. Durand has borrowed the idea of an epicletic hymn from there, included one in both his episcopal and presbyteral rites, but changed the preference to the sequence, *Veni sancte spiritus*.

iv. other additions

At the conclusion of the consecration prayer with the head anointing formulary in its midst, Durand inserts into his pontifical texts several other new elements: the consecrator begins chanting Psalm 133 ("Behold how good") and its antiphon during the anointing of the hands;[73] he includes the usual prayer for episcopal hand anointing (*God and father of our lord Jesus Christ* = PRG.LXIII.37 where it was used for the "confirmation" of the thumb) but Durand uses the prayer both for the anointing of the hands and thumb. It is only after this anointing that the elect may be called *consecratus*.

The bishop of Mende also sees a need for the consecrator to bless the crozier and ring during the ordination rite itself before they may be given to the newly ordained. He composes new formulas for those blessings:

PGD.I.XIV.39. . . . Blessing of the crozier. Prayer. "God sustainer of human weakness. . . ."

PGD.I.XIV.41. Blessing of the ring. Prayer. "Creator and preserver of the human race. . . ."

The *PGD* includes the giving of the gospel book to the new bishop, a practice first cited in the *PRG* and then continued in the *PRXII* and the *PRC*. But after that Durand adds an intriguing rubric:

PGD.I.XIV.44. And presently in certain churches the consecrator opens the book of the gospels [which is] between the hands of the *consecratus* and sees a prognostication, about which one must not be anxious.

The consecrator opens the gospel book at random and exhorts the new bishop regarding events predicted in the Scripture text.[74] This rubric (fortunately!) does not continue in the tradition.

For the offertory of the Mass, Bishop Durand copies (from the *PRXII.X.32* and the *PRC.XI.γ33*) the list of gifts to be brought forward to the consecrator by the newly ordained himself: two loaves of bread, two pitchers full of wine, two lit candles, and other customary items. But only the bishop of Mende wants to impress upon the reader that this action was instituted for the episcopal ordination rite by Pope Melchiades (+314)!

While at the conclusion of the Mass, the *PRC* describes the imposition of the miter on the new bishop by the consecrator in silence, Guillaume Durand takes this opportunity to expand those rubrics. He creates a blessing for the miter and creates another formulary for its imposition, the wording of the latter providing the reader with a vivid sense of Durand's allegorial imagination which sees in the design of the miter a fearsome and radiant helmet:

PGD.I.XIV.56. . . . Lord, we place on the head of this your bishop and champion the helmet of protection and salvation, so that with face adorned and head armed with the horns of both testaments, he may appear fearsome to the adversaries of truth and, by the bounty of your grace, may he be their mighty enemy, you who endowed the face of Moses your servant, adorned from the fellowship of your discourse, with the brightest horns of your splendor and truth and commanded a crown to be placed upon the head of your high priest Aaron + . Through. Amen.

He inserts both these new elements before the prayer after Communion.

After the final blessing of the assembly by the consecrator, Durand creates still more rites. There is a new blessing for the episcopal gloves and a new formulary for their imposition which he has constructed around the image of Jacob, "his hands covered with the skins of young goats." Durand then retrieves the ritual of the enthronement of the new bishop[75] (whether this is his cathedra or not) and adds the singing of the *Te Deum* during it.

And finally, Durand adds another prayer by the consecrator and a solemn pontifical blessing of the people by the new bishop, omits any mention of the threefold *multos annos*, and provides for the taking of the oath to the metropolitan.

e. CONSECRATION PRESENTATION: STRUCTURE

The complexities Durand creates in the rite occur after the presentation. Its structure is quite simple.

PGD

2nd stage

Consecration Presentation

	introit
	episcopal vestments
	collect to gradual
presentation:	two bishops
proclamation of consensus and consecration:	
	Episcopum oportet
	bidding *MF*
consecration:	litany
	gospel book
	laying on of hands
	Accipe spiritum sanctum
	Propitiare
	consecration prayer
	consecration continues

C. CONCLUSION

For all of its contributions to the evolution of medieval episcopal liturgy, the *PGD* is often severely criticized. Salmon's evaluation is typical:

> When [Durand] changes something of the *PRC*, it is not to return to a more traditional element nor to simplify. On the contrary, he overloads the ceremonial, already sufficiently ample, with new rites, new formularies, chants, and detailed rubrics. When he is not innovating pure and simple, he is drawing from other non-Roman, probably Gallican, books. He has given the Roman pontifical this complicated and somewhat redundant form which, by wanting to increase the ceremony's solemnity, he only weighed down by concealing or making secondary the essential parts.[76]

Observation of the evolution of the presentations of the bishop-elect after Durand's redaction justifies Salmon's judgment:

PRG	PRXII	PRC	PGD
1st stage	*1st stage*	*1st stage*	*1st stage*
Selection	**Selection**	**Selection**	**Selection**
Presentation	**Presentation**	**Presentation**	**Presentation**
Sunday	Sunday	Sunday	Sunday
presentation	presentation	presentation	presentation
			2 bishops
			postulation
			elevate this
			presbyter
examination	examination	examination	examination
proclamation of	**proclamation of**	**proclamation of**	**proclamation of**
consensus and	**consensus and**	**consensus and**	**consensus and**
consecration	**consecration**	**consecration**	**consecration**
with the agreement/	with the agreement/	with the agreement/	[ ]
he may be ordained	he may be ordained	he may be ordained	
		[α β *Episcopum oportet*]	
2nd stage	*2nd stage*	*2nd stage*	*2nd stage*
Consecration	**Consecration**	**Consecration**	**Consecration**
Presentation	**Presentation**	**Presentation**	**Presentation**
Sunday	Sunday	Sunday	Sunday
introit to gradual	introit to gradual	introit to gradual	introit
episcopal vestments	episcopal vestments	episcopal vestments	episcopal vestments
			collect to gradual
presentation	**presentation**	**presentation**	**presentation**
2 bishops	2 bishops	2 bishops	2 bishops
proclamation of	**proclamation of**	**proclamation of**	**proclamation of**
consensus and	**consensus and**	**consensus and**	**consensus and**
consecration	**consecration**	**consecration**	**consecration**
Servanda est	[ ]	[γ *Episcopum oportet*]	*Episcopum oportet*
[CD: with the			
agreement/he may			
be ordained]			
[AV: optional sermon]			
bidding *MF*	bidding *MF*	bidding *MF*	bidding *MF*
consecration	**consecration**	**consecration**	**consecration**
litany	litany	litany	litany
gospel book	gospel book	gospel book	gospel book
laying on of hands	laying on of hands	laying on of hands	laying on of hands
			Accipe spiritum
			sanctum
Propitiare	*Propitiare*	*Propitiare*	*Propitiare*
consecration	consecration	consecration	consecration
prayer	prayer	prayer	prayer
consecration	consecration	consecration	consecration
continues	continues	continues	continues

Within the Selection Presentation, Durand adds a postulation dialogue which allows a formalized testimony to the worthiness of the elect, but he then weakens it by eliminating the name of the vacant see and by removing mention of the relationships between those who testify. He also legitimates the omission of a proclamation of consensus and consecration rather than preserve any of the previous proclamations:

OR34/35/36/35B Because the desires of all have agreed upon you, today you will abstain and tomorrow, if it is pleasing to God, you would be consecrated.

MF Seruanda est. . . . By the will of the Lord, therefore, in place of N. of pious memory, with the testimony of the presbyters and of the whole clergy and with the advice of the citizens and those assembled, we believe that the reverend N. should be elected. . . .

PRG/PRXII/PRC And thus examined and well prepared with the consent of the clerics and laity and the agreement of the bishops of the entire province . . . he may be ordained.

The bishop of Mende deletes any such expression of consensus achieved and instead directs the elect to kiss the hand of the consecrator:

*PGD.*I.XIV.20. And the scrutiny thus finished, the above-mentioned bishops, who earlier led and presented the elect, bring him to the consecrator whose hand is reverently kissed.

It is this reverence to the consecrator which introduces the consecration stage, not a proclamation of consensus.

Within the Consecration Presentation, in the elements before the bidding, the changes are less momentous. As is clear from the time of the *PRG,* the proclamation of consensus and consecration does not fulfill its original function well. The earlier *PRG* recensions maintain some sense of the importance of this ritual element and place the exhortation, *Servanda est,* at this point.

But the bipartite nature of the proclamation (consensus *and* consecration, leading to the bidding) was abandoned early on. After sorting through the other models (optional sermon, repetition of the proclamation from the selection stage, the bidding by itself), Durand makes the understandable choice of *Episcopum oportet.* Thus by Durand's hand, expression of consensus in the presentation of the bishop-elect is kept to a standardized, ritualized minimum:

*PGD.*I.XIV.16.
. . . And the consecrating [bishop] says:

Do you know him to be worthy?
The bishops respond:
As far as human frailty permits [one] to know, we know and we believe him to be worthy.

Chapter 5 will trace the two stages of the ordination process, now well canonized in structure, through the *editio princeps* of Piccolomini and Burchard created for Pope Innocent VIII and the post-Tridentine *editio typica* of Pope Clement VIII.

Texts of the Pontifical of Guillaume Durand:

In prima de personarum benedictionibus, ordinationibus et consecrationibus agitur.
In secunda parte de consecrationibus et benedictionibus aliarum tam sacrarum quam prophanarum rerum agitur.
In tertia parte de quibusdam ecclesiasticis officiis agitur.

PGD.I.X.1. Sacri et maiores ordines sunt subdiaconatus, diaconatus, et presbiteratus. Episcopalis autem ordo sub appellatione sacrorum ordinum simpliciter non intelligitur, quoniam illa summitas sacerdotii culmen et apex atque thronus dicitur dignitatis.

Roman Selection Presentation:

PGD.I.XIV. De examinatione, ordinatione et consecratione episcopi.

1. . . . Sabbato namque ante dominicam ad consecrandum illum statutam, hora vespertina, metropolitanus resideat super faldistorium in atrio ecclesie, . . . Et suffraganei episcopi duo ad minus ad hoc specialiter convocati a dextris et a sinistris eius super faldistoria similiter resideant, . . .

2. Tunc archipresbiter vel archidiaconus ecclesie ad quam est electus, . . . deductus hinc et inde a duobus canonicis eiusdem ecclesie veniunt coram metropolitano. . . .

5. Benedictione itaque completa, interrogat eos metropolitanus. Et suffraganei etiam eadem tacite dicunt: Fili mi, quid postulas?
Respondet archidiaconus: Ut Deus et dominus noster concedat nobis pastorem. Interrogatio: Habetis vestrum? Respondet: Habemus. Interr.: Est de ipsa ecclesia aut de alia? Resp.: De ipsa. Interr.: Quid vobis complacuit in illo? Resp.: Sanctitas, castitas, humilitas, benignitas et omnia que Deo placita sunt.
Interr.: Habetis decretum? Resp.: Habemus. Et metropolitanus dicit: Legatur.

7. Sane decreto lecto, prosequitur metropolitanus et dicit: Videte ne aliquam promissionem vobis fecerit, quia simoniacum et contra canones est. Resp.: Absit. Et metropolitanus dicit: Ducatur. . . .

8. Accensis autem cereis, electus adhuc ieiunus, pluviali vel planeta si sit mos paratus, ducitur processionaliter coram metropolitano, precedentibus eum canonicis ecclesie ad quam est electus, archidiacono et archipresbitero ecclesie metropolitane hinc inde deducentibus eum. . . .

11. Tunc interrogat eum metropolitanus: Fili mi, quid postulas?
Respondet electus: Sanctissime pater, confratres mei elegerunt me, licet indignum, sibi preesse pastorem. . . .

12. . . . Resp.: Absit. Et metropolitanus dicit: Tu videris. Quia ergo omnium vota in te conveniunt, hodie abstinebis et cras, Deo annuente, consecraberis. Resp.: Precepisit, domine. Sed, si expediat, dispenset cum illo ut comedat. Tunc deputat ei aliquem discretum de sua ecclesia confessorem, cui peccata sua confiteatur.

13. . . . Tunc, illo surgente et data per metropolitanum benedictione Sit nomen domini, et cet., discedant singuli ad domos suas. Quedam tamen ecclesie non faciunt premissum serotinum scrutinium, sed, mane die dominico, proceditur prout sequitur.

18. Ecclesia romana, que non curat de scrutinio serotino, incipit hic officium consecrationis, priusquam fiat confessio ante missam.

PRC.XI.5. . . . Beatissimo pape Ill.apostolice sedis dignitate conspicuo, clerus et populus Ill. ecclesie totius devotionis famulatum.

PGD.I.XIV.6. . . . Reverendissimo in Christo patri domino Ill. metropolice sedis dignitate conspicuo capitulum illius ecclesie totius devotionis famulatum.

Gallican Selection Presentation:

14. Dominica itaque die sequenti, circa mediam tertiam, metropolitanus intrans ecclesiam, in qua debet consecrari electus, ingreditur vestibulum seu sacrarium, induens pontificalia indumenta, sicut missam celebraturus. Deinde egreditur e sacrario cum episcopis presentibus indutis amictibus, albis vel superpelliciis, stolis et cappis seu pluvialibus, cum mitris et cambucis et cum diaconis et subdiaconis et reliquis ministris, prout est mos procedendi sollempniter in dominicis diebus ad missam.

15. Et electus, paratus amictu, alba vel superpellicio, stola, cinctorio et pluviali tantum, deductus a duobus episcopis hinc et inde post eos, sicque usque ante altare procedunt. Tunc consecrator resident super faldistorium coram altare, verso dorso ad ipsum altare. Ceteri quoque episcopi super sua faldistoria hinc inde a dextris et sinistris eius inferius in choro ecclesie seriatim sedent, quasi chorum facientes, libros pontificales super genua tenentes.

16. Deinde duo episcopi ductores, stantes in inferiori parte chori ecclesie post episcopos, medium tenentes electum contra faciem consecratoris, offerunt illum sibi, alta voce dicentes: Reverende pater, postulat sancta mater ecclesia catholica ut hunc presbiterum ad onus episcopatus sublevetis.

Et consecrans dicit: Scitis illum esse dignum?

Respondent episcopi: Quantum humana fragilitas nosce sinit, scimus et credimus illum esse dignum.

Respondent consecrator et alii: Deo gratias.

17. . . . Et consecrator media voce, in modum lectionis, incipit sequentem examinationem Cartaginensis concilii. Ceteri vero episcopi prosequuntur submissa voce et dicunt quecumque dixerit consecrator. Et omnes debent tunc mitras tenere et sedere.

18. Ecclesia romana, que non curat de scrutinio serotino, incipit hic officium consecrationis, priusquam fiat confessio ante missam. Die tamen precedenti, indicitur consecrando ieiunium et ei aliquis cardinalis deputatur confessor.

19. Examinatio que incipitur absolute. Antiqua sanctorum patrum. . . .

. . . Vis beato Petro apostolo cui a Deo data est potestas ligandi atque solvendi, eiusque vicariis romanis pontificibus atque sancte Bituricensi ecclesie michique eius ministro et successoribus meis fidem, subiectionem et obedientiam secundum canonicam auctoritatem exhibere? . . .

20. Expleto itaque scrutinio, prefati duo episcopi, qui prius deduxerunt et presentaverunt electum, ducunt eum ad consecratorem et osculatur reverenter manus illius. . . .

Consecration Presentation:

21. Facta itaque confessione, metropolitanus ascendit ad altare, cantore antiphonam ad introitum inchoante. Premissi vero episcopi ductores ducunt illum post altare. Quo ibi demisso, redeunt ad sedes suas in choro in ordine episcoporum et archidiaconus et acoliti induunt illum sandalia, dalmaticam, casulam et omnia pontificalia, anulo, mitra et cirothecis exceptis.

22. Illud autem notandum est quod ecclesia romana propter ordinationes episcoporum numquam mutat officium diei. Dicit tamen pro officio consecrationis collectam Adesto suplicationibus nostris, et cet., et infra actionem et postcommunionem infrascriptas. Alie vero ecclesie plures dicunt missam de spiritu sancto et alie dicunt missam sequentem. . . .

23. . . . Oratio. Adesto. . . .

24. Lectio epistole beati Pauli apostoli ad Timotheum. . . .

25. Finito graduali, premissi duo episcopi, qui eum prius deduxerunt, planetis induti deducunt eum ad gradus ante altare. Tunc consecrator, sedens ante medium altaris, versus ad illum dicit:

Episcopum oportet iudicare, interpretari, consecrare, confirmare ordinare, offerre et baptizare.

26. Deinde stans dicit ad circumstantes:

Oratio. Oremus, dilectissimi nobis, ut huic viro . . . largitatem. Per. Resp.: Amen.

27. Et mox tam consecrator, quam episcopi et electus accumbunt super faldistoria, coram altari, ita quod electus maneat a sinistris consecratoris. Ministri etiam et alii se super stramenta prosternunt et cantor incipit letaniam dicens: Kyrie eleison, et. cet., prosequendo totam. Require supra, sub ordinatione subdiaconi.

28. Postquam autem, dixerit: Ut obsequium servitutis nostre, et cet., sibique a choro responsum fuerit, tunc consecrator ab accubitu surgens et ad consecrandum se volvens, baculum pastoralem cum sinistra tenens, dicit primo:

Ut hunc presentem electum bene + dicere digneris. Te rogamus, audi nos. Secundo dicit: Bene + dicere et sancti + ficare digneris
Tercio dicit: Bene + dicere et sancti + ficare et consecrare + digneris,

producendo semper signum crucis super illum, idemque faciunt et dicunt ceteri episcopi, prostrati tamen semper manentes, choro etiam semper hec eadem respondente. Deinde iterum accumbit, cantore resumente letaniam et dicente: Ut nos exaudire digneris, et cet., prosequendo totam.

29. Qua finita, surgunt omnes et, consecratore ante altare stante, vultu ad chorum verso et electo ante illum genu flectente, consecrator aperit codicem evangeliorum, ponens illum super caput et scapulas consecrandi, et duo episcopi sustinent illum, littera ex parte inferiori manente.

30. Tunc ordinator imponit utramque manum super caput illius dicens: Accipe spiritum sanctum. Idemque faciunt et dicunt omnes episcopi, tam tenentes librum quam alii successive.

31. Quo facto, illo genu flectente, dicit ordinator media voce et etiam alii episcopi, submissa tamen voce, cum ipso:
Oratio. Propitiare. . . .

32. Deinde consecrator dicit voce mediocri, iunctis manibus ante pectus, et alii etiam episcopi, tenentes libros, idem dicunt voce submissa:
Prephatio. Per omnia secula seculorum, etc. Vere dignum, etc. Honor omnium dignitatum . . . unguenti rore sanctifica.

33. Hic incipiat consecrator, flexis genibus, sequentiam Veni sancte spiritus.
Et mox surgens, dum cantatur, mittit crisma in caput illius in modum crucis, circumligato prius capite lineo panno retorto . . . legendo: Ungatur et consecretur caput tuum celesti benedictione in ordine pontificali. In nomine pa+tris et fi+lii et spiritus + sancti. Amen. Pax tecum. Et cum spiritu tuo. Et si plures sunt qui consecrantur, hoc in persona cuiuslibet singulariter repetatur. Sed et secundum morem quarumdam ecclesiarum, omnes episcopi qui adsunt similiter perungunt successive caput illius manibus et singuli dicunt: Inungatur et consecretur, et cet., ut supra. Quod nec iuri nec ecclesie romane consuetudini consentaneum est.

34. Expleta unctione et finita sequentia, pontifex iterum resumat in pristino tono et dicat: Hoc, domine, copiose in caput eius. . . .

35. Post hec consecrator inchoat, scola prosequente, antiphonam: Unguentum in capite. . . . Ps. Ecce quam bonum. . . .

36. Inchoata autem antiphona, mox confirmat et inungit ambas manus illius et pollices cum crismate . . . , sicut in unctione manuum sacerdotis, que fit cum oleo, supra, in Titulo de ordinatione sacerdotis, dictum est. Et perungendo dicit: Oratio. Deus et pater domini nostri Iesu Christi. . . .

37. In quibusdam tamen ecclesiis palma dextre manus tantum inungitur cum crismate et oleo simul mixtis, primo per consecratorem et postea per omnes episcopos successive. Et deinde pollex eiusdem manus ungitur cum crismate tantum per solum consecratorem. Hoc tamen nec ius nec ecclesie romane mos commendat.

44. Et mox in quibusdam ecclesiis consecrator aperit librum evangeliorum inter manus consecrati et videt pronosticum, de quo non est curandum.

49. Tunc consecratus offert ex institutione Melchiadis pape et de more offert duos panes, duas amphoras vino plenas et duos cereos accensos et alia consueta.

56. . . . Imponimus, domine, capiti huius antistitis et agoniste tui galeam munitionis et salutis, quatinus decorata facie et armato capite cornibus utriusque testamenti terribilis appareat adversariis veritatis et, te ei largiente gratiam, impugnator eorum robustus existat, qui Moysi famuli tui faciem ex tui sermonis consortio decoratam lucidissimis tue claritatis ac veritatis cornibus insignisti et capiti Aaron pontificis tui tyaram imponi iussisti +. Per. Amen.

Text from presbyteral ordination:
PGD.I.XIII.25. . . . Accipe spiritum sanctum, quorum remiseris peccata remittuntur eis et quorum retinueris retenta erunt.

Text from diaconal ordination:
PGD.I.XII.10. . . . Accipe spiritum sanctum ad robur et ad resistendum diabolo et temptationibus eius.

NOTES

[1] Hereafter *PRXII*.

[2] In addition to the specific references cited in footnotes in the three paragraphs that follow, I have also relied on information provided by Vogel, *Medieval Liturgy*, 249–251.

[3] "la souche commune de tous les livres épiscopaux romains du XIIe siècle. . . ." Vogel and Elze, *PRG* III, 51.

[4] ". . . la famille romaine . . . un groupe spécial, dont les membres sont facilement reconnaissables." Andrieu, *PRXII*, 9.

[5] Kleinheyer, *Die Priesterweihe*, 171.

[6] ". . . bisher noch sehr wenig organisch in den Ritus eingebaut waren." Ibid., 173.

[7] It is noteworthy that the later Roman rite never validated the aberration of the *PRG's* placement of episcopal ordination rites (i.e., forty chapters *after* the presbyteral rites), but immediately returned them to the position they held in the earlier *ordines romani*, i.e., after the rite of presbyteral ordination while still keeping them outside the *cursus*. See Pierre Jounel, "Le nouveau rituel d'ordination," *LMD* 98 (1969) 64.

[8] Andrieu, *OR* IV, 80; Vogel describes the work further as "an excellent example of what happened to an RGP during the XI century at Rome before the Gregorian liturgists attempted to compile a new book. . . ." *Medieval Liturgy*, 265, n. 276.

[9] ". . . un authentique *ordo* romain décrivant la séance du samedi soir." Andrieu, *PRXII*, 12; Kleinheyer, *Die Priesterweihe*, 168, n. 7.

[10] Manuscripts B C O record that the elect enters alone, while L explains that Roman custom has the elect presented by a deacon on his right and a subdeacon on his left.

[11] Andrieu, *PRXII*, 12.

[12] ". . . non erano rari i casi di uno stesso documento che prescrivesse i due diversi tipi d'esame." Santantoni, *L'Ordinazione episcopale*, 128.

[13] Roger Reynolds, "The *De Officiis VII Graduum:* Its Origins and Early Medieval Development," *Mediaeval Studies* 34 (1972) 113–151.

[14] Ibid., 117.

[15] Ibid., 128.

[16] Quotations from this paragraph are from Reynolds, "The *De Officiis VII Graduum*," 135, 145, and 150.

[17] Bradshaw, *Ordination Rites*, 39.

[18] Comparison of the *PRXII* combined prayer for hand and thumb with the two separate texts in the *PRG* and *OR35B* reveals a fascinating and subtle theology at work. The *PRG* included a formula to confirm the thumb. Andrieu explains the logic: the thumb need only be "confirmed," having already been consecrated (along with the whole hand) at presbyteral ordination. For some reason, the more recent recensions of the *PRG* also added *consecratio manuum*, a text from presbyteral ordination of *MF. OR35B* preserved both texts. The compiler of the *PRXII* noted the redundancy and solved it with precision. The *PRG* presbyteral prayer is excised, and the episcopal formula for the thumb is retained but expanded so that the hand is appropriately "confirmed" and the thumb itself deliberately consecrated with chrism in the sign of the cross. See Andrieu, "La carrière ecclésiastique des papes et les documents liturgiques du moyen âge," *RSR* 21 (1947) 105.

[19] There are qualifying commentaries, as we will see, in both the Pontifical of the Roman Curia and the Pontifical of Guillaume Durand.

[20] The caution against ordaining *curiales* was first cited in *OR34*.28 but is originally from the fourth century. Mention of them in manuscripts from the twelfth century marks this part of the rite as "an archaic formula, mechanically reproduced in the chancelleries, although it no longer corresponded to the practices of the times." ("[U]ne formule archaïque, machinalement reproduite dans les chancelleries, bien qu'elle ne répondît plus aux usages du temps.") Andrieu, *OR* III, 577 and 579.

[21] Vogel, *Medieval Liturgy*, 251.

[22] "Il faut donc conclure qu'un liturgiste travaillant à Rome, ayant sous les yeux un pontifical de la forme B C O, résolut d'en donner une édition revue et augmentée. Il refondit les rubriques et enregistra un certain nombre de détails nouveaux, qu'il connaissait pour les avoir lui-même directement observés au cours de cérémonies accomplies en sa présence dans la cité apostolique. Peut-être même, en certains cas, ne se borna-t-il pas à rapporter des usages constatés et hasarda-t-il des innovations personnelles, qui lui semblaient souhaitables et justifiées. En un temps où maints détails du cérémonial, trop sommairement décrits dans les livres courants, cherchaient encore leur forme définitive, de telles initiatives, de la part d'un liturgiste autorisé, n'avaient rien d'anormal." Andrieu, *PRXII*, 103–104.

[23] *PRG*.LXIII.1 (emphasis added).

[24] Vogel, *Medieval Liturgy*, 251.

[25] "Cet examen gallican fait double emploi avec le *scrutinium serotinum* romain, et l'on comprehend que, retenu par la liturgie romaine, il ait évincé le dit *scrutinium*." Batiffol, "La liturgie du sacre des évêques dans son évolution historique," *RHE* 23 (1927) 750.

[26] "L'ancien rituel romain des ordinations tombe en désuétude et les clercs instruits considèrent comme seul normal celui que décrivent les livres francs ou germains et notamment le pontifical romano-germanique." Andrieu, *OR* I, 514.

[27] "Le Pontificale du XIIe siècle et celui de la Curie au XIIIe siècle . . . ont toujours la cérémonie du samedi soir; elle a lieu en principe dans l'atrium de l'église." Salmon, "Le rite du sacre des évêques," 33.

[28] ". . . tandis qu'autrefois il avait lieu tout entier la veille, dans les pontificaux du XIIe, du XIIIe siècle et dans celui de Guillaume Durand, il sera transféré en grande partie au jour même du sacre." Ibid., 34.

[29] "Dort war es freilich ein Relikt; denn spätestens mit dem *PRG* richtet man sich auch in Rom nach anderen Traditionen." Kleinheyer, "Ordinationen und Beauftragungen," 31 n. 22.

[30] Vogel, *Medieval Liturgy*, 266.

[31] Andrieu, *PRXII*, 12.

[32] Hereafter *PRC*.

[33] Andrieu, *PRC*, iii.

[34] Vogel, *Medieval Liturgy,* 252.

[35] "Une famille . . . cohérente. . . . Sans aucun doute, ils dépendent tous d'un commun ancêtre." Andrieu, *PRC,* 299.

[36] Adrien Nocent, "Storia dei libri liturgici romani," in *Anàmnesis 2: La Liturgia, panorama storico generale,* Salvatore Marsili, Jordi Pinell, Achille Triacca, Tomaso Federici, Adrien Nocent, Burkhard Neunheuser (Torino: Marietti, 1988) 167–168.

[37] Kleinheyer, *Die Priesterweihe,* 176.

[38] Vogel, *Medieval Liturgy,* 252.

[39] ". . . mais la source où il puisa surtout fut le Pontifical de la Curie." Andrieu, *PGD,* 311.

[40] Andrieu, *PRC,* 234.

[41] Puniet explains the suppression of the *scrutinium.* "It had completely disappeared since the papal chapel had adopted the Roman pontifical. It no longer had the right to remain in this collection for the usage of all the bishops since no bishop whatever could claim to examine the election of a candidate which the sovereign pontiff himself had nominated or at least confirmed." ("Il a complètement disparu depuis que la chapelle papale a adopté le Pontifical romain. Il n'avait plus de titre à demeurer dans ce recueil à l'usage de tous les évêques, puisqu'un évêque quelconque ne pouvait plus prétendre examiner l'élection d'un candidat que le souverain pontife lui-même avait nommé ou au moins confirmé.") "Consécration épiscopale," 2584.

[42] Provisions in this scrutiny for the possibility of the elect not being a presbyter and possibly being a widower are surprising in the thirteenth century. Andrieu signals the unusual quality of these additions by the use of brackets in the text itself and mention in the apparatus of how many manuscripts omit these words. No wonder this scrutiny had fallen into disuse!

[43] The meticulous Lateran liturgist has carefully added the amice, alb, maniple, stole, cincture, and cope to the simple *PRXII* rubric: The elect is dressed in sacred vestments (no. 9).

[44] Thomas O'Meara, "Emergence and Decline of Popular Voice in the Selection of Bishops," in *The Choosing of Bishops,* ed. W. Bassett (Hartford, Connecticut: The Canon Law Society of America, 1971) 30.

[45] "Formule bizarre, qui n'est pas une monition et dont on ne voit pas à qui elle s'adresse." See "La liturgie du sacre des évêques dans son évolution historique," 757.

[46] The elaborations of the consecration stage added by the *PRG* and by the *PRXII* are preserved in the *PRC;* there are no additional innovations except for the increase in grandeur of the offertory gifts presented to the pope. There is an explicit attempt in manuscripts O H Y to change the practice of praying the consecration prayer *in modum prephationis* (no. 24) back to its original and simpler form: for example, *add. corr. in marg.: in tono prephationis* . . . (no. 24 in the apparatus). However, this attempt was not successful until the reform of 1968.

[47] *L'Ordinazione episcopale,* 51 n. 3.

[48] "Dopo aver accertata la regolarità dell'elezione, l'esaminatore mirava ad assicurarsi che gli elettori, oltre ad aver scelto liberamente, avessero anche scelto bene." Ibid., 132.

[49] ". . . servirà solo a ricordare al consacrando, nell'imminenza della sua ordinazione, quali saranno i suoi nuovi doveri e le sue nuove responsabilità." Ibid., 128.

[50] Hereafter *PGD*.

[51] "In den Jahren 1292–1295 entsteht in der kleinen Bischofsstadt Mende in Südfrankreich ein Pontifikale, das für die weitere Entwicklung der Pontifikalliturgie von ähnlich entscheidender Bedeutung werden sollte wie das *PRG*, das *Pontificale Guilelmi Durandi (PDG)*." Kleinheyer, *Die Priesterweihe*, 189.

[52] Pierre de Puniet, *The Roman Pontifical*, trans. M. Harcourt (London: Longmans, Green, and Company, 1932) 39. Written for the instruction of the clergy on the meaning of the liturgical rites they celebrated, the *Rationale* is "an extensive work that marks the high point of the allegorical interpretation of the liturgy in the Middle Ages." Herman Wegman, *Christian Worship in the East and West*, trans. G. Lathrop (New York: Pueblo, 1985) 219.

[53] Andrieu, *PGD*, 10.

[54] For example the blessing of cemeteries and the consecration of patens and chalices.

[55] For example rites and ceremonies such as the liturgy of Holy Saturday, the *ordo* for parish visitations, and directives as to when the Creed is said.

[56] The statement of the *PGD* in this regard is consistent with the teaching of Thomas Aquinas (+1274), as will be briefly mentioned at the beginning of chapter 6.

[57] Marc Dykmans, *Le Pontifical Romain révisé au XVe siècle*, ST 311 (Città del Vaticano: Biblioteca Apostolica Vaticana, 1985) 10–11, n. 3, provides an extensive chart enumerating the *PRG–PGD* parallels.

[58] Vogel, *Medieval Liturgy*, 252.

[59] Andrieu, *PGD*, 311–312.

[60] ". . . il tocco definitivo all'ormai complesso e confuso rito, canonizzato poi con il Pontificale romano pubblicato prima da Clemente VIII." "L'evoluzione storica dei riti delle ordinazioni," *EL* 83 (1969) 77.

[61] Batiffol, "La liturgie due sacre des évêques dans son évolution historique," the two-page chart following page 763; and Salmon, "Le rite du sacre des évêques," passim.

[62] "Souvent, après avoir décrit l'usage romain, il rapporte celui qu'on suit ailleurs. . . . Parfois même c'est l'usage romain qui vient en second lieu, celui qui a été exposé précédemment semblant être considéré comme plus normal." Andrieu, *PGD*, 16.

[63] Salmon describes this new question as "a bit enigmatic and not very elegant" ("un peu énigmatique et pas très élégant"). He preferred the formula from *OR35B*: What are all the things you are rightly concerned about, brother? "Le rite du sacre des évêques," 33.

[64] Durand adds an interesting note after the text of the decree, encouraging dioceses to use the decree form he drafted in his *Speculum iudicale*.

[65] Piccolomini-Burchard will insert it in the Roman Pontifical of 1485 but only after the texts of the rite itself. The *scrutinium* was completely suppressed in the pontifical published by the Dominican Albert Castellani in Venice in 1520, but then returned to the appendix of Book III in 1572, under the title and in the place it continued to have for almost four more centuries: "Regarding the evening scrutiny which the ancients used before the elect was to be consecrated a bishop." Puniet, "Consécration épiscopale," 2584.

[66] Joseph Lécuyer includes a note about the choice of this hour in his article, "Le sacrement de l'épiscopat," *Divinitas* 1 (1957) 235. He recalls that in the Pseudo-Decretals Saint Anaclet attributed the canonical decision to reserve the third hour on Sunday for conferring episcopal ordination to the fact that at this hour the Spirit descended upon the apostles on Pentecost.

[67] The postulation dialogue in the appendix of *Robert* was from a source prepared for the Province of Rouen. *Robert*'s editor believes the appendix dates from the eleventh century. See pp. 128–129 for comments about the similar text from Martène's *Ordo X*.

[68] Mario Righetti suggests a later source for the blessing in a variant of the *PRC* presbyteral ordination rite. While Righetti is correct about the presence of the blessing in the apparatus, Andrieu notes that the addition is made by a fourteenth-century hand. This suggests that the blessing in this one variant may be the result of the mutual borrowing of the *PRC* from an earlier copy of the *PGD*, and not the other way around. See *I Sacramenti–I Sacramentali* 413, n. 84.

[69] Salmon, "Le rite du sacre des évêques," 37.

[70] It was the very solemnity of this act which was its undoing in the 1968 reform. Annibale Bugnini writes in *The Reform of the Liturgy 1948–1975*, trans. M. O'Connell (Collegeville: Liturgical Press, 1990) 720, n. 28: "[T]he solemn blessing given to the bishop elect [by the consecrator] (who was wearing his miter and holding his pastoral staff) during the litany could give the impression that this was the moment of greatest solemnity; for this reason the action was eliminated."

[71] There are traces of the "Receive the holy spirit" statements that Durand added to the episcopal, presbyteral and diaconal ordination rites in variants of the *PRC*. But since only one variant in each rite carries the statement, since Andrieu's apparatus for episcopal ordination states that the addition is fifteenth century, and since Andrieu himself gives no indication of the *PRC* being a source for these elements, I will again suggest that this is a matter of the later *PRC* copyists bringing in new material from the *PGD*.

[72] It is easy to see, given its place and the solemn manner in which the words are pronounced, how this ritual element overshadows the true sacramental form. See Lécuyer, "Commentarium," *N* 4 (1968) 214, and also James Puglisi's critique: "[t]he addition of this sentence effectively obscures the epiclesis that is pronounced later; and it adds nothing of value to the preceding text." *Contemporary Rites and*

General Conclusions, 14. But what might have been the original impetus for the creation of the new statement in presbyteral ordination? The rite in the *PRC* already contained the statement "Receive power to offer sacrifice to God . . ." but no explicit mention of the power to absolve. Durand remedies what he saw to be a serious lack.

[73] The "Behold how good" and its antiphon (and the hand anointing prayer from presbyteral ordination) are also found in one variant of the γ recension of the *PRC*. But since only one manuscript (and a more recent one) includes these elements, I will consider this part of the borrowing that the later recensions of the *PRC* took from the *PGD*.

[74] See C. B[raga], "Commentarius: *De Ordinatione Episcopi,*" EL 83 (1969) 53, n. 29 and Salmon, "Le rite du sacre des évêques," 39.

[75] The ritual seating of the new bishop was first seen in *OR34.42* and described in Archbishop Hincmar's letter. Prayers to accompany it are found in the *PRG.LXII.5* and in the English books: *The Benedictional of Archbishop Robert, Pontificale Lanalatense,* and the Pontificals of *Dunstan, Egbert,* and *Magdalen College*. See Santantoni, *L'Ordinazione episcopale,* 290–295.

[76] "Lorsqu'il change quelque chose au pontifical de la Curie, ce n'est pas pour reprendre un élément plus traditionnel our pour simplifier, au contraire. Il surcharge le cérémonial, déjà assez ample, de nouveaux rites, de nouvelles formules, de chants, de rubriques détaillées; lorsqu'il n'innove pas purement et simplement, il puise dans d'autres livres, non romains, probablement gallicans. Il a donné au Pontifical romain cette tournure compliquée et un peu redondante, qui, en voulant augmenter la solennité de la cérémonie, ne fait que l'alourdir, en cachant ou en faisant passer au second plan les parties essentielles." "Le rite du sacre des évêques," 44–45.

Chapter 5

The Consecrator says.
Do you have the apostolic mandate?

The Presentation of the Bishop-elect in the *Editio Princeps* (1485) and in the *Editio Typica* (1595)

I. The Presentation of the Bishop-Elect in the Roman Pontifical of 1485[1]

A. THE *PR1485* AND THE RITUAL CONTEXT OF EPISCOPAL ORDINATION

Throughout the fourteenth century, and particularly during the period of the Avignon Papacy (1309–1377), the Pontifical of Guillaume Durand was frequently copied and rapidly gained acceptance among bishops of the neighboring dioceses and provinces. It was inevitable that it would soon encounter copies of the *PRC* which had been brought from Rome to Avignon by the papal Curia.[2] Hybrid editions of both pontificals began to appear as the two rival books borrowed rituals, texts, and rubrics from each other, supplementing specific deficiencies from the other work.

But ultimately, experienced liturgists preferred the work of Guillaume Durand. Useful far beyond one small French diocese, the *PGD* came to be recognized for its superior conformity to canon law and to Roman liturgical custom.[3] When Innocent VIII (+1492) commissioned his masters of ceremonies to create an official edition of the pontifical, it was to the *PGD* that the liturgists turned. And, as Andrieu points out, it was the *PGD* that most bishops had already adopted by then.[4]

Agostino Patrizzi Piccolomini, master of ceremonies for both Paul II and Innocent VIII, acknowledged the extent of his respect for and replication of Durand's pontifical. His letter dedicating the new pontifical to

Innocent VIII expressed the care with which he and his colleague, John Burchard of Strasbourg (who did most of the work⁵), followed the *PGD:*

I was for some time deterred from this task both by the very difficulty of it and especially by respect for the authority of Guillaume Durand, Bishop of Mende, who published the Pontifical that most bishops use nowadays. . . . I should think it a crime to tamper with his text, except that many additions, omissions and corruptions of later date are found in books that purport to give his text; and besides Durand himself had in mind compiling his work not the universal Church but rather the church of Mende, of which he had charge. We, however, following him as far as has been possible, and everywhere adhering to the ritual and ordinal of the Holy Apostolic See, have used many different manuscripts, and like bees that visit many flowers have gathered from different sources to build up a single body.⁶

The Pontifical of Piccolomini and Burchard, using the same title as the *PGD* ("the book of pontifical *ordos*"), was published in 1485 and was the first official (but not yet obligatory) edition of the Roman Pontifical, the *editio princeps.*

The *PR1485* follows the division of the rites into three books which Guillaume Durand initiated. The first book, which consists of blessings, ordinations, and consecrations of persons, presents in ascending order the rituals for minor orders (doorkeeper, lector, exorcist, and acolyte, having removed to the appendix the rite for psalmist from the *PGD*) and the ordination rites for the three sacred orders (subdeacon, deacon, and presbyter). The texts for the consecration of a bishop come after the ordination rites.

B. ANALYSIS OF THE LITURGICAL UNITS

1. *Selection Presentation*

a. SELECTION PRESENTATION: TEXT

PR1485 [f. 30 v.-50 v.] Regarding the consecration of the elect as a bishop.

f. 32 r. . . . Therefore at the suitable hour the Consecrator: elect: the assisting bishops and others who ought to take part in the consecration assemble at the church: and the consecrator having done the prayer goes up before the altar to the faldstool prepared in his chapel on the left side of the altar namely the epistle [side]: as is the practice. And it is made ready there according to the practice. The elect with the assisting bishops goes to his chapel and there receives the appropriate vestments: namely if mass is sung he receives: Amice[,] alb: cincture: maniple: stole in the manner of a priest and cope.

f. 32 v. . . . The elect thus prepared with his biretta is led into the middle among the bishops prepared and mitered. . . .

[The elect and assisting bishops make their reverence to the consecrator; the seating arrangements for the elect and bishops are described.]

The elect without biretta: and the assisting bishops without miters: and the senior assistant [bishop] says toward the consecrator.

Reverend father: holy mother catholic church asks: that you elevate this presbyter present to the responsibility of the episcopacy.
The consecrator says.
Do you have the apostolic mandate.
The senior assistant bishop responds.
We have.
The consecrator says.
Let it be read.

Then the Notary of the consecration receiving the mandate from the hand of the assisting bishop. reads [it] from beginning to end. Meanwhile all sit with heads covered.

When the mandate has been read through by the notary the Consecrator says.

Thanks be to God.

Then with all seated in their places as has been said.

The consecrator in a moderate voice in the manner of a reading begins the following examination of the council. of Carthage: which he ought to always read as it appears [in the text] in the singular: even if there are several examined together. The assisting bishops however say in subdued voice whatever the Consecrator says: and then all ought to hold [their] miters and sit.

Examination.
Antiqua sanctorum patrum. . . .

f. 33. r . . . Question. Will you promise fidelity: submission and obedience to blessed Peter the apostle to whom the power to bind and to loose was given by God: and to his vicars the Roman pontiffs: according to canonical authority.
He responds. I will.

f. 34. r . . . And when the examination has been finished the above-mentioned assisting. bishops lead the elect to the Consecrator whose hand is reverently kissed.

b. SELECTION PRESENTATION:
   "REGARDING THE CONSECRATION OF THE ELECT AS A BISHOP"
   For the first time in its long written history, the rite for the ordination of a bishop is given a title referring to only half of its constitutive

elements, "consecration."[7] We have followed the evolution of the title of the episcopal rite from "Again how a bishop is ordained" (OR34) and "How a bishop is to be ordained in the roman church" (the PRG) to "The order for calling and examining or consecrating the elect as a bishop" (OR35B) and "Regarding the examination, ordination and consecration of a bishop" (the PGD). For the title of the *editio princeps,* Piccolomini-Burchard have deliberately chosen to change the name of the rite to "Regarding the consecration of the elect as a bishop."

Two separate issues lie behind this change. First, any reference in the title to the selection stage of ordination has been removed, as well as any indication that ordination is a two-stage process. Episcopal ordination has been reduced to the consecration liturgy, although elements of the selection remain. Second, the new title is a clear indication that in fact the episcopal rite is not considered an ordination, i.e., is not considered part of the sacrament of holy orders. The three sacred orders do not include the episcopacy. This rite is the ecclesial act of elevating someone to episcopal dignity: it is understood to be consecration, not ordination. It is this new designation, "the consecration of the elect as a bishop," which will be taken up into the Roman Pontifical of 1595.[8]

C. SELECTION PRESENTATION:
  THE ROMAN EVENING SCRUTINY

A second definitive shift in these texts is Piccolomini-Burchard's decision to move the scrutiny out of its initial place in the rite. The PRC and the PGD had both indicated that the scrutiny had fallen into disuse, although both Pontificals continued to include the texts at the beginning of the rite. The PR1485 moves the scrutiny to a separate chapter at the end of the rite, immediately after the act of reverence to the consecrator (*ad multos annos),* along with an opening commentary that this scrutiny ritual is no longer in use:

PR1485.f 50 v Regarding the evening scrutiny which the ancients used
And because with our episcopal ordination we have said the evening scrutiny which the churches of antiquity used is not to be any more in use. . . .

The Selection Presentation begins just as in the PGD, with the postulation dialogue and Gallican examination, *Antiqua sanctorum patrum.*

d. SELECTION PRESENTATION: RUBRICS

Both Puniet and Vogel[9] cite as one of the purposes for revising and supplementing Durand's work the need for greater precision and completeness in the rubrics. Piccolomini-Burchard's efforts in this area are remarkably comprehensive. Centuries later, "Dom Guéranger pointed out that the Congregation of Rites . . . never had to make any corrections or alterations in Burchard's rubrics."[10] Compared to the *PGD*, there is a veritable explosion of comments, canonical prescriptions, and rubrical directives throughout the rite; the introduction alone adds another three and a half pages of text before the ritual even begins.

One marked change from earlier rites is the introduction of two separate chapels as locations for elements of the consecration Mass. Initial elements of the Mass occur simultaneously in the consecrator's (larger) chapel and in the elect's (smaller) chapel while the consecration rite itself takes place in the church proper. Following the offertory, however, the consecrator and the new bishop concelebrate at the main altar.

The directives for the use of the miter are also extensive; for example, Burchard specifies that the consecrator wears the miter for the bidding, litany, laying on of hands, and *Accipe Spiritum sanctum,* lays it aside for *Propitiare* and the consecration prayer, puts it on again for the anointing of the head, and lays it aside once again for the remaining section of the consecration prayer. There is also provision made for the consecrator to recite the entire liturgy rather than having it solemnly sung.[11] The majority of these new rubrical texts will also be brought into the Roman Pontifical of 1595.

e. SELECTION PRESENTATION:
  ABSENCE OF RELATIONSHIPS

On a Sunday or a feast day morning, in the church where the consecration is to be held, the consecrator, bishop-elect, at least two assistant bishops, and those who are to be present assemble. The directives in this regard are purposely vague. There is no reference to the presence of the faithful of the vacant see, the suffragans, nor the metropolitan; the church building itself has no necessary relationship to the elect, the consecrator, or the bishops. The relationship between the new bishop and the sees attesting his worthiness no longer finds expression in the rubrics.

The elect is still vested as a presbyter at this point and is presented by two bishops to the consecrator. When all are seated, there is a short pause. Then the assistant bishops and the elect rise, and the senior assistant bishop voices the postulation to the consecrator in words taken from the *PGD:*

PR1485.f 32. v . . . Reverend father: holy mother catholic church asks: that you elevate this presbyter present to the responsibility of the episcopacy.

At this point however the dialogue changes radically from the earlier rituals we have studied. The consecrator's response is not "Do you know him to be worthy?" *(PGD)* nor "Acclaim this man, chosen by the testimony of good works, as most worthy of the priesthood . . ." *(Servanda est* of *MF* and the *PRG*). The consecrator proclaims nothing on his own authority but asks for only the papal mandate to be read:

PR1484.f 32. v The consecrator says. Do you have the apostolic mandate.
The senior assistant bishop responds. We have.
The consecrator says. Let it be read.

The words of this very brief exchange are similar to another dialogue from the Roman scrutiny copied from *OR34* into *OR35, OR36,* and *OR35B:*

OR34.22. And again he says: Do you have the decree?
They respond: We do.
23. And, when they present it, he commands the chaplain that it be read again.

and also:

OR35B.2. He asks: Do you have the decree?
They respond: We do.
And the *apostolicus* says: Let it be read.

In the case of these *ordines,* the decree to be read aloud was the written expression of the electors' consensus as part of the selection process, verification of an election properly conducted, and the unanimous postulation for the candidate's ordination. The mandate referred to in the *PR1485,* however, is not a consensual document but the expression of papal choice of the elect and "the permission to proceed to the consecration."[12]

Rather than seeking a confirmation of his worthiness from those who postulate the consecration of the elect ("Do you [plural] know him to be worthy?"), the consecrator asks for the one guarantee necessary: the papal mandate. The alteration in the text is evident in this comparison:

PGD.I.XIV.16.	*PR1485.f 32.v*
Reverend father,	Reverend father:
holy mother catholic church asks	holy mother catholic church asks:
that you elevate	that you elevate

this presbyter	this presbyter present
to the responsibility	to the responsibility
of the episcopacy.	of the episcopacy.
Do you know him to be worthy?	Do you have the apostolic mandate.
As far as human frailty permits [one]	We have.
to know, we know and believe that he	Let it be read.
is worthy.	

Piccolomini-Burchard, while respecting Durand's text, recognized components of a ritual dialogue which no longer bore resemblance to ecclesiastical reality. When bishops began to depend solely upon papal appointment for the right of jurisdiction, the words verifying the papal appointment were introduced into the consecration ritual. The postulation in the *PR1485* is a mere ceremonial introduction to the rite: neither the name of the local church nor the elect is included; the senior assistant bishop who recites the postulation text represents no postulating or consenting ecclesial community (or communities).

Following the reading of the mandate, the consecrator has no response that is related to his own episcopal office. He simply responds: "Thanks be to God," the words that remain from the original dialogue of Guillaume Durand but now restricted to the consecrator alone. The assistant bishops and other members of the assembly are silent.

PGD.I.XIV.16.	*PR1485*.f 32.v
The consecrator and others respond:	The consecrator says.
Thanks be to God.	Thanks be to God.

In the *PR1485* it is the papal mandate that announces the prior choice of the elect and provides the only testimony to his worthiness from any of the sees involved. The mandate and not a proclamation of consensus allows the consecration to proceed. "This same mandate replaces the former election of the bishop by the clergy and by the people,"[13] a change of tremendous significance dating from approximately the fourteenth century when the Holy See reserved to itself the selection of bishops (or at least their canonical institution).[14]

f. SELECTION PRESENTATION: EXAMINATION

Following the presentation and postulation, the examination first introduced in the *PRG* as "the examination according to the Gauls" begins immediately. The same erroneous description of it from the *PGD* (i.e., that this is the examination according to the Council of Carthage) is repeated in this text.

The wording of the promise of fidelity returns to the text found in the *PRC*. There is no mention of the metropolitan as there was in the pontifical of Guillaume Durand (in which the metropolitan identifies himself as the minister of the local church):

PGD.I.XIV.19.	*PR1485 f 33.r*
Will you promise fidelity, submission and obedience	Will you promise fidelity: submission and obedience
to blessed Peter the apostle to whom	to blessed Peter the apostle to whom
the power to bind and to loose	the power to bind and to loose
was given by God,	was given by God:
to his vicars the roman pontiffs	to his vicars the Roman pontiffs:
and to me his minister of the holy church of Besançon	
and to my successors	
according to canonical authority?	according to canonical authority.

Whereas the *PRC* was specifically compiled for use at the Lateran and for use of churches related to the pope as metropolitan, the purpose of the *editio princeps* was far broader. It was "an edition that was to be submitted as authentic to all the bishops of the Latin world."[15] And yet no provision is made to maintain Durand's inclusion of the metropolitan within the examination of the elect. It seems that by 1485 even the consecrator has no necessary relation to the elect; he is most likely not his metropolitan. Leon Strieder names the change that is at work in the slight but significant shifts between the *PGD* and the *PR1485*, "[T]he grounding of the ordination of either presbyters or bishops in the service of a particular local or universal church is often diminished in favor of a more personal commitment to the person of the pope."[16] The voices of the sees involved are almost silent.

g. SELECTION PRESENTATION:
PROCLAMATION

Piccolomini-Burchard continue another pattern from the *PGD:* there is no proclamation of consensus and consecration after the examination.

The elect is merely led by the two bishops to the consecrator whose hand he kisses (a rubric appearing first in the *PRC* and borrowed by Guillaume Durand).[17]

We have observed the evolution of the proclamation at the conclusion of the Roman scrutiny or the Gallican examination through many forms. The Roman pattern involved the pope (or metropolitan) declaring:

OR34.30. . . . Because the desires of all have agreed upon you, today you will abstain and tomorrow, if it is pleasing to God, you will be consecrated.

The Gallican pattern specified many of those coming to consensus in the selection of the candidate within the vacant see:

MF.9.35. . . . By the will of the Lord, therefore, in place of N., of pious memory, with the testimony of the presbyters and of the whole clergy and with the advice of the citizens and of those assembled, we believe that the reverend N. should be elect. . . . Therefore, dearly beloved brethren, acclaim this man, chosen by the testimony of good works, as most worthy of the priesthood, crying out your praises together, and say: He is worthy.

The later Germanic pattern manifests the same critical importance of acknowledging the consensus reached by the sees involved. The proclamation, borrowed from the words of *SEA*, always followed the examination:

PRG.LXIII.17. And thus examined and fully prepared with the consent of the clerics and laity and the agreement of the bishops of the entire province and especially of the metropolitan or by [his] authority or presence he may be ordained.

Even when the Roman pontificals of later centuries (the *PRXII*, the *PRC*) removed references to the metropolitan, the proclamation remained substantially intact. In the *PR1485*, however, Piccolomini-Burchard are faithful to Durand and omit any proclamation of consensus and consecration, and thereby omit another vital expression of the consensus on which episcopal ordination used to rest.

h. SELECTION PRESENTATION:
STRUCTURE

The first stage of the ordination is completed (presentation, postulation, examination) but with no proclamation of consensus and consecration to introduce the consecration liturgy. We saw this break with tradition in the *PGD* which inserted a new postulation dialogue in which the consecrator asked for testimony of the elect's worthiness. The *PR1485* omitted the core of this dialogue and substituted the reading of the only testimony now necessary: the papal mandate.

The remainder of the structure is intact; all of these elements continue to occur before the Mass begins. The absence of any proclamation of consensus, however, indicates how substantially the purpose of the first presentation has shifted: from expression and completion of communal consensus to verification of papal appointment and formulaic recitation of the examination.

PR1485

1st stage

Selection Presentation

	Sunday
presentation:	two bishops
postulation:	elevate this presbyter
	mandate
	examination
proclamation of consensus and consecration:	
	[ ]

2. Consecration Presentation

a. CONSECRATION PRESENTATION: TEXT

PR1485 f. 34. v Then the Consecrator with miter removed with the ministers turned toward the altar makes the confession in the usual manner: with the elect remaining at his left and all the bishops standing before their chairs they make [the confession] similarly with their clerics: and so when the confession has been made the Consecrator goes up to the altar[,] it is kissed and he incenses it in the usual manner. Then he goes to his chair and proceeds with the mass as far as the *Alleluia* or to the last verse of the Tract exclusively: if the *Alleluia* is not sung.

[rubrics follow for a mass that is not sung]

The assisting bishops then lead the elect to his chapel: and there with the cope removed the Acolytes vest him: Sandals. . . . Then he receives the pectoral cross: and stole adjusted for him so that it may hang from his shoulders. Then he is vested in tunic, dalmatic and chasuble: wearing these he goes up to his altar [in his chapel]: where standing in the middle among the assisting bishops. with uncovered head he reads the entire office of the mass up to the *Alleluia*. or to the last verse of the Tract exclusively: and he does not ever turn toward the people when he says The lord be with you as at other masses he would be accustomed to do.

It is to be noted however that the Roman church for episcopal ordinations never changes the office of the day: one nevertheless says the collect for the office of the consecration after the collect of the day. . . .

Introitus. [text and music follow]

f. 35. v . . . *Adesto.* . . .

A reading from the epistle of blessed paul the apostle to Timothy.

f. 36. r The assisting bishops again lead the elect to the Consecrator:

[The elect and bishops make a second reverence before the consecrator.]

Then all sit as before and the Consecrator sitting with miter on [and] turned to him says.

[*Episcopum oportet*] A bishop is to: judge: interpret: consecrate: ordain: offer: and baptize.

Then with all rising the consecrator standing with miter on says this preface to those present.

Oremus dilectissimi nobis: . . .

And immediately both the Consecrator and the assisting bishops recline upon the faldstools: and seats with [their] mitres: the Elect prostrates at the left of the consecrator: the ministers also: and all the others kneel. Then the cantor begins the litany saying: *kyrieleison* and so on. . . .

[The consecrator offers the threefold blessings for the elect toward the end of the litany, making the sign of the cross over him with the assisting bishops.]

f. 36. v . . . When it is finished all rise and with the Consecrator before his fald-stool standing with miter [on] the Elect rises and kneels before him. Then the Consecrator having received the book of the gospels saying nothing imposes that [book] open upon the neck and shoulders of the elect with the assisting bishops helping. in such a way that the lower part of the book [touches] the neck of the elect's head: one of the chaplains of the elect having knelt behind him: keeping the text facing downward: the book is to be continually held until it is to be handed over to the elect into [his] hands.

Then the Consecrator and assisting bishops touch the head of the *consecrandus* with both hands saying these words [once] only.

Accipe spiritum sanctum.

When this has been done the Consecrator in moderate voice standing with miter removed says the prayer.

Propiciare. . . .

Then in moderate voice with hands extended before [his] chest he chants this preface.

f. 37. r For ever and ever. They respond. Amen. The Lord be with you. . . .

f. 37. v . . . honor of every dignity. . . .

f. 39. r . . . Complete the fullness of your ministry in your priest, and equipped with all the adornments of glory, hallow him with the dew of heavenly unction.

If held here within the Ro[man]. cu[ria]. the apostolic Subdeacon for the consecration. Or if held outside the Roman curia: [then] one of the chaplains of the pontiff: binds the head of the elect with one of the longer of the eight napkins mentioned above: and the Consecrator kneeling begins the hymn turned to the altar.

Veni creator spiritus.

f. 39. v Then he dips his right thumb into the holy chrism offered to him by one of the ministers: and anoints the head of the elect kneeling before him having formed first the sign of the cross over the entire crown [of the head]: then spreading [it over] the rest of the crown saying by reading meanwhile.

May your head be anointed and consecrated by the heavenly blessing in the pontifical order. In the name of the fa+ther and of the son+ and of the holy+ spirit. Amen. Peace be with you. They respond. And also with you.

[If there are others, they are also anointed. The pontiff cleans his thumb, removes his miter while the hymn finishes. The pontiff continues singing the prayer]

May it flow down, O lord, richly upon his head. . . .

b. CONSECRATION PRESENTATION:
   INTRODUCTORY RITES

In place of the consecrator's proclamation of consensus and consecration as introduction to the consecration liturgy, we find only the silent reverence of the consecrator by the elect. The first act of the second stage of the ordination (the consecration) begins with the pre-Mass confession, i.e., the *Confiteor* with its attendant prayers recited in dialogue form.[18] For the ritual described in these texts, the consecrator and elect recite the prayers together; the other bishops pray the penitential dialogue with their own clerics.

The consecrator then moves to his chapel and begins to celebrate the Mass up through the end of the gradual; the elect does the same in his chapel after being vested as a bishop. His episcopal vesture includes the subdeacon's tunic, deacon's dalmatic, and presbyter's chasuble and maniple, as well as the episcopal pectoral cross.

Again following the *PGD*, the compilers of the *PR1485* note that the Roman Church never changes the office of the day for episcopal ordinations; the proper collect for the consecration is recited after the collect for the day. The proper collect continues to be *Adesto* (= *SVe* 942). The epistle (1 Tim 3:1-7 and Titus 2:10) and gradual follow.

c. CONSECRATION PRESENTATION:
ABSENCE OF THE SECOND PROCLAMATION OF CONSENSUS

The two assistant bishops who accompanied the elect for the first presentation now lead him forward again to the consecrator. And once again the proclamation of consensus and consecration which marked the earlier Roman and Gallican rites is omitted.

OR34 had joined the proclamation of consensus to the bidding for the prototype of the Roman statement:

OR34.38. . . . The clergy and people of the city of N. consenting, with their neighboring sees, have chosen for themselves N., the deacon, or presbyter, to be consecrated bishop. Therefore let us pray for this man, that our God and lord Jesus Christ may grant to him the episcopal chair for ruling over his church and all the people.

And the Gallican model combined both proclamation and bidding in the extended Gallican bidding in the *MF*:

MF.9.39. Dearly beloved brethren, let us beseech God . . . for this his servant whom he has willed to exalt in the church and to place in the seat of the elders, by the harmonious decisions which he has inspired and by the loyal wishes spread forth among his people and by the testimony of their voices, setting him with the princes of his people; at their unanimous prayer may he now adorn this same man with the high priesthood. . . .

That he who is to be raised up over the elect, chosen by all, may be made fit by each and every hallowed and hallowing rite, may we be aided by the most earnest and unanimous prayers of all in this rite of his consecration and of our supplication. . . .

In place of either of these is now the *Episcopum oportet* unit first introduced into this position in the rite by manuscript O of the *PRXII*. Piccolomini-Burchard faithfully copy this unit from the *PGD* (but omitting the episcopal duty *confirmare*):

PR1485.f 36. r *[Episcopum oportet]* The bishop is to: judge: interpret: consecrate: ordain: offer: and baptize.

Redactors throughout the centuries who adapted the texts of the *ordines romani* and the early Gallican texts have equated the second proclamation of consensus and consecration by the consecrator with the liturgical unit of a simple allocution by the consecrator. The *PRXII*, for example, had nothing with which to replace *Servanda est* and left the space empty, moving immediately to the bidding; the *PRC* α β did the same, while *PRC* γ substituted the *Episcopum oportet* unit as the (basis for an ?) allocution to the people on episcopal ministry. This is the unit that Durand mandates but makes it an admonition to the elect alone. This evolution maintains the external structure (keeping a proclamation by the consecrator in this position) but highlights the loss of the purpose of the original proclamation: expression of the communion of consensus among the sees involved as to the choice of the elect and thus the introduction of the consecration that would necessarily follow.

Piccolomini-Burchard next decide that the bidding which follows *Episcopum oportet* is not an oration (as the *PGD* has it) but a preface. It is addressed to those present (a return to the rubrics of the *PRC*) and ends with the misleading collect form it picked up from the *PRC: per Christum dominum nostrum.*

d. CONSECRATION:

EVOLUTION OF THE ELEMENTS

The litany is begun and includes Durand's threefold blessing of the elect by the consecrator and other bishops who then place the open gospel book upon the neck and shoulders of the elect. The papal liturgists refine Durand's directives to mention that the assistant bishops are to say nothing at this point, and one of the chaplains of the elect (not the bishops) is to hold the book in place during the rituals that follow.

The consecrator and assistant bishops impose hands on the head of the *consecrandus*, saying only *"Accipe spiritum sanctum."* The Roman collect, *Propiciare*, follows. The consecrator, with moderate voice, is to chant the conclusion to the collect, then the preface dialogue, and the consecration prayer until the words:

PR1485.f 39. r Complete the fullness of your ministry in your priest, and equipped with all the adornments of glory, hallow him with the dew of heavenly unction.

Following rubrics from the *PGD*, the *PR1485* directs the binding of the elect's head in linen strips by one of the chaplains; the consecrator then intones the hymn, *Veni creator spiritus* (not the sequence, *Veni sancte spiritus*, from the *PGD*[19]) and anoints the head of the elect with chrism while offering the accompaning formulary, "May your head be anointed and consecrated. . . ." And if there are several to be consecrated, the consecrator repeats this with each one individually.

The consecration prayer then recommences; following it and Psalm 133, the elect's[20] hands are anointed[21] with chrism with both accompanying prayers ("May these hands be anointed" = *MF*.8.34 [presbyteral ordination] and "God and father of our lord Jesus Christ" = the *PRG*.LXIII.37). Only at the conclusion of this latter prayer is the elect finally designated *consecratus*, an explicit indication that the anointings during the consecration were considered essential elements of episcopal consecration by the theologians of this age.

Piccolomini-Burchard duplicate the explanatory rites from the *PGD*: blessing and giving of the crozier, blessing and giving of the ring, giving of the gospel book, each element with its own spoken formula. The kiss of peace marks the end of this part of the consecration; it is exchanged only between the consecrator and *consecratus* and between the assistant bishops and the *consecratus*.

The new bishop (in his own chapel) and the consecrator then return to the celebration of the Mass beginning with the *Alleluia*. The full text of the gospel is given but incorrectly cited as being from Matthew. It is rather Mark 6:6-13, the traditional gospel for episcopal ordination drawn from the *PRG*.LXIII.50.

The *PR1485* repeats the insistence from Guillaume Durand that the offering of two loaves of bread, two full pitchers of wine, and two lighted candles is a tradition instituted by Pope Melchiades. The new bishop leaves his chapel for the offertory and then concelebrates the rest of the Mass at the main altar with the consecrator:

PR1485.f 45. v Then the Consecrator washes [his] hands and goes up to the altar. The *Consecratus* however [goes] to the back part of the epistle side of the altar and standing there in the middle among the assisting bishops having before him his missal he says and does everything at the same time with the Consecrator just as [it is] in the missal.

Three explanatory rites occur after the final blessing of the Mass: the blessing and imposing of the miter (moved from its position after Communion in the *PGD*), the blessing and giving of the gloves (each element with its own formula), and the enthronement of the new bishop either in his cathedra or in the faldstool of the consecrator (if he is not consecrated in his own cathedral) as the *Te Deum* is sung. A final antiphon, a collect, the pontifical blessing by the *consecratus,* and the threefold *ad multos annos* reverence to the consecrator bring the rite to an end.

e. CONSECRATION PRESENTATION: STRUCTURE

> *PR1485*
>
> *2nd stage*
>
> **Consecration Presentation**
> | | |
> | --- | --- |
> | | introit to gradual |
> | | episcopal vestments |
> | **presentation:** | two bishops |
> | **proclamation of consensus and consecration:** | |
> | | *Episcopum oportet* |
> | | bidding *MF* |
> | **consecration:** | litany |
> | | gospel book |
> | | laying on of hands |
> | | *Accipe spiritum sanctum* |
> | | *Propiciare* |
> | | consecration prayer |
> | | consecration continues |

3. *Conclusion*

Structurally, the *PR1485,* the *editio princeps,* reproduces Durand's work almost exactly. But two textual changes are notable. In the postulation dialogue, the shift in the source of testimony to the worthiness of the elect from two (unidentified) bishops (in the *PGD*) to the papal mandate, and, in the examination of the elect, the excision of the mention of the metropolitan and his see, serve to underscore the increasing control of the selection of bishops by the apostolic see and the marked decline of participation by any of the other sees involved. The liturgical texts express and help consolidate that control.

The best rationale for the state of the evolution of the episcopal ordination rite in the *PR1485* is the canonical commentary which Piccolomini-Burchard place at the very beginning of the rite. In difficult and inelegant Latin, it sets forth the juridical and ecclesiological under-pinnings for the rite and thus for this arrangement of the texts:

*PR1485.*f 30. v-31. r Regarding the consecration of the elect as a Bishop.

Since provisions for Cathedral churches: either Metropolitan: or patriarchal: or the confirmation of elections to them: pertain by full right of law today to the apostolic see: and by the same [right of law] it is again provided to churches widowed of a pastor: so that elections solemnized by those who have the canonical privilege to do so are confirmed.

Therefore the scrutiny which is called evening and the examination on the previous day which is mentioned in the ancient pontifical books: this we decide is to be omitted. It seems improper: and totally absurd: that those matters which by the supreme pontiff: and his sacred senate have been established: approved and examined should be examined again by lesser tribunals: hence these [procedures] [found] in this place are set aside as superfluous: . . . .

The text describes the authority of the apostolic see in two situations of episcopal selection current at the time. Providing the bishop for metropolitan or patriarchal cathedrals or confirming the election of such a bishop belongs to the apostolic see by full right of law. In the case of a "widowed church" whose bishop may be chosen by an election occurring under special canonical privilege, the right of confirming that bishop-elect also belongs to the apostolic see. It is for this reason that the Saturday evening scrutiny from *OR34* and its examination found in the ancient pontifical books have been set aside.

Patrizzi Piccolomini and John Burchard, in good company with other canonists and theologians of the late fifteenth century in reflecting on the selection of bishops, held as unassailable the ecclesiastical polity of their own times. From this perspective, "the supreme pontiff and his sacred senate" have sole authority to provide the principal bishops for a region according to a process understood to be the genuine tradition of the Roman Church. In the face of this staunch conviction, the notion of collaboration or consensus with any "lesser courts" of the neighboring sees in the formal selection of bishops must have appeared "totally absurd" precisely because that interference after the fact would have so explicitly violated authentic church teaching.

The Roman and Gallican traditions, however, rested on an inverted ecclesiology: the participation of the vacant see occurred first, with the neighboring sees and metropolitan see also to be taken into account. It was only at the end of the consensual selection process, after all sees were convinced that the elect was worthy, that the final confirmation was spoken by the consecrator and the approval given for the second stage to begin.

Given the authors' juridical and ecclesiological framework, however, it is easy to understand why the papal mandate is now ritually the center of the postulation dialogue. The evolution from the earliest texts has been substantial:

Roman	Gallican	PR1485
1st stage	*1st stage*	*1st stage*
Selection Presentation	**Selection Presentation**	**Selection Presentation**
Saturday	Saturday	Sunday
presentation	**presentation**	**presentation**
vacant see		2 bishops
postulation		postulation
grant us a patron		elevate this presbyter
decree		mandate
examination	examination	examination
proclamation of	**proclamation of**	**proclamation of**
consensus and	**consensus and**	**consensus and**
consecration	**consecration**	**consecration**
desires of all/	*Servanda est*	[ ]
you will be consecrated		
2nd stage		
Consecration Presentation	**Consecration Presentation**	**Consecration Presentation**
Sunday	Sunday	Sunday
introit to gradual	presentation	introit to gradual
episcopal vestments	episcopal vestments	episcopal vestments
presentation	introit to collect	presentation
archdeacon		2 bishops
proclamation of	**proclamation of**	**proclamation of**
consensus and	**consensus and**	**consensus and**
consecration	**consecration**	**consecration**
clergy + people	chosen by all/	*Episcopum oportet*
+ bishops consent/		
bidding OR34	extended bidding	bidding *MF*
consecration	**consecration**	**consecration**
litany	litany	litany
	gospel book	gospel book
	laying on of hands	laying on of hands
		Accipe spiritum sanctum
Propitiare	*Propitiare*	*Propitiare*
consecration prayer	consecration prayer	consecration prayer
consecration continues	consecration continues	consecration continues

As we shall see, Piccolomini-Burchard's structure moves almost intact into the Roman Pontifical of 1595.

Texts of the Roman Pontifical of 1485:

Deterruit me ab hoc opere aliquandiu tum rei ipsius difficultas tum maxime Gulielmi Durantis Episcopi Mimatensis auctoritas, qui pontificalem librum quo maxime hoc tempore utuntur antistites edidit. . . . Cuius editioni manus apponere piaculum ducerem, nisi post ea tempora multaque addita pleraque intermissa, plurima vero viciata reperirentur, et nisi ipse Durantes non tam universalis ecclesie quam Mimatensis cui praeerat, in suo opere rationem habuisset. Nos vero illum quantum potuimus secuti, adhibitis pluribus ac diversis exemplaribus ritum atque ordinem quem sacrosancta servat apostolica sedes ubique tenentes, tamquam ex diversis floribus ad instar apum alia ex aliis excerpsimus, atque unum quasi confecimus corpus.

Selection Presentation:

PR1485 [f. 30 v.-50 v.]

f 30. v-31. r De consecratione electi in episcopum.

Quoniam ecclesiam Cathedralium: siue Metropolitanarum: ac patriarchalium prouisiones: seu electionum ad illas confirmationes: ad sedem apostolicam hodie pleno iure pertinent: et ab eadem ecclesiis pastore induatis: uel de nouo prouidetur: ut electiones ab illis quibus et priuilegio licet canonice celebrate confirmantur. Ideo scrutinium quod serotinum appellatur et pridianam illam examinationem que in antiquis pontificalibus libris habetur: hic pretermittedam esse censuimus. Inconueniens quippe videtur: et omnino absurdum: ut que a summo pontifice: ac sacro senatu statuta: approbata: atque examinata sunt a minoribus tribunalibus iterum examinentur: p[ro]inde illis in hoc loco ut superfluis dimissis:

f. 32 r. . . . Hora igitur competenti Consecrator: electus: assistentes episcopi et alii qui consecrationi interesse debent ad ecclesiam conueniant: et consecrator facta oratione ante altare ascendit ad faldistorium in capella sua ad sinistrum cornu altaris videlicet epistole preparatum: ut moris est. Ibique ex more paratur. Electus vero cum assistentibus episcopis vadit ad capellam suam et ibi capit paramenta opportuna: videlicet si missa cantatur accipit: Amictum albam: cingulum: manipulum: stolam: in modum sacerdotis et pluuiale.

f. 32 v. . . . Electus vero cum suo birreto ducitur sic paratus medius inter episcopos paratos: et mitratos: . . . Electus sine birreto: et assistentes episcopi sine mitra:

et senior assistentium versus ad consecratorem dicit.
Reuerende pater: postulat sancta mater ecclesia catholica: ut hunc presentem presbyterum ad onus episcopatus subleuetis.
Consecrator dicit. Habetis mandatum apostolicum.
Respondet episcopus senior assistentium. Habemus.
Consecrator dicit. Legatur.

Tunc Notarius consecratoris accipiens mandatum de manu episcopi assistentis. legit a principio ad fine. Interim sedent omnes tectis capitibus.

Mandato per notarium perlecto Consecrator dicit. Deo gratias.

Deinde omnibus in locis suis ut dictum est sedentibus.

Consecrator media voce in modum lectionis incipit sequentem examinationem Carthaginensis. concilii: que legi debet semper sicut iacet in singulari: etiam si plures simul examinarentur. Assistentes vero episcopi submissa voce dicunt quecunque dixerit Consecrator: et omnes debent tunc mitras tenere et sedere.

Examen.
Antiqua sanctorum patrum. . . .

f. 33. r . . . Interrogatio. Vis beato Petro apostolo cui a deo data est potestas ligandi atque soluendi: eiusque vicariis Romanis pontificibus: fidem: subiectionem et obedientiam secundum canonicam auctoritatem exhibere. R. Volo.

f. 34. r . . . . Expleto itaque examine, praefati assistentes. episcopi ducunt electum ad Consecra-

f. 34. v torem cuius manum reuerenter osculatur.

*PR1485.*f 50 v . . . De scrutinio serotino quo antiqui utebantur
Et quoniam in nostra ordinatione episcopali diximus scrutinium serotinum quo antiquitus ecclesie utebantur non esse amplius in usu. . . .

Consecration Presentation:

PR1485 f. 34. v Tunc Consecrator deposita mitra cum ministris ad altare conuersus facit solito more confessionem: electo a sinistris eius manente et omnes episcopi ante sedes suas stantes faciunt similiter cum clericis suis: facta itaque confessione Consecrator ascendit ad altare osculatur et incensat illud more solito. Deinde vadit ad sedem suam et procedit in missa usque ad Alleluia ut vltimum versum Tractus exclusiue: si Alleluia non dicitur.

Episcopi vero assistentes ducunt electum ad capellam suam: et ibi deposito pluuiali Acoliti induunt illum: Sandalia. . . . Tum accipit crucem pectoralem: et stolam ei aptatur ut ab humeris pendeat. Deinde tunicella, dalmatica et casula induitur: quibus indutus accedit ad suum altare: ubi stans medius inter episcopos assistentes. detecto capite legit totum officium misse usque ad Alleluia. vel ultimum versum Tractus exclusiue: neque unquam vertit se ad populum cum dicit dominus vobiscum ut in eliis missis fieri solet.

Est autem notandum quod ecclesia Romana propter ordinationes episcoporum nunquam mutat officium diei: dicit tamen post collectam diei pro officio consecrationis collectam.

Introitus.

f. 35. v Adesto. . . .

Lectio epistole beati pauli apostoli ad Thimoteaum.

f. 36. r . . . Assistentes episcopi iterum ducunt electum ad Consecratorem: . . .

Tum sedent omnes ut prius et Consecrator sedens cum mitra versus ad illum dicit. Episcopum oportet: iudicare: interpretari: consecrare: ordinare: offerre: et baptizare.

Deinde omnibus surgentibus consecrator stans cum mitra dicit ad circumstantes hanc prefationem.

Oremus dilectissimi nobis: . . . .

Et mox tam Consecrator quoque assistentes episcopi accumbunt super faldistorium: et sedilia sua cum mitris: Electus vero prosternat se a sinistris consecratoris: ministri etiam: et alii omnes genuflectant. Tunc cantor incipit letaniam dicens: kyrieleison et cetera. . . .

f. 36. v . . . Qua finita surgant omnes et Consecratore ante faldistorium suum cum mitra stante Electus surgit et ante eum genuflectit. Tunc Consecrator accepto libro euangeliorum illum apertum adiuuantibus episcopis assistentibus nihil dicens imponit super ceruicem et spatulas electi ita quod inferior pars libri ceruicem capitis electi: littera ex parte inferiori manente: quem vnus ex capellanis electi retro ipsum genuflexus: quousque liber ipse eidem electo in manus tradendus sit continuo sustineat.

Deinde Consecrator et assistentes episcopi ambabus manibus caput consecrandi tangant dicentes hec verba tantum.

Accipe spiritum sanctum.

Quo facto Consecrator media voce stans deposita mitra dicat orationem.

Propiciare. . . .

Deinde voce mediocri extensis manibus ante pectus dicat hanc prefationem.

f. 37. r Per omnia secula seculorum. R. Amen. V. Dominus vobiscum. . . .

f. 37. v . . . honor omnium dignitatum. . . .

f. 39. r . . . Comple in sacerdote tuo ministerii tui summam et ornamentis totius glorificationis instructum celestis vnguenti rore sanctifica.

Hic si in Ro. cu. fit consecratio Subdiaconus apostolicus. Uel si extra Romanam curiam fit: vnus ex capellanis pontificis: liget caput electi cum vna ex longioribus mappulis de octo superius dictis: et Consecrator flexis genubus versus ad altare incipit hymnum. Veni creator spiritus.

f. 39. v Tum pollicem suum dextrum intingit in sanctum crisma per vnum ex ministris sibi oblatum: et caput electi coram se genuflexi inungit formatus primo signum crucis per totam coronam: deinde reliquum corone liniendo interim legendo dicens.

Ungatur et consecretur caput tuum celesti benedictione in ordine pontificali. In nomine pa+tris et fi+lii et spiritus+sancti. Amen. Pax tibi. R. Et cum spiritu tuo. . . .

Hoc domine copiose in caput eius influat. . . .

f. 45. v Deinde Consecrator lavat manus et accedit ad altare. Consecratus uero ad posterius cornu Epistole altaris. et ibi stans medius inter Episcopos assistentes. ante se habens missale suum. simul cum Consecratore dicit. et facit omnia prout in missali.

II. The Presentation of the Bishop-Elect in the Roman Pontifical of 1595[22]

A. THE *PR1595* AND THE RITUAL CONTEXT OF EPISCOPAL ORDINATION

The texts we are to consider, Botte's "point of departure" for the 1968 reform, have elicited a spectrum of adulation and detraction since their publication. For example, in the introduction to his authoritative volume of history and commentary on the *Pontificale Romanum*, Puniet exalts every text in the work in superlative fashion. The Pontifical of his day is, he insists:

> . . . the most authentic, the most firmly built on the data of tradition, and the only one which, being invested with the sovereign sanction of the Roman pontiffs, has won universal and indisputable authority; a faithful witness to divine truth, a trustworthy interpreter of the words of life, a visible bond which knits us ever more closely to the centre of unity.[23]

J. D. Crichton, on the other hand, is specifically critical of the texts we are to consider. "The former rite of consecration was one of the most complicated of the Roman liturgy and except to the connoisseur of ceremonial (and there were such), wearisome and largely incomprehensible."[24] Let us examine aspects of the immediate history of this remarkable document which so claimed Puniet's devotion but did not inspire Crichton's.

More than a century after the publication of the *editio princeps*, the *PR1485*, Clement VIII (+1605) had reproduced the texts of that earlier Pontifical almost word for word when he set out "to do for the Pontifical what Pius V had done for the Missal and Breviary."[25] The Pontifical of Clement VIII was published in 1595 and promulgated by the apostolic constitution *Ex quo in Ecclesia Dei* on February 10th of the following year.[26]

The *PR1595* was an exclusive document—the first to abrogate use of all previous pontificals of the Latin Church,[27] the first *editio typica* of the *Pontificale Romanum*. The invariability of the pontifical texts after 1595 was key to Pope Clement's design. The constitution of promulgation exacts strict compliance:

Establishing that the aforesaid Pontifical must at no time be changed in whole or in part, or have anything added to it or taken away, and that whosoever must exercise the pontifical functions, or otherwise must do or execute the matters that receive mention in the above-mentioned Pontifical, are held by their performance and execution by the prescript and directive of this Pontifical, and that no one on whom the duty of exercising and doing these things has been imposed can satisfy this obligation of the law apart from the observance of the formulas which are contained in this Pontifical.[28]

Although there were to be four other *editiones typicae* throughout the four centuries that followed until the Second Vatican Council (i.e., the pontificals of Urban VIII [1645], Benedict XIV [1752], Leo XIII [1888], and the pontifical corrected by John XXIII [1961/1962[29]]), it was the text of the *PR1595* itself which remained virtually unaltered until 1968.

The lengthy and detailed rubrical and canonical instructions which serve as introductory commentary to the rite of episcopal consecration in the *PR1595* contain precise information about its ritual context. Volume I of the *PR1595* ("Regarding persons") duplicates the contents which the *PR1485* copied from the *PGD*. It begins with the rite "Regarding those to be Confirmed"; the extensive *cursus honorum* of "Regarding those on whom Orders are to be Conferred" follows. The minor orders are door-keeper, lector, exorcist, and acolyte; they lead to the three sacred orders: subdeacon, deacon, and presbyter.

The *PR1595* retains the new name of the rite given by Piccolomini-Burchard: "Regarding the consecration of the Elect as a Bishop." It does not fall within the sequence of ordination rites but follows them as a separate chapter.

The prescribed day for the consecration is a Sunday or the feast day of an apostle (or even the feast day of a saint by papal concession). If celebrated outside of Rome, the consecration may occur in any number of places: preferably the cathedral of the new bishop, but also anywhere within that province, or in the cathedral of the consecrator.

B. ANALYSIS OF THE LITURGICAL UNITS

1. *Selection Presentation*

a. SELECTION PRESENTATION: TEXT

PR1595 p. 75 Regarding the Consecration of the elect as a bishop.

No one is to be Consecrated unless first the Consecrator is sure of the commission to consecrate, either by Apostolic letters, if he be outside the curia, or by verbal commission given by the supreme Pontiff to the Consecrator, if the Consecrator himself is a Cardinal.

The day chosen for consecration should be a Sunday or the feast day of the Apostles, or even a feast day if the supreme Pontiff will especially grant this; and it is fitting, that the Consecrator as well as the Elect, should fast on the preceding day.

The consecration, if it is to be performed outside of the Roman curia, should be celebrated in the Church, to which he has been promoted, or within the province, if it can be conveniently done.

In the Church, where the consecration is to be held, two chapels are prepared, a larger one for the Consecrating [bishop], and

p. 76 a smaller one for the Elect.

p. 77 Accordingly at the appropriate hour the Consecrator, Elect, the Assisting Bishops, and the others, who ought to take part in the consecration, assemble at the Church . . .

The Elect however with the Assisting Bishops goes to his chapel and there obtains the appropriate vestments, namely, if Mass is sung, amice, alb, cincture, stole in the manner of a Priest, and cope. . . .

[Rubrics follow for a Mass that is recited.]

When everything is ready the Consecrator goes up to before the altar, and there sits in the middle on the faldstool, turning [his] back to the altar. The Elect however vested and wearing his biretta, is led between the two assisting Bishops vested and mitered. . . .

[The Elect and Bishops make a reverence before the Consecrator.]

p. 78 When they are thus placed, and after a short period of silence, they rise, the Elect without biretta, and the assisting Bishops without miters, and the senior Assistant [Bishop] turned to the Consecrator says:

Most reverend Father, holy mother Catholic Church asks that you elevate this Presbyter present to the responsibility of the Episcopacy.
The Consecrator says.
Do you have the Apostolic mandate?
The senior Assistant Bishop responds.
We have.
The Consecrator says.
Let it be read.

p. 79 The the notary of the Consecrator receiving the mandate from the hand of the Assisting Bishop, reads [it] from beginning to end. Meanwhile all sit, with heads covered.

226

When the mandate has been read through by the notary,
the Consecrator says. Thanks be to God.

[The text of the oath is provided should this need to be done before the person of this Consecrator pp. 79–81.]

p. 82 Then when the Elect and the Assistant [Bishops] are seated in their places as it was stated, the Consecrator in a clear voice reads the following examination, which should always be read, as it appears [in the text], in the singular, even if several are examined together. The Assisting Bishops in a subdued voice however say, whatever the Consecrator says, and all ought to then hold [their] miters and sit.

Examination.
Antiqua sanctorum patrum. . . .

p. 83 Will you promise fidelity, submission, and obedience, in all things to blessed Peter the Apostle, to whom the power to bind and to loose was given by God; and to his Vicar our Lord, Lord N. Pope N. and his successors, the Roman Pontiffs, according to canonical authority?

[The questions continue, pp. 83–85.]

p. 85 And when the examination is finished, the Assisting Bishops mentioned above lead the Elect to the Consecrator, before whom he kneels, his hand is reverently
p. 86 kissed.

b. SELECTION PRESENTATION:
   OTHERS WHO OUGHT TO BE PRESENT AT THE CONSECRATION

The list of those present comprises a select number: the consecrator with three chaplains and two acolytes, the elect and his chaplains, two assistant bishops and their chaplains, the notary, several subdeacons, and any others who should attend. Is there evidence of the assembly? Is there evidence of the ecclesial relationships between those present?

The term "all" does appear several times in the rite: "All respond Amen," for example, or "all rising." However, "all" also refers to the bishops present in a rubric regarding miters: "Again all sit, with heads covered." The only two references to the explicit presence of the non-ordained involve directives for the elect at the opening greeting of the Mass in his chapel ("he does not turn toward the people") and the consecrator's final blessing ("The consecrator . . . solemnly blesses the people.") The presence of some of the faithful may be presumed but in the text of the *PR1595* is not rubrically significant.[30]

The relationships among the ministers themselves and between the ministers and the assembly are not rubrically significant either. The consecrator is not necessarily the elect's metropolitan; the two assistant bishops are not necessarily suffragans of the metropolitan nor "fellow servants" (OR34) or "fellow brothers" (OR35B) of the elect; representatives of the vacant See are not necessarily present and participating. Some initial directives in the rite indicate a preference for the celebration to occur somewhere in the diocese to which the elect has been promoted, or elsewhere within his province, if this is convenient. The consecration is celebrated in no particular church for no particular church by no particular church.

c. SELECTION PRESENTATION:
  VARIATIONS FROM THE *PR1485*

Very little of significance changes in the rite of consecration between the *PR1485* and the *PR1595*. The Roman evening scrutiny, which the *PR1485* removed from the rite itself into a chapter immediately following the rite, is placed in the *PR1595* in the appendix to Volume III ("Regarding ecclesiastical offices"). There it remained for almost four centuries under the title "Regarding the evening scrutiny which the ancients celebrated before the elect was consecrated as a bishop."[31]

The postulation dialogue occurs at the very beginning of the liturgy; the wording is that of the *PR1485* except that the consecrator is addressed more deferentially as "Most reverend father":

PR1485. f 32. v	PR1595 pp. 78–79
Reverend father:	Most reverend Father,
holy mother catholic church asks:	holy mother Catholic Church asks,
that you elevate	that you elevate
this presbyter present to the	this Presbyter present to the
responsibility of the episcopacy.	responsibility of the episcopacy.
The Consecrator says:	The Consecrator says.
Do you have the apostolic mandate.	Do you have the Apostolic mandate?
The senior assisting bishop responds.	The senior Assisting Bishop responds.
We have.	We have.
The Consecrator says.	The Consecrator says.
Let it be read.	Let it be read.
. . . When the mandate has been read	. . . When the mandate has been read
by the nostary	by the notary,
the Consecrator says.	the Consecrator says.
Thanks be to God.	Thanks be to God.

The postulation continues to be made by two assistant bishops not necessarily related to the elect nor to the vacant see. The papal mandate remains the only witness to the worthiness of the bishop-elect.

Then the *PR1595* includes the text of the oath, presented here as an option for "those bishops in the Papal States and in countries that had such relationships with Rome."[32] Then the consecrator begins the examination, *Antiqua sanctorum Patrum*.

While the ritualized dialogue between consecrator and elect remains substantially that copied from the *PR1485* (originally from the *PRG*), one set of questions invites comparison:

PR1485. f 33. r	*PR1595* p. 83
Will you promise fidelity: submission and obedience	Will you promise fidelity, submission, and obedience, in all things
to blessed Peter the apostle to whom the power to bind and to loose was given by God: and to his vicars	to blessed Peter the Apostle, to whom the power to bind and to loose was given by God; and to his Vicar our Lord, Lord N. Pope N. and his successors,
the Roman pontiffs: according to canonical authority.	the Roman Pontiffs according to canonical authority?

In the *PR1485*, the promise of fidelity, submission, and obedience is to the Roman pontiffs as a whole, a "more general and impersonal use of the plural form of vicar, [giving] a broader ecclesial sense to the position of the vicar of Peter."[33] But in the later Pontifical of 1595, the promise is *in all things*[34] and specifically made to the individual person of the present pope as well as his successors. The later promise underscores once again the relationship that is most significant in episcopal ordination of this century: the elect's selection by and obedience to the present pope.

Let us extend the comparison further and examine the same promise as included in the *PGD*:

PGD.I.XIV.19	*PR1485* f 33. r	*PR1595* p. 83
Will you promise fidelity, submission and obedience	Will you promise fidelity: submission and obedience	Will you promise fidelity, submission, and obedience, in all things,
to blessed Peter the	to blessed Peter the	to blessed Peter the

PGD.I.XIV.19	PR1485 f 33. r	PR1595 p. 83
apostle to whom the power to bind and to loose was given by God,	apostle to whom the power to bind and to loose was given by God:	Apostle, to whom the power to bind, and to loose was given by God;
and to his vicars	and to his vicars	and to his Vicars our Lord, Lord N. Pope N. and his succesors,
the roman pontiffs and to me his minister of the holy church of Besançon and my successors according to canonical authority?	the Roman pontiffs: according to canonical authority.	the Roman Pontiffs according to canonical authority?

The promise of fidelity is increasingly restricted: from one made to all the vicars of Peter *and* to the metropolitan (minister of the local church) *and* to his successors to the promise in the *PR1595* made to the present pope and his successors. Absent is any reference to the local church or to the metropolitan, such vital participants in the selection and consecration of bishops in earlier liturgical traditions.

2. *Consecration Presentation*

a. CONSECRATION PRESENTATION: TEXT

PR1595 p. 86 Then the Consecrator, with miter removed, turned together with the ministers to the altar, makes, in the customary way, the Confession, the Elect remaining at his left; and all the Bishops standing before their chairs similarly make the Confession with their chaplains. When the Confession is done, the Consecrator goes up to the altar, and it is kissed, and the Gospel to be said in the Mass; and he incenses the altar, in the customary way. Then he goes to his chair, or faldstool, and proceeds in the Mass up to the *Alleluia,* or the last verse of the Tract, or the Sequence exclusively.

[Rubrics follow for a recited Mass.]

The Assisting Bishops however lead the Elect to his chapel, and there when the cope is removed, Acolytes vest him in sandals, the customary Psalms, and prayers being read, if he has not taken them earlier. Then he receives the pectoral cross, and the stole is adjusted for him, so that it may hang from [his] shoulders. Then he is vested in tunic, dalmatic, chasuble, and maniple; . . . .
Prayer. *Adesto.* . . .

p. 87 The Assisting Bishops however again lead the Elect to the Consecrator. . . . And the Consecrator sitting with miter, turned to him, says.

[Episcopum oportet] A Bishop to judge, interpret, consecrate, ordain, offer, baptize, and confirm.

Then with all rising, the Consecrator standing with miter, says to those standing around. *Oremus, fratres.* . . .

p. 88 Then the cantor, or, if the office is to be read, the Consecrator begins the litany. . . .

p. 89 Then the Consecrator, having received the book of the Gospels, saying nothing, imposes that [book] open upon the head and shoulders of the Elect, with the Assistant Bishops helping; in such a way that the lower part of the book touches the neck of the Elect's head, one of the chaplains of the Elect, having knelt behind him, keeping the text facing downward, the book is to be continually held until it is to be handed over to the Elect into [his] hands. Then the Consecrator, and Assisting Bishops, touches the head of the one to be consecrated with both hands, saying.

Accipe Spiritum sanctum.

When this is done, the Consecrator standing, with miter removed, says.

Propitiare. . . .

p. 90 For ever and ever. R. Amen. The Lord be with you. . . .

p. 91 . . . honor of every dignity. . . .

p. 94 If the consecration is held in the Roman curia, the Apostolic Subdeacon, or one of the chaplains of the Pon-
p. 95 tiff binds the head of the Elect with one of the longer napkins, from the eight mentioned above; and the Consecrator, kneeling, toward the altar begins the hymn, the other things continuing. *Veni creator Spiritus.* . . .

p. 96 When the anointing has been completed, the Pontiff cleans off [his] thumb with a little bit of bread; and when the previously mentioned hymn has finished, with miter removed, he rises; and in a clear voice continues, saying. May it flow down, Lord, richly upon his head. . . .

p. 103 and he anoints with Chrism both hands joined together of the Elect kneeling before him, in the form of a cross, . . . and immediately he anoints the palms of the Elect completely, saying. May these hands be anointed. . . .

p. 107 Receive the Gospel, and go, preach to the people entrusted to you; for God is powerful to increase his grace within you, God who lives and reigns with God the Father in the unity of the holy Spirit. For ever and ever. R. Amen. Finally the Consecrator receives the *Consecratus* for the kiss of peace; and the Assisting Bishops individually [do] similarly, saying to the *Consecratus*.
Peace be with you. And he himself responds to each one. And with your spirit. Then he proceeds with Mass up to the Offertory inclusively. The *Consecratus* does the same in his chapel.

p. 112 Then the Consecrator rises, and takes the *Consecratus* by the right hand; and the first of the Assisting Bishops [takes him] by the left, and they enthrone him, putting him
p. 113 sitting in the faldstool, from which the Consecrator has stood up; or, if this was done in the *Consecratus'* own Church, they enthrone him in the customary Episcopal chair. . . . Then the Consecrator, standing toward the altar, with miter removed, begins the Hymn, the other things continuing, up to the end. *Te Deum laudamus.*
When the hymn has been begun, the *Consecratus* is lead by the Assisting Bishops with miters through the Church; and he blesses everyone; . . .

b. CONSECRATION PRESENTATION:
 VARIATION FROM THE *PR1485*

Following the pattern of the *PR1485*, after the examination the Mass begins. The bishop-elect vests in episcopal garb (the threefold symbol of ordained ministry: tunic, dalmatic, and chasuble with the addition of episcopal sandals and pectoral cross) and celebrates the Mass in his chapel up to the gospel acclamation. The opening prayer is *Adesto* (= *SVe* 942).

The two assistant bishops present the bishop-elect to the consecrator a second time for the consecration stage. The consecrator reads the *Episcopum oportet* unit which earlier pontificals had substituted for any proclamation of consensus before the consecration begins. The *PR1595* text reintroduces the episcopal responsibility "to confirm" from the *PGD* which had been omitted in the *PR1485*.

Bidding *MF* follows, still (incorrectly) given the formal ending of a collect, and the litany begins. Guillaume Durand's innovation of the consecrator's triple blessing continues to take place at the end of the litany. Before the litany oration *(Propitiare)*, the two assistant bishops hold the gospel book over the neck and shoulders of the elect, and while one of the elect's chaplains holds the book in place, the two bishops with the consecrator impose hands on the elect, saying *Accipe Spiritum sanctum* as Durand prescribed.

The composite consecration prayer is sung with the preface dialogue; the elect's head is bound with linen strips and anointed midway during the prayer with a separate anointing formulary. As the anointing continues and the consecrator washes his hands, the hymn *Veni Creator Spiritus* is sung. The consecration prayer resumes; following it, the elect's hands are anointed with chrism. Only at the end of the two anointing formularies is the elect called *consecratus.*

Just as in the *PR1485*, the explanatory rites take place: the blessing and giving of the crozier and ring, the kiss of peace exchanged with the consecrator and assistant bishops, the resumption of the Mass in separate chapels up to the presentation of the elaborate gifts of two heavy torches, containers of bread and barrels of wine decorated in silver and gold, one set with the coat of arms of the consecrator, one with those of the elect.

After communion, the miter and gloves are blessed and given to the new bishop who is then enthroned (in the consecrator's faldstool or in the *cathedra* of the newly ordained). The consecrator intones the *Te Deum* and the new bishop blesses those present; he greets the consecrator with *ad multos annos* and then begins to recite the first chapter of John's Gospel.[35]

3. Conclusion

The structure of episcopal ordination in the rite of the *PR1595* remains that of the earlier pontifical, Piccolomini-Burchard's *editio princeps*:

PR1595

1st stage

Selection Presentation

	Sunday
presentation:	two bishops
postulation:	elevate this presbyter
	mandate
	examination
proclamation of consensus and consecration:	
	[ ]

2nd stage

Consecration Presentation

	Sunday
	introit to gradual
	episcopal vestments
presentation:	two bishops
proclamation of consensus and consecration:	
	Episcopum oportet
	bidding *MF*
consecration:	litany
	gospel book
	laying on of hands
	Accipe Spiritum sanctum
	Propitiare
	consecration prayer
	consecration continues

Although it owes almost every one of its elements to the *editio princeps*, it is this Roman Pontifical of 1595 (the *editio typica*) which Botte and Study group 20 take as their "point of departure" for the reform of episcopal ordination after the conciliar mandate that both ceremonies and texts of the ordination rites be revised. We will study that reform in relation to the *editio typica* in chapter 6.

Texts of the Roman Pontifical of 1595:

Selection Presentation:

PR1595 p. 75 De Consecratione electi in episcopvm.

Nemo Consecrari debet, nisi prius constet Consecratori de commissione consecrandi, sive per literas Apostolicas, si fit extra curiam, sive per commissionem viuae vocis oraculo a summo Pontifice Consecratori factam, si Consecrator ipse sit Cardinalis.

Statuta die consecrationis, quae debet esse Dominica, vel natalitium Apostolorum, vel etiam festiua, si summus Pontifex hoc specialiter indulserit: et tam Consecrator, quam Electus conueniens est, vt praecedenti die ieiunent.

Consecratio, si extra curiam Romanam fiat, in Ecclesia, ad quam promoti fuerint, aut in prouincia, si commode fieri poterit, celebretur.

In Ecclesia, vbi fiet consecratio, ornantur duae capellae, maior pro Consecrante, et

p. 76 minor pro Electo.

p. 77 Hora igitur competenti Consecrator, Electus, Assistentes Episcopi, et alij, qui consecrationi interesse debent, ad Ecclesiam conueniunt. . . . Electus vero cum Assistentibus Episcopis vadit ad capellam suam, et ibi capit paramenta opportuna, videlicet, si Missa cantatur, amictum, albam, cingulum, stolam in modum Sacerdotis, et pluuiale. . . .
Omnibus itaque paratis, Consecrator accedit ante altare, et ibi in medio sedet super faldistorium, vertens renes altari. Electus vero cum suo bireto ducitur sic paratus, medius inter Assistentes sibi Episcopos paratos, et mitratos, . . .

p. 78 Cum sic locati fuerint, et aliquantulum quieuerint, surgunt, Electus sine bireto, et Assistentes Episcopi sine mitris, et senior Assistentium versus ad Consecratorem, dicit.

Reuerendissime Pater, postulat sancta mater Ecclesia Catholica, vt hunc praesentem Presbyterum ad onus Episcopatus subleuetis.
Consecrator dicit.
Habetis mandatum Apostolicum?
Respondet Episcopus senior Assistentium.
Habemus.

Consecrator dicit.
Legatur.

p. 79 Tum notarius Consecratoris accipiens mandatum de manu Episcopi Assistentis, legit a principio ad finem. Interim sedent omnes, tectis capitibus. Mandato per notarium perlecto, Consecrator dicit. Deo gratias.

p. 82 Deinde Electo, et Assistentibus, in locis suis (vt dictum est) sedentibus, Consecrator intelligibili voce legit sequentem examinationem, quae legi debet semper, sicut iacet, in singulari, etiam si plures simul examinentur. Assistentes vero Episcopi submissa voce dicunt, quaecumque dixerit Consecrator, et omnes debent tunc mitras tenere, et sedere.

Examen.
Antiqua sanctorum Patrum. . . .

p. 83 Vis beato Petro Apostolo, cui a Deo data est potestas ligandi, ac soluendi; eiusque Vicario Domino nostro, Domino N. Papae N. suisque successoribus, Romanis Pontificibus fidem, subiectionem, et obedientiam, secundum canonicam auctoritatem, per omnia exhibere?

p. 85 Expleto itaque examine, praefati Assistentes Episcopi ducunt Electum ad Consecratorem, coram quo genuflexus, eius manum reuerenter oscu
p. 86 latur.

Consecration Presentation:

p. 86 Tunc Consecrator, deposita mitra, cum ministris ad altare conuersus, facit, solito more, Confessionem, Electo a sinistris eius manente;
et omnes Episcopi ante sedes suas stantes faciunt similiter Confessionem cum capellanis suis. Facta itaque Confessione, Consecrator ascendit ad altare, et osculatur illud, et Euangelium in Missa dicendum; et incensat altare, more solito. Deinde vadit ad sedem suam, vel faldistorium, et procedit in Missa vsque ad Alleluia, siue vltimum versum Tractus, vel Sequentiae exclusiue. . . .
Episcopi vero Assistentes ducunt Electum ad capellam suam, et ibi deposito pluuiali, Acoliti induunt illum sandalia, ipso Psalmos, et orationes consuetas legente, si prius illa non accepit. Tum accipit crucem pectoralem, et stola ei aptatur, vt ab humeris dependeat. Deinde tunicella, dalmatica, casula, et manipulo induitur; . . .

Oratio. Adesto. . . .

p. 87 Assistentes vero Episcopi iterum ducunt Electum ad Consecratorem. . . . et Consecrator sedens cum mitra, versus ad illum, dicit.
Episcopum oportet iudicare, interpretari, consecrare, ordinare, offerre, baptizare, et confirmare.
Deinde omnibus surgentibus, Consecrator stans cum mitra, dicit ad circumstantes.
Oremus, fratres. . . .

p. 88 Tum cantor, vel, si officium fit legendo, Consecrator incipit Litanias. . . .

p. 89 Tum Consecrator, accepto libro Euangeliorum, illum apertum, adiuuantibus Episcopis Assistentibus, nihil dicens imponit super ceruicem et scapulas Electi; ita quod inferior pars libri ceruicem capitis Electi tangat, littera ex parte inferiori manente, quem vnus ex capellanis Electi, post illum genuflexus, quousque liber ipse eidem Electo in manus tradendus sit, continue sustinet.

Deinde Consecrator, et Assistentes Episcopi, ambabus manibus caput consecrandi tangunt, dicentes.

Accipe Spiritum sanctum.

Quo facto, Consecrator stans, deposita mitra, dicit.

Propitiare. . . .

p. 90 Per omnis saecula saeculorum. R. Amen. Dominus vobiscum. . . .

p. 91 . . . honor omnium dignitatum. . . .

p. 94 Si in Romana curia fit consecratio, Subdiaconus Apostolicus, vel vnus ex capellanis Pon-

p. 95 tificis ligat caput Electi cum vna ex longioribus mappulis, de octo superius dictis; et Consecrator, flexis genibus, versus ad altare incipit, caeteris prosequentibus, hymnum. Veni creator Spiritus. . . .

p. 96 Expleta vnctione, Pontifex pollicem cum medulla panis paululum abstergit; et finito hymno praedicto, deposita mitra, surgit; et in pristina voce prosequitur, dicens.

Hoc, Domine, copiose in caput eius influat. . . .

p. 103 et Electo ante ipsum genuflexo inungit ambas manus simul iunctas cum Chrismate, in modum crucis, . . et mox inungat totaliter palmas Electi, dicens.

Vngantur manus istae. . . .

p. 107 Accipe Euangelium, et vade, praedica populo tibi commisso; potens est enim Deus, vt augeat tibi gratiam suam, qui viuit, et regnat cum Deo Patre in vnitate Spiritus sancti Deus. Per omnia saecula saeculorum. R. Amen. Demum Consecrator recipit Consecratum ad osculum pacis; similiter et Assistentes Episcopi singuli, dicentes ipsi Consecrato.

Pax tibi.

Et ipse respondet singulis.

Et cum spiritu tuo.

. . . Deinde procedit in Missa vsque ad Offertorium inclusiue. Idem facit Consecratus in capella sua.

p. 112 Tum surgit Consecrator, et accipt Consecratum per manum dextram; et primus ex Assistentibus Episcopis per sinistram, et intronizant eum, ponendo ipsum ad

p. 113 sedendum in faldistorio, de quo surrexit Consecrator; vel, si id fiat in Ecclesia propria Consecrati, intronizant eum in sede Episcopali consueta. . . .

Deinde versus ad altare Consecrator, deposita mitra, stans incipit, caeteris vsque ad finem prosequentibus, Hymnum. Te Deum laudamus.

Incepto hymno, Consecratus ducitur ab Assistentibus Episcopi cum mitris per Ecclesiam; et ominibus benedicit; . . .

NOTES

[1] Hereafter *PR1485*.

[2] Andrieu, *PGD*, 17.

[3] Dykmans, *Le Pontifical romain*, 9–10.

[4] ". . . la plupart des évêques l'avaient déjà adopté." Andrieu, *PGD*, 19.

[5] Vogel, *Medieval Liturgy*, 255. See also Vogel and Elze, *PRG* III, 54, n. 107: "Il est certain que c'est Burchard qui a fait le travail, car dans les éditions subséquentes le nom de l'évêque, tandis que celui du maître des cérémonies demeure sur la page du titre"; and their comment that Burchard was more informed than anyone on the liturgy in use in Rome during his time: "personne plus que Burchard n'était au fait de la liturgie en usage de son temps à Rome."

[6] Text in John Bligh, *Ordination to the Priesthood* (New York: Sheed and Ward, 1956) 28.

[7] The only other place this title is used is in the *SVe* to designate the prayer texts for the rite, XXVIII: "Consecration of Bishops."

[8] While Piccolomini-Burchard deliberately change the title of the rite to "consecration," within the extensive commentary they add they occasionally refer to "episcopal ordination."

[9] Puniet, *The Roman Pontifical*, 45–46; Vogel, *Medieval Liturgy*, 256.

[10] Puniet, *The Roman Pontifical*, 45.

[11] Walter Clancy explains the canonical understanding that he believes justifies this preference: "Although it is fitting that Orders be conferred with solemnity, it is not necessary that the Mass of ordination be a solemn Pontifical Mass. The ordaining prelate may offer simply a low Mass. Indeed, because of the length of the ceremony, this practice has become more or less the rule." *The Rites and Ceremonies of Sacred Ordination (Canons 1002–1005): A Historical Conspectus and a Canonical Commentary* (Washington, D.C.: The Catholic University of America Press, 1962) 84–85.

[12] ". . . la permission de procéder à la consécration." Puniet, "Consécration épiscopale," 2584.

[13] "Ce même mandat remplace l'ancienne élection de l'évêque par le clergé et par le peuple." V. Leroquais, *Les Pontificaux manuscrits*, LXXXV.

[14] "[L]a décision pontificale élevant quelqu'un à l'épiscopat. . . . Ce changement eut lieu vers le XIVe siècle, lorsque le Saint-Siège se fût [sic] réservé la [sic] choix des évêques ou au moins leur institution canonique." Salmon, "Le rite du sacre des évêques," 34, n. 10.

[15] Puniet, *The Roman Pontifical,* 45.

[16] Leon Strieder, *The Promise of Obedience: A Ritual History* (Collegeville: Liturgical Press, 2001) 40.

[17] Andrieu, *PGD,* 379, n. 20.

[18] Joseph Jungmann describes the evolution of the *Confiteor,* "this confession before each Mass," in his *The Mass of the Roman Rite: Its Origins and Development (Missarum Sollemnia),* I, trans. F. Brunner, replica edition (Westminster, MD: Christian Classics Inc., 1986) 298–311 (especially n. 56) which mentions the practice enjoined by various general chapters of the Dominicans down to the sixteenth century. Guillaume Durand, the Dominican, composed the rubrics for the confession that Piccolomini-Burchard copy at this point.

[19] Andrieu points out in the apparatus that several manuscripts mention the hymn *Veni creator spiritus* as an alternative.

[20] Note that the candidate is still called *electus* even after the laying on of hands and consecration prayer.

[21] The *PR1485* omits all reference to consecration or "confirmation" of hands and thumbs; they are simply "anointed."

[22] Hereafter *PR1595.*

[23] Puniet, *The Roman Pontifical,* xiii.

[24] J. D. Crichton, *Christian Celebration,* vol. II: *The Sacraments* (London: Geoffrey Chapman, 1979) 147.

[25] Vogel, *Medieval Liturgy,* 269, n. 300.

[26] Puniet, *The Roman Pontifical,* 50.

[27] Gerard Austin, *The Rite of Confirmation: Anointing with the Spirit* (New York: Pueblo, 1985) 22. And also see Vincent Leroquais who reminds us: "Before 1596, each particular Church possessed its own [pontifical], often different from its neighbor." ("Avant 1596, chaque Eglise particulière possédait le sien, souvent différent du voisin.") *Les Pontificaux manuscrits,* III.

[28] Statuentes Pontificale praedictum nullo umquam tempore, in toto, vel in parte mutandum, vel ei aliquid addendum, aut omnino detrahendum esse, ac quoscumque, qui Pontificalia munera exercere, vel alias, quae in dicto Pontificali continentur, facere, aut exequi debent, ad ea peragenda, et praestanda, ex huius Pontificalis praescripto, et ratione teneri, neminemque ex iis, quibus ea exercendi, et faciendi munus impositum est, nisi formulis, quae hoc ipse Pontificali continentur servatis, satisfacere posse. Text and translation from Clancy, *The Rites and Ceremonies of Sacred Ordination,* 21.

[29] Martin Klöckener, *Die Liturgie der Diözesansynode,* LQF 68 (Münster: Aschendorff, 1986) 324. Anhang IV contains excellent information: "The printed editions of the pontificals since 1485," 324–329. I am indebted to Fr. Ephrem Carr, O.S.B, for this source.

[30] Absence of references to the faithful in the rubrics of the *PR1595* should not be surprising in an *ordo* of the post-Tridentine period. Burkhard Neunheuser, for example, observes how Pius V (for the Roman Missal of 1570) directed that

almost every reference to the faithful be systematically eliminated from John Burchard's *Ordo Missae* of almost a century earlier. The "low Mass" or "private Mass" of the *ordo* of Pius V "becomes the norm for all eucharistic celebrations." A similar excising of rubrics may well have occurred in the creation of the post-Tridentine pontifical. See Burkhard Neunheuser, "The Relation of Priest and Faithful in the Liturgies of Pius V and Paul VI," in *Roles in the Liturgical Assembly,* Saint Serge Liturgical Conference XXIII (New York: Pueblo, 1981) 209.

[31] Puniet, "Consécration épiscopale," 2584.

[32] Strieder, *The Promise of Obedience,* 47.

[33] Ibid.

[34] Originally part of the text of the examination of the *PRG*.LXIII.12.

[35] By the fifteen and sixteenth centuries, this was a common practice as a type of blessing after the chasuble was removed. See Jungmann, *The Mass of the Roman Rite,* II, 450, n. 17, but also 447–451 for the history of the use of the Last Gospel.

Chapter 6

All Say:
Thanks be to God:

The Presentation of the Bishop-Elect in the Rite of Episcopal Ordination according to the Reform of the Second Vatican Council

I. Doctrinal and Theological Preludes to *Ordination of a Bishop* 1968

In the nearly five hundred years between the *editio princeps* of the episcopal ordination rite published in the Roman Pontifical of 1485 and the *editio typica* of the rite revised by decree of the Second Vatican Ecumenical Council and published by the authority of Pope Paul VI in 1968, significant doctrinal and theological questions were debated, defined, and continued to vex theologians, liturgists, and canonists alike. Discussion of some of the principal issues in their historical context follows. All of them contribute to the theological foundations which made the revised rite of 1968 possible.

A. DECREE TO THE ARMENIANS 1439

The only official pronouncement on the matter and form of ordination made before the Council of Trent is found in the *Decree to the Armenians,* ratified as the Bull *Exsultate Domino* of Pope Eugene IV on 22 November 1439 at the Council of Florence. Concerning the precise nature of the sacrament of orders, the *Decree* restates the Thomistic positions that the three sacred orders are the presbyterate, diaconate, and subdiaconate, the matter is the *traditio instrumentorum* (the handing over of the "instruments" proper to the liturgical ministry of each order), and the form is the specific text accompanying the *traditio.*

Thomas Aquinas had constructed his theology of orders from this premise:[1]

ST Suppl. Q 37 art. 2 . . . But the Orders derive their sacramental nature from their relation to the greatest of the sacraments [Eucharist], and consequently the number of Orders depends on this.

His conclusions then logically followed:

ST Suppl. Q 37 art. 3 . . . In this sense there are only three sacred Orders, namely the priesthood and diaconate, which exercise an act about the consecrated body and blood of Christ, and the subdiaconate, which exercises an act about the consecrated vessels.

ST Suppl. Q 37 art. 5 . . . The conferring of power is effected by giving them something pertaining to their proper act. And since the principal act of a priest is to consecrate the body and blood of Christ, the priestly character is imprinted at the very giving of the chalice under the prescribed form of words.

In explaining his theology of the episcopacy, Thomas asserted that the concept of order has two distinct meanings: "sacrament" and "hierarchical office which involves sacred actions." He concluded that in terms of possessing hierarchical powers which are higher than those of presbyters, the episcopate is an order. But since a bishop's elevation imparts no sacramental character, the episcopate is not a sacramental order.[2]

The *Decree to the Armenians*, then, faithful to Thomistic thought, summarized and promulgated "the *fides* of the Church with regard to orders as it was understood in the Middle Ages":[3]

The sixth [order] is the sacrament of orders. Its matter is the object by whose handing over the order is conferred. So the priesthood is bestowed by the handing over of a chalice with wine and a paten with bread; the diaconate by the giving of the book of the gospels; the subdiaconate by the handing over of an empty chalice with an empty paten on it; and similarly for the other orders by allotting things connected with their ministry. The form for a priest is: Receive the power of offering sacrifice in the church for the living and the dead, in the name of the Father and of the Son and of the holy Spirit. The forms for the other orders are contained in full in the Roman pontifical.[4]

But for all the clarity of its definitions, the *Decree to the Armenians* did not finally resolve all questions regarding the proper matter and form of the ordination rites nor did it resolve the questions about the nature of the episcopacy (with which the *Decree* did not specifically concern itself). In fact: "the most weighty argument against the binding force of the

Decretum pro Armenis is the continuation of the controversy in the West. Certainly the writers before, during and after the Council of Trent did not consider the matter closed."[5]

B. THE COUNCIL OF TRENT, SESSION XXIII, 1563

A. Duval provides a concise summary of the unresolved issues regarding the episcopacy that faced the Council fathers of Trent. The debates came to a climax in the discussions between October 1562 and July 1563:

> Is the episcopate of divine institution or not? Is episcopal jurisdiction derived directly from Christ? What is the role of the Pope in its transmission? How is the superiority of the episcopate over the priesthood to be defined? Is the episcopate a *verus et proprius ordo,* conferred by a *verum sacramentum* or not? Is it in the simple priest or in the bishop that the true conception of the *sacerdos ecclesiae sanctae catholicae* is realised, a conception in which the *sacerdotes minores* would be but collaborators . . . ?[6]

Thus faced with "pressing problems in the wake of Reformation criticism of the offices of the Church . . . [and] uncertainties concerning episcopal office,"[7] and caught between "a fear of conciliarism"[8] on the one hand and "the latent 'presbyterianism' of certain Thomistic theologians"[9] on the other, the Council of Trent would not be drawn into a decisive formulation on the nature of the episcopacy.

However, the council was not completely silent on the subject. Session Twenty-three (15 July 1563) promulgated four chapters and eight canons on the doctrine of the sacrament of order. Its teachings included: there are seven orders in the list of which the bishop is not included (Chapter II); the bishop belongs to the hierarchical order of the church, is ranked higher than priests, and has additional powers to confirm and to ordain (IV); neither the consent nor the calling nor the authority of the people are required in the ordination of bishops (IV);[10] it is the authority of the pope alone which promotes presbyters to the episcopacy *(canon 8).*

Not needing to define the matter and form of this rite, the council simply ratified that order is truly a sacrament, conferring its particular graces by words and external signs (III), but in canons 4 and 5 the council also admonished those who would question the strict necessity of bishops to say *Accipe Spiritum Sanctum* and to perform the sacred anointings. In response to so many unresolved issues, theological debate only increased

242

in the post-Tridentine climate, "with the gathering of force for the inclusion of episcopacy in the sacrament of order.["]

C. *APOSTOLICAE CURAE ET CARITATIS* 1896

In the context of his letter regarding Anglican orders celebrated according to the Edwardian ritual, Leo XIII indicated the direction of shifting theological opinion. His statement about the sacramental nature of the episcopacy is clear:

> The episcopacy . . . most truly belongs to the sacrament of order and is a priesthood of excelling dignity.[12]

He cites the phrases "high priesthood" and "apex of sacred ministry," used by both the fathers of the church and Roman liturgical books to refer to the bishop, as the warrants for his statement.[13]

D. *EPISCOPALIS CONSECRATIONIS* 1944

By his apostolic constitution *Episcopalis Consecrationis*[14] of 30 November 1944, Pius XII clarified the status of the two bishops participating with the principal consecrator in episcopal ordination. The Pope's text declared that the two bishops presenting the bishop-elect were themselves consecrators and not merely "Assisting Bishops" (as they were called in the *PR1485* and the *PR1595*):

> . . . Although, when the essential rites are performed, only one bishop is required and suffices for the validity of an episcopal consecration, nevertheless, the two bishops who, from ancient custom and according to the prescription of the "Roman Pontifical," assist at the consecration—being themselves consecrators and thus henceforth to be called co-consecrators—should with the aforementioned consecrator not only touch the head of the elect with both hands and say *Accipe Spiritum Sanctum*, but, having made at an appropriate time the mental intention of conferring episcopal consecration together with the bishop consecrator, recite the prayer *Propitiare* with the entire preface that follows, and also, throughout the whole rite read in a low voice everything the consecrator reads or chants, except the prayers prescribed for the blessing of the pontifical vestments which are imposed in the rite of consecration.[15]

Note the large number of elements that Pius XII has decreed for the co-consecrators: mental intention to consecrate, laying on of hands and entire consecration prayer, but also *Accipe Spiritum Sanctum*, the litany oration *(Propitiare)*, and everything else that the principal consecrators says or sings (except for the formularies for gloves and miter). Further clarification regarding the nature of the rite itself, however, would finally come with a papal document three years later.

E. SACRAMENTUM ORDINIS 1947

With such intensity did the debates over the nature of the episcopacy and the essential elements of ordination continue that by the promulgation of the apostolic constitution of Pius XII, *Sacramentum Ordinis* (30 November 1947),[16] five centuries after the *Decree to the Armenians,* the theological viewpoint on both issues had completely reversed itself. *Sacramentum Ordinis* presupposes the sacramental nature of the consecration of bishops and signals this conclusion by including the "ordination or consecration of a bishop" in the three sacred orders it defines.

The contentions which *Sacramentum Ordinis* settled were not only theological but pastoral and canonical. The centuries following the *Decree to the Armenians* saw an unceasing stream of requests for repetition of various elements of the ordination rites to remedy defects of matter and form. Bishops and priests throughout the Latin Church grew increasingly anxious that the minute and complex prescriptions for their ordinations' validity may not have been meticulously adhered to.[17]

By the beginning of the twentieth century, the pastoral and canonical crisis was severe. Several factors figured in the solution. The commission named in 1907 by Pius X for the creation of the new Code of Canon Law championed the cause.[18] Also of vital importance to the shift in theological understanding was the study by the Dutch curial cardinal Willem Marinus van Rossum, covering 385 theologians from the thirteenth century to the beginning of the twentieth. His vast and masterful work, *De essentia sacramenti ordinis* (Freiburg, 1914), supported the biblical and patristic position that the laying on of hands and ordination prayer were the essential elements of ordination.[19] A third factor was the printing of early liturgical books (by Jean Morin, Edmund Martène, and Michel Andrieu) that "opened the eyes of dogmatic theologians to the comparatively recent origin" of the *traditio instrumentorum.*[20] Botte enthusiastically heralds the 1947 constitution as of profound significance in the area of sacramental theology: it marked the primacy of tradition over speculation![21]

For the ordination of bishop, *Sacramentum Ordinis* declares:

5. Finally, in the ordination or consecration of a bishop the matter is the imposition of the hands which is done by the bishop consecrator. The form consists in

the words of the "preface," of which the following are essential and therefore required for validity: "Complete the fullness of your ministry in your priest, and equipped with all the adornments of glory, hallow him with the dew of heavenly unction."[22]

No longer does the elect become *consecratus* only after the anointing of his head and hands; the primacy of the laying on of hands and ordination prayer was restored. Furthermore, the *entire* "preface" (ordination prayer) constituted the form, although one particular sentence of the prayer is identified as necessary for validity.

Writing in 1959 from long experience with theological issues of ordination in the Church of England, E. C. Ratcliff summarizes the critical importance of this decree:

> The effect of *Sacramentum Ordinis* is to reconnect the laying-on of hands with the ancient Ordination Prayer proper to each Order, so that the laying-on of hands is the 'matter' and the substantive petition the 'form', of the Sacrament. Roman theory is now in substantial accord with the Greco-Russian. The Ordination Prayer determines the meaning of the laying-on of hands. Whatever the Rites might appear to suggest to the contrary, the essential act of Ordination is laying-on of hands with prayer.[23]

F. *VARIATIONES IN RUBRICIS PONTIFICALIS ROMANI* 1950

The Sacred Congregation of Rites prepared a decree for the changes to be made in the rubrics of the *Roman Pontifical* in accordance with the two apostolic constitutions. The most important changes are these three:[24] from the first chapter ("Regarding the conferring of orders") the deletion of the words "He is to warn the ordinands that they touch the instruments, by means of whose handing over the character is imprinted"; in the rite of episcopal ordination, use of the word *consecratus* immediately after the consecration prayer; and the highlighted words of the essential part of the form with the insistence that the words be recited (not sung) simultaneously by the principal consecrator and co-consecrators.

The prescriptions of this decree and of the two previous apostolic constitutions are the reasons for the slightly revised edition of "Regarding the Consecration of the Elect as a Bishop" produced in the 1962 edition of the *Roman Pontifical*.[25] Besides the changes mentioned above, the previous term, "assisting Bishops," became "co-consecrating Bishops."

G. *SACROSANCTUM CONCILIUM* 1963

In his commentary on the 1968 ordination rites, Bruno Kleinheyer remarks that this work of the reform corresponds faithfully to the direction of the council.[26] Particular articles to which the new rites are faithful include the following:[27]

SC 14. In the reform and promotion of the liturgy, this full and active participation by all the people is the aim to be considered before all else; . . .

SC 21. In this reform both texts and rites should be so drawn up that they express more clearly the holy things they signify and that the Christian people, as far as possible, are able to understand them with ease and to take part in the rites fully, actively, and as befits a community.

SC 31. The revision of liturgical books must ensure that the rubrics make provision for the parts belonging to the people.

SC 76. Both the ceremonies and texts of the ordination rites are to be revised. The address given by the bishop at the beginning of each ordination or consecration may be in the vernacular.

When a bishop is consecrated, all the bishops present may take part in the laying on of hands.

And in a fine preview of the theological statements to come in *Lumen Gentium*,[28] *Sacrosanctum Concilium* declares:

SC 41. The bishop is to be looked upon as the high priest of his flock. . . . Therefore all should hold in great esteem the liturgical life of the diocese centered around the bishop, especially in his cathedral church; . . . .

All the themes and principles listed above will be easily recognized in the revised liturgical texts of the *Ordination of a Bishop 1968*.

H. *LUMEN GENTIUM* 1964

In an article entitled "Observations on Episcopacy in the Light of Vatican II," Karl Rahner writes: "There can be no doubt that the dogmatic Constitution on the Church is the most significant achievement of Vatican II in so far as the immediately practical results of the Council are concerned. Within this Constitution, the teaching on the episcopacy is the most important sector."[29] Key statements of that teaching include the following:[30]

LG 21. This Council teaches that episcopal consecration bestows the fullness of the sacrament of orders, that fullness of power, namely, which in both the

Church's liturgical practice and the language of the Fathers is called the high priesthood, the summit of the sacred ministry.

LG 26. Marked with the fullness of the sacrament of orders, a bishop is "the steward of the grace of the supreme priesthood. . . ."

LG 27. The bishops, as vicars and legates of Christ, govern the particular churches assigned to them. . . . The pastoral charge, that is, the permanent and daily care of their sheep, is entrusted to them fully; nor are they to be regarded as vicars of the Roman Pontiff; for they exercise the power which they possess in their own right and are called in the truest sense of the term prelates of the people whom they govern.

In the statements of *Lumen Gentium*, a balanced theology of the episcopacy is recovered and clarified: the bishop as successor to the apostles is fully priest, constituted head of the local church by sacramental ordination, not by delegation. On the other hand, the genuine exercise of this authority is established in and through union with the Roman pontiff and the college of bishops.

In its euchological and rubrical texts, *Ordination of a Bishop 1968* expresses in ritual form the theological principles of the conciliar documents, while maintaining conformity with the earlier apostolic constitutions and curial decree of 1944, 1947, and 1950.

II. *Ordination of a Bishop* 1968 [31]

A. *OB1968* AND THE RITUAL CONTEXT OF EPISCOPAL ORDINATION

After a lengthy and circuitous exploration, we return to the point of origin of this study—the reform of the episcopal ordination rites after the Second Vatican Council and to Botte's own description of the task:

> The reform of these rites posed some ticklish problems. The Pontifical took shape progressively, from the fifth to the end of the thirteen centuries, to a great extent outside Rome. It contained elements of very different origin and value. The essential element, that is, the laying on of hands, was somewhat buried under a pile of secondary rites. Furthermore, certain formulas were inspired by medieval theology and needed correction. . . . The instructions given by the Council prescribed restoring simplicity and genuineness to the rites, so that the rites and prayers might catechize the people on holy orders. For this reason we set aside the radical solution of restoring the ordinations to the fifth century state by suppressing the secondary rites

added on through the ages. When judiciously chosen, these rites
could be an element of catechesis. So we took the Roman Pontifical
as it stood as our point of departure, and critiqued it to determine
what could be retained of the Roman tradition.[32]

Through the much wider lens provided by the previous chapters, the
focus of this work turns to an examination of the 1968 rite as a reform of
the 1595 rite. Some introductory comments on the title, arrangement,
and order of the three ordination rites begins this presentation.

While some elements of "the Roman tradition" (to use Botte's term)
were retained, other elements were recovered and restored. For example,
OB1968 deliberately reclaims the traditional Roman and Gallican word
"ordination" to describe the nature of this rite for so many centuries
misplaced and misidentified as "consecration." United again with the
ordination texts for presbyters and deacons, the episcopal rite underscores by its placement the equality of its sacramental status and the
nature of the episcopacy itself as one of the three holy orders. The significance of the return to the sacramental language of "ordination" in the
title is somewhat undermined, however, by the retention of the terms
"principal consecrator," "consecrating bishops," and "consecration
prayer" throughout the liturgical texts.

The arrangement of the three ordination rites within the ritual book by
which they were promulgated is itself distinctly different. Although the
title of the revised rite ("Ordination of a Deacon, a Presbyter, and a Bishop")
lists the orders in their singular form, the layout of the rites within the
ritual book recovers the preeminent importance of the relationship of the
bishop to the local church: that is, there are many presbyters and deacons
ordained for a diocese but only one bishop. The theology of the episcopate
has controlled the preference for the presentation of the rites: "Ordination
of Deacons," "Ordination of Presbyters" followed by "Ordination of a
Bishop." In the majority of instances, only one bishop would be ordained
at any one time since he would be ordained within a vacant see to serve
that vacant see. The Foreword to the *Roman Pontifical* (1978) reiterates the
preference: "The rites are first given as they are generally celebrated
when several men are admitted into the order of deacons or priests or
when the bishop of the local church . . . is ordained. Next, rites are given
for exceptional circumstances. . . ."[33]

The order in which the three rites are listed, however, remains the
ascending order (deacon, presbyter, bishop) which "appears in the
Missale Francorum and becomes customary from the time of the Romano-

Germanic Pontifical. . . . The doctrine of Vatican II on the episcopacy would rather suggest the reverse order."[34]

The revised ordination rites were promulgated by the apostolic constitution of Pope Paul VI, *Pontificalis Romani,* of 18 June 1968. Referring to the "controversy and . . . anxiety of conscience" that prevailed before *Sacramentum Ordinis* in 1947, Paul VI established the matter and form for the conferring of each order. Regarding the ordination of a bishop, he decreed:

> Finally, in the ordination of a bishop, the matter is the laying on of hands upon the head of the bishop-elect by the consecrating bishops, or at least by the principal consecrator, which is done in silence before the consecratory prayer; the form consists of the words of the consecratory prayer, of which the following belong to the nature of the rite and are consequently required for validity:
> So now pour out upon this chosen one that power which is from you, the governing Spirit whom you gave to your beloved Son, Jesus Christ, the Spirit given by him to the holy apostles, who founded the Church in every place to be your temple for the unceasing glory and praise of your name.[35]

The matter (as determined by *Sacramentum Ordinis*) is the laying on of hands; the form is the ordination prayer. The precise words of course reflect the new 1968 text. The freedom initially made possible by the radical recovery of the essential elements of ordination by Pius XII and now reconfirmed by Paul VI opened the doors for Botte and Study group 20 to "drastically simplify"[36] the ordination rites after the council. No ritual elements beyond the laying on of hands and ordination prayer were strictly necessary. Secondary elements from the 1595 rite could be judiciously chosen to serve simply as desirable explanatory rites to illuminate theological facets of episcopal ministry.

After a brief analysis of the *praenotanda* and the reversal of ecclesial perspective it presents, we examine the Selection and Consecration Presentations.

B. ANALYSIS OF THE LITURGICAL UNITS

1. *Praenotanda*

a. PRAENOTANDA: TEXT

OB1968 Introduction

1. The ordination of a bishop should take place on a Sunday or holy day when a large number of the faithful can attend, unless pastoral reasons suggest another day, such as the feast of an apostle.

2. The principal consecrator must be assisted by at least two other consecrating bishops, but it is fitting for all the bishops present together with the principal consecrator to ordain the bishop-elect.

3. Two priests assist the bishop-elect.

4. It is most appropriate for all the consecrating bishops and the priests assisting the bishop-elect to concelebrate the Mass with the principal consecrator and with the bishop-elect. . . .

6. . . . The bishop-elect wears all the priestly vestments, the pectoral cross, and the dalmatic. . . .

7. The blessing of the ring, pastoral staff, and miter ordinarily takes place at a convenient time prior to the ordination service.

9. b) The ordination should usually take place at the bishop's chair; or, to enable the faithful to participate more fully, seats for the principal consecrator and consecrating bishops may be placed before the altar or elsewhere. Seats for the bishop-elect and his assisting priests should be placed so that the faithful may have a complete view of the liturgical rites.

11. The liturgy of the word takes place according to the rubrics.

b. PRAENOTANDA

Being the first of the sacraments revised after the council, the ordination rites did not benefit from the pattern later set by the *General Instruction of the Roman Missal* (1969) of a comprehensive theological and rubrical introduction. The ordination rites are preceded only by the apostolic constitution promulgating them *(Pontificalis Romani)*. Each individual rite begins with brief, separate, rubrical notes for *praenotanda*.

Besides giving careful attention to principles enunciated by *SC* (particularly participation of the faithful, simplicity, and clarity of rites and texts, and the organic relationship between former and revised rites), Botte and members of Study group 20[37] were convinced of the catechetical power of the rites:

> In fact, the rites in their structure and particular parts should also have a didactic function; they should therefore be clear in their organization and contain a series of gestures and words that express sure teaching. . . . [The church's] formulas . . . are intended not simply for the conferral of a sacrament but also for the instruction of the faithful through the rite.[38]

Thus several times throughout the brief *praenotanda,* the presence of the faithful and their ability to observe the rite are mentioned: a strikingly different ecclesial perspective from the *PR1595* whose rubrics have no reference to the faithful. Preference for the participation and understanding of the faithful, for example, affect even the use of the *cathedra;* the people are to have a complete view of the rite. On the other hand, the provisions made for participation of the faithful in *OB1968* seem to be predominantly ocular.

c. THE DAYS FOR ORDINATION

While *OB1968* retains the ancient tradition of Sunday as the preferred day for ordination, it greatly expands other possibilities to any feast day. For the first time in any ordination rite the preference for the choice of day is to be determined by the presence of a large number of the faithful. From the opening words of the *praenotanda,* the principle stated by *SC* 31 takes effect: rubrics are to take the role of the people into account.

d. THREE BISHOPS

The ancient tradition of the presence of three bishops remains, yet (following *SC* 76) all bishops present ordain the elect. The "Assisting Bishops" of the *PR1595* (having been made co-consecrators by *Episcopalis Consecrationis*, 1944) are here replaced by two priests. The significance of the (minimum of) three bishops for purposes of consensus is not recovered by *OB1968* since the revised rite does not identify the bishops nor their relationship to the vacant see nor to the elect.

e. THE VACANT SEE

References to the vacant see, rare in the liturgical texts after the *ordines romani, Missale Francorum,* and the *PRG,* make their reappearance in these brief *praenotanda* of 1968. The preference for the site of the ordination is the elect's own church; the preference for principal celebrant at the concelebration of the eucharistic liturgy is the newly ordained.[39] Both points reflect the principle of *SC* 41: the liturgical life of the diocese finds its center in the bishop, particularly as he celebrates the Eucharist in his cathedral church with his priests, deacons, and other ministers in the midst of his people. Thus the presence and concelebration of priests from the vacant see is highlighted in the introductory texts. These presbyters are the only ministers so identified, however. The ecclesial relationship of the principal consecrator, other bishops, participating priests, deacons, and faithful to the vacant see is left unstated.

f. CONCELEBRATION

Concelebration of the Eucharist had been prescribed for the new bishop and the consecrator since the *PRXII*:[40]

PRXII.X.32. He offers two loaves [of bread] and a flask of wine to his consecrator and returning to the altar celebrates Mass with him.

The *PRCγ* employs stronger language:

PRC.XI.34. [The] *consecratus* . . . must concelebrate with the celebrating consecrator.

Guillaume Durand places the *consecratus* between two assisting bishops and in detail specifies:

PGD I.XIV.50. [He is] concelebrating and making the gestures and in a subdued voice saying all that the consecrator does and says.

Concelebration in the far more inclusive sense of the 1965 *Rite of Concelebration* is the norm envisioned here and includes all bishops and priests present concelebrating with the newly ordained and the principal consecrator.

g. PONTIFICAL INSIGNIA

The short, clear, unencumbered rites characterized by the noble simplicity called for in *SC* 34 are well exemplified by the reform of the blessing of the pontifical insignia. *OB1968* omits the texts for the blessing of the crozier and ring from the explanatory rites that followed the consecration in the *PR1595* and omits the texts for the blessing of the miter and gloves that took place after the consecrator's final blessing. The new insignia blessing (for ring, crozier, and miter only) is brief, simple, and christological; it occurs at any convenient time before the ordination.

h. THE LITURGY OF THE WORD:
LOSS OF THE SELECTION PRESENTATION

"The liturgy of the word takes place according to the rubrics" (no. 11). With these few words, the ancient and traditional structure of episcopal ordination is overturned. For the first time in any liturgical rite since *OR34*, the Selection Presentation is dislocated: it is moved from its place *before* the consecration liturgy to *within* the consecration liturgy. The text of the Selection Presentation from the *PR1595* remains intact, but it is now subsumed into the Consecration Presentation. For the first time since the sixth century, episcopal ordination in the Roman Church retains not even a remnant of its traditional two-stage structure. Only one presentation of the bishop-elect remains: the anomaly of a Consecration Presentation with an introductory Selection Presentation text.

In a praiseworthy attempt to simplify the three ordination rites, Study group 20 decided to standardize the arrangement of several elements within all three of the rites. A model homily (an element drawn from presbyteral and diaconal ordination rites), for example, is created for episcopal ordination; an examination of the candidates before the bidding (drawn from episcopal ordination) is created for the presbyteral and diaconal rites. The liturgical elements of the sacrament of ordination in all three rites now take place following the gospel.

The structural reconfiguring that followed from this choice unnecessarily obliterates an ancient distinction between the three orders according to which the minister's liturgical role determined the placement of the ordination rite within the liturgy.[41] But even more significant is the fact that the standardization removed a fundamental component of the structure of episcopal ordination: its first stage, the selection. The elect enters already vested as bishop—even before the postulation! The deciding voice has already spoken; the selection occurred well before this consecration liturgy began.

On the other hand, one might suggest that the Selection Presentation, even though it retained its earlier position, ceased to be an authentic expression of communal consensus by the thirteenth century (if not earlier) and it unambiguously ceased to be meaningful by the time of the *PR1485* (as that juridical introduction made explicit). It could be said that Botte and Study group 20 by simplification and standardization brought the liturgy of episcopal ordination into line with ecclesiastical reality. Yet critical opportunities to recover as well as to retain some aspects of "the Roman tradition" as Botte understood it passed unheeded.

2. *Consecration Presentation*

a. CONSECRATION PRESENTATION: TEXT

OB1968 Ordination of a Bishop

13. The ordination of a bishop begins after the gospel. While all stand, the hymn *Veni, Creator Spiritus* is sung, or another hymn similar to it, depending on local custom.

15. The bishop-elect is led by his assisting priests to the chair of the principal consecrator, before whom he makes a sign of reverence.

16. One of the priests addresses the principal consecrator:

Most Reverend Father, the Church of N. asks you to ordain this priest, N., for service as bishop.

If the bishop-elect is not to be ordained as a residential bishop:

Most Reverend Father, our holy mother the Catholic Church asks you to ordain this priest, N., for service as bishop.

The principal consecrator asks him:
Have you a mandate from the Holy See?
He replies:
We have.
Principal consecrator:
Let it be read.

Everyone sits while the document is read.

17. After the reading, all present say:

Thanks be to God,

or give their assent to the choice in some other way, according to local custom.

18. Then the principal consecrator, while all are sitting, briefly addresses the clergy, people, and the bishop-elect on the duties of a bishop. He may use these words: . . .

19. The bishop-elect then rises and stands in front of the principal consecrator, who questions him:

[Antiqua sanctorum Patrum] An age-old custom of the Fathers decrees that a bishop-elect is to be questioned before the people on his resolve to uphold the faith and to discharge his duties faithfully. . . .

Are you resolved to build up the Church as the body of Christ and to remain united to it within the order of bishops under the authority of the successor of the apostle Peter?

Are you resolved to be faithful in your obedience to the successor of the apostle Peter?

20. Then all stand, and the bishop, without his miter, invites the people to pray:
[Oremus, dilectissimi nobis] My dear people, let us pray that almighty God in his goodness will pour out his grace upon this man whom he has chosen to provide for the needs of the Church.

21. The bishop-elect prostrates himself. . . .

22. After the litany, the principal consecrator alone stands and, with hands joined, sings or says:

[Propitiare] Lord, be moved by our prayers. Anoint your servant with the fullness of priestly grace, and bless him with spiritual power in all its richness.

24. The principal consecrator lays his hands upon the head of the bishop-elect, in silence. After him, all the other bishops present do the same.

25. Then the principal consecrator places the open Book of the gospels upon the head of the bishop-elect; two deacons, standing at either side of the bishop-elect, hold the Book of the Gospels above his head until the prayer of consecration is completed.

26. Next the principal consecrator, with his hands extended over the bishop-elect, sings the prayer of consecration or says it aloud:

God the Father of our Lord Jesus Christ, Father of mercies and God of all consolation. . . .

Before an analysis of the text is undertaken, let us compare the structure of the presentation of the bishop-elect in the 1968 revision with the presentations of the bishop-elect from the *PR1595*. The comparison will serve as a reference for the commentary that follows. The sections in brackets indicate those structural elements drawn from the Selection Presentation now placed within the Consecration Presentation:

PR1595	*OB1968*
1st stage	*1st stage*
Selection Presentation	
Sunday	
presentation:	
two bishops	
postulation:	
elevate this presbyter	
mandate	
examination	
proclamation of consensus	
and consecration:	
[ ]	
2nd stage	*2nd stage*
Consecration Presentation	**Consecration Presentation**
	Sunday
introit to gradual	entrance song to gospel
episcopal vestments	episcopal vestments

PR1595	OB1968
	[Selection Presentation
presentation:	presentation:
two bishops	two presbyters
	postulation:
	ordain this presbyter
	mandate]
	address
proclamation of consensus	proclamation of consensus
and consecration:	and consecration:
Episcopum oportet	[ ]
	examination
bidding *MF*	bidding *MF*

b. CONSECRATION PRESENTATION:
ONE PRESENTATION

All remnants of a separate selection stage of ordination having been removed by the 1968 reform, there is now but one presentation of the bishop-elect: he is presented for consecration. The structural element within which the postulation is made, however, is drawn from the Selection Presentation. It is not a little ironic that as *OB1968* restored the constitutive importance of the vacant see in the postulation, it has suppressed the ritual structure of the selection stage which allowed the vacant see its prominence and participation.

c. CONSECRATION PRESENTATION:
VACANT SEE

Comparison here will underscore this important ecclesiological shift: the recovery of the ritual inclusion of (at least the name of) the vacant see. No longer is it "holy Mother Catholic Church" who asks for the ordination of this presbyter but the vacant see, "the Church of N." The recovery (from *OR34.21*) of presbyters as "assistants" to the elect provides the possibility that these two priests may represent another link to the vacant see.

PR1595 pp. 78–79	*OB1968.16–17*
. . . and the senior Assistant [bishop] turned to the Consecrator, says.	One of the priests addresses the principal consecrator:

PR1595 pp. 78–79	OB1968.16–17
Most reverend Father,	Most Reverend Father,
holy mother Catholic Church asks you	the Church of N. asks you
to elevate this Presbyter present to	to ordain this priest, N.,
the responsibility of the Episcopacy.	for service as bishop.
The Consecrator says.	The principal consecrator asks him:
Do you have the Apostolic mandate?	Have you a mandate from the Holy See?
The senior Assistant Bishop responds.	He replies:
We have.	We have.
The Consecrator says.	Principal consecrator:
Let it be read.	Let it be read. . . .
. . . When the mandate has been read by the notary,	After the reading,
the Consecrator says.	all present say:
Thanks be to God.	Thanks be to God,
	or give their assent to the choice in
	some other way, according to local custom.

The one voice in the selection of the bishop-elect, however, remains that of the apostolic see by means of the mandate. No recovery of a broader understanding of "the Roman tradition" of selection was yet possible; the substitution of the papal mandate for a consensus of testimony regarding the worthiness of the elect (set firmly in place by the *PR1485*) remains in force.

d. CONSECRATION PRESENTATION:
   OMISSION OF PLURAL OF MAJESTY

Although forms of the word "consecrate" are retained in *OB1968*, the verb in the postulation is deliberately changed to "ordain." Bugnini's description of the textual alteration in this verb is instructive: "The Pope's first request concerned a point of style: not to use the *plural* of majesty in the request that the consecrating bishop proceed to the ordination; that is, put the Latin verb in the singular, not the plural (*ordines* instead of *ordinetis*).—A very appropriate suggestion."[42]

e. CONSECRATION PRESENTATION:
   "ALL . . . GIVE THEIR ASSENT TO THE CHOICE"

In yet another admirable attempt to enhance the participation of the faithful in the ordination rite, the authors of the reformed rite change the speaker of "Thanks be to God" from the consecrator to all present. As an inclusion of the faithful, this rubrical shift can be appreciated. The words are further identified as constituting the faithful's assent to the choice of the elect. Ideally arising from the midst of an assembly significantly representative of the local church, a resounding proclamation of "Thanks be to God" may be a significant element of the ritual. As a liturgical element which recognizes the voice of the clergy and people in the choice of the elect, this is a positive step.

As was indicated previously in the analysis of the postulation dialogue brought into episcopal ordination by Guillaume Durand, "Thanks be to God" was the ritual conclusion spoken by all present at the conclusion of the testimony regarding the worthiness of the elect during the selection stage.

Pontifical of Besançon	PGD.I.XIV.16	PR1485.32.v	PR1595 p. 79
And all respond.	The consecrator and others respond.	. . . the Consecrator says.	The Consecrator says.
Thanks be to God.	Thanks be to God.	Thanks be to God.	Thanks be to God.

OB1968 (unwittingly?) restores the earlier Gallican tradition of giving these words to all present, yet two concerns regarding this revision remain: the identity of the assembly and the sequence of their assent within the rite.

There is no absolute, ecclesiological significance to the fact that those present (friends and relatives of the elect? others?) assent to the prior selection of the candidate. One constitutive voice in the traditional selection process was that of the faithful of the vacant see, not the voice of any assembly of the faithful gathered for the occasion.

Even should the assembly be composed of large numbers of the clergy and people of the vacant see, the placement of their response in the structure of the rite is not yet the traditional one. In OB1968 the choice of the bishop-elect is announced by the apostolic mandate; the assembly assents to the previous choice. The sequence of these elements is the reverse of that observed in the earlier Roman and Gallican traditions. Many voices participated in the selection of the candidate; the apostolic see contributed to, confirmed, and concluded the consensual selection process. OB1968 begins with the reading of the apostolic mandate that makes the prior choice explicit; the assembly assents ritually after the fact, not as a constitutive voice, not even as a formulaic voice, in the earlier stage of the ordination process.

f. CONSECRATION PRESENTATION:
VENI, CREATOR SPIRITUS

Botte and the members of Study group 20 attempted to remove the hymn, *Veni, Creator Spiritus,* from its position in the *PR1595.* Botte explains the reasons: "It was sung immediately after the laying on of the hands, when it was time for the anointing of the candidate. This was a misrepresentation since it led to the belief that the Spirit had not yet come and that the essential rite was beginning."[43] The group considered moving the hymn to another time during the rite. But because of its nature as an invocation of the Holy Spirit, the most appropriate place for it was after the bidding and before the ordination prayer. This place and function had been traditionally and appropriately filled by the litany of saints, now in its revised form made even more fitting: it invites participation of the faithful and contains the three specific intercessions for "this chosen man" formerly offered personally by the consecrator. Paul VI decided to retain the hymn despite good reasons for its omission. It is now sung at the beginning of the presentation of the bishop-elect between the proclamation of the gospel and the postulation dialogue as the elect is presented by the two presbyters.[44]

g. CONSECRATION PRESENTATION:
ADDRESS

For the first time since the exhortation, *Servanda est* of the *Missale Francorum,* a model text of an address is provided for episcopal ordination. The authors of the revised rite, taking the *PR1595* as their point of departure, find an address at the beginning of presbyteral and diaconal ordination rites and decide to provide a similar model for the episcopal rite. Emil Lengeling composed the substance of the text to which Botte then gave "a more harmonious literary shape."[45]

In *OB1968* the sample address, "Consider carefully the position in the Church," exists as a newly created unit within the structure of the Consecration Presentation after the postulation and before the examination. The new text, so carefully crafted as catechesis for the faithful on the meaning of episcopal ordination, could have been deliberately written to replace the *Episcopum oportet* unit from the earlier pontificals *(PRXII–PR1595).* *Episcopum oportet,* a brief list of episcopal responsibilities, would then have found a solid parallel in the 1968 address:

*OB1968.*18. Then the principal consecrator . . . briefly addresses the clergy, people, and the bishop-elect on the duties of a bishop. . . .

Botte and Study group 20 seemed unaware of the existence of this earlier allocution and thus were not intending to replace it. But as the reformed rite stands, there is no proclamation of consensus and consecration in episcopal ordination. The proclamation from the Selection Presentation removed by Guillaume Durand is never replaced; the proclamation from the Consecration Presentation was omitted from the *PRXII* and replaced by the *PRC* with *Episcopum oportet*. With more ample time (as well as more felicitous times), the authors of the reformed rite may have retained something of "the Roman tradition" by providing a model address faithful to the ancient structure of that element: a proclamation of consensus and consecration. The texts of such a proclamation from *OR34* and the exhortation, *Servanda est* from the *Missale Francorum* and the *PRG*, would have served as outstanding inspiration.

h. CONSECRATION PRESENTATION:
EXAMINATION

The last element drawn from the former Selection Presentation structure is the text of the examination. Its opening words continue to be those taken from the "examination for the ordination of a bishop according to the Gauls": *Antiqua sanctorum patrum* (*OR35B* and the *PRG* [B G K L]).

OR35B.12/*PRG*.LXIII.a.(12)	*OB1968*.19
The age-old instruction of the holy fathers teaches and decrees that he who is chosen to the order of the episcopacy, especially, as we read in the Carthaginian canon, shall be most diligently examined beforehand concerning his faith. . . .	An age-old custom of the Fathers decrees that a bishop-elect is to be questioned before the people on his resolve to uphold the faith and to discharge his duties faithfully.

Botte explains how the revision of the examination was accomplished:[46]

> [T]he examination which precedes the ordination of the bishop . . .
> is an old tradition which was kept by the Pontifical. The one conse-
> crating asked a series of questions of the candidate before the people.
> Undoubtedly this venerable custom should be kept, but the examina-
> tion aimed at orthodoxy of the candidate in light of heresies today
> having only historical interest. We thought it preferable to have the
> examination cover the commitment of the bishop to the church and

his people. I drafted a questionnaire which I submitted for review to my consultors. We proposed it to the Commission which received it well and helped us finalize it. It serves as a useful complement to the address of the consecrator.

In his explanation of the questions for the elect, note Botte's use of the phrase "before the people." This phrase appears for the first time in the 1968 *Antiqua sanctorum patrum* text. Those responsible for the reform are laudably committed to the inclusion of the faithful in a variety of ways throughout the new rite. What appears to be less recognized, however, is the traditional nature of the structure of the examination.

The Gallican model concludes the Selection Presentation with the examination of the elect (still vested as presbyter), followed by the statement from *Statuta Ecclesiae Antiqua,* authorizing the ordination to proceed once consensus is achieved by clergy, people, neighboring bishops, and metropolitan. In the early Roman model, the examination was also an essential element of the Selection Presentation. The faithful of the vacant see were not the *observers* of the examination; rather, it was the people themselves with their clergy who *were examined* as to the worthiness of the elect and the legitimacy of his election. Only when the "apostolic lord" accepted the examination of the people and clergy did the examination of the elect begin. The faithful of the vacant see then did not so much attend the examination but participate in it as a constitutive voice, as the canon of Celestine I recalls: "No bishop may be imposed on the unwilling" (*PRG*.LXIII.18).

Besides the addition of "before the people," the authors of the revised rite also subtly but significantly rewrote the description of the one being examined. The traditional text calls him "he who is to be chosen for the order of the Episcopacy." The examination takes place within the Selection Presentation as part of the process of consensus regarding the worthiness of the one so chosen. The text of *OB1968* reflects the fact that the selection stage of ordination no longer exists. The decision regarding the episcopal status of the elect has already been made: he is bishop-elect before he is presented for the examination "before the people."

Let us consider the questions of the examination themselves. The earlier texts contain nine questions regarding the elect's moral behavior and nine related to the orthodoxy of his faith. By the time of the *PR1595,* however, the fourth question (asking for fidelity, submission, and obedience to the metropolitan and his successors) has been removed. The original third question:

PR1595, p. 83 Will you promise fidelity, submission, and obedience in all things to blessed Peter the Apostle, to whom the power to bind and to loose was given by God; and to his Vicar our Lord, Lord N. Pope N. and his successors, the Roman Pontiffs according to canonical authority?

is considerably revised and refocused to read:

OB1968.19. Are you resolved to build up the Church as the body of Christ and to remain united to it within the order of bishops under the authority of the successor of the apostle Peter?

As a condition for its approval of this new examination form in November 1967, the Congregation for the Doctrine of the Faith stated that "the candidate should be expressly asked about his determination to give obedience to the Roman Pontiff."[47] Thus an additional question was added to the rite:

OB1968.19. Are you resolved to be faithful in your obedience to the successor of the apostle Peter?

Of the eight questions in the PR1595, only one survives in the reformed rite:

PR1595 p. 84	OB1968.19
Will you be kind and compassionate in the name of the lord to the poor and to strangers and to all who are in need?	Are you resolved to show kindness and compassion in the name of the Lord to the poor and to strangers and to all who are in need?

i. CONSECRATION PRESENTATION:
   THE BIDDING

The Consecration Presentation concludes with the bidding which has held this hinge position since the *Missale Francorum*. The revised text returns to the original Latin words of the address, "dilectissimi nobis [our dearly beloved]," rather than "dearest brothers" of the PR1595, and removes the inaccurate ending. OB1968 will translate this phrase as "my dear people." From the early eighth century, then, these words have gathered the prayers of the assembly for the consecration of the bishop-elect:

MF, PRG, PRXII, PRC, PGD, PR1485, PR1595, OB1968
Oremus . . . ut huic viro, utilitati ecclesiae providens, benignitas omnipotentis
Dei gratiae tuae tribuat largitatem.

OB1968.20
My dear people, let us pray that almighty God in his goodness will pour out his
grace upon this man whom he has chosen to provide for the needs of the Church.

The presentation of the bishop-elect is complete; the bidding introduces
the formal elements of the consecration itself: litany, laying on of hands,
and ordination prayer.

j. THE CONSECRATION:
FURTHER REVISED ELEMENTS[48]

When Bruno Kleinheyer, assessing the 1968 reform of the episcopal
ordination rite, concluded that "in the whole history of the liturgy of
ordination there has never been a reform comparable to this,"[49] he was
addressing the choice of the ordination prayer from *Apostolic Tradition* to
replace the ancient composite prayer text from the *Missale Francorum* and
the Old Gelasian Sacramentary. While undeniably the most extraordinary element of the reform, the choice of the *Apostolic Tradition* prayer[50]
only heads a long list of other revisions, among which are:

- a more concise litany sung by cantors and people with the option of
  including names important to the vacant see and to the elect;

- restoration of *Propitiare* as the litany collect;

- elimination of *Accipe Spiritum Sanctum* before the ordination prayer;

- elimination of the preface dialogue before the ordination prayer;

- the laying on of hands in silence by all bishops present;

- two deacons (not the assisting bishops) hold the gospel book over the
  head of the elect;

- anointing of the head of the newly ordained after (rather than within)
  the ordination prayer with a new, simple formula;

- elimination of the anointing of hands and thumb;

- presentation of the gospel book with new formula before any other
  insignia;

- inversion of the order in which the insignia are presented: the ring,
  miter (without formula), and crozier;

- seating of the new bishop on his *cathedra;*
- sign of peace exchanged between the newly ordained and the other bishops;
- elimination of the elaborate ritual offering of candles, bread and wine in favor of the gifts presented by members of the local church;[51]
- an opportunity for the *ordinatus* to address those present before the final blessing;
- *Hanc igitur* provided for Eucharistic Prayer I;
- new form of the solemn blessing.[52]

Commentary by three of the rite's authors will serve as a fitting conclusion to this analysis of the *OB1968*. Bernard Botte, the *relator* of Study group 20, realistically wrote:

> We worked in the spirit of Vatican II, careful to preserve the Church's authentic tradition but also to restore to the rites their authenticity and simplicity in order that they be accessible to the Christian people. . . . Of course this did not settle all the problems, but it provided a solid foundation for extensive reflection.[53]

Joseph Lécuyer reminded readers of the commitment to the catechetical values that guided much of their work:

> I sincerely believe that the revision was made with the greatest fidelity to the principles and spirit of the Second Vatican Council and that not only the clergy but all the faithful will thus be significantly helped to better understand the mission of those called to serve the people of God as deacons, priests or bishops.[54]

And in a sweeping historical judgment, Bruno Kleinheyer did not hesitate to insist: "In this millennium, no reform (if you can call the various reworkings of these rites that) was so abundant in theological rationale as well as in pastoral concerns as the current one."[55]

Texts of De Ordinatione Episcopi 1968:

OB1968 Praenotanda

1. Ordinatio Episcopi fiat cum fidelium quam maxima frequentia die dominico vel festo, nisi rationes pastorales alium diem, ex. gr. festum Apostolorum, suadeant.

2. Episcopus Consecrator principalis debet saltem alios duos Episcopos conse-crantes adhibere; sed decet ut omnes Episcopi praesentes una cum Consecratore principali Electum ordinent.

3. Electo assistant duo Presbyteri.

4. Valde convenit, ut omnes Episcopi consecrantes necnon Presbyteri Electo assis-tentes cum Consecratore principali et cum Electo Missam concelebrent. . . .

6. . . . Electus induit omnia paramenta sacerdotalia necnon crucem pectoralem et dalmaticam. . . .

7. Benedictio anuli, baculi pastoralis et mitrae, tempore opportuno, ante ipsam ordinationem, de more peragitur.

9. b) Ordinatio Electi fiat de more ad cathedram; si autem propter participationem fidelium opus est, parentur sedes pro Consecratore principali et Episcopis consecrantibus ante altare vel alio opportuniore loco; sedes autem pro Electo et Presbyteris ei assistentibus sic parentur, ut actio liturgica a fidelibus bene conspici queat.

11. Liturgia verbi peragitur ad normam rubricarum.

Consecration Presentation:

13. Dicto Evangelio, incipit Ordinatio Episcopi. Omnibus stantibus, canitur hymnus Veni, Creator Spiritus, vel alius hymnus huic respondens, iuxta locorum consuetudines.

15. Electus a Presbyteris ipsi assistentibus adducitur ante sedem Consecratoris principalis, cui reverentiam facit.

16. Unus e Presbyteris alloquitur Consecratorem principalem his verbis:

Reverendissime Pater, postulat Ecclesia N., ut Presbyterum N. N. ad onus Episcopatus ordines.

Si vero agitur de Episcopo ordinando non residentiali:

Reverendissime Pater, postulat sancta Mater Ecclesia Catholica, ut Presbyterum N. N. ad onus Episcopatus ordines.

Consecrator principalis illum interrogat, dicens:
Habetis mandatum Apostolicum?
Ille respondet:
Habemus.
Consecrator principalis:
Legatur.

17. Tunc legitur mandatum, omnibus sedentibus. Quo perlecto, omnes dicunt:
Deo gratias,
vel alio modo, iuxta morem regionis, electioni assentiunt.

18. Deinde Consecrator principalis, omnibus sedentibus, breviter alloquitur clerum ac populum necnon Electum de munere Episcopi; quod facere potest his verbis: . . .

19. Post allocutionem, Electus surgit et stat ante Consecratorem principalem, qui illum interrogat his verbis:

Antiqua sanctorum Patrum institutio praecipit, ut, qui Episcopus ordinandus est, coram populo interrogetur de proposito fidei servandae et muneris exsequendi. . . .

Vis corpus Christi, Ecclesiam eius, aedificare et in eius unitate cum Ordine Episcoporum, sub auctoritate successoris beati Petri Apostoli, permanere?

Vis beati Petri Apostoli successori oboedientiam fideliter exhibere?

Vis pauperibus et peregrinis omnibusque indigentibus propter nomen Domini affabilem et misericordem te praebere?

22. Litaniis expletis, solus Consecrator principalis surgit et, manibus iunctis, dicit:

Propitiare. . . .

24. Consecrator principalis imponit manus super caput Electi, nihil dicens. Similiter faciunt post eum et ceteri Episcopi.

25. Deinde Consecrator principalis imponit librum Evangeliorum apertum super caput Electi; duo Diaconi, a dexteris et sinistris Electi stantes, tenent librum Evangeliorum supra caput ipsius usquedum oratio Consecrationis finiatur.

26. Tunc Consecrator principalis, extensis manibus, dicit orationem Consecrationis:

Deus et Pater Domini nostri Iesu Christi, Pater misericordiarum et Deus totius consolationis. . . .

III. *Ordination of a Bishop* 1990 [56]

One of the best ways to acknowledge two key changes in *Ordination of a Bishop* from 1968 to 1990 is to quote from the decree by which the new rite was promulgated:

The rites of Ordination by which ministers of Christ and stewards of the mysteries of God are constituted in the Church, revised in accord with the norms of the Second Vatican Council (see *SC*, art. 76), were published in the first *editio typica* in 1968 under the title *De Ordinatione Diaconi, Presbyteri et Episcopi*.

But now, in view of the experience acquired from the liturgical reform, it has been judged opportune to prepare a second *editio typica*, which has the following distinct elements that differ from the earlier edition.

1. This second edition, like the other liturgical books, is provided with introductions, in order to present the doctrine concerning the sacrament and to bring out more clearly the structure of its celebration.

2. The structure of this book is changed in such a way that it begins with the Bishop, who has the fullness of the sacrament of Holy Orders, in order to convey more clearly the idea that priests are the Bishop's co-workers and that deacons are ordained for his ministry.[57]

The revisions of the 1968 episcopal rite published in 1990 are primarily rubrical. In his evaluation of the *editio typica altera*, Ferdinando Dell'Oro explains that the 1990 rite is not "a 'reform of the reform,' but only a general and ordered standardization of these books with the necessary coordination and enrichment of the texts and rites."[58] Nevertheless, the revisions are not unimportant. Besides the inversion of the orders in the title of the rite *(Rites of Ordination of a Bishop, of Priests, and of Deacons)* and the significant addition of the substantial *Praenotanda,* there are other elements worth noting.

The vocabulary has been standardized: the presiding bishop is renamed the "principal ordaining Bishop"; the former "consecrating bishops" are "ordaining Bishops"; the "Consecration prayer" has become the "Ordination Prayer."

The participation of the local church is more explicitly defined in several key articles, one of the most important being that of an expanded description of the presbyters who present the bishop-elect:

OB1990.17. Two priests of the diocese for which the Bishop-elect is being ordained assist him in the celebration of his Ordination; and, in the name of the local Church, one of these priests requests the principal ordaining Bishop to confer Ordination on the Bishop-elect. Along with the Bishop ordained in this celebration and the other Bishops, these two priests and, to the extent possible, even other priests, particularly those of the same diocese, concelebrate the Liturgy of the Eucharist.

To the structure of the presentation of the bishop-elect is thereby partially restored the identity of those making the presentation as it was first described in *OR34:* they are representatives of the vacant see. It is the local church itself who asks for the ordination of the elect, as no. 24 so concisely states:

OB1990.24. After the Gospel reading, the local Church, in the person of one of its priests, requests the ordaining Bishop to ordain the Bishop-elect.

The explicit identification of the two presbyters as being from the local church helps restore the voice of the local church in the ordination. The restoration is partial, however, since although the presbyters present the elect and one of them makes the postulation, they have not participated in choosing the elect nor has the local church in whose name they now speak.

The preference for the participation of the local church is expanded and strengthened at numerous additional points in *OB1990*. Section III of the general *Praenotanda*, for example, specifies the adaptation of the ordination rites to be made for the needs of the particular regions, with respect for the genius and traditions of the various peoples, for local circumstances and conditions (*OB1990.11*). The episcopal conference will determine (among other ritual elements) the form of the assembly's assent at the conclusion of the postulation dialogue.

In the *Praenotanda* specific to episcopal ordination, the faithful of the local church are urged to pray for the one to be chosen bishop and to continue to pray for him after his selection:

OB1990.15. It is the duty of all the faithful to pray for the one to be elected their Bishop and for the Bishop once elected.

And before the ordination liturgy takes place, there should be careful preparation of all the various communities of the local church:

OB1990.20. All the communities of the diocese for which the Bishop is to be ordained should be made ready in an appropriate manner for the celebration of the Ordination.

For the liturgy itself, the *Praenotanda* mandates that the clergy and faithful of the local church in great numbers are to be invited:

OB1990.15. Since the Bishop is constituted for the sake of the entire local Church, the clergy and other faithful are to be invited to his Ordination, so that as many as possible may take part in the celebration.

During the liturgy, no longer is it the case that "the principal consecrator" decides who presides at the Eucharist that follows the ordination. It is in the person of the new bishop, when ordained in his own church (now an even stronger preference[59]), that the liturgical life of the local church is renewed; he is its center and focus of unity. He presides over this first Eucharist with the faithful of his see in the company of his presbyters, deacons, and other ministers:

OB1990.27. Within his own diocese it is most fitting that the newly ordained Bishop preside at the concelebration of the Liturgy of the Eucharist. . . .

Several other refinements present in *OB1990* are worthy of mention. The insignia of ring, miter, and croizer no longer require prior blessing; their *traditio* during the ordination suffices (no. 28); the kiss of peace exchanged between the newly ordained and all the bishops is aptly described as the seal on his reception into the college of bishops (no. 26); inserts into Eucharistic Prayers II, III, and IV (as the equivalent of the *Hanc igitur* in the Roman Canon) are provided for the first time (no. 59).

Three other additions are less appreciated. While no. 12 of *OB1968* provided (appropriately) for the omission of both the Creed and the general intercessions,[60] *OB1990* inserts the recitation of the Creed into the celebration of ordination when rubrics call for it (no. 58). The insertion creates an awkward embolism between the sign of reception into the order of bishops and the preparation of the gifts, a rather inexplicable awkwardness since no. 23 clearly states that the ordination rite is celebrated *between* the Liturgy of the Word and the Liturgy of the Eucharist.

Several liturgical commentators have remarked positively on the omission of the formulas for blessing and imposing the miter in *OB1968*. In the *PR1595* formula for imposing the miter (written by Guillaume Durand), the Consecrator reminded the new bishop that his miter was the helmet of protection and salvation, the horns of both biblical testaments, the brightest rays of Moses' face, and Aaron's high priestly tiara.[61] *OB1968* wisely chose to mark the imposition of the miter with silence. The revised rite of 1990 reintroduces a formula for this ritual act:

OB1990.53. Receive the miter, and may the splendor of holiness shine forth in you, so that when the chief shepherd appears you may deserve to receive from him an unfading crown of glory.

Pierre Jounel wryly comments that the newly determined symbolism for the miter is closer to Amalarius and Guillaume Durand than *Lumen Gentium*.[62] The separation of the *traditio* of the ring from that of the crozier (from *OB1968*) is a questionable act itself, but it is made more so by the additional formula to accompany the imposition of what is essentially an ornamental head-covering. In a sardonic understatement, Bruno Kleinheyer concludes that one can certainly be of two minds as to whether this new explanatory formula is an improvement over the one in the *PR1595!* [63]

One final comment is in order regarding the permission extended in *OB1990.96* to parents and relatives *(parentes et propinqui)* of the new bishop to receive Communion under both kinds. While a certain graciousness underlies this permission, one might wonder at the theology at work here. Why would the invitation be directed only to parents and relatives? Why would not the invitation be extended to the faithful of the local church to whom the bishop has been joined in profound nuptial relationship (no. 51) and over whom he now keeps watch as shepherd (no. 54)?[64]

The slight textual and rubrical revisions of *OB1990*, while conforming the rite more closely to the theology of the episcopacy in *Lumen Gentium*, retained the untraditional structure of the presentation of the bishop-elect first created for *OB1968:*

OB1990

1st stage

2nd stage

Consecration Presentation

Sunday
entrance song to gospel
episcopal vestments

[**Selection Presentation**
presentation:
two presbyters
postulation:
ordain this presbyter
mandate]

address
proclamation of consensus and consecration:
[   ]
examination
bidding *MF*
consecration: litany
Propitiare
laying on of hands
gospel book
consecration prayer
consecration continues

And while restoring significant opportunities for "full, conscious and active participation" (*SC* 14) of the assembly in the ordination liturgy, *OB1990* retained the untraditional structure of ordination as only a one-stage process, that of consecration.

Decree by the Congregation for Divine Worship and Discipline of the Sacraments:[65]

Ritus Ordinationum, quibus Christi ministri et dispensatores mysteriorum Dei in Ecclesia constituuntur, iuxta normas Concilii Vaticani II (cf. *SC*, 76) recogniti, anno 1968 in prima editione typica promulgati sunt sub titulo *De Ordinatione Diaconi, Presbyteri et Episcopi.*

Nunc vero, attenta experientia, quae e liturgica oritur instauratione, opportunum visum est alteram parare editionem typicam, quae relatione habita ad priorem sequentia praebet elementa peculiaria:

1. Haec editio ditata est *Praenotandis,* sicut ceteri libri liturgici, ut exponatur doctrina de sacramento et structura celebrationis clarius eluceat.

2. Dispositio libri immutata est, ita ut initium sumendo ab Episcopo, qui plenitudinem sacri Ordinis habet, melius intellegatur quomodo presbyteri eius sint cooperatores et diaconi ad eius ministerium ordinentur.

Texts of De Ordinatione Episcopi 1990:

15. Officium est omnium fidelium orare pro Episcopo suo eligendo et electo. . . . Cum Episcopus pro tota Ecclesia locali constituatur, ad eius Ordinationem clerici aliique fideles invitandi sunt, ut quam maxima frequentia celebrationi intersint.

17. Duo presbyteri dioecesis, pro qua electus ordinatur, ei in celebratione Ordinationis assistunt: nomine Ecclesiae localis unus ex eis ab Episcopo ordinante principali petit, ut electo Ordinationem conferat. Una cum Episcopo in hac celebratione Ordinato aliisque Episcopis hi duo presbyteri et, in quantum fieri potest, etiam alii presbyterii praesertim eiusdem dioecesis liturgiam eucharisticam concelebrant.

20. Convenit ut omnes communitates dioecesis, pro qua Episcopus ordinatur, ad celebrationem Ordinationis apto modo praeparentur.

21. Episcopus, qui tamquam caput cuidam dioecesi praeficitur, in ecclesia cathedrali ordinetur.

24. Dicto Evangelio, Ecclesia localis per unum ex presbyteris suis ab Episcopo ordinante principali petit, ut electum ordinet.

27. Summe convenit, ut Episcopus intra fines propriae dioecesis ordinatus concelebrationi in liturgia eucharistica praesideat. . . .

53. Accipe mitram, et clarescat in te splendor sanctitatis, ut, cum apparuerit princeps pastorum, immarcescibilem gloriae coronam percipere merearis.

NOTES

[1] Translation is by Fathers of the English Dominican Province in St. Thomas Aquinas, *Summa Theologica,* vol. 3 (New York: Benziger Brothers, Inc., 1948) 2691 (art. 2); 2692 (art. 3); 2695 (art. 5).

[2] Ibid., 2704–2705. *ST* Suppl. Q. 40, art. 5. states in part: "Wherefore since the bishop has not a higher power than the priest, in this respect the episcopate is not an Order. . . . Hence although at his promotion a bishop receives a spiritual power in respect of certain sacraments, this power nevertheless has not the nature of a character. For this reason, the episcopate is not an Order, in the sense in which an Order is a sacrament." Article 5 also includes this rationale: "The greater Orders are not conferred except on Saturdays. But the episcopal power is bestowed on Sundays. Therefore it is not an Order."

[3] Piet Fransen, "Orders and Ordination," *Sacramentum Mundi,* vol. 4, gen. ed. A. Darlap (New York: Herder and Herder, 1969) 317.

[4] Translation is from *Decrees of the Ecumenical Councils,* volume I: *Nicaea I to Lateran V,* ed. N. Tanner (London: Sheed and Ward Limited, 1990 and Washington, D.C.: Georgetown University Press, 1990) *549–*550.

[5] Walter Clancy, *The Rites and Ceremonies of Sacred Ordination,* 38.

[6] "The Council of Trent and Holy Orders," in Botte and others, *The Sacrament of Holy Orders,* 243.

[7] Edward Kilmartin, *Church, Eucharist and Priesthood* (New York: Paulist Press, 1981) 5.

[8] Arthur Henderson, *Ordained Ministry in the American Lutheran and Roman Catholic Churches,* 111.

[9] Alexandre Ganoczy, "'Splendours and Miseries' of the Tridentine Doctrine of Ministries," in *Office and Ministry in the Church, Concilium,* vol. 80, eds. B. Van Iersel and R. Murphy (New York: Herder and Herder, 1972) trans. R. Wilson, 85.

[10] Note the unusual use of the word *ordination* in relation to bishops for these doctrinal statements when the liturgical use in the *PR1485* is exclusively *consecration.*

[11] Kenan Osborne, *Priesthood: A History of Ordained Ministry in the Roman Catholic Church* (New York: Paulist Press, 1988) 261.

[12] Translation from Osborne, *Priesthood,* 296.

[13] Ibid.

[14] *AAS* 37 (1945) 131.

[15] Translation by Clancy, *The Rites and Ceremonies of Sacred Ordination,* 97–99, from *AAS* 37 (1945) 132.

[16] *AAS* 40 (1948) 5–7.

[17] Defects included (for presbyteral ordination): omission of both occurrences of the laying on of hands or of one of them or of one part of the first; lack of physical contact in the laying on of hands; omission of the *traditio instrumentorum;* lack of physical contact in the *traditio;* lack of the consecration of the chalice; lack of bread or wine or their invalidity. See G. Lachello, "La costituzione apostolica 'Sacramentum Ordinis,'" *La Scuola Cattolica* 77 (1949) 124. After *Sacramentum Ordinis,* ninety possible cases of nullity for defect of form were suppressed! See Bernard Botte, "La Constitution apostolique 'Sacramentum ordinis,'" *LMD* 16 (1948) 128. Thanks to Dr. Martin Connell for asking this question.

[18] F. Hürth, "Contenuto e significato della Costituzione Apostolica sopra gli ordini sacri," *La Civiltà Cattolica* 99 (1948) II, 620.

[19] Balthasar Fischer, "Das Gebet der Kirche als Wesenselement des Weihesakramentes," *LJ* 20 (1970) 173; Adam, *Foundations of Liturgy*, 211.

[20] Bligh, *Ordination to the Priesthood*, 47.

[21] Botte, "La Constitution apostolique 'Sacramentum ordinis,'" 128.

[22] Translation by Clancy, *The Rites and Ceremonies of Sacred Ordination*, 104–105, from *AAS* 40 (1948) 7. Translation of the prayer from Bradshaw, *Ordination Rites*, 216 (adapted for the text from *PR1485*).

[23] Edward Craddock Ratcliff, "Schemes of Union, the Ministry and Forms of Ordination," in *E. C. Ratcliff: Reflections on Liturgical Revision*, ed. D. Tripp (Bramcote, Nottingham: Grove Books, 1980) 30.

[24] Kleinheyer, "La riforma degli ordini sacri," 9, n. 6.

[25] *Pontificale Romanum, pars prima, editio typica* (Typis Polyglottis Vaticanis, 1962).

[26] Kleinheyer, "La riforma degli ordini sacri," 8–9: "Si vedrà così che questo lavoro di riforma si è attentuto fedelmente alle indicazioni del Concilio."

[27] The analysis of the ordination texts below will indicate more specifically how these articles have been implemented. Citations from *Sacrosanctum Concilium* [hereafter *SC*] are from *Documents on the Liturgy: 1963–1979, Conciliar, Papal, and Curial Documents* [hereafter *DOL*], International Commission on English in the Liturgy (Collegeville: Liturgical Press, 1982) 1:8, 9, 10, 18, 12–13.

[28] David Power, *Ministers of Christ and His Church*, 127.

[29] *Concilium* 3/1 (1965) 10, trans. Theodore Westow.

[30] *Lumen Gentium* [hereafter, *LG*] no. 27 is taken from *Vatican Council II: The Conciliar and Post Conciliar Documents*, gen. ed. Austin Flannery (Wilmington, Delaware: Scholarly Resources Inc., 1975) 382–383.

[31] Hereafter *OB1968*.

[32] Botte, *From Silence to Participation*, 134.

[33] International Commission on English in the Liturgy, "Foreword," *Roman Pontifical* (Vatican City: Vatican Polyglot Press, 1978) xiv–xv.

[34] Gy, "Ancient Ordination Prayers," 76. Kleinheyer notes that the ordination rites of 1968 were published *before* the decision was made to suppress the minor orders, so that an ascending order for the last three rites would have been understandable. "Ordinationsfeiern," 88. A later study group formed in 1974, this time with Kleinheyer as *relator* and Botte as consultant, attempted to improve several deficiencies in the layout of the rites, including the restoration of descending order. "The climate was not favorable . . . and the material ended up . . . in the archives!" See Bugnini, *The Reform of the Liturgy*, chapter 42 on Holy Orders, 707–723. The quotation above is from p. 723. The inversion of this order will be accomplished by the 1990 revision.

[35] Translation by International Commission on English in the Liturgy from "Apostolic Constitution: Approval of New Rites for the Ordination of Deacons, Presbyters, and Bishops" in the *Roman Pontifical* (1978) 153.

³⁶ Bradshaw, "Recent Developments," in *The Study of Liturgy* (1992) 397.

³⁷ Bruno Kleinheyer, Joachim Nabuco, Cyrille Vogel, Emil Lengeling, Pierre Jounel, and Joseph Lécuyer. See Bugnini, *The Reform of the Liturgy,* 707 n. 1.

³⁸ Ibid., 708–709.

³⁹ If the elect's church is not the site, he does not become principal celebrant but (returning to the rubrics of *OR34* and the *PRG*), he takes up the first seat among the other bishops.

⁴⁰ See Pierre Jounel, *The Rite of Concelebration of Mass and of Communion under Both Species,* trans. Desclée Company Inc. (New York: Desclée, 1967) 23 and Salmon, "Le rite du sacre des évêques," 40–41.

⁴¹ The pope was ordained before the *Gloria* that he might intone the chant and then preside over the entire liturgy; a deacon was ordained between the epistle and gospel that he might take up his liturgical role of chanting the gospel. Jounel, "Le nouveau rituel d'ordination," 67. Bradshaw describes another primitive pattern: a bishop was ordained at the beginning of the liturgy in order to preside over all of it; presbyters were ordained before the anaphora that they might participate in the prayer; deacons were ordained before the distribution of Communion, etc. See "Theology and Rite *AD* 200–400," 357.

⁴² Bugnini, *Reform of the Liturgy,* 712–713.

⁴³ Botte, *From Silence to Participation,* 138.

⁴⁴ Besides Botte's memoirs, see also Bugnini, *The Reform of the Liturgy,* 715–716.

⁴⁵ Botte, *From Silence to Participation,* 136. For a list of the precise scriptural, conciliar, and patristic references in the text, see C. Braga, "Commentarius: *De Ordinatione Episcopi,* 46–47. In his memoirs, Botte relates a story of presenting the draft of this new address when a member of the *Consilium* remarked, "The old address was better." Botte of course challenged him to state where this address was found in the Pontifical. Getting a stunned look in response, Botte added: "Don't look, it's not worth your time—there never was an address for the ordination of a bishop in the Pontifical. A little discreet laughter was heard, followed by silence. Our address was approved without any difficulty." *From Silence to Participation,* 127–128.

⁴⁶ Ibid., 137.

⁴⁷ Bugnini, *The Reform of the Liturgy,* 712.

⁴⁸ Many fine commentaries have been written on the 1968 reform of episcopal ordination. Besides Bugnini's masterful *The Reform of the Liturgy,* particularly instructive are the following: J. D. Crichton, "Holy Orders," in *The Sacraments;* C. Braga, "Commentarius: *De Ordinatione Episcopi*"; Botte, "L'ordination de l'évêque"; Frederick McManus, "The New Rite for Ordination of Bishops," *American Ecclesiastical Review* 159 (1968) 410–416; International Commission on English in the Liturgy, "Ordination of a Bishop (The Roman Pontifical)," *N* 17 (1981) 197–216; Jounel, "Le nouveau rituel d'ordination"; Kleinheyer, "La riforma degli ordini sacri"; Emil Lengeling, "Teologia del sacramento dell'ordine nei testi nel nuovo rito," *RL* 56 (1969) 25–54.

[49] Translation cited in J. D. Crichton, *The Sacraments,* 142 from "L'ordination des prêtres," *LMD* 98 (1969) 94.

[50] As far back as 1940, Botte praises the theology of the ordination prayer from the *Apostolic Tradition:* "One cannot but admire the completeness and vigor of this prayer. It is never equaled by any of those which succeed it, and nowhere else will we find the theology of the episcopate expressed in such clear liturgical formulae." ("Quant à cette prière, on ne peut qu'admirer sa plénitude et sa vigueur. Elle ne sera égalée par aucune autre et l'on ne trouvera nulle part ailleurs la théologie de l'épiscopat exprimée en des formules liturgiques plus claires.") "Le sacre épiscopal," 24. It is a conviction he will be able to realize twenty-eight years later.

[51] Frederick McManus, ed., *Thirty Years of Liturgical Renewal: Statements of the Bishops' Committee on the Liturgy* (Washington, D.C.: United States Catholic Conference, 1987) 118.

[52] *OB1968* includes the restoration of the threefold solemn blessing first seen in episcopal ordination in the *PRG*.LXIII.56 [with a second form added in manuscripts C D V]). The triple blessing was part of the proposed form of the *missa normativa; OB1968* is its debut. McManus, "The New Rite of Ordination of Bishops," 412; Brandolini, "L'evoluzione storica dei riti delle ordinazioni," 82.

[53] "Nous avons travaillé dans l'espirit de Vatican II, soucieux de garder la tradition authentique de l'Eglise, mais aussi de rendre aux rites leur vérité et leur simplicité, pour qu'ils soient accessibles au peuple chrétien. . . . Bien sûr, cela ne résout pas tous les problèmes; mais cela fournit une base solide pour une réflexion approfondie." Botte, "L'ordination de l'évêque," 126.

[54] "Je pense sincèrement que la révision a été faite avec le maximum de fidélité aux principes et à l'espirit du Concile Vatican II et que non seulement le clergé, mais tous les fidèles seront ainsi largement aidés pour mieux comprendre la mission de ceux qui sont appelés à servir le peuple de Dieu comme diacres, comme prêtres ou comme évêques." Lécuyer, "Commentarium," 219.

[55] "Nell'ultimo millennio, nessuna riforma, se così si possono chiamare le diverse rielaborazioni di questi riti, fu così ricca di motivazioni teologiche ed insieme di preoccupazioni pastorali, come quella di oggi." Kleinheyer, "La riforma degli ordini sacri," 24.

[56] Hereafter *OB1990. Ordination of a Bishop* in *Rites of Ordination of a Bishop, of Priests, and of Deacons* (Washington, D.C.: United States Conference of Catholic Bishops, 2003) 5–63.

[57] Decree, 29 June 1989, in *Rites of Ordination of a Bishop, of Priests, and of Deacons,* vii.

[58] "Non si tratta di una 'riforma della riforma,' ma soltanto di una generale e ordinata omologazione di questi libri con le necessarie integrazioni e arricchimenti dei testi e dei riti." "La *Editio typica altera* del Pontificale Romano delle Ordinazioni: I novi *Praenotanda,*" *RL* 78 (1991) 333.

⁵⁹ *OB1990.21*. The Bishop who is placed as head of a particular diocese should be ordained in the cathedral church.

⁶⁰ The intercessions are included in the litany and the omission of the Creed allows a seamless joining of the ordination rite to the Liturgy of the Eucharist. Bruno Kleinheyer, "Weiheliturgie in neuer Gestalt," *LJ* 18 (1968) 228. The International Commission on English in the Liturgy appropriately explains the 1968 omission of the Creed in its commentary: "The profession of faith is omitted since the Church's faith is proclaimed in the ordination liturgy." "Ordination of a Bishop," 201–202.

⁶¹ And signifying all these things, it signifies nothing. See A.-M. Rouget, "Les nouveaux rituels d'ordination," *LMD* 94 (1968) 188.

⁶² "La nouvelle édition typique du rituel des ordinations," *LMD* 186 (1991) 11.

⁶³ "Ordinationsfeiern," 102.

⁶⁴ A similar perspective mars the introduction to the model addresses of both *Ordination of Deacons* and *Ordination of Priests* 1968 and 1990. The ordaining bishop speaks to the assembly not as members of the local church but as relatives and friends of the ordinandi (e.g., "Beloved brothers and sisters: because these our sons, who are your relatives and friends, are now to be advanced to the Order of Priests . . ." from *Ordination of Priests* 1990, no. 123): a telling indication of the underlying ecclesiology at work. Rubrics regarding the assembly may be appropriately restored to the rites, but the absence of ecclesial relationships to the elect remains evident in the texts. I am grateful to Dr. Paul Bradshaw for this insight.

⁶⁵ *De Ordinatione Episcopi, Presbyterorum, et Diaconorum*, iii.

Conclusion

The purpose of this lengthy conclusion is threefold: to offer a modest presentation of some key historical realities in order to better understand the impact of the political and social forces upon the liturgical texts; to highlight some of the profound ecclesiological realities expressed in the evolving liturgical texts; and, in light of this study of the structure of episcopal ordination, to comment on future reform of episcopal ordination rites within the Roman Catholic Church.

I. The Historical Context

Underlying the evolution of the liturgical texts examined in the previous chapters are the powerful forces of ecclesial and political history which influenced the contours of the selection process and which gradually restricted the number of ecclesial communions contributing to consensus. We observed above how the consenting voices within the selection process of the bishop-elect are identified in the ritual component of the proclamation of consensus and consecration. How were the traditional voices configured? How were the constitutive voices diminished? What historical factors contributed to the changes evident in the liturgical texts?

A. TRADITIONAL ECCLESIAL COMMUNION: LOCAL SEE, NEIGHBORING SEES, AND METROPOLITAN SEE

As an element of the Consecration Presentation, the early Roman model (exemplified by *OR34*) created this proclamation of consensus and consecration which was to be recited by the pope in his role as metropolitan:

OR34.38. The clergy and people of the city of N. consenting, with their neighboring sees, have chosen for themselves N., the deacon, or presbyter, to be consecrated bishop. And therefore let us pray for this man. . . .

The hybrid rite of the *PRG* copied into its Selection Presentation the proclamation from the fifth-century Gallican *Statuta Ecclesiae Antiqua:*

PRG.LXIII.f. (17) And thus examined and full prepared with the consent of the clerics and laity and the agreement of the bishops of the entire province and especially of the metropolitan or by [his] authority or presence he may be ordained.

The exhortation from the *Missale Francorum (Servanda est)* took hold in the Consecration Presentation of the *PRG*:

PRG.LXIII.28. By the will of the Lord, therefore, in place of N., of pious memory, with the testimony of the presbyters and of the whole clergy and with the advice of the citizens and of those assembled, we believe that the reverend N. should be elected. . . . Therefore, dearly beloved brethren, acclaim this man, chosen by the testimony of good works, as most worthy of the priesthood, crying out your praises together, and say: He is worthy.

The *PRXII*, compiled for Roman usage, copied the same proclamation for its Selection Presentation from the *PRG*, and then removed the reference to the metropolitan:

PRXII.X.12. Therefore thus examined and well prepared, with the consent of the clerics and laity and the agreement of the bishops of the entire province, in the name of the lord he may be ordained.

The *PRC* then brought the identical proclamation into its texts, also minus the unnecessary metropolitan reference.

It was the work of Guillaume Durand which provided evidence of the new role of the cathedral chapter in episcopal selection, a role created as part of the Gregorian reform of the eleventh and twelfth centuries and mandated by Lateran IV (1215).[1] Durand completely omitted the proclamation above, replaced it with the *Episcopum oportet* unit, and included mention of the cathedral chapter in the decree presented to the metropolitan. He did not, however, specify any papal involvement in the choice of the new bishop. The metropolitan addresses the two (suffragan?) bishops and calls for their testimony:

PGD.I.XIV.16
Reverend father, holy mother catholic church asks that you elevate this presbyter to the responsibility of the episcopacy.

Do you know him to be worthy?
As far as human frailty permits [one] to know we know and we believe him to be worthy.
Thanks be to God.

By the end of the fifteenth century, the liturgical texts of the *PR1485* reflected a more restricted canonical reality. The proclamation of consensus and consecration had been reduced to the reading of the papal mandate; the local see, neighboring sees, and metropolitan see did not elect nor consent:

PR1485.f 32. v
Reverend father: holy mother catholic church asks: that you elevate this presbyter present to the responsibility of the episcopacy.
Do you have the apostolic mandate.
We have.
Let it be read.

Changes in liturgical texts during the medieval period often reflected fluctuating social, political, and economic factors rather than theological ones. Certainly the ideal of communal consensus as the basis for the selection of a bishop was well established in numerous ecclesiastical canons and decrees. Archbishop Rufinus of Sorrento, for example, writing in the mid-twelfth century summarizes the traditional understanding:

> In the election of a bishop, these five things are especially to be
> considered: the wishes of the citizens, the testimony of the people,
> the choice of those in high positions and of the regular clergy,
> the election of the clerics, the confirmation of the metropolitan and
> of the comprovincial bishops.[2]

The subverting forces belonged to other realms than ecclesiology.
The chaotic situation of uneducated laity on the diocesan level as well as the shifting allegiances within church-state relationships took their toll. The various strands of overlapping jurisdictions within these relationships included the secular rulers, the waning power of the metropolitan, and expanding papal authority. The entanglements of all three factors are difficult to unravel; however, some elements of development may be presented separately.

B. THE VOICE OF SECULAR AUTHORITIES

Hervé-Marie Legrand succinctly describes a key principle of the development under study when he writes: "Elections [were] not abandoned for theological reasons. The progressive decay of ancient institutions is explained . . . by the constant pressure of the political authorities."[3] As the bishop himself becomes a prince of the state as well as the church, so the secular princes, kings, and eventually emperors, guaranteed a voice in episcopal selection as members of the laity, used that voice to dominate the proceedings. Irresistibly drawn by the economic and social power inherent in the large landholdings of bishops and abbots, the princes, kings, and emperors sought and won the right to control episcopal office and thus church property.

Robert Benson identifies the motivation for the increasing interference of civil rulers in episcopal selection with these opening words of his historical study, *The Bishop-Elect:*[4]

> During the High Middle Ages the episcopate was, like monarchy, a universal governing institution throughout Latin Christendom. The double role—ecclesiastical and secular—of most bishops heightened the historical importance of episcopacy and the episcopate. Every bishop was a successor of the Apostles and a prince of the Church, possessing both sacramental and jurisdictional powers, and with a solemn responsibility for the salvation of Christian souls. Moreover, most bishops were also princes of this world, whose duties demanded the combined talents of a politician, an administrator, and even sometimes (at least until the twelfth century) a soldier. Many bishops bore the rank and title of prince or baron, and their bishoprics held vast lands and far-reaching powers of secular jurisdiction. The monarchy's highest officials and advisers were often drawn from the episcopate. Bishops governed for the ruler, furnished much of his army, and provided indispensable support. In short, the episcopate was inextricably enmeshed in the machinery of monarchical govern-ment, and a history of the medieval episcopate would necessarily include a large part of medieval Europe's political history.

This "materialization of office"[5] opened the door to investiture of the bishop by the civil ruler, an investiture of the new bishop with ring and crozier which "constituted not only the confirmation of the bishop-elect but also the formal 'grant of the bishopric.'"[6] The rights of the metro-politan were consequently severely restricted to simply consecrating the man chosen by secular authority after having presided at a scrutiny that was largely ceremonial.[7]

It is ironic that royal authorities exerted their power in the episcopal selection process precisely as laity, a right preserved by venerable tradition as a constitutive element of the vacant see. Indeed, the prince, king or emperor was the layman "elected by God" whose responsibility it was to exercise supervision over the civil affairs of the church by divine right.[8] As the balance of power shifted beyond the ecclesiastical arena and the might of feudal states exerted itself in episcopal appointments in an absolute way, papal authority necessarily intervened against selection processes manipulated by monarchies.

As a cornerstone of his reform, Gregory VII (+1085) attempted to restore the ancient ideal of free canonical elections by clergy and people by removing the dominant voice of the local monarch and returning some responsibility for episcopal choice to the local see. "For Gregory VII the church's election was the only 'gate of the sheepfold' (John 10:1-10) through which the true bishop could come to his flock."[9] However the electoral structure on the local level was severely reduced to the most important nobles and prelates who would comprise the cathedral chapter; the vast majority of clergy and laity were deprived of their voice.

Into his policies, however, Gregory set the distinction between election by the clergy and consent by the people.[10] The *Decretum* of Gratian in approximately 1140[11] would diminish the laity's participation even further as part of its aim to reduce the pointless meddling of uneducated laity and "the caprice of princes."[12] The goal to drastically reduce and subdue royal control of episcopal elections without denying other members of the laity their legitimate voice proved impossible; the silence of all lay voices was the sacrifice paid to end royal interference. Thomas O'Meara explains:

> The *Decretum* of Gratian begins the formulation of a new electoral system which received its rules and procedures under Innocent III (+1216) and Gregory IX (+1241). Only this system of church structure with no trace of communal pluralism in the selection of bishops would be known to Thomas Aquinas, Albert the Great and Bonaventure. With some qualifications, only this form projects an orthodox image at the Council of Trent vis-à-vis the "innovations of the Reformers." . . .[13]

Even the cathedral chapters, established as a remedy for lay domination and the divisive wrangling of political rivalries and authorized to conduct episcopal elections, "in the long run, . . . proved just as susceptible to turbulence, discord, and lay domination."[14]

C. LOSS OF THE VOICE OF THE METROPOLITAN

As noted in the earlier chapters above, the presence of other bishops at the two-stage ordination process was an expression of their consensus in the act of selection, and their testimony to the shared apostolic faith of the newest member of their college. Legrand comments: "By their presence and their action, the neighboring bishops bear witness to the identity in matters of faith and apostolic ministry of the church, celebrating the ordination with the apostolic Church throughout space and time."[15]

What further evolution of this dynamic affects the particular role of the metropolitan? The voices comprising the first two elements of the communion of consensus in the earliest liturgical rites we have examined are those of the vacant see and neighboring sees. "The metropolitan's confirmation and ordination was the third and final factor";[16] they ordained their suffragans without recourse to any other see,[17] as the texts of the *PRG* and the *PGD* confirm. Klaus Schatz identifies the interplay of these three expressions of ecclesial communion as "the primary form of episcopal collegiality."[18] The political ambitions of secular authority were the first to threaten and undermine the metropolitan level of collegial reality, and later papal attempts to force its restoration only assured its permanent destruction.

"The embeddedness of the Church in the power structure,"[19] drawing in like a powerful magnet the heavily vested interests of every level of secular authority, also destroyed in its wake the ancient collegial system of the metropolitan province and its synods. These were replaced with royal control. One voice alone possessed the authority to overturn this corrupt system and to free the church from the quagmire of the medieval system of feudal government and society.

Tracing the evolution of papal influence and the decline of the metropolitan, Schatz insightfully states that "the excessive growth of the primacy was in great part the result of the non-functioning of other Church structures. . . ."[20] Overwhelmed by the political, economic, and military consequences of an imperial episcopacy, the ecclesial communion of local, neighboring, and metropolitan sees collapsed; the resulting vacuum helped to create and advance the power of a centralized and centralizing papacy.

Although the goal of the Gregorian reform in restoring canonical elections of bishops was not to substitute papal appointment for the former royal appointments, the reforms themselves uncovered the striking weaknesses of the provincial and local ecclesial structures. One aspect of the reform, for example, was the reinstitution of the metropolitan's role of final confirmation in episcopal selection. But the new ecclesial structures did not reflect actual ecclesial reality; structures may have been restored but the foundation of the ancient ecclesial communion which had given rise to the structures no longer existed. Metropolitans set in place and shored up by secular rulers and wearing the pallium as an insignia of papal delegation[21] were mere figureheads in a newly mandated ecclesial structure. Cathedral chapters, themselves often divided in political factions and unable to elect, appealed to Rome (and not to the metropolitan) for definitive rulings:

> More objectivity and justice were expected from the Roman curia than from local church authorities, which were by nature more dependent on the power centers of the particular place. A similar phenomenon appeared quite often in the election of bishops. The absence of any spirit of ecclesial community in local church institutions increasingly led to the transfer of decisions to Rome.[22]

D. THE VOICE OF THE APOSTOLIC SEE

As we consider this last strand in the tightly woven tapestry of medieval church-state relations, Legrand's summary is an aid to proper perspective. He writes: "The direct nomination of virtually all Catholic bishops by the pope does not derive from his primacy, but from historical circumstances which allowed the pope to remove it from the hands of the civil authorities."[23] Against the corruption and political intrigues that enmeshed the Curia, the institution of cathedral chapters seemed a commendable remedy. But when partisan battles and financial ambitions erupted among the canonical electors, the situation called for "the aloofness and broad policy of the popes."[24]

This "broad policy" increasingly drew into its purview the ecclesiastical relationships and responsibilities left in early ages to the metropolitans and their provincial synods. Papal authority expanded to include the following: the pope was immediate superior to all archbishops; certain sees were directly subject to the pope; through papal legates, the pope could inhibit chapter elections, allow postulations and translations; by a system of papal provisions and reservations, by his powers of exclusive jurisdiction over contested chapter elections, the pope controlled the disposition of the most important bishoprics; by the granting of the pallium to metropolitans, a network of papal vicars was created, intermediaries between the emperors and the pope.

As instances of church-state disputes increased (Innocent IV against Emperor Frederick II, for example), the canonical election process for entire regions was suspended, replaced by papal selection alone.

> [I]n this way the idea that papal appointment of bishops as something quite normal became fully accepted. When the cathedral chapter continued to choose the bishop, it did so no longer on the basis of local church autonomy, but because it was assigned this task by the pope as a matter of papal privilege.[25]

Financial advantage for the Curia further strengthened the appeal of reserving episcopal appointments to the apostolic see. The large annual incomes paid by new bishops from their lucrative benefices became so commonplace that finally "Pope Urban V drew the line in 1363 by reserving all archbishoprics, bishoprics, and abbacies with incomes above a certain sum (!) to the curia. . . . From then on in the Latin Church the principle was that bishops were canonically appointed by the pope."[26] Even when particular states retained the monarchy's role in the choice of bishop, the ecclesiastical appointment was made from Rome, not from the cathedral chapter.[27]

Canonical consequences followed naturally from this political arrangement: order and jurisdiction were two separate and distinct realities. Episcopal consecration was understood to confer powers of sanctifying in the church, membership in the episcopal college, and (some theologians speculated) even universal jurisdiction, but the authority of local diocesan jurisdiction (*potestas jurisdictionis*) was conferred absolutely by papal appointment.[28]

The Gregorian ideal of the free election of bishops, though expressive of the most authentic ecclesiological principles and the most venerable Christian tradition, was no match for the political and economic dynamics created by an imperial episcopacy only to be overridden by an imperial papacy. These examples of vigorous centralized administration, carried out and sustained under the growing authority of papal primacy, would remain the preeminent models for understanding episcopal selection by the council fathers of Trent and Vatican I. Theology and practice agreed: "The pope appoints bishops, and if in the past other ecclesiastical authorities such as patriarchs or metropolitans had exercised that right, it was only because the power had been delegated to them by the pope. Of course such an interpretation bore no relation to the real events of history."[29]

II. The Theological Context

The structure of the presentation of the bishop-elect reveals the very nature of the sacrament of ordination as a two-stage process, not the laying on of hands and consecration prayer only.

> [O]rdination [is] essentially a process and not merely a rite, a process accomplished over time and not just in a brief sacramental moment, a process that begins with the Church's discernment of God's call to an individual for a particular ministry within a specific Christian community, continues with the community's prayer for the bestowal of the gifts and graces necessary for the effective discharge of that office, and culminates in the acceptance by the people of the new minister's role among them, expressed in their assent to his or her performance of the liturgical functions belonging to the particular office.[30]

The structure of the presentation of the bishop-elect also reveals participation of the local see to be a constitutive element of both stages of the process. The importance then of studying the presentation of the bishop-elect lies not so much in the particularities of the structure it discloses but in the nature of the church the structure expresses, in the ecclesiology made manifest in the ritual acts, or (as Legrand so eloquently expresses it) in the "ecclesiology elaborated from its liturgical base. . . ."[31] The structure of the presentation of the bishop-elect expresses a theology of the church as communion, as a "layered reality"[32] and as "a communion of communions,"[33] a theology of the episcopacy as ikon and servant of that communion, and a theology of ordination as epiclesis.[34]

The ecclesial communion of the church is expressed, renewed and deepened by the two-stage ordination rite "by which the Holy Spirit establishes particular relationships within the communion of the Church,"[35] relationships revealed and strengthened by the consensual testimony to the worthiness of the elect by the local see (clergy and people), neighboring sees, metropolitan see, and apostolic see: "relationships which both constitute and manifest the order of the Church as a communion of communions."[36]

The new bishop is an ikon and servant of that communion. United to his local church by nuptial bonds of mutual consent, he is the focus of its unity. Through the rituals of the ordination expressive of the communion of consensus, he also "becomes the real representative of his church to others, and receives the task of representing the whole Church in his own church: he is the principal instrument of the conciliarity of the Church."[37] The "fullness" of his priesthood lies in the communion of relationships his very person makes manifest: the communion within the episcopal college "which sacramentalizes the communion of particular churches."[38]

The presence and power of the Holy Spirit is the operative principle behind each stage of the ordination process. Study of the ancient rites in particular uncovers consistent evidence that ordination is in no sense either self-appointment nor community appointment.[39] Ordination has nothing to do with the electoral principles of democracy and majority vote. God chooses by the church's selection and God ordains by the church's prayer. "God announces and accomplishes the divine will through the church's election and its ordination; the church's action makes known and realizes God's provident gift."[40]

The requisite communion of consensus is created and sustained only by the Holy Spirit: the ground of ordination is epicletic communal choice (Selection) and epicletic communal prayer (Consecration). "Ordination constitutes an *epiclesis*"[41] for the role of the Holy Spirit permeates the entire process. The consensus of the participating sees is a gift of the Spirit at work within each expression of communion: in the prayer preceding the selection, in the electors' discernment of the *charismata* within the elect, in the various canonical and liturgical acts of selecting the one whom God has chosen as worthy of the episcopacy.[42]

In the acts of consecration, God responds to the community's prayer (silence [as in *Apostolic Tradition*] or the litany) with a fresh outpouring of the Holy Spirit upon the elect through the laying on of hands and epicletic prayer:

*SVe.*947 [H]allow [him] with the flow of heavenly unction . . . so that the power of your Spirit may both fill [him] within and surround [him] without.

*OB*1990.47 Pour out now upon this chosen one that power which is from you, the Spirit of governance whom you gave to your beloved Son, Jesus Christ, the Spirit whom he bestowed upon the holy Apostles. . . .

The person of the bishop, then, as leader of the community is in a unique sense "a visible sign in the community of the Spirit's presence. . . ."[43]

The epicletic nature of ordination continues to be evident in the acts of the community's reception of the new bishop: reception expressed both by the ancient manner of exchanging the sign of peace and by the culminating celebration of the Eucharist.[44] Explaining the *pax* exchanged among those who share Christ's own Spirit, Gregory Dix states with conviction:

A genuine election by his own Church and the free acceptance of him by all its members as their bishop (symbolized by the kiss of peace given to him by all immediately after his consecration . . .) were as much a *sine qua non* for the episcopate as consecration itself. (I do not think this puts the matter too strongly.)[45]

Bradshaw agrees and describes the significance of the kiss of peace in the early Christian centuries:

[I]t functioned as a 'sealing' of the whole process: the bishop initiated it by greeting the newly ordained with a kiss, and the rest of the clergy and people then followed suit, in order to give symbolic expression of their acceptance of the new minister, which is a vital part of the whole ordination process.[46]

Following the Spirit-guided acts of ordination, representatives of the communions of consensus celebrate the Eucharist at which the newly ordained bishop presides. This final act of ordination realizes the reception of the *ordinatus;* celebration of the Eucharist by the local church "is not only a proclamation, but a ratification of the appointment and installation of the new bishop."[47]

III. Future of the Reform

The 1968 revision of the ordination rites was extraordinary in scope, heroic in vision and practical application, and remarkable in the power of its effects down to our own day. Any commentary offered here arises from appreciation and awe at what was accomplished, not from disrespect. From the vantage point of several decades and of the preceding pages, however, some weaknesses in the reform may be observed.

Overriding any specific objections are two general criticisms: the starting point of the reform and its overall method. To take "the Roman Pontifical as it stood for our point of departure," as Botte explained,[48] unnecessarily restricted the parameters of the revision to one base text alone and thus to simply suppressions, regroupings, and substitutions of various elements of that single text. As to the method of the revision, Botte summarized it as primarily a critique of the existing Roman Pontifical "to determine what could be retained of the Roman tradition."[49] But elements of the 1595 rite appear to have been analyzed as individual and discreet entities, not as components which function within unified structures of the Roman tradition, structures expressive of ecclesiological significance.

But the starting point and method of liturgical reform in one era need not be that of the next. In fact, a more comprehensive knowledge of the history of the development of episcopal ordination may offer impetus to further reform and renewal of ordination within the Roman Rite.

A. PRINCIPLES OF REFORM

Relying on this belief, I recommend the focus of the next generation of liturgical reformers include the following three principles enunciated by *Sacrosanctum Concilium* and the *General Instruction of the Roman Missal*.

SC 23. That sound tradition may be retained and yet the way remain open to legitimate progress, a careful investigation is always to be made into each part of the liturgy to be revised. This investigation should be theological, historical, and pastoral. Also the general laws governing the structure and meaning of the liturgy must be studied in conjunction with the experience derived from recent liturgical reforms and from the indults conceded to various places.[50]

A more extensive historical investigation into each part of the rite of episcopal ordination to be revised, with an eye particularly to the structure and the meaning expressed therein, would be an excellent starting point for future reform. Special attention would then also be paid to the local churches' experiences of the 1968 and 1990 reforms.

Although directed to the Eucharist, the perspective of *SC* 50 may be aptly applied to the ordination rites:

SC 50. For this purpose the rites are to be simplified, due care being taken to preserve their substance; elements that, with the passage of time, came to be duplicated or were added with but little advantage are now to be discarded; other elements that have suffered injury through accident of history are now, as may seem useful or necessary, to be restored to the vigor they had in the tradition of the Fathers.[51]

As I hope the previous chapters have shown, the two-stage process of episcopal ordination belongs to the substance of that sacrament, and thus belongs to "the tradition of the Fathers." Restoration of the selection stage and of the communion of consensus that lies at its core appears to be both "useful and necessary" to the life of the entire church.

An even more fitting article is that of no. 9 from the Preamble of the *General Instruction of the Roman Missal* that picks up the thought of *SC* 50 as if it were part of the same conversation:

GIRM 9. For this reason, the "norms of the holy Fathers" requires not only the preservation of what our immediate forebears have passed on to us, but also an understanding and a more profound study of the Church's entire past and of all the ways in which her one and only faith has been set forth in the quite diverse human and social forms prevailing in the Semitic, Greek, and Latin areas. Moreover, this broader view allows us to see how the Holy Spirit endows the People of God with a marvelous fidelity in preserving the unalterable deposit of faith, even amid a very great variety of prayers and rites.[52]

A profound study and understanding of the church's *entire* past would be the necessary foundation for any future reform, continuing the marvelous fidelity inspired by the Spirit and expressed in diverse ritual forms throughout history.

B. RECOMMENDATIONS

1. *Selection*

The restoration of a consensual process of selection of the new bishop would be the most challenging area of any reform. No longer excessively pressured by the same degree of political interference by kings and emperors, no longer prey to a vacuum of leadership on local and provincial levels, the sees participating in the selection could draw upon the foundation of their solid ecclesial bonds to create a selection process through which the inspiration of the Holy Spirit might freely move. The local see, neighboring sees, metropolitan see, and apostolic see all have wisdom, experience, and prayer to contribute in a consensual process of selection which would express and deepen their communion. Thomas O'Meara expresses this hope in much the same terms:

> The Christian must be aware that society and culture may have matured to the point where participation and pluralism are normal. Education and the communications' revolution would be central factors here. If this is true, then we can return to the more sophisticated and religious directions of the New Testament, return there not because anything old is better, but because historical and political maturity allows us to attempt again the lofty ideal of the Gospel.[53]

Creative interpretation of three articles from the *OB1990* might open the door to wider possibilities of participation by the local see; I will discuss these in reverse order: nos. 20, 15, and 11.

OB1990.20. All the communities of the diocese for which the Bishop is to be ordained should be made ready in an appropriate manner for the celebration of the Ordination.

Since ordination itself consists of two distinct but inseparable stages, the best preparation for the celebration of the sacrament would be communal prayer by all the communities of the diocese, in the context of which they would participate in some way in the selection of the bishop-elect.

OB1990.15. It is the duty of all the faithful to pray for the one to be elected their Bishop and for the Bishop once elected.

Communal epicletic prayer must be the heart of the selection process as it is of the consecration. It bears repeating that a selection process in a Christian context owes nothing to the methods of political democracy. Because it is God who chooses and God who ordains through the ministries of the participating sees, a climate of profound openness and trust, of self-sacrifice and discernment (whose ground can only be furrowed by communal prayer) must reign in all the ecclesial communions involved in the selection.

The specific arrangements as to how consensus is achieved would be established:

OB1990.11. . . . [w]ith due regard for local circumstances and conditions, and for the genius and traditions of the various peoples. . . .

Although certainly not with the selection process in mind, no. 11 begins its list of particular areas of authority for the conferences of bishops with an adaption which might be expanded to encompass the venerable tradition of the Roman Church:

OB1990.11. . . . a) to establish in what way the community, in keeping with regional customs, is to indicate its assent to the election of the candidates. . . .

During the last century, the "communion of communions" has recovered much of its traditional integrity which was a hallmark of the first four Christian centuries. The relationships between the local see, neighboring sees, metropolitan see, and apostolic see, created and sustained by the Spirit of the risen Lord, well articulated by Vatican Council II, well expressed and deepened by the liturgical life centered around the bishop, are in place; they await only the spark of courageous experimentation to retrieve the traditional structure of the sacrament of ordination.

2. *Revised structure*

Restoration of the selection process would first aim at reclaiming the structure of the Selection Presentation from its present position in the *OB1990*. The extended period of time necessary for a consensual selection process could come to a ritual conclusion immediately before the consecration liturgy (perhaps the day before), and comprise the presentation of the bishop-elect by members of the local see to the ordaining bishops, the postulation dialogue with opportunities to testify to the worthiness of the elect ("Do you know him to be worthy?") by representatives of the local see, neighboring sees (if any are absent), metropolitan see (if he would not be present the following day), and the reading of the papal mandate. The examination of the elect, which the *OB1990* more fittingly recast as promises, would occur in the presence of all. A new proclamation of consensus and consecration would be written, expressive of the ecclesial communions that chose the elect and that testified he is worthy, a proclamation that would then announce the consecration to follow, inviting the elect as well as all the local church and the ordaining bishops to fast and pray.

The consecration liturgy would begin with the elect in episcopal vestments and with simplified introductory rites, proclamation of a first reading, and singing of the psalm (and, if desired, proclamation of a second reading).[54] The second presentation of the bishop-elect by representatives of the local see to the ordaining bishops would then occur. The principal ordaining bishop would offer an address on the meaning of the ministry of bishop in the life of the church, concluding it with a second newly composed proclamation of consensus and consecration to which would be joined the bidding, introducing the litany of saints.

The remaining elements of the consecration would be celebrated as they are presented in the *OB1990*, except for the following:

(a) the silent laying on of hands would be done by all the bishops present, but culminating in the imposition of hands by all three ordaining bishops during the ordination prayer itself, thus recovering the ancient union of the laying on of hands and prayer;[55]

(b) after the presentation of the Book of the Gospels, the newly ordained would receive the nuptial ring with its formula, the crozier with its formula; the miter would be placed on his head in silence (returning to the plan of the *OB1968*);

(c) following the kiss of peace exchanged between the new bishop and the bishops present (more accurately, the sign of reception into the episcopal order[56]), there would occur a second sign of reception, the signs of peace exchanged between the new bishop and representatives of the presbyters, deacons, and laity of the local church;[57]

(d) elements from the concluding rites of the *OB1990*.61-63 would be moved forward: the procession of the new bishop through the church as he blesses all present and the *Te Deum* [or another hymn according to local custom] is sung; the solemn enthronement of the new bishop in the *cathedra*; the proclamation of the *Alleluia* and the gospel; the new bishop's first homily from the *cathedra* in the midst of this "communion of communions"; the Liturgy of the Eucharist proceeding as usual, drawing to a close with the solemn blessing for the rite by the newly ordained bishop.

3. *Spirit of reform*

There are no better words to sum up both the spirit in which this entire study was undertaken and the spirit in which future reform would proceed than those spoken by Paul VI in an address to the members and *periti* of the Consilium, 13 October 1966.[58] His words are both challenge and hope for the work that lies ahead:

> Our own thoughts turn often to your exacting and discerning work for the revision of the liturgy according to the mind of the Council. Three points come to mind about the performance of a task so complex and demanding such prudence.
>
> Your first charge is an investigation into the sacred rites of long usage in the Church, which you are then to revise and to put into an improved form. The investigation presents no special problems, since the ceremonies are well known; it does, nevertheless, require certain qualities of spirit. One is a reverence for the sacred that prompts us to honor the ceremonies used by the Church in worshiping God. Another is respect for tradition, which has passed on a priceless heritage worthy of veneration. Necessary as well is a sense of history, which has bearing on the way the rites under revision were formed, on their genuine meaning, either as prayer or as symbol, and on other similar points.

No predisposition to change everything without reason must govern this investigation, nor a hastiness, typical of the iconoclast, to emend and revise everything. The guides must be a devout prudence and a reverence combined with wisdom. The search must be for what is best rather than for what is new. With the new, whatever bears the treasures of the most inspired ages of faith should receive preference over present-day inventions. Nevertheless, the voice of the Church today must not be so constricted that it could not sing a new song, should the inspiration of the Holy Spirit move it to do so.

The Holy Spirit flourishes in the holy church as the words of the ordination prayer of 1990 remind us: ". . . through your Son Jesus Christ, through whom glory and power and honor are yours with the Holy Spirit in the holy Church, now and for ever and ever" (no. 47). May the holy Spirit guide the holy church through future reforms to restore the sacrament of ordination to "the vigor [it] had in the tradition of the Fathers" (*SC* 50) that it may be the sacrament in which the consensus of ecclesial communion is fully experienced and expressed by every see involved, in both the selection and the consecration of the bishop-elect.

NOTES

[1] Daniel Galliher, *Canonical Elections* [dissertation submitted to The Catholic University] (Somerset, Ohio: Rosary Press, 1917) 17; Salmon, "Le rite sacre des évêques," 32.

[2] Vivian Green, "Elections, church," 422.

[3] "Theology and the Election of Bishops in the Early Church," 34.

[4] Benson's remarks are found on page 3 of his study.

[5] Friedrich Kempf, "Prelacies and the Secular Powers," in *The Church in the Age of Feudalism,* eds. F. Kempf, H.- G. Beck, E. Ewig and J. Jungmann, vol. III of *The History of the Church,* gen. eds. H. Jedin and J. Dolan (New York: Seabury Press, 1980) 276.

[6] Robert Benson, "Election by Community and Chapter: Reflections on Co-Responsibility in the Historical Church," *J* 31 (1971) 59.

[7] Kempf, "Prelacies and the Secular Powers," 288.

[8] Uta-Renate Blumenthal, *The Investiture Controversy,* 34.

[9] Klaus Schatz, *Papal Primacy: From Its Origins to the Present* (Collegeville: Liturgical Press, 1996) 97.

[10] Robert Benson, "Election by Community and Chapter," 61.

[11] Jean Gaudemet, "Bishops: From Election to Nomination," trans. I. McGonagle, in Huizing, *Electing Our Own Bishops,* 10.

[12] Ibid., 11.

[13] "Emergence and Decline of Popular Voice in the Selection of Bishops," 31.

[14] Benson, "Election by Community and Chapter," 80.

[15] "Theology and the Election of Bishops in the Early Church," 37.

[16] O'Meara, "Emergence and Decline of Popular Voice in the Selection of Bishops," 28.

[17] George Tavard, "Episcopacy and Apostolic Succession according to Hincmar of Rheims," 614.

[18] Schatz, *Papal Primacy*, 69.

[19] Ibid., 72. The following paragraphs draw heavily on Schatz' compelling analysis.

[20] Ibid.

[21] Ibid., 81.

[22] Ibid.

[23] "Theology and the Election of Bishops in the Early Church," 41.

[24] The information contained in this paragraph is drawn from Geoffrey Barraclough, *The Medieval Papacy* (n.p.: Harcourt, Brace and World, Inc., 1968) 121, 288, 309; and Kempf and others, *The Church in the Age of Feudalism,* 166.

[25] Schatz, *Papal Primacy*, 99.

[26] Ibid., 100.

[27] Ibid.

[28] Seamus Ryan, "Episcopal Consecration: Trent to Vatican II," *ITQ* 33 (1966) 133, 144; also see Augustine McDevitt, "The Episcopate as an Order and Sacrament on the Eve of the High Scholastic Period," *Franciscan Studies* 20 (1960) 96–148; J. James Cuneo, "The Power of Jurisdiction: Empowerment for Church Functioning and Mission Distinct from the Power of Orders," *J* 39 (1979) 183–219; and M. McGough, "The Immediate Source of Episcopal Jurisdiction: A Tridentine Debate," *The Irish Ecclesiastical Record* 86 (1956) 82–97; 87 (1957) 91–109; 88 (1957) 306–323.

[29] Schatz, *Papal Primacy*, 100.

[30] Paul Bradshaw, "Ordination as God's Action through the Church," in *Anglican Orders and Ordinations,* ed., D. Holeton (Cambridge: Grove Books Limited, 1997) 9.

[31] Preface to Puglisi, *Epistemological Principles and Roman Catholic Rites,* xvii.

[32] Schatz, *Papal Primacy*, 180.

[33] Susan Wood, "Priestly Identity: Sacrament of the Ecclesial Community," *W* 69 (1995) 118.

[34] Puglisi, *Epistemological Principles and Roman Catholic Rites,* 194.

[35] John Zizioulas, "Ordination—A Sacrament? I. An Orthodox Reply," *Concilium* 4/8 (1972) 34–35.

[36] Wood, "Priestly Identity," 118.

[37] Legrand, "Theology and the Election of Bishops in the Early Church," 37.

[38] Wood, "Priestly Identity," 118.

[39] Kenan Osborne, *Priesthood,* 122.

[40] McGoldrick, "Orders, Sacrament of," 900.

[41] J. J. von Allmen cited in Ralph Quere, "The Spirit and the Gifts Are Ours," *Lutheran Quarterly* 27 (1975) 330. Also see Chanoines Réguliers de Mondaye, "L'Evêque d'après les prières d'ordination," 755, for an excellent list of references to the Spirit in ordination rites of East and West.

[42] That the choice is God's is explicitly clear in sections of the two traditional consecration prayers: *SVe* 947 And, therefore, to these your servants whom you have chosen for the ministry of the high-priesthood, we beseech you, O Lord, that you would bestow this grace . . . ; *Apostolic Tradition* 3 Bestow, knower of the heart, Father, on this your servant, whom you have chosen for the episcopate, to feed your holy flock. . . . Bradshaw and others, *The Apostolic Tradition,* 30.

[43] Godfrey Diekmann, "The Laying on of Hands: The Basic Sacramental Rite," *Proceedings of the Catholic Theological Society of America* 29 (1974) 341. Jean Corbon continues this theme when he writes that "ordained ministers are there primarily to serve the *epiclesis*, for they are servants of the Spirit who acts with power." *The Wellspring of Worship,* trans. M. O'Connell (New York: Paulist Press, 1988) 6.

[44] In describing reception as the traditional third element of ordination, Edward Kilmartin cites a petition in the Syriac tradition of ordination which "asks that the community receive the grace to welcome the ordinand as a gift of the Spirit." *Christian Liturgy: Theology and Practice* (Kansas City, Missouri: Sheed and Ward, 1988) 198 n. 13.

[45] "The Ministry in the Early Church," 199.

[46] Bradshaw, "Ordination as God's Action," 11.

[47] Thomas Krosnicki, "The Reception/Installation of a Bishop," *N* 15 (1979) 271.

[48] Botte, *From Silence to Participation,* 134.

[49] Ibid.

[50] *DOL* 1:9.

[51] *DOL* 1:14.

[52] International Commission on English in the Liturgy, *General Instruction of the Roman Missal* (Washington, D.C.: United States Conference of Catholic Bishops, 2003) 10.

[53] "Emergence and Decline of Popular Voice in the Selection of Bishops," 32.

[54] The traditional place for the ordination after epistle and psalm is maintained for two reasons: to respect the dynamic of the original Scripture passages which pertain to one becoming a bishop at a future time and to allow the new bishop to preside over the proclamation of the gospel and to give the homily. (This of course would not be the placement of the ordination rites for presbyters nor for deacons.)

[55] See Bradshaw, *Ordination Rites,* 33: "Certainly, the more ancient sources all agree that the imposition of hands was originally performed during the time that the prayer was being offered for the ordinand."

[56] *OB1990*.26 The fraternal kiss that the newly ordained Bishop receives from the principal ordaining Bishop and from all the Bishops seals, so to speak, his admittance into the College of Bishops.

[57] This action would signal the retrieval of the patristic gesture at this point which was "intended to express the acceptance by the community of their new relationship with the ordained." Bradshaw, "Theology and Rite *A.D.* 200–400," 361.

[58] The author is indebted to Anscar Chupungco, O.S.B, for the inspirational use of the conclusion of this quotation in his article, "A Church Caught between Tradition and Progress" in *The Renewal That Awaits Us*, eds. E. Bernstein and M. Connell (Chicago: Liturgy Training Publications, 1997) 11 and 16. Translation is from *DOL* 84:223–224. Original text is found in *AAS* 58 (1966) 1145–1146.

Bibliography

I. Sources

A. SCRIPTURE

The New Oxford Annotated Bible. New Revised Standard Version. New York: Oxford University Press, 1991.

B. LITURGICAL TEXTS

Andrieu, Michel. "Le sacre épiscopal d'après Hincmar de Reims." *RHE* 48 (1953) 22–73.

_____, ed. *Le Pontifical romain au moyen-âge. I. Le Pontifical romain du XIIe siècle.* ST 86. Città del Vaticano: Biblioteca Apostolica Vaticana, 1938; reprinted, 1983.

_____, ed. *Le Pontifical romain au moyen-âge. II. Le Pontifical de la Curie romaine au XIIIe siècle.* ST 87. Città del Vaticano: Biblioteca Apostolica Vaticana, 1940; reprinted, 1984.

_____, ed. *Le Pontifical romain au moyen-âge. III. Le Pontifical de Guillaume Durand.* ST 88. Città del Vaticano: Biblioteca Apostolica Vaticana, 1940; reprinted, 1984.

_____, ed. *Le Pontifical romain au moyen-âge. IV. Tables Alphabétiques.* ST 99. Città del Vaticano: Biblioteca Apostolica Vaticana, 1941; reprinted, 1985.

_____, ed. *Les Ordines romani du haut moyen âge. I. Les Manuscrits.* SSL Etudes et Documents 11. Louvain: Spicilegium sacrum Lovaniense, 1931; reprinted, 1957.

_____, ed. *Les Ordines romani du haut moyen âge. III. Les Textes (Suite) (Ordines XIV–XXXIV).* SSL Etudes et Documents 24. Louvain: Spicilegium Sacrum Lovaniense, 1951; reprinted, 1961.

_____, ed. *Les Ordines romani du haut moyen âge. IV. Les Textes (Suite) (Ordines XXXV–XLIX).* SSL Etudes et Documents 28. Louvain: Spicilegium Sacrum Lovaniense, 1956.

Banting, H.M.J., ed. *Two Anglo-Saxon Pontificals (The Egbert and Sidney Sussex Pontificals).* Henry Bradshaw Society, v. 104. London: Henry Bradshaw Society, 1989.

Botte, Bernard, ed. *La Tradition apostolique de Saint Hippolyte: essai de reconstitution.* 5. Auflage. Eds. A. Gerhards and S. Felbecker. *LQF* 39. Münster: Aschendorff, 1989.

Bradshaw, Paul, Maxwell Johnson, and L. Edward Phillips. *The Apostolic Tradition: A Commentary.* Minneapolis: Augsburg Fortress, 2003.

_____, ed. *The Canons of Hippolytus.* Trans. Carol Bebawi. Alcuin/GROW Liturgical Study 2. Bramcote, Nottingham: Grove Books Limited, 1987.

Conn, Marie. "The Dunstan and Brodie (Anderson) Pontificals: An Edition and Study." PH.D. diss., University of Notre Dame, 1993.

Coquin, René-Georges. *Les Canons D'Hippolyte. Patrologia Orientalis* XXXI.-Fascicule 2. Paris: Firmin-Didot et Cie, 1966.

De consecratione electi in Episcopum. In Pontificalis ordinis liber incipit in quo ea tantum ordinata sunt que ad officium pontificis pertinent. . . . Romae: apud Steph. Planck, 1485.

De consecratione Electi in Episcopum. In Pontificale romanum Clementis VIII P.M. iussu restitutum atque editum. Romae: Iacobum Lunam, impensis Leonardi Parasoli et Sociorum, 1596. Paris, Bibl. Fac. O.P. Rés XVI A.- 2° Centre international de publications oecuméniques des liturgies. Un corpus des liturgies chrétiennes sur microfiches.

De Ordinatione Diaconi, Presbyteri et Episcopi. In Pontificale Romanum, ex decreto Sacrosancti Oecumenici Concilii Vaticanii II instauratum, auctoritate Pauli PP. VI promulgatum. Editio typica. Urbs Vaticana: Typis Polyglottis Vaticanis, 1968.

De Ordinatione Episcopi, Presbyterorum et Diaconorum. Editio typica altera. Città del Vaticano: Libreria Editrice Vaticano, 1990.

Deshusses, Jean, ed. *Le Sacramentaire Grégorien. Ses principales formes d'après les plus anciens manuscrits. I.* Deuxième édition. Spicilegium Friburgense 16. Fribourg: Editions universitaires, 1979.

Doble, Gilbert, ed. *Pontificale Lanaletense (Bibliothèque de la ville de Rouen a. 27. Cat. 368).* Henry Bradshaw Society, v. 74. London: Henry Bradshaw Society, 1937.

Dumas, A. and Deshusses, J., eds. *Liber Sacramentorum Gellonensis.* CCL 159-159A. Turnhout: Brepols, 1981.

International Commission on English in the Liturgy. *The Roman Pontifical.* Vatican City: Vatican Polyglot Press, 1978.

_____. *Rites of Ordination of a Bishop, of Priests, and of Deacons.* Second Typical Edition. Washington, D.C.: United States Conference of Catholic Bishops, 2003.

Martène, Edmund. *De antiquis ecclesiae ritibus libri.I.* Editio secunda. Antwerp: Bry, 1736. Reprinted at Hildesheim: Georg Olms, 1967.

Mohlberg, Leo Cunibert, Eizenhöfer, Leo, and Siffrin, Petrus, eds. *Liber sacramentorum romanae aeclesiae ordinis anni circuli (Cod. Vat. Reg. lat. 316/Paris Bibl. Nat. 7193, 41/56) (Sacramentarium Gelasianum).* Third edition. RED, series maior 4. Roma: Herder, 1981.

_____. *Missale Francorum (Cod. Vat. Reg. lat. 257).* RED, maior. Fontes II. Roma: Herder, 1957.

_____. *Sacramentarium Veronense (Cod. Bibl. Capit. Veron. LXXXV [80]).* Third edition. RED, series maior 1. Roma: Herder, 1978.

Munier, C., ed. *Statuta ecclesiae antiqua.* CCL 148. Pp. 162–188. Turnhout: Brepols, 1963.

Ordination of a Bishop. In *Rites of Ordination of a Bishop, of Priests, and of Deacons.* 5–63. Washington, D.C.: United States Conference of Catholic Bishops, 2003.

Pontificale Romanum. Pars prima. Editio typica. Typis Plyglottis Vaticanis, 1962.

Saint-Roch, Patrick, ed. *Liber Sacramentorum Engolismensis: Le Sacramentaire gélasien d'Angoulême.* CCL 159C. Turnhout: Brepols, 1987.

Vogel, Cyrille and Elze, Reinhard, eds. *Le Pontifical romano-germanique du dixième siècle. I. Le Texte (I–XCVIII).* ST 226. Città del Vaticano: Biblioteca Apostolica Vaticana, 1963.

_____. *Le Pontifical romano-germanique du dixième siècle. III. Introductiion générale et Tables.* ST 269. Città del Vaticano: Biblioteca Apostolica Vaticana, 1972.

Warren, F. E., ed. *The Leofric Missal as used in the Cathedral of Exeter during the Episcopate of its first bishop A.D. 1050–1072.* Oxford: Clarendon Press, 1883.

Wilson, H. A., ed. *The Benedictional of Archbishop Robert.* Henry Bradshaw Society, v. 24. London: Henry Bradshaw Society, 1903.

C. MAGISTERIUM

International Commission on English in the Liturgy. *Documents on the Liturgy: 1963–1979. Conciliar, Papal, and Curial Documents.* Collegeville: Liturgical Press, 1982.

_____. *General Instruction of the Roman Missal.* Washington, D.C.: United States Conference of Catholic Bishops, 2003.

Pius XII. *Episcopalis Consecrationis. AAS* 37 (1945) 131–132.

_____. *Sacramentum Ordinis. AAS* 40 (1948) 5–7.

Sacra Congregatio Rituum. *Variationes in Rubricis Pontificalis Romani. AAS* 42 (1950) 448–455.

Tanner, Norman, ed. *Decrees of the Ecumenical Councils.* Volume I: *Nicaea I to Lateran V.* London: Sheed and Ward Limited, 1990 and Washington, D.C.: Georgetown University Press, 1990.

Vatican Council II. *Vatican Council II: Conciliar and Post Conciliar Documents.* Gen. ed. Austin Flannery. Wilmington, Delaware: Scholarly Resources Inc., 1975.

II. Studies

A. BOOKS AND ARTICLES CITED

Adam, Adolf. *Foundations of Liturgy: An Introduction to its History and Practice.* Trans. M. O'Connell. Collegeville: Liturgical Press, 1992.

Alberigo, Giuseppe and Weiler, Anton. *Election and Consensus in the Church. Concilium* 77. New York: Herder and Herder, 1972.

Andrieu, Michel. "La carrière ecclésiastique des papes et les documents liturgiques du moyen âge." *RSR* 21 (1947) 90–120.

_____. "L'onction des mains dans le sacre épiscopal." *RHE* 26 (1930) 343–347.

Aquinas, Thomas. *Summa Theologica.* Volume III. Trans. Fathers of the English Dominican Province. New York: Benzinger Brothers, Inc., 1948.

Austin, Gerard. *The Rite of Confirmation: Anointing with the Spirit.* New York: Pueblo, 1985.

B. D. L. "Constitution apostolique sur le rôle des évêques coconsécrateurs." *LMD* 5 (1946) 107–110.

Barraclough, Geoffrey. *The Medieval Papacy.* [n.p.]: Harcourt, Brace and World, Inc., 1968.

Batiffol, Pierre. "La liturgie du sacre des évêques dans son évolution historique." *RHE* 23 (1927) 733–763.

Benson, Robert. "Election by Community and Chapter: Reflections on Co-Responsibility in the Historical Church." *J* 31 (1971) 54–80.

_____. *The Bishop-Elect: A Study in Medieval Ecclesiastical Office.* Princeton, New Jersey: Princeton University Press, 1968.

Bligh, John. *Ordination to the Priesthood.* New York: Sheed and Ward, 1956.

Blumenthal, Uta-Renate. *The Investiture Controversy: Church and Monarchy from the Ninth to the Twelfth Century.* Philadelphia: University of Pennsylvania Press, 1988.

Botte, Bernard. *From Silence to Participation.* Trans. J. Sullivan. Washington, D.C.: Pastoral Press, 1988.

_____. "La Constitution apostolique 'Sacramentum Ordinis.'" *LMD* 16 (1948) 124–129.

_____. "Le nouveau rituel d'ordination." *QL* 49 (1968) 273–278.

_____. "L'ordination de l'évêque." *LMD* 98 (1969) 113–126.

_____. "L'ordre d'après les prières d'ordination." *QL* 35 (1954) 166–179.

_____. "Le rituel d'ordination des *Statuta Ecclesiae Antiqua.*" *Recherches de théologie ancienne et médiévale* 11 (1939) 223–241.

_____. "Le sacre épiscopal dans le rite romain." *QL* 25 (1940) 22–32.

_____ and others. *The Sacrament of Holy Orders.* Collegeville: Liturgical Press, 1962.

Bradshaw, Paul. "Medieval Ordinations." In *The Study of Liturgy* (1992). Jones and others, 369–379.

_____. "Ordination as God's Action through the Church." In *Anglican Orders and Ordinations.* Ed. D. Holeton, 8–15. Cambridge: Grove Books Limited, 1997.

_____. *Ordination Rites of the Ancient Churches of East and West.* New York: Pueblo, 1990.

_____. "Recent Developments." In *The Study of Liturgy* (1992). Jones and others, 391–398.

_____. "Shifting Scholarly Perspectives." In his *The Search for the Origins of Christian Worship,* 1–20. Second edition. New York: Oxford University Press, 2002.

_____. "Theology and Rite AD 200–400." In *The Study of Liturgy* (1992). Jones and others, 355–362.

B[raga]., C. "Commentarius: *De Ordinatione Episcopi.*" *EL* 83 (1969) 42–66.

Brandolini, Luca. "L'evoluzione storica dei riti delle ordinazioni." *EL* 83 (1969) 67–87.

Brown, Raymond. *Priest and Bishop: Biblical Reflections.* New York: Paulist Press, 1970.

Bugnini, Annibale. *The Reform of the Liturgy 1948–1975.* Trans. M. O'Connell. Collegeville: Liturgical Press, 1990.

Chanoines Réguliers de Mondaye. "L'évêque d'après les prières d'ordination." In Congar, *L'Episcopat et l'Eglise universelle,* 739–780.

Chavasse, Antoine. *Le Sacramentaire Gélasien (Vaticanus Reginensis 316)*. Tournai: Desclée, 1958.

Chupungco, Anscar. "The Church Caught between Tradition and Progress." In *The Renewal That Awaits Us*. Eds. E. Bernstein and M. Connell, 3–17. Chicago: Liturgy Training Publications, 1997.

Clancy, Walter. *The Rites and Ceremonies of Sacred Ordination (Canons 1002–1005): A Historical Conspectus and a Canonical Commentary*. Washington, D.C.: The Catholic University of America Press, 1962.

Congar, Yves and Dupuy, B. - D. *L'Episcopat et L'Eglise universelle*. Unam Sanctam 39. Paris: Cerf, 1962.

Corbon, Jean. *The Wellspring of Worship*. Trans. M. O'Connell. New York: Paulist Press, 1988.

Crichton, James Dunlop. *Christian Celebration*. Vol. II: *The Sacraments*. London: Geoffrey Chapman, 1979.

Cuneo, J. James. "The Power of Jurisdiction: Empowerment for Church Functioning and Mission Distinct from the Power of Orders." *J* 39 (1979) 183–219.

De Clerck, Paul. "La prière gallicane 'Pater Sancte' de l'ordination épiscopale." In *Traditio et Progressio*, 163–176. Studia Anselmiana 95. Analecta Liturgica 12. Roma: Pontificio Ateneo S. Anselmo, 1988.

Dell'Oro, Ferdinando. "La *Editio typica altera* del *Pontificale Romano* delle ordinazioni: I nuovi *Praenotanda*." *RL* 78 (1991) 281–335.

Diekmann, Godfrey. "The Laying on of Hands: The Basic Sacramental Rite." *Proceedings of the Catholic Theological Society of America* 29 (1974) 339–351.

Dix, Gregory. "The Ministry in the Early Church." In *The Apostolic Ministry: Essays on the History and the Doctrine of Episcopacy*. Ed. K. Kirk, 185–303. Second edition. London: Hodder and Stoughton, 1962.

Duval, A. "The Council of Trent and Holy Orders." In *The Sacrament of Holy Orders*. Botte and others, 219–258.

Dykmans, Marc. *Le Pontifical romain révisé au XVe siècle*. ST 311. Città del Vaticano: Biblioteca Apostolica Vaticana, 1985.

Ellard, Gerald. *Ordination Anointings in the Western Church Before 1000 A.D.* Cambridge, Massachusetts: Mediaeval Academy of America, 1933.

Ferraro, Giuseppe. *Le Preghiere di ordinazione al diaconato, al presbiterato, e all'episcopato*. Napoli: Edizioni Dehoniane, 1977.

Fischer, Balthasar. "Das Gebet der Kirche als Wesenselement des Weihesakramentes." *LJ* 20 (1970) 166–177.

Fransen, Piet. "Orders and Ordination." *Sacramentum Mundi*. Vol. 4. Gen. ed. A. Darlap, 305–327. New York: Herder and Herder, 1969.

Galliher, Daniel. *Canonical Elections*. [Dissertation submitted to Catholic University.] Somerset, Ohio: Rosary Press, 1917.

Ganoczy, Alexandre. "'Splendors and Miseries' of the Tridentine Doctrine of Ministries." Trans. R. Wilson. In *Office and Ministry in the Church*. *Concilium* 80. Eds. B. Van Iersel and R. Murphy, 75–86. New York: Herder and Herder, 1972.

Gaudemet, Jean. "Bishops: From Election to Nomination." Trans. I. McGonagle. In *Electing Our Own Bishops*. Eds. Huizing and Walf, 10–15.

Green, Vivian. "Elections, Church." In *The Dictionary of the Middle Ages*. Volume 4. Gen. ed. Joseph Strayer, 421–425. New York: Charles Scribner and Sons, 1982.

Gy, Pierre-Marie. "Ancient Ordination Prayers." In *Ordination Rites: Past and Present*. Eds. Vos and Wainwright, 70–93.

Hawkins, Frank. "The Early History of the Roman Rites of Ordination." In *The Study of Liturgy* (1978). Jones and others, 362–365.

Henderson, Arthur. *Ordained Ministry in the American Lutheran and Roman Catholic Churches: A Study in Theological Method and a Proposal for Mutual Recognition*. Ann Arbor, Michigan: University Microfilms International, 1985.

Houssiau, Albert. "La formation de la liturgie romaine du sacre épiscopal." *Collectanea Mechliniensia* 33 (1948) 276–284.

Huizing, Peter and Walf, Knut, eds. *Electing Our Own Bishops*. New York: Seabury, 1980.

Hürth, F. "Contenuto e significato della Costituzione Apostolica sopra gli ordini sacri." *La Civiltà Cattolica* 99/II (1948) 614–628.

International Commission on English in the Liturgy. "Ordination of a Bishop (The Roman Pontifical)." *N* 17 (1981) 197–216.

Jones, Cheslyn, Wainwright, Geoffrey, Yarnold, Edward and Bradshaw, Paul. *The Study of Liturgy*. Revised edition. New York: Oxford University Press, 1992.

Jounel, Pierre. "La nouvelle édition typique du rituel des ordinations." *LMD* 186 (1991) 7–22.

_____. "Le nouveau rituel d'ordination." *LMD* 98 (1969) 63–72.

_____. "Ordinations." In *The Sacraments*. Trans. M. O'Connell. Eds. R. Cabié and others, 139–179. Vol. III of *The Church at Prayer*. Gen. ed. A.-M. Martimort. Collegeville: Liturgical Press, 1988.

_____. *The Rite of Concelebration of Mass and of Communion under Both Species.* Trans. Desclée Company, Inc. New York: Desclée, 1967.

Jungmann, Joseph. *The Mass of the Roman Rite: its Origins and Development (Missarum Sollemnia).* Trans. F. Brunner. 2 vols. Replica edition. Westminster, Maryland: Christian Classics, Inc., 1986. From the original edition: New York: Benzinger Brothers, 1951/1955.

Kavanagh, Aidan. "Reflections on Confirmation." *Professional Approaches in Christian Education* 17 (February 1986) 16–19.

Kempf, F., H.-G. Beck, E. Ewig, and J. Jungmann. *The Church in the Age of Feudalism.* Volume III of *History of the Church.* Gen. eds. Hubert Jedin and John Dolan. Trans. A. Biggs. New York: Seabury Press, 1980.

Kilmartin, Edward. *Christian Liturgy: Theology and Practice.* Kansas City, Missouri: Sheed and Ward, 1988.

_____. *Church, Eucharist and Priesthood.* New York: Paulist Press, 1981.

_____. "Episcopal Election: The Right of the Laity." In *Electing Our Own Bishops.* Eds. Huizing and Walf, 39–43.

Kirsch, Johann. "Palatini." *The Catholic Encyclopedia.* Eds. Charles Herbermann and others. Volume XI, 417. New York: Robert Appleton Company, 1911.

Kleinheyer, Bruno. *Die Priesterweihe im römischen Ritus: eine liturgie-historische Studie.* Trier: Paulinus, 1962.

_____. "La riforma degli ordini sacri." *RL* 56 (1969) 8–24.

_____. "Ordinationen und Beauftragungen." In *Sakramentliche Feiern II.* B. Kleinheyer, B. Severus, and R. Kaczynski, 7–65. Teil 8: *Gottesdienst der Kirche: Handbuch der Liturgiewissenschaft.* Regensburg: Pustet, 1984.

_____. "Ordinationsfeiern." *LJ* 41 (1991) 88–118.

_____. "Weiheliturgie in neuer Gestalt." *LJ* 18 (1968) 210–229.

Klöckener, Martin. *Die Liturgie der Diözesansynode.* LQF 68. Münster: Aschendorff, 1986.

Krosnicki, Thomas. "The Reception/Installation of a Bishop." *N* 15 (1979) 266–277.

Lécuyer, Joseph. "Commentarium." *N* 4 (1968) 213–219.

_____. "Le sacrement de l'épiscopat." *Divinitas* 1 (1957) 221–251.

_____. "Note sur la liturgie du sacre des évêques." *EL* 66 (1952) 369–372.

Legrand, Hervé-Marie. "Theology and the Election of Bishops in the Early Church." Trans. R. Wilson. *Concilium* 7/8 (1972) 31–42.

Lengeling, Emil. "Teologia del sacramento dell'rdine nei testi del nuovo rito." *RL* 56 (1969) 25–54.

Leroquais, Vincent. *Les Pontificaux manuscrits des bibliothèques publiques de France.* Volumes I–III. Paris: [n.p.], 1937.

McDevitt, Augustine. "The Episcopate as an Order and Sacrament on the Eve of the High Scholastic Period." *Franciscan Studies* 20 (1960) 96–148.

McGoldrick, Patrick. "Orders, Sacrament of." In *The New Dictionary of Sacramental Worship.* Ed. P. Fink, 896–908. Collegeville: Liturgical Press, 1990.

McGough, M. "The Immediate Source of Episcopal Jurisdiction: A Tridentine Debate." *The Irish Ecclesiastical Record* 86 (1956) 82–97; 87 (1957) 91–109; 88 (1957) 306–323.

McManus, Frederick. "The New Rite for Ordination of Bishops." *American Ecclesiastical Review* 159 (1968) 410–416.

_____, ed. *Thirty Years of Liturgical Renewal: Statements of the Bishops' Committee on the Liturgy.* Washington, D. C.: United States Catholic Conference, 1987.

Metzger, Marcel. "Nouvelles perspectives pour la prétendue *Tradition apostolique.*" *EO* 5 (1988) 241–259.

Mitchell, Nathan. *Mission and Ministry: History and Theology in the Sacrament of Order.* Wilmington, Delaware: Michael Glazier, 1986.

Munier, Charles. "Une forme abrégée du rituel des ordinations des *Statuta Ecclesiae Antiqua. RSR* 32 (1958) 79–84.

Neunheuser, Burkhard. "The Relation of Priest and Faithful in the Liturgies of Pius V and Paul VI." Trans. M. O'Connell. In *Roles in the Liturgical Assembly,* 207–219. New York: Pueblo, 1981.

Nocent, Adrien. "Storia dei libri liturgici romani." In *Anàmnesis 2: La Liturgia: panorama storico generale.* S. Marsili; J. Pinell; A. M. Triacca; T. Federici; A. Nocent; B. Neunheuser, 147–183. Torino: Marietti, 1988.

O'Meara, Thomas. "Emergence and Decline of Popular Voice in the Selection of Bishops." In *The Choosing of Bishops.* Ed. W. Bassett, 21–32. Hartford, Connecticut: The Canon Law Society of America, 1971.

Osborne, Kenan. *Priesthood: A History of the Ordained Ministry in the Roman Catholic Church.* New York: Paulist Press, 1988.

Porter, H. Boone. *The Ordination Prayers of the Ancient Western Churches.* London: SPCK, 1967.

Power, David. *Ministers of Christ and his Church: The Theology of the Priesthood.* London: Geoffrey Chapman, 1969.

_____. "Power and Authority in Early Christian Centuries." In *That They May Live: Power, Empowerment and Leadership in the Church.* Ed. M. Downey, 25–38. New York: Crossroad, 1991.

Puglisi, James. *The Process of Admission to Ordained Ministry: A Comparative Study.* Volume I: *Epistemological Principles and Roman Catholic Rites.* Trans. M. Driscoll and M. Misrahi. Collegeville: Liturgical Press, 1996. Volume III: *Contemporary Rites and General Conclusions.* Trans. M. Misrahi. Collegeville: Liturgical Press, 2001.

Puniet, Pierre de. "Consécration épiscopale." *Dictionnaire d'Archéologie Chrétienne et de Liturgie.* Volume III/2. Col. 2579–2604. Gen. Eds. F. Cabrol and H. Leclercq. Paris, 1914.

_____. *The Roman Pontifical.* Trans. M. Harcourt. London: Longmans, Green and Company, 1932.

Quere, Ralph. "The Spirit and the Gifts Are Ours: Imparting or Imploring the Spirit in Ordination Rites? *The Lutheran Quarterly* 27 (1975) 322–346.

Rahner, Karl. "Observations on Episcopacy in the Light of Vatican II." Trans. T. Westow. *Concilium* 3/1 (1965) 10–14.

Rasmussen, Niels. "Unité et diversité des Pontificaux latins au VIIIe, IXe et X siècles." In *Liturgie de L'Eglise particulière et liturgie de L'Eglise universelle,* 393–410. Bibliotheca "Ephemeridies Liturgicae" "Subsidia" 3. Roma: Edizioni Liturgiche, 1976.

Ratcliff, Edward Craddock. "A Note on Schemes of Union, the Ministry and Forms of Ordination." In *E. C. Ratcliff: Reflections on Liturgical Revision.* Ed. D. Tripp, 27–32. Bramcote, Nottingham: Grove Books, 1980.

Reiss, John. *The Time and Place of Sacred Ordination: A Historical Synopsis and a Commentary.* Washington, D.C.: The Catholic University of America Press, 1953.

Reynolds, Roger. "The *De Officiis VII Graduum*: Its Origins and Early Medieval Development." *Mediaeval Studies* 34 (1972) 133–151.

Righetti, Mario. *Manuale di Storia Liturgica.* Vol. IV: I *Sacramenti—I Sacramentali.* Milano: Àncora, 1953.

Roguet, A.- M. "Les nouveaux rituels d'ordination." *LMD* 94 (1968) 179–189.

Rordorf, Willy. "L'Ordination de l'évêque selon *la Tradition apostolique* d'Hippolyte de Rome." *QLP* 55 (1974) 137–150.

Roulin, Eugène. *Vestments and Vesture: A Manual of Liturgical Art.* St. Louis: B. Herder Book Company, 1933.

Ryan, Seamus. "Episcopal Consecration: Trent to Vatican II." *ITQ* 33 (1966) 133–150.

Salmon, Pierre. "Le rite du sacre des évêques dans les pontificaux du moyen âge." In *Miscellanea Giulio Belvederi,* 27–45. Collezione "Amici delle

Catacombe" XXIII. Città del Vaticano: Società "Amici delle Catacombe" presso Pontificio Istituto di Archeologia Cristiana, 1954–1955.

Santantoni, Antonio. *L'Ordinazione episcopale: storia e teologia dei riti dell'ordinazione nelle antiche liturgie dell'Occidente*. Studia Anselmiana 69. Analecta Liturgica 2. Roma: Editrice Anselmiana, 1976.

Schatz, Klaus. *Papal Primacy: From Its Origins to the Present*. Trans. J. Otto and L. Maloney. Collegeville: Liturgical Press, 1996.

Strieder, Leon. *The Promise of Obedience: A Ritual History*. Collegeville: Liturgical Press, 2001.

Taft, Robert. "How Liturgies Grow: The Evolution of the Byzantine Divine Liturgy." In his *Beyond East and West: Problems in Liturgical Understanding,* 167–192. Washington, D.C.: Pastoral Press, 1984.

_____. "The Structural Analysis of Liturgical Units: An Essay in Methodology." In his *Beyond East and West: Problems in Liturgical Understanding,* 151–164. Washington, D.C.: Pastoral Press, 1984.

Talley, Thomas. *The Origins of the Liturgical Year*. New York: Pueblo, 1986.

Tavard, George. "Episcopacy and Apostolic Succession according to Hincmar of Rheims." *TS* 34 (1973) 594–623.

Vogel, Cyrille. *Medieval Liturgy: An Introduction to the Sources*. Translated and revised by W. Storey and N. Rasmussen. Washington, D.C.: Pastoral Press, 1986.

_____. "Précisions sur la date et l'ordonnance primitive du *Pontifical Romano-Germanique*." *EL* 74 (1960) 145–162.

Vos, Wiebe and Wainwright, Geoffrey, eds. *Ordination Rites: Past and Present* (= *SL* 13/2, 3, 4). Rotterdam: The Liturgical Ecumenical Center Trust, 1980.

Wegman, Herman. *Christian Worship in East and West: A Study Guide to Liturgical History*. Trans. G. Lathrop. New York: Pueblo, 1985.

Wood, Susan. "Priestly Identity: Sacramental of the Ecclesial Community." *W* 69 (1995) 109–127.

Zizioulas, John. "Ordination—A Sacrament? I. An Orthodox Reply." *Concilium* 4/8 (1972) 33–40.

Index